SOMETHING
ABOUT THE
AUTHOR®

Something about
the Author *was named
an "Outstanding
Reference Source,"
the highest honor given
by the American
Library Association
Reference and Adult
Services Division.*

ISSN 0276-816X

J
R
928
V. 69

something ABOUT THE AUTHOR®

**Facts and Pictures about Authors
and Illustrators of Books for Young People**

EDITED BY
DONNA OLENDORF

VOLUME 69

Gale Research Inc. • *DETROIT* • *LONDON*

NAPA CITY - COUNTY LIBRARY
1150 Division Street
Napa, Ca. 94559-3396

STAFF

Editor: Donna Olendorf

Associate Editor: Sonia Benson

Senior Editor: Hal May

Sketchwriters: Marilyn K. Basel, Barbara Carlisle Bigelow, Joanna Brod, Bruce Ching, Elizabeth A. Des Chenes, Kathleen J. Edgar, Marie Ellavich, David M. Galens, Kevin Hile, David P. Johnson, Janice E. Jorgensen, James F. Kamp, Denise E. Kasinec, Thomas Kozikowski, Sharon Malinowski, Margaret Mazurkiewicz, Mark F. Mikula, Michelle M. Motowski, Tom Pendergast, Susan Reicha, Mary K. Ruby, Pamela L. Shelton, Kenneth R. Shepherd, Diane Telgen, Polly A. Vedder, and Thomas Wiloch

Index Coordinator: James F. Kamp

Research Manager: Victoria B. Cariappa

Research Supervisor: Mary Rose Bonk

Editorial Associates: Reginald A. Carlton, Clare Collins, Andrew Guy Malonis, and Norma Sawaya

Editorial Assistants: Mike Avolio, Patricia Bowen, Rachel A. Dixon, Shirley Gates, Sharon McGilvray, and Devra M. Sladics

Production Manager: Mary Beth Trimper

External Production Assistant: Mary Winterhalter

Art Director: Arthur Chartow

Keyliner: C. J. Jonik

Library of Congress Catalog Card Number 62-52046

ISBN 0-8103-2279-X ISSN 0276-816X

Printed in the United States of America.

Published simultaneously in the United Kingdom by Gale Research International Limited
(An affiliated company of Gale Research Inc.)

Contents

Introduction

Something about the Author (*SATA*) is an ongoing reference series that deals with the lives and works of authors and illustrators of children's books. *SATA* includes not only well-known authors and illustrators whose books are widely read, but also those less prominent people whose works are just coming to be recognized. This series is often the only readily available information source for emerging writers or artists. You'll find *SATA* informative and entertaining whether you are a student, a librarian, an English teacher, a parent, or simply an adult who enjoys children's literature for its own sake.

What's Inside SATA

SATA provides detailed information about authors and illustrators who span the full time range of children's literature, from early figures like John Newbery and L. Frank Baum to contemporary figures like Judy Blume and Richard Peck. Authors in the series represent primarily English-speaking countries, particularly the United States, Canada, and the United Kingdom. Also included, however, are authors from around the world whose works are available in English translation. The writings represented in *SATA* include those created intentionally for children and young adults as well as those written for a general audience and known to interest younger readers. These writings cover the entire spectrum of children's literature, including picture books, humor, folk and fairy tales, animal stories, mystery and adventure, science fiction and fantasy, historical fiction, poetry and nonsense verse, drama, biography, and nonfiction.

Obituaries are also included in *SATA* and are intended not only as death notices but as concise views of people's lives and work. Additionally, each edition features newly revised and updated entries for a selection of *SATA* listees who remain of interest to today's readers and who have been active enough to require extensive revision of their earlier biographies.

Two Convenient Indexes

In response to suggestions from librarians, *SATA* indexes no longer appear in each volume, but are included in alternate (odd-numbered) volumes of the series, beginning with Volume 57.

SATA continues to include two indexes that cumulate with each alternate volume: the Illustrations Index, arranged by the name of the illustrator, gives the number of the volume and page where the illustrator's work appears in the current volume as well as all preceding volumes in the series; the Author Index gives the number of the volume in which a person's Biographical Sketch or Obituary appears in the current volume as well as all preceding volumes in the series.

These indexes also include references to authors and illustrators who appear in Gale's *Yesterday's Authors of Books for Children, Children's Literature Review,* and the *Something about the Author Autobiography Series.*

Easy-to-Use Entry Format

Whether you're already familiar with the *SATA* series or just getting acquainted, you will want to be aware of the kind of information that an entry provides. In every *SATA* entry the editors attempt to give as complete a picture of the person's life and work as possible. A typical entry in *SATA* includes the following clearly labeled information sections:

- *PERSONAL:* date and place of birth and death, parents' names and occupations, name of spouse, date of marriage, and names of children, educational institutions attended, degrees received, religious and political affiliations.

- *ADDRESSES:* complete home, office, and agent's address.

- *CAREER:* name of employer, position, and dates for each career post; military service.

- *MEMBER:* memberships and offices held in professional and civic organizations.

- *AWARDS, HONORS:* literary and professional awards received.

- *WRITINGS:* title-by-title chronological bibliography of books written and/or illustrated, listed by genre when known; lists of other notable publications, such as plays, screenplays, and periodical contributions.

- *WORK IN PROGRESS:* description of projects in progress.

- *SIDELIGHTS:* a biographical portrait of the author's development, either directly from the person—and often written specifically for the SATA entry—or gathered from diaries, letters, interviews, or other published sources.

- *FOR MORE INFORMATION SEE:* references for further reading.

- *EXTENSIVE ILLUSTRATIONS:* photographs, movie stills, manuscript samples, book covers, and other interesting visual materials supplement the text.

How a SATA Entry Is Compiled

A *SATA* entry progresses through a series of steps. If the biographee is living, the *SATA* editors try to secure information directly from him or her through a questionnaire. From the information that the biographee supplies, the editors prepare an entry, filling in any essential missing details with research and/or telephone interviews. When necessary, the author or illustrator is sent a copy of the entry to check for accuracy and completeness.

If the biographee is deceased or cannot be reached by questionnaire, the *SATA* editors examine a wide variety of published sources to gather information for an entry. Biographical and bibliographic sources are consulted, as are book reviews, feature articles, published interviews, and material sometimes obtained from the biographee's family, publishers, agent, or other associates. Entries compiled entirely from secondary sources are marked with an asterisk (*).

We Welcome Your Suggestions

We invite you to examine the entire *SATA* series, starting with this volume. Please write and tell us if we can make *SATA* even more helpful to you. Send comments and suggestions to: The Editor, *Something about the Author,* Gale Research Inc., 835 Penobscot Bldg., Detroit, Michigan 48226.

Acknowledgments

Grateful acknowledgment is made to the following publishers, authors, and artists whose works appear in this volume.

RICHARD ADAMS. Photograph (c) 1990 by Peter Hirst-Smith.

JAN ADKINS. Cover illustration by Jan Adkins from her *Deadline for Final Art.* Walker Publishing Company, Inc., 1990. Copyright (c) 1990 by Jan Adkins. Reprinted by permission of Curtis Brown Ltd./ Photograph by Sally Stone Halvorson.

TEDD ARNOLD. Photograph courtesy of Tedd Arnold.

MOLLY BANG. Illustration by Molly Bang from her *The Paper Crane.* Greenwillow Books, 1985. Copyright (c) 1985 by Molly Garrett Bang. Reprinted by permission of Greenwillow Books, a division of William Morrow & Company, Inc./ Title page drawing by Molly Bang from her *Yellow Ball.* William Morrow & Company, 1991. Copyright (C) 1991 by Molly Bang. Reprinted by permission of Morrow Junior Books, a division of William Morrow & Company, Inc./ Illustration by Molly Bang from her *Ten, Nine, Eight.* Mulberry Books, 1991. Copyright (c) 1983 by Molly Bang. Reprinted by permission of Greenwillow Books, a division of William Morrow & Company, Inc./ Photograph courtesy of William Morrow & Company.

MARION DANE BAUER. Cover of *On My Honor,* by Marion Dane Bauer. Copyright (c) 1986 by Marion Dane Bauer. Cover illustration by Michael Conway. Used by permission of Dell Books, a division of Bantam Doubleday Dell Publishing Group, Inc./ Photograph courtesy of Marion Dane Bauer./ Movie still courtesy Highgate Pictures, a division of Learning Corporation of America.

NICOLA BAYLEY. Illustration by Nicola Bayley from *The Tyger Voyage,* by Richard Adams. Text copyright (c) 1976 by Richard Adams. Illustrations copyright (c) 1976 by Nicola Bayley. Reprinted by permission of Random Century Group Ltd./ Photograph by John Hilton.

BYRD BAYLOR. Jacket of *Hawk, I'm Your Brother,* by Byrd Baylor. Jacket illustration (c) 1976 by Peter Parnall. Reprinted with the permission of Charles Scribner's Sons, an imprint of Macmillan Publishing Company./ Jacket of *The Desert Is Theirs,* by Byrd Baylor. Copyright (c) 1975 by Byrd Baylor. Jacket illustration copyright (c) 1975 by Peter Parnall. Illustrations by Peter Parnall. Reprinted with the permission of Charles Scribner's Sons, an imprint of Macmillan Publishing Company./ Photograph courtesy of Byrd Baylor.

STEVE BEINICKE. Illustration by Steve Beinicke from *Andrew and the Wild Bikes,* by Allen Morgan. Annick Press, Ltd., 1990. Text copyright (c) 1990 by Allen Morgan. Illustrations copyright (c) 1990 by Steve Beinicke. Reprinted by permission of Annick Press Ltd.

ANN BLADES. Illustration by Ann Blades from her *Mary of Mile 18.* Copyright (c) 1971 by Ann Blades. Reprinted by permission of Tundra Books Inc./ Photograph courtesy of Ann Blades.

JOAN W. BLOS. Cover of *A Gathering of Days,* by Joan W. Blos. Charles Scribner's Sons, 1979. Copyright (c) 1979 by Joan W. Blos. Jacket illustration by Honi Werner. Reprinted with the permission of Charles Scribner's Sons, an imprint of Macmillan Publishing Company./ Photograph courtesy of Joan W. Blos.

BARBARA HOOD BURGESS. Photograph courtesy of Barbara Hood Burgess.

PATRICIA CALVERT. Cover of *The Money Creek Mare,* by Patricia Calvert. Copyright (c) 1981 by Patricia Calvert. Jacket illustration by Ruth Sanderson. Reprinted by permission of Ruth Sanderson./ Photograph courtesy of Patricia Calvert.

AIDAN CHAMBERS. Photograph by Lydia van der Meer.

KAY CHORAO. Illustration by Kay Chorao from her *Lemon Moon.* Copyright (c) 1983 by Kay Chorao. Reprinted by permission of Holiday House, Inc./ Photograph courtesy of Kay Chorao.

LUCILLE CLIFTON. Cover of *Everett Anderson's Nine Month Long,* by Lucille Clifton. Copyright (c) 1978 by Lucille Clifton. Illustrations by Ann Grifalconi. Reprinted by permission of Henry Holt and Company, Inc./ Jacket of *Everett Anderson's Goodbye,* by Lucille Clifton. Henry Holt and Company, 1988. Text copyright (c) 1983 by Lucille Clifton. Illustrations copyright (c) 1983 by Ann Grifalconi. Reprinted by permission of Henry Holt and Company, Inc./ Photograph by Layle Silbert.

MARGUERITE HENRY. Cover of *King of the Wind,* by Marguerite Henry. Rand McNally & Company, 1970. Copyright (c) 1948 by Rand McNally & Company. Illustrations by Wesley Dennis. Illustrations copyright (c) 1947. Copyright renewed 1976 by Morgan and Charles Reid Dennis. Reprinted with the permission of Macmillan Publishing Company./ Photograph from *A Pictorial Life Story of Misty,* by Marguerite Henry. Rand McNally & Company, 1976. Copyright (c) 1976 by Marguerite Henry./ Cover of *Brighty of the Grand Canyon,* by Marguerite Henry. Checkerboard Press, 1963. Copyright (c) 1963 Macmillan Publishing Company. Cover illustration by Wesley Dennis. Reprinted with the permission of Macmillan Publishing Company./ Photograph courtesy of Marguerite Henry.

NAT HENTOFF. Cover of *The Day They Came to Arrest the Book,* by Nat Hentoff. Delacorte, 1982. Copyright (c) 1982 by Nat Hentoff. Reprinted by permission of Dell Books, a division of Bantam Doubleday Dell Publishing Group, Inc./ Cover of *Does This School Have Capital Punishment?,* by Nat Hentoff. Delacorte Press, 1981. Copyright (c) 1981 by Marnate Productions. Used by permission of Delacorte Press, a division of Bantam Doubleday Dell Publishing Group, Inc./ Photograph courtesy of Nat Hentoff.

JAMAKE HIGHWATER. Jacket of *Ceremony of Innocence,* by Jamake Highwater. Jacket art by Blackbear Bosin, copyright (c) 1985 by Nola Bosin Kimble. Jacket (c) 1985 by Harper & Row, Publishers, Inc. Reprinted by permission of HarperCollins Publishers./ Jacket of *I Wear the Morning Star,* by Jamake Highwater. Jacket art (c) 1986 by David P. Bradley. Jacket (c) 1986 by Harper & Row, Publishers, Inc. Reprinted by permission of HarperCollins Publishers./ Jacket of *Eyes of Darkness,* by Jamake Highwater. Jacket painting (c) 1985 by David Montiel. Reprinted by permission of Lothrop, Lee & Shepard Books, a division of William Morrow & Company, Inc./ Jacket of *Anpao: An American Odyssey,* by Jamake Highwater. Jacket painting by Fritz Scholder. Reprinted by permission of HarperCollins Publishers./ Photograph by Henry Kurth.

LILLIAN HOBAN. Cover by Lillian Hoban from her *Arthur's Christmas Cookies.* Copyright (c) 1972 by Lillian Hoban. Reprinted by permission of HarperCollins Publishers./ Illustration by Lillian Hoban from her *It's Really Christmas.* Copyright (c) 1982 by Lillian Hoban. Reprinted by permission of Greenwillow Books, a division of William Morrow & Company, Inc./ Illustration from *Nora and Mrs. Mind-Your-Own-Business,* by Johanna Hurwitz. Morrow Junior Books, 1991. Text copyright (c) 1977 by Johanna Hurwitz. Illustrations copyright (c) 1991 by Lillian Hoban. Reprinted by permission of Morrow Junior Books, a division of William Morrow & Company, Inc.

ROSE IMPEY. Photograph courtesy of Rose Impey.

JUDY JACOBS. Photograph courtesy of Judy Jacobs.

FAITH JAQUES. Illustrations by Faith Jaques from her *Tilly's House.* Margaret K. McElderry Books, 1979. Text and illustrations copyright (c) 1979 by Faith Jaques. Reprinted by permission of William Heinemann Limited.

DOLORES JOHNSON. Photograph by Elizabeth Kine, courtesy of Dolores Johnson.

CHARLES KEEPING. Illustration by Charles Keeping from his *Sammy Streetsinger.* Oxford University Press, 1984. Copyright (c) 1984 by Charles Keeping. Reprinted by permission of Oxford University Press./ Illustration by Charles Keeping from *Beowulf,* by Kevin Crossley-Holland. Oxford University Press, 1982. Text copyright (c) 1982 by Kevin Crossley-Holland. Illustrations copyright (c) 1982 by Charles Keeping. Reprinted by permission of Oxford University Press./ Photograph courtesy of Charles Keeping.

HILARY KNIGHT. Illustration by Hilary Knight from *Kay Thompson's Eloise,* by Kay Thompson. Copyright (c) 1955 by Kay Thompson. Copyright renewed (c) 1983 by Kay Thompson. Reprinted by permission of the publisher, Simon and Schuster, New York./ Photograph by Otto Maya.

KATHRYN LASKY. Cover of *Sugaring Time,* by Kathryn Lasky. Aladdin Books, 1986. Text copyright (c) 1983 by Kathryn Lasky. Cover photograph copyright (c) 1983 by Christopher G. Knight. Reprinted with the permission of Macmillan Publishing Company./ Jacket of *Fourth of July Bear,* by Kathryn Lasky. Morrow Junior Books, 1991. Text copyright (c) 1991 by Kathryn Lasky. Illustrations copyright (c) 1991 by Helen Cogancherry. Reprinted by permission of Morrow Junior Books, a division of William Morrow & Company./ Photograph by Christopher Knight.

ELIZABETH LEVY. Jacket of *Frankenstein Moved in on the Fourth Floor,* by Elizabeth Levy. Harper & Row, Publishers, 1979. Text copyright (c) 1979 by Elizabeth Levy. Jacket illustration copyright (c) 1979 by Mordecai Gerstein. Reprinted by permission of HarperCollins Publishers./ Photograph by Andrew Strawcutter.

J. PATRICK LEWIS. Photograph courtesy of J. Patrick Lewis.

KIM LONG. Photograph courtesy of Kim Long.

BERNIE MACKINNON. Photograph of Bernie MacKinnon.

ROSALIE MAGGIO. Photograph courtesy of Rosalie Maggio.

SOMETHING ABOUT THE AUTHOR

ADAMS, Richard 1920-

PERSONAL: Full name is Richard George Adams; born May 9, 1920, in Newbury, Berkshire, England; son of Evelyn George Beadon (a surgeon) and Lilian Rosa (Button) Adams; married Barbara Elizabeth Acland, September 26, 1949; children: Juliet Vera Lucy, Rosamond Beatrice Elizabeth. *Education:* Attended Bradfield College, Berkshire; Worcester College, Oxford, B.A., 1948, M.A., 1953. *Religion:* Church of England.

ADDRESSES: Office—26 Church St., Whitchurch, Hampshire, England. *Agent*— David Highman Associates Ltd., 5-8 Lower John St., London W1R 4HA, England.

CAREER: Worked in Ministry of Housing and Local Government, London, 1948-68; Department of the Environment, London, Assistant Secretary, 1968-74; full-time writer, 1974—. Writer-in-residence, University of Florida, Gainesville, 1975, and Hollins College, 1976. *Military service:* British Army, 1940-45.

MEMBER: Royal Society for the Prevention of Cruelty to Animals (former president).

AWARDS, HONORS: Carnegie Medal, 1972, and Guardian Award, 1973, both for *Watership Down;* California Young Readers' Association Award, 1977.

WRITINGS:

NOVELS

Watership Down, Rex Collings, 1972, Macmillan, 1974.

RICHARD ADAMS

Shardik, Allen Lane-Rex Collings, 1974, Simon & Schuster, 1975.
The Plague Dogs, illustrated by A. Wainwright, Allen Lane-Rex Collings, 1977, Knopf, 1978.

Watership Down, Adams's award-winning novel about a group of rabbits in search of a home, was released as a full-length animated film by Avco-Embassy in 1978.

The Girl in a Swing, Knopf, 1980.

Maia, Viking, 1984, Knopf, 1985.

The Bureaucats, illustrated by Robin Jacques, Viking Kestrel, 1985.

Traveller, Knopf, 1988.

POETRY

The Tyger Voyage, illustrated by Nicola Bayley, Knopf, 1976.

The Adventures and Brave Deeds of the Ship's Cat on the Spanish Maine: Together with the Most Lamentable Losse of the Alcestis and Triumphant Firing of the Port of Chagres, illustrated by Alan Aldridge and Harry Willock, Knopf, 1977.

The Legend of Te Tuna, Sylvester and Orphanos, 1982.

EDITOR

Grimm's Fairy Tales, illustrated by Pauline Ellison, Routledge, 1981.

Richard Adams's Favorite Animal Stories, illustrated by Beverly Butcher, Octopus, 1981.

The Best of Ernest Thompson Seton, Fontana, 1982.

(And contributor) *Occasional Poets: An Anthology,* Viking, 1986.

OTHER

(With Max Hooper) *Nature through the Seasons,* illustrated by David Goddard and Adrian Williams, Simon & Schuster, 1975.

(Contributor) Lin Carter, editor, *Kingdoms of Sorcery,* Doubleday, 1976.

(With Hooper) *Nature Day and Night,* illustrated by Goddard and Stephen Lee, Viking, 1978.

(Compiler) *Sinister and Supernatural Stories,* Ward Locke, 1978.

The Watership Down Film Picture Book, Macmillan, 1978.

(Author of introduction) Georgi Vladimov, *Faithful Ruslan,* translated by Michael Glenn, Simon & Schuster, 1979.

The Iron Wolf and Other Stories (folktales), illustrated by Yvonne Gilbert and Jennifer Campbell, Allen Lane, 1980, also published as *The Unbroken Web,* Crown, 1980.

(With Ronald Lockley) *Voyage through the Antarctic,* Allen Lane, 1982, Viking, 1986.

A Nature Diary, Viking, 1986.

A Book of British Music Festivals, Riverdale, 1988.

The Day Gone By, Knopf, 1991.

ADAPTATIONS: Watership Down was released as a full-length animated film by Avco-Embassy, 1978.

SIDELIGHTS: For fans of fantasy, Richard Adams is best known as the author of *Watership Down,* the story of a group of rabbits in search of a safe home. Considered by many critics to be a modern classic, *Watership Down*'s exceptional scope and imagination blur the distinction between juvenile and adult literature. Adams did not set out to be a fantasy writer; in fact, he spent over twenty-five years in government service before becoming a full-time author. He originally wrote *Watership Down* to entertain his two young daughters. When the book became a runaway success, Adams was encouraged to explore other literary genres, including poetry. Due to the fantastic situations and characters found in much of his work, Adams has often been categorized as a "children's writer," a distinction he dislikes. In an essay for *Twentieth-Century Children's Writers,* Adams writes: "I do not, myself, recognize a distinction between publications for children and adults. It has always seemed to me that there are only books and readers.... In my view, the distinction may do more harm than good by deterring children from reading books which they would enjoy if left to themselves but which they have been told are 'for adults.'"

Much of the appeal of *Watership Down* lies in Adams's depiction of the main characters: a small band of rabbits who are forced to find a new home when their old one is destroyed. The rabbit leaders—Hazel, courageous Bigwig, clairvoyant Fiver, and clever Blackberry—must defend the site of the new warren from many potential disasters, including threats from mankind and invasion by another rabbit group led by the evil general Woodwart. After a number of adventures that result in great personal loss, the small company is finally able to set up a new home at Watership Down. Strong animal characters in suspenseful situations are also found in *The Plague Dogs, Shardik,* and *Traveller.* Adams's recurring use of animal protagonists is largely the result of his deep love for wildlife and the outdoors. "I am a country man," Adams told Jonathan Cooper of *People.* "Birds, flowers, and the march of seasons are everything to me."

Critics have responded favorably to Adams's unique view of nature. A reviewer for the *Times Literary Supplement* claims that *Watership Down* "has all the originality and depth so often lacking in children's novels." Leon Garfield of *Spectator* concurs: "*Watership Down* is a grand, epic adventure.... The natural world is observed and rendered with wonderful precision; and the character of the wandering band of rabbits ... becomes part of one's own experience as one progresses through the book." And Diana Waggoner, writing about both *Watership Down* and *Shardik* in *The Hills of Faraway: A Guide to Fantasy,* notes that "Adams's potential is enormous and, probably, almost untapped as yet ... if he can live up to his potential, he will be a major figure."

Adams has also received critical attention for his books that do not feature animal characters. In *The Girl in a Swing,* Adams depicts a haunted and doomed love affair; *Maia* centers on a young woman's sexual awakening in a fictional country. When composing his books, Adams often refers to the literary influences of his childhood, including Rudyard Kipling, Ernest Thompson Seton, and John Bunyan. "I believe writing is rather like chess in the respect that although there are certain rules to bear in mind, a lot of these should really be torn up at discretion," Adams comments in an essay for *The Thorny Paradise: Writers on Writing for Children.* "As far as learning how to do it goes, there is no substitute for continually studying the games of great players.... I

would say, beware of the principles and rules about writing for children—the value of an established order and all that. One can easily get so blinkered by the rules that one can no longer judge a book by the light of the heart. That light, of course, is what is used by the children themselves."

WORKS CITED:

Adams, Richard, "Some Ingredients of *Watership Down,*" *The Thorny Paradise: Writers on Writing for Children,* edited by Edward Blishen, Kestrel Books, 1975, pp. 163-73.
Adams, Richard, *Twentieth-Century Children's Writers,* edited by D. L. Kirkpatrick, St. Martin's, 1975, pp. 9-10.
"The Burrowers," *Times Literary Supplement,* December 8, 1972, p. 1489.
Cooper, Jonathan, "Richard Adams Follows Up *Watership Down* and *Shardik* with an Erotic Epic Called *Maia,*" *People,* March 11, 1985.
Garfield, Leon, "Burrow in Berkshire," *Spectator,* February 3, 1973, p. 141.
Waggoner, Diana, "Some Trends in Fantasy," *The Hills of Faraway: A Guide to Fantasy,* Atheneum, 1978, pp. 36-64.

FOR MORE INFORMATION SEE:

BOOKS

Butts, Dennis, editor, *Good Writers for Young Readers,* Hart-Davis, 1977, pp. 114-43.
Children's Literature Review, Volume 20, Gale, 1990, pp. 10-32.

PERIODICALS

Bulletin of the Center for Children's Books, November, 1976.
Horn Book, June, 1973; August, 1974.
New York, March, 1974.
Publishers Weekly, April 15, 1974.*

*   *   *

ADKINS, Jan 1944-

PERSONAL: Born November 7, 1944, in Gallipolis, OH; son of Alban Blakemore (a contractor) and Dixie Lee (Ellis) Adkins; married Deborah Kiernan, September 14, 1968 (died in June, 1976); married Dorcas Sheldon Peirce, December, 1977; children: (first marriage) Sally; (second marriage) Samuel Ulysses; stepchildren: Robbie. *Education:* Ohio State University, B.A., 1969.

ADDRESSES: Home—591 Front St., Marion, MA 02738. *Office*—*National Geographic,* National Geographic Society, 17th St. and M St., Washington, DC 20036. *Agent*—Perry Knowlton, Curtis Brown Ltd., 575 Madison Ave., New York, NY 10022.

CAREER: Author and illustrator. Ireland & Associates Architects, Columbus, OH, designer, 1963-66; writer, graphic designer, and illustrator, 1969—; math and

JAN ADKINS

science teacher in Mattapoisett, MA, 1969-70; Buzzard Inc. (advertising agency), Marion, MA, vice-president and art director, 1974-76; *National Geographic* (magazine), Washington, DC, assistant art director.

AWARDS, HONORS: Brooklyn Museum Art citations, 1972, 1973, and 1974; Lewis Carroll Shelf Award, University of Wisconsin, and National Book Award nomination, both 1972, for *The Art and Industry of Sand Castles;* Children's Book Showcase awards, Children's Book Council, 1974, for *Toolchest,* and 1976, for *Inside;* Children's Science Book Award, New York Academy of Sciences, 1981, for *Moving Heavy Things.*

WRITINGS:

The Art and Industry of Sandcastles, Walker & Co., 1970.
The Craft of Making Wine, Walker & Co., 1971.
How a House Happens, Walker & Co., 1972.
The Craft of Sail, Walker & Co., 1973.
Toolchest: A Primer of Woodcraft, Walker & Co., 1973.
Small Gardener: Big Surprise, Ginn, 1974.
The Bakers: On Making Bread, Scribner, 1975.
Inside: Seeing beneath the Surface, Walker & Co., 1975.
(Illustrator) Laurence Pringle, *Chains, Webs, and Pyramids: The Flow of Energy in Nature,* Crowell, 1975.
Luther Tarbox (fiction), Scribner, 1977.
Moving On: Stories of Four Travelers, Scribner, 1978.
Symbols: A Silent Language, Walker & Co., 1978.
Wooden Ship, Houghton, 1978.
The Art and Ingenuity of the Woodstove, Everest House, 1978.
Moving Heavy Things, Houghton, 1980.

The Wood Book: An Entertaining, Interesting, and Even Useful Compendium of Facts, Notions, Opinions, and Sentiments about Wood and Its Growing, Cutting, Working, and Burning, Little, Brown, 1980.
Heavy Equipment, Scribner, 1980.
Letterbox: The Art and History of Letters, Walker & Co., 1981.
A Storm without Rain (young adult novel), Little, Brown, 1983.
Workboats, Macmillan, 1985.
Cookie (mystery novel), Harper, 1988.
Deadline for Final Art, (mystery novel), Walker & Co., 1990.
Solstice: A Mystery of the Season (novel), Walker & Co., 1990.

Contributor to periodicals, including *Cricket, Harper's, Mother Earth News, Sail, Smithsonian,* and *Woodenboat.*

SIDELIGHTS: Both an author and an illustrator, Jan Adkins is widely known for his inviting, informative books on such diverse subjects as sand castles, woodworking, baking, construction, and calligraphy. He has also written fiction for young adults and older readers. Flavored with whimsical humor, his books win praise

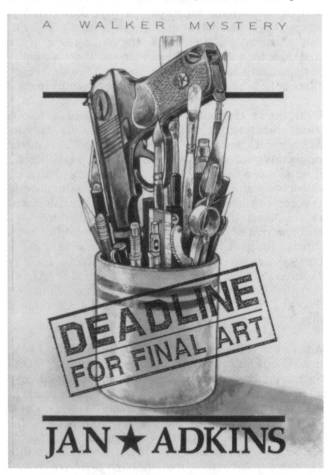

An intrigue between the United States and the Soviet Union in *Deadline for Final Art* is one of the many diverse subjects of Adkins's later fiction. (Cover illustration by Adkins.)

for their clear, detailed illustrations, originality, enthusiasm, and thorough research.

Among Adkins's best-known books is his first, *The Art and Industry of Sandcastles*. On one level a practical as well as fanciful guide to building with wet sand, the book also serves as an introduction to the history and structure of real castles and to life in medieval times. Adkins illustrated the work with his own drawings of historical castles and their sand counterparts, and he also hand-lettered the text. Judging the book an unusual, even unlikely, combination of elements, reviewers nonetheless delighted in its originality and hailed it as an imaginative, well-made, and definitive guide.

In subsequent works Adkins brought the same combination of skillful drawing, lucid explanation, and novelty to bear on a wide range of subjects. With each book he introduced his readers to the specific tools involved in different activities, the correct terms for procedures, and the various properties of materials. While admiring the scope of his books, reviewers sometimes expressed concern that Adkins was including too much technical information, which they felt might prove daunting or simply incomprehensible to young readers. In an interview with Norma Bagnall published in *Language Arts*, Adkins presented his view of the issue: "Something that bothers me about writing for children is that an editor will try to expunge everything that a child would not understand. I don't want children to understand everything; I want them to read the book.... If children understand everything the first time around, they'll throw the book away, and they ought to." By not condescending to his audience, Adkins has produced introductory books that critics often find as suitable for adults as for young people.

Fiction gave Adkins another outlet for his wide-ranging interests and the accuracy, attention to detail, and skillful illustration praised in his nonfiction. His novel *A Storm without Rain*, for example, draws upon his knowledge of sailing and shipbuilding, both previously featured in nonfiction books. Set in eastern Massachusetts, the story follows the adventures of teenager Jack Carter, who begins a short sailing trip in the late twentieth century and ends up in 1904. In his family's shipyard he meets his own grandfather, then a teenager himself, and together the two boys try to find a way for Jack to return to his own time. Writing in the *New York Times Book Review*, Jane Langton commended Adkins for including details about shipbuilding and turn-of-the-century Massachusetts that add to the tale's credibility. She also hailed Adkins's "memorable" illustrations, which with the text create "an authentic background." The critic concluded, "The reader puts down the book with admiration for craftsmanship—for that of the boatbuilders ... and for that of the writer, who honed his fanciful tale so authentically." In later novels Adkins explored subjects including time travel and family relationships in Maine and intrigue between the United States and the Soviet Union.

WORKS CITED:

Bagnall, Norma, interview with Adkins, *Language Arts*, May, 1980, pp. 560-66.
Langton, Jane, review of *A Storm without Rain* in *New York Times Book Review*, September 18, 1983, p. 39.

FOR MORE INFORMATION SEE:

BOOKS

Children's Literature Review, Volume 7, Gale, 1984, pp. 17-28.

PERIODICALS

Cricket, May, 1977, p. 54.*

*   *   *

ALLEN, Alex B.
See HEIDE, Florence Parry

*   *   *

ARNOLD, Tedd 1949-

PERSONAL: Born January 20, 1949, in Elmira, NY; son of Theodore Arnold (a machinist) and Gabriela (Rosno) Arnold; married Carol Clark (a teacher), August 15, 1971; children: Walter, William. *Education:* University of Florida, B.F.A.

ADDRESSES: Agent—Peter Elek Agency, P.O. Box 223, Canal St. Station, New York, NY 10013.

CAREER: While in Tallahassee, FL, worked as a textbook illustrator, 1973-78, and creative director and owner of a graphic design studio, 1978-81; Cycles USA, Tallahassee, advertising art director, 1981-84; Workman Publishing, New York City, book designer, 1984-85; free-lance author and illustrator in Elmira, NY, 1985—. *Military service:* U.S. Army Reserve, medic, 1969-75.

WRITINGS:

FOR CHILDREN

(And illustrator) *Sounds*, Little Simon, 1985.
(And illustrator) *Opposites*, Little Simon, 1985.
(And illustrator) *Actions*, Little Simon, 1985.
(And illustrator) *Colors*, Little Simon, 1985.
(And illustrator) *My First Drawing Book*, Workman Publishing, 1986.
(And illustrator) *No Jumping on the Bed!*, Dial Books for Young Readers, 1987.
(And illustrator) *My First Play House*, Workman Publishing, 1987.
(And illustrator) *My First Play Town*, Workman Publishing, 1987.
(And illustrator) *Ollie Forgot*, Dial Books for Young Readers, 1988.
(And illustrator) *Mother Goose's Words of Wit and Wisdom: A Book of Months*, Dial Books for Young Readers, 1990.

TEDD ARNOLD

(And designer of samplers) *Cross-Stitch Patterns for Mother Goose's Words of Wit and Wisdom Samplers to Stitch,* New American Library/Dutton, 1990.

(And illustrator) *The Signmaker's Assistant,* Dial Books for Young Readers, 1992.

The Simple People, illustrated by Andrew Shachat, Dial Books for Young Readers, 1992.

FOR CHILDREN; ILLUSTRATOR

Helen Witty, *Mrs. Witty's Monster Cookies,* Workman Publishing, 1983.

Ron Atlas, *Looking for Zebra; Hotel Zoo: Happy Hunting from A to Z,* Little Simon, 1986.

Atlas, *A Room for Benny,* Little Simon, 1987.

Rena Coyle, *My First Baking Book,* Workman Publishing, 1988.

Anne Kostick, *My First Camera Book,* Workman Publishing, 1989.

David Schiller and David Rosenbloom, *My First Computer Book,* Workman Publishing, 1991.

WORK IN PROGRESS: The Twin Princes, a children's book for Dial Books for Young Readers; writing and illustrating another children's book, *Green Wilma,* for Dial Books; illustrating *My First Garden Book* by Carole Ottesen for Workman Publishing.

SIDELIGHTS: Tedd Arnold told *SATA:* "It still comes as a great surprise to me that I'm now an author. I've always drawn pictures, taken art classes and thought of myself as an artist. In school, my cartoons graced many a desktop, chalkboard, and math paper. (The teachers and the girls always noticed.) In the army, extra duty could be avoided by letting the sergeants know how nice the barracks would look with 'inspirational' murals painted on the walls. After college, I quickly learned that art-related jobs were more comfortable than construction-related jobs. And even today I find that drawing pictures for books is a great way to avoid doing real work.

"Back in college, I began writing titles across the bottoms of my drawings. The titles became lengthy, growing into sentences and paragraphs. The drawings and writings were like fragments of stories, pages torn from books. My interest in the words developed into a renewed interest in an old love—comics. It was in the form of comics that I first explored storytelling.

"However, the writing was always for the pictures. The pictures were the real thing, the reason for being, the fun. Which is why the label of 'author' still feels like brand new dress shoes, while 'artist' feels like well-worn, street-running, tree-climbing, can-kicking, ball-park sneakers. But don't we all just love a new pair of shoes!"

FOR MORE INFORMATION SEE:

PERIODICALS

Growing Point, July, 1989, p. 5196.
Language Arts, April, 1988, p. 415.
New Yorker, November 30, 1987, p. 140-141.
School Library Journal, October, 1987, p. 110; December, 1988, p. 79; November, 1990, p. 76.
Times Literary Supplement, April 7, 1989, p. 380.

B

BANG, Molly 1943-
(Garrett Bang)

PERSONAL: Full name is Molly Garrett Bang; born December 29, 1943, in Princeton, NJ; daughter of Frederik Barry (a research physician) and Betsy (an author, translator, and scientist; maiden name, Garrett) Bang; married Richard H. Campbell (an acoustics engineer), September 27, 1974; children: Monika. *Education:* Wellesley College, B.A., 1965; University of Arizona, M.A., 1969; Harvard University, M.A., 1971.

ADDRESSES: Home—89 Water St., Woods Hole, MA 02543.

CAREER: Author, illustrator, and translator. Doshisha University, Kyoto, Japan, teacher of English, 1965-67; Asahi Shimbun, New York, NY, interpreter of Japanese, 1969; Baltimore Sunpapers, Baltimore, MD, reporter, 1970. Illustrator and consultant for UNICEF, Johns Hopkins Center for Medical Research and Training, and Harvard Institute for International Development.

AWARDS, HONORS: Notable book award from American Library Association, 1977, for *Wiley and the Hairy Man,* and 1980, for *The Grey Lady and the Strawberry Snatcher;* honor book award for illustration from *Horn Book,* 1980, for *The Grey Lady and the Strawberry Snatcher,* 1984, for *Dawn,* and 1986, for *The Paper Crane;* Caldecott Honor Book Award, 1981, for *The Grey Lady and the Strawberry Snatcher* and, 1983, for *Ten, Nine, Eight;* Kate Greenaway Honor Award, 1983, for *Ten, Nine, Eight;* Hans Christian Andersen Award nomination, and *Boston Globe/Horn Book* Award for Illustration, both 1988, for *The Paper Crane.*

WRITINGS:

BOOKS FOR CHILDREN; SELF-ILLUSTRATED

(Compiler) *The Goblins Giggle, and Other Stories* (folktales from France, China, Japan, Ireland, and Germany), Scribner, 1973.

(Under name Garrett Bang; translator and compiler) *Men from the Village Deep in the Mountains, and Other Japanese Folk Tales,* Macmillan, 1973.

(Editor) *Wiley and the Hairy Man* (adapted from an American folktale by mother, Betsy Bang), Macmillan, 1975.

(Editor) *The Buried Moon and Other Stories* (folktales from China, Japan, England, and India), Scribner, 1977.

The Grey Lady and the Strawberry Snatcher, Four Winds, 1980.

(Adaptor and editor) *Tye May and the Magic Brush* (Chinese folktale), Greenwillow, 1981.

Ten, Nine, Eight, Greenwillow, 1983.

(Adaptor) *Dawn* (Japanese folktale), Morrow, 1983.

(Adaptor) *The Paper Crane* (Chinese folktale), Greenwillow, 1985.

Delphine, Morrow, 1988.

Picture This: Perception and Composition, Little, Brown, 1991.

Yellow Ball, Morrow, 1991.

ILLUSTRATOR

Betsy Bang, translator and editor, *The Old Woman and the Red Pumpkin: A Bengali Folk Tale,* Macmillan, 1975.

B. Bang, translator and editor, *The Old Woman and the Rice Thief,* Greenwillow, 1977.

B. Bang, translator and editor, *Tuntuni, the Tailor Bird,* Greenwillow, 1978.

B. Bang, translator and editor, *The Demons of Rajpur,* Greenwillow, 1980.

Judith Benet Richardson, *David's Landing,* Woods Hole Historical Collection, 1984.

Sylvia Cassedy and Suetake Kunihirs, translators, and *Red Dragonfly on My Shoulder,* Harper, 1992.

OTHER

Also author and illustrator of numerous health care manuals.

SIDELIGHTS: Molly Garrett Bang is a talented and prolific author and illustrator of many popular books for children. A well-traveled and educated person, Bang

Author-illustrator Molly Bang.

reflects in her books her love and extensive study of foreign lands, people, and folklore. While she has published many unique adaptations of numerous legends, Bang is perhaps most recognized for her tales steeped in mystery and yet branded with her unique sense of humor.

Bang's love for books was kindled early. Her mother, Betsy, is a writer and has adapted and translated several folktales (five of which her daughter Molly illustrated). Bang's parents also maintained an extensive library and frequently presented each other with copies of Arthur Rackham's handsomely illustrated books for special occasions, such as birthdays and anniversaries. Rackham's illustrations fascinated Bang and planted the idea that illustration would someday be a lovely profession for her.

For years Bang kept the desire of illustrating books in the back of her mind while she pursued a variety of subjects and interests in high school and college. After graduating from Wellesley College with a degree in French, Bang went to Japan to teach English at Doshisha University in Kyoto for eighteen months. She returned to the United States to work on master's degrees in Oriental Studies from the University of Arizona and from Harvard University. Bang then went back overseas to illustrate health manuals for rural health projects for UNICEF, the Johns Hopkins Center for Medical Research and Training, and the Harvard Institute for International Research, in such cities as Calcutta, India and Dacca, Bangladesh, and in the West African republic of Mali.

After working with UNICEF, Johns Hopkins, and Harvard, Bang came back to the United States and initiated her career as illustrator by gathering and illustrating a group of tales she had read during her

travels overseas. Published in 1973, *The Goblins Giggle, and Other Stories* is the first of many Bang books that successfully incorporate Bang's fascination with international folklore and legends with her love of mystery and suspense. In her *School Library Journal* review of *The Goblins Giggle, and Other Stories,* Margaret A. Dorsey comments that these "five spooky folk tales—two Japanese, two European, one Chinese—are smoothly told and greatly enhanced by full- or double-page black-and-white illustrations.... This is a charming collection in which humans triumph over supernatural adversaries after a few suitably chilling thrills." And a critic for the *New York Times Book Review* states that "Molly Bang has a splendid feeling for general chill, and her choices are all scary but end comfortably so as not to keep anyone awake for long. Her illustrations are unique and intriguing."

The Goblins Giggle, and Other Stories was just the first of many books that reveal Bang's captivation with folktales that are rich in mystery and suspense. In such popular and award-winning books as *Wiley and the Hairy Man, The Grey Lady and the Strawberry Snatcher, Dawn,* and *The Paper Crane,* Bang has either breathed new life into original fables or created her own yarns with her rare skill as a gifted and sensitive writer and versatile illustrator.

In *Wiley and the Hairy Man,* Bang recreates a black American folktale she found while travelling in the South. Set in Alabama, *Wiley and the Hairy Man* is a quaint story of a young boy and his mother terrorized by a scary swamp monster. After several frightful encounters, the pair resourcefully overcome their fear to fend off the monster. "The tale has all the best elements of entertainment—humor, suspense, action, and ethnic

A contemporary folk tale, *The Paper Crane,* **written and illustrated by Bang, skillfully blends Western characterization with Asian folklore themes.**

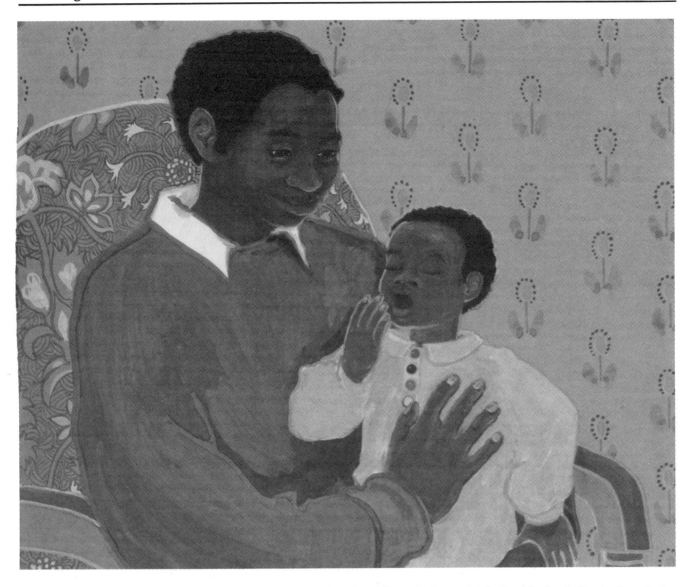

Best known for her folklore retellings, Bang has also produced a well-received counting book with simple illustrations that count down to bedtime. (From *Ten, Nine, Eight* written and illustrated by Bang.)

color—with the stylistic simplicity befitting an easy reader," writes Judith Goldberger in *Booklist*. Goldberger continues to note that "flourishes are accomplished via illustrations in moss-grey, black, and white.... It is hard to imagine a reader unaffected by this book's punch."

Another book that captured both the public and critic's attention is Bang's picture book, *The Grey Lady and the Strawberry Snatcher*. Recipient of numerous awards and honors, *The Grey Lady and the Strawberry Snatcher* is a delightfully intriguing and dramatic story of an old woman who is relentlessly pursued by a bizarre, strawberry stealing creature. Patricia Jean Cianciolo remarks in *Picture Books for Children* that *The Grey Lady and the Strawberry Snatcher* "is filled with surprises, lively humor, and suspense. Its unusual colors and its characters are ethnically indeterminate, but the whole is strongly suggestive of a folktale from India. The skillfully executed, impressionistic illustrations, so full of

meticulous, often startling details, offer an exciting visual treat to the readers of this wordless book."

Denise M. Wilms comments in a *Booklist* review of *The Grey Lady and the Strawberry Snatcher* that "a wordless picture book depends on eerie art and high drama for holding its scrutinizers, and they will be held.... Bang's art is a sum of disparate colors, patterns, and spreads of gray that unexpectedly blend. None of her figures is conventional: the tropical-type setting is peopled by warm brown faces and hot colors. Backgrounds point to a variety of ethnic motifs—a Persian rug, an Indian woman on a skateboard, a Buddha-like figure smiling out of a shop window, a banjo-picking grandfather at the gray lady's house. It's a visual jigsaw that somehow balances and holds beyond the story line."

In *Dawn* and *The Paper Crane* Bang retells classic folktales in contemporary settings. *Dawn* is Bang's updated version of the old Japanese tale of "The Crane

Bang's 1991 picture book, *Yellow Ball,* **invites youngsters to journey far from shore and explore the open sea.**

Wife"—a yarn about a young man who rescues an injured Canadian goose. After nursing the bird back to health, he releases the animal. A beautiful young woman suddenly appears and the two fall in love, marry, and have a daughter, Dawn. After the man breaks a promise to his wife, she turns back into the Canadian goose he had saved years ago and is taken away by a flock of geese. The father and daughter are left with their grief and sadness. The daughter then sets sail to find her mother.

Bulletin of the Center for Children's Books contributor Zena Sutherland writes in her review of *Dawn* that "Bang's story is a variant of a traditional folk theme, the

animal-mate who resumes his or her original shape; the author has made a touching and effective tale of this, and has illustrated it handsomely." "As in many good folktales," Michael Dirda writes in the *Washington Post Book World,* "the boatmaker's ambition leads to disaster for all concerned. What makes this version so powerful are, of course, Bang's illustrations. Watercolors alternate with pencil and charcoal drawings ... and the whole book [is] pleasingly designed.... This is a haunting picture book, as affecting to adults as it is entrancing for children."

Also based on a classic Chinese legend, *The Paper Crane* is the story of an act of kindness being rewarded by a magical gift. Bang tells of a restaurant that is losing all of its business because a super highway is built that bypasses the building. Late one evening a poor stranger enters the restaurant and is treated to a delicious meal by the owner and his son. To thank them for their kindness, the stranger makes a crane out of a paper napkin and presents it to the two men with the instructions that the crane will come to life and dance for them when they clap their hands. Word spreads about the dancing crane, and swarms of customers flock to the restaurant, saving the business from closing.

Patricia Dooley states in *School Library Journal* that "here is that very rare treat, a contemporary folk tale that feels just right. Bang gives a modern setting and details to the consoling story of a good man, deprived by unlucky fate of his livelihood, whose act of kindness and generosity is repaid by the restoration of his fortunes, through the bringing to life of a magical animal—the paper crane." And Hanna B. Zeiger explains in a *Horn Book* review of *The Paper Crane:* "In a world in which we use the word *gentle* to describe everything from laxatives to scouring powder, Molly Bang has restored dignity to the word with her truly gentle tale of *The Paper Crane....* The book successfully blends Asian folklore themes with contemporary Western characterization."

While she is gratified that so many young readers have been tickled, thrilled, and delighted by her books, Bang is concerned that not all children have equal access to the enormous variety of books published yearly for children. "Ways need to be found," Bang explains to Robert D. Hale in *Horn Book,* "to get books to children beyond the privileged class." Bang cites the budget restrictions of both public and school libraries as one of the reasons lower income children often find reading a difficult skill to master. Bang also told Hale that "too many children don't know how to use a book, because they aren't given the chance to learn. If they only have flimsy paperbacks, they never experience the feel of a real book. Because they are less available to people who are poor, books become less relevant. In the midst of all this self-congratulation we have to think about that."

WORKS CITED:

Cianciolo, Patricia Jean, "The Imaginative World: *The Grey Lady and the Strawberry Snatcher,*" *Picture Books for Children,* American Library Association, 1981, p. 151.

Dirda, Michael, review of *Dawn, Washington Post Book World,* October 9, 1983, pp. 10-11.

Dooley, Patricia, review of *The Paper Crane, School Library Journal,* December, 1985, p. 66.

Dorsey, Margaret A., review of *The Goblins Giggle, and Other Stories, School Library Journal,* January, 1974, p. 45.

Review of *The Goblins Giggle, and Other Stories, New York Times Book Review,* January 13, 1974, p. 8.

Goldberger, Judith, review of *Wiley and the Hairy Man, Booklist,* July 15, 1976, p. 1601.

Hale, Robert D., "Musings," *Horn Book,* November/December, 1989, pp. 806-807.

Sutherland, Zena, review of *Dawn, Bulletin of the Center for Children's Books,* January, 1984, pp. 82-83.

Wilms, Denise M., review of *The Grey Lady and the Strawberry Snatcher, Booklist,* July 15, 1980, pp. 1673-1674.

Zeiger, Hanna B., review of *The Paper Crane, Horn Book,* January, 1986, p. 45.

FOR MORE INFORMATION SEE:

BOOKS

Children's Literature Review, Volume 8, Gale, 1985.

*   *   *

BAUER, Marion Dane 1938-

PERSONAL: Born November 20, 1938, in Oglesby, IL; daughter of Chester (a chemist) and Elsie (a kindergarten teacher; maiden name, Hempstead) Dane; married Ronald Bauer (an Episcopal priest), June 25, 1959 (divorced); children: Peter Dane, Elisabeth Alison. *Education:* Attended La Salle-Peru-Oglesby Junior College, 1956-58, and University of Missouri, 1958-59; University of Oklahoma, B.A., 1962. *Politics:* Democrat. *Religion:* Episcopalian.

ADDRESSES: Home—8861 Basswood Rd., Eden Prairie, MN 55344. *Agent*—Carol Mann Literary Agency, 168 Pacific St., Brooklyn, NY 11201.

MARION DANE BAUER

In Bauer's *On My Honor*, a boy faces some tough moral choices after the drowning of his friend. (Cover illustration by Michael Conway.)

CAREER: High school teacher, Waukesha, WI, 1962-64; Hennepin Technical Center, Minneapolis, MN, instructor in creative writing for adult education program, 1975-78; instructor, University of Minnesota Continuing Education for Women, 1978—, and Institute for Children's Literature, 1982—.

MEMBER: Authors Guild of Authors League of America, Society of Children's Book Writers.

AWARDS, HONORS: American Library Association Notable Book Award, 1976, and Japanese Library Association Award, both for *Shelter from the Wind;* Gold Kite Honor Book Award, Society of Children's Book Writers, 1979, for *Foster Child;* Jane Addams Peace Association Award, 1984, for *Rain of Fire;* Notable Children's Book Award, American Library Association, and Best Books list, *School Library Journal,* both 1986, both for *On My Honor;* Newbery Honor Book Award, and British Children's Book Award runner-up, both 1987, both for *On My Honor.*

WRITINGS:

Shelter from the Wind, Clarion Books, 1976.
Foster Child, Clarion Books, 1977.
Tangled Butterfly, Clarion Books, 1980.

"Rodeo Red and the Runaway," an *ABC Afterschool Special,* was based on Bauer's 1976 novel, *Shelter from the Wind.*

Rain of Fire, Houghton, 1983.
Like Mother, Like Daughter, Ticknor & Fields, 1985.
On My Honor, Ticknor & Fields, 1986.
Touch the Moon, Ticknor & Fields, 1987.
A Dream of Queens and Castles, Houghton, 1990.

ADAPTATIONS: An *ABC Afterschool Special,* "Rodeo Red and the Runaway," was based on *Shelter from the Wind. On My Honor* has been released on videocassette by Random House.

WORK IN PROGRESS: Face to Face (a novel); *What's Your Story: A Young Person's Guide to Writing Fiction.*

SIDELIGHTS: Marion Dane Bauer is the author of a number of books that deal with the sometimes harsh realities of growing up. Although some of Bauer's novels feature fantastic themes and situations, the majority of her works, such as *Rain of Fire* and *On My Honor,* focus on young people who must learn to cope with traumatic events in everyday life. Bauer's fiction is often drawn from personal experiences, featuring places she has lived in or visited often; as a result, her books have a special sense of detail. Sometimes Bauer is happy with the finished product; other times, she can't wait to begin a new project. Above all, Bauer is simply happy to be able to tell stories. "I have been given the most splendid gift I can imagine," she wrote in an essay for *Something about the Author Autobiography Series* (*SAAS*). "My dreams have been able to reach out to other people. And my life has been touched in return."

Bauer grew up in a small Illinois prairie town. Thanks largely to her mother's creative nature, Bauer had a childhood that she once described as "idyllic." She was a dreamer, spending a great deal of time writing stories both in her head and on paper. (Bauer considers her first "penned" work to be a poem dedicated to her teddy bear.) As time went on, there was less and less time for Bauer to spend on her writing; first came college, then marriage and a family. Writing remained Bauer's self-proclaimed "secret vice" until her daughter began grade school. Bauer then started visiting the local library to read up on current trends in children's literature. Eventually, she began work on *Foster Child,* a novel loosely based on her experiences as a foster parent.

The eventual publication of *Foster Child* gave Bauer the boost of confidence that she needed. More novels followed, including *Shelter from the Wind* and *Touch the Moon.* Critics praised Bauer's ability to handle sensitive subjects with conviction and care. *Rain of Fire,* Bauer's story about a young boy's relationship with his older brother who has just returned from action in World War II, was lauded by a reviewer for the *Bulletin of the Center for Children's Books* as "serious, but not somber, beautifully laminated and perceptive in unfolding the intricacies of human relationships ... it has good pace and momentum within its tight frame." Similarly, *On My Honor* explores human reaction to tragedy. When two friends impulsively swim in a forbidden and dangerous river and one boy drowns, the survivor must make some difficult decisions at a very confusing moment. Claudia Lepman-Logan, writing in *Horn Book,* noted that the moral dilemma at the core of *On My Honor* makes for "an exciting reading experience," largely due to the novel's "richness and strength."

Bauer's willingness to deal with tough issues is balanced at times by her sense of whimsy. In works such as *Touch the Moon,* in which a young girl creates a vivid fantasy life that includes a magical horse, Bauer explores a theme of reality versus illusion. In her *SAAS* entry, Bauer remarked: "One of the things to know about themes in fiction is that no story speaks Truth. They all portray individual truths. And almost any theme that can be explored and justified in fiction has its opposite which is equally 'true.' A student once came to me ... and commented that the theme of her work consistently was, 'You don't have to accept reality; try fantasy.' An appropriate piece of wisdom to convey, surely."

Many of Bauer's works feature a moral choice. Some of these choices result in small consequences; others have greater repercussions. Bauer feels that it is important to teach children that such choices are important. "To have hope [children] must believe that the choices they make matter, that they have the power to change human history," Bauer told *Horn Book.* She added that she is "convinced that one of the most fundamental experiences of being human is the discovery each of us makes in our cribs: that we are alone.... Fiction can cut through our isolation ... because fiction can move us inside another human being, allow us to share the thoughts and feelings and to see the world through those other eyes."

WORKS CITED:

Bauer, Marion Dane, "Peace in Story, Peace in the World," *Horn Book,* November/December, 1987.
Bauer, Marion Dane, *Something about the Author Autobiography Series,* Volume 9, Gale, 1990, pp. 1-16.
Lepman-Logan, Claudia, "Books in the Classroom: Moral Choices in Literature," *Horn Book,* January/February, 1989, pp. 108-111.
Review of *Rain of Fire, Bulletin of the Center for Children's Books,* November, 1983.

FOR MORE INFORMATION SEE:

BOOKS

Holtze, Sally Holmes, editor, *Fifth Book of Junior Authors,* Wilson, 1983, pp. 24-27.

PERIODICALS

Bulletin of the Center for Children's Books, October, 1986.
School Library Journal, March, 1987, p. 78; November, 1987, pp. 33-34.
Wilson Library Bulletin, April, 1987, pp. 48-49.

*   *   *

BAYLEY, Nicola 1949-

PERSONAL: Born August 18, 1949, in Singapore; daughter of Percy Howard (a company director) and Ann Barbara (Crowder) Bayley; married John Hilton (a barrister), December 21, 1979; children: Felix Percy Howard. *Education:* Attended St. Martin's School of Art; Royal College of Art, diploma, 1974.

ADDRESSES: Home—London, England.

CAREER: Illustrator of children's books. *Exhibitions:* St. Martin's School of Art, 1967-71, and Royal College of Art Graduate Exhibition, 1971-74.

AWARDS, HONORS: Kate Greenaway Medal commendation, 1981, Children's Choice Award, Children's Book Council and International Reading Association, 1982, and Bologna Book Fair Prize, 1983, all for *The Patchwork Cat;* Kurt Maschler Award runner-up, Book Trust in London, 1983, for *The Mouldy.*

WRITINGS:

SELF-ILLUSTRATED CHILDREN'S BOOKS

(Compiler) *Nicola Bayley's Book of Nursery Rhymes,* J. Cape, 1975, Knopf, 1977.
(Compiler) *One Old Oxford Ox* (counting book), Atheneum, 1977.

(Compiler) "Copycats" series (includes *Parrot Cat, Polar Bear Cat, Elephant Cat, Spider Cat,* and *Crab Cat*), Knopf, 1984.

(Compiler) *As I Was Going Up and Down and Other Nonsense Rhymes,* Macmillan, 1986.

(Compiler) *Hush-a-Bye Baby and Other Bedtime Rhymes,* Macmillan, 1986.

(Compiler) *Bedtime and Moonshine: Lullabies and Nonsense,* Macmillan, 1987.

ILLUSTRATOR

Richard Adams, *The Tyger Voyage,* Knopf, 1976.

Christopher Logue, adapter, *Puss in Boots* (pop-up book), J. Cape, 1976, Greenwillow, 1977.

Russell Hoban, *La Corona and the Tin Frog, and Other Tales,* J. Cape, 1978, Merrimack, 1981.

William Mayne, *The Patchwork Cat,* Knopf, 1981.

Mayne, *The Mouldy,* Knopf, 1983.

Paul Manning, "Merry-Go-Rhymes" series (includes *Cook, Fisherman, Clown,* and *Boy*), Walker, 1987, Macmillan, 1988.

Antonia Barber, *The Mousehole Cat,* Macmillan, 1990.

SIDELIGHTS: Nicola Bayley fills her works for young children with elegantly detailed and lushly colored illustrations. Many of her books contain collections of nursery and nonsense rhymes which are accompanied by delicate, miniature pictures. Bayley's illustrations have also found their way into the works of other authors, and it was one of her drawings that motivated Richard Adams to write *The Tyger Voyage.* Bayley is "a brilliant young English artist whose pictures glow like late-medieval manuscripts," describes Alison Lurie in the *New York Times Book Review.* And a *Junior Bookshelf* reviewer asserts: "Bayley belongs to one of the oldest traditions in children's books.... Her art is mannered, but very well-mannered, exquisite and in perfect taste."

Bayley was born in Singapore in 1949, but spent her childhood in both China and Hampshire, England. As a student at an English boarding school, she was excused from sports and games because of "growing pains." Instead, she spent most of her afternoons in the art room, receiving encouragement from both her parents and her art teachers. Originally planning to be a fashion designer, Bayley sent out a portfolio of fashion and textile designs to a variety of art schools. Accepted at St. Martin's School of Art in London, she took a number of graphic design courses before concentrating in her final years on illustration. From St. Martin's, Bayley went to the Royal College of Art, also in London, where she continued her education and further developed her style of illustration.

Upon graduating, Bayley began working for Jonathan Cape, the publisher of her first book, *Nicola Bayley's Book of Nursery Rhymes.* "Enchanting detail, a Victorian style, and luminous colors" fill this collection of twenty-two Mother Goose rhymes, relates Ruth M. McConnell in *School Library Journal.* "There is a great variety of fanciful pattern, with each turning of the page a surprise." Bayley's next work for Jonathan Cape came

Nicola Bayley and her son Felix.

in the form of Richard Adams' *The Tyger Voyage.* The book was a result of Bayley's depiction of the old rhyme, "Three Thick Thumping Tigers Taking Toast for Tea." Her painting so inspired Adams that he wrote his narrative poem around it, and Bayley rendered the rest of the illustrations.

In her following works, Bayley retells and collects the writings of others, adding her own illustrations. Her retelling of *One Old Oxford Ox* was published in 1977, and consists of "an alliterative counting rhyme tailored to trip the tongue, and the pictures shine from wide creamy borders," points out Karla Kuskin in the *New York Times Book Review.* "These miniature vistas have such melting brightness they might be fashioned of stained glass." In her *Hush-a-Bye Baby and Other Bedtime Rhymes,* Bayley collects twelve rhymes from Mother Goose, along with American and German traditional rhymes. "Toys, angels, animals and grotesques are set in beautifully suggested landscapes or interiors in a little book which is a joy to handle and investigate," concludes Margery Fisher in *Growing Point.*

Bayley's "Copycats" series, published in 1984, consists of several small books featuring a cat who imagines himself to be a variety of other animals in such titles as *Crab Cat, Polar Bear Cat,* and *Elephant Cat.* The cat, one of Bayley's favorite animals to illustrate, begins by

Bayley's illustration of a nursery rhyme inspired Richard Adams to write *The Tyger Voyage*, which Bayley subsequently illustrated.

describing all the benefits of being the other animals. But as soon as he encounters something negative, such as being wet and cold as a penguin cat, he quickly turns back into a regular cat. "A few words serve to link pictures which seem to exist mainly to demonstrate the resilience of cat-nature and the beauty of action and posture, with a gentle humour to remove any taint of sentimentality," observes Fisher in her *Growing Point* review of the series. Andrew Clements, writing in *New Statesman*, finds the series "enchanting," and full of "sequences of ravishing fantastical illustrations."

Bayley lives and works in London, creating her illustrations in a studio once used by Arthur Rackham, a renowned English artist and illustrator. She produces her paintings using a technique known as stippling, which consists of dotting paint onto a surface with a brush in thousands of tiny dabs. Preferring to work with water colors on cartridge paper, Bayley claims that the hardest part of her work is at the rough draft stage: "I use my brain for them," explains Bayley in an essay for *Illustrators of Children's Books: 1967-1976*. "After that it's mindless though absorbing. It's almost painting by numbers. I just fill in what I've drawn."

WORKS CITED:

Bayley, Nicola, essay in *Illustrators of Children's Books: 1967-1976,* compiled by Lee Kingman and others, Horn Book, 1978.
Clements, Andrew, "A Serious Business," *New Statesman,* December 7, 1984, p. 30.
Fisher, Margery, "Amusing the Little Ones?," *Growing Point,* November, 1984, pp. 4332-35.
Fisher, "Nursery Books," *Growing Point,* May, 1985, pp. 4438-39.
Kuskin, Karla, "Picture Books," *New York Times Book Review,* November 13, 1977, pp. 57-58.
Lurie, Alison, "The Classics Remain," *New York Times Book Review,* November 13, 1977, p. 31.
McConnell, Ruth M., review of *Nicola Bayley's Book of Nursery Rhymes, School Library Journal,* December, 1977, p. 42.
Review of *One Old Oxford Ox, Junior Bookshelf,* February, 1978, pp. 13-14.

FOR MORE INFORMATION SEE:

PERIODICALS

Junior Bookshelf, April, 1985, p. 77.
Publishers Weekly, December 9, 1983, p. 51.
School Library Journal, February, 1984, pp. 61-62; March, 1985, p. 146.
Washington Post Book World, November 13, 1977, pp. E1-E2.*

*   *   *

BAYLOR, Byrd 1924-
(Byrd Baylor Schweitzer)

PERSONAL: Born March 28, 1924, in San Antonio, TX; children: two sons. *Education:* Attended University of Arizona.

ADDRESSES: Home—Arizona.

CAREER: Author of books for children and adults. Worked variously as a reporter for an Arizona newspaper and as an executive secretary for the Association for Papago Affairs.

AWARDS, HONORS: Caldecott Honor Book, American Library Association, and Steck-Vaughn Award, Texas Institute of Letters, both 1973, for *When Clay Sings;* Catlin Peace Pipe Award, 1974, for *They Put on Masks;* Art Books for Children Citation, Brooklyn Public Library, 1976, for *Everybody Needs a Rock;* Steck-Vaughn Award, New York Academy of Sciences Younger Honor, Caldecott Honor Book, and *Boston Globe-Horn Book* Honor Book for Illustration, all 1976, and Art Books for Children Citation, 1977, 1978, and 1979, all for *The Desert Is Theirs;* Caldecott Honor Book, 1977, for *Hawk, I'm Your Brother,* and 1979, for *The Way to Start a Day;* Steck-Vaughn Award, 1978, for *Guess Who My Favorite Person Is;* Outstanding Arizona Author, 1985; *When Clay Sings* and *Everybody Needs a Rock* were named notable books by the American Library Association.

BYRD BAYLOR

WRITINGS:

FOR CHILDREN, EXCEPT AS NOTED; UNDER NAME
  BYRD BAYLOR, EXCEPT AS NOTED

(Under name Byrd Baylor Schweitzer) *Amigo,* illustrated by Garth Williams, Macmillan, 1963.

(Under surname Schweitzer) *One Small Blue Bead,* illustrated by Symeon Shimin, Macmillan, 1965.

(Under surname Schweitzer) *The Chinese Bug,* illustrated by Beatrice Darwin, Houghton, 1968.

(Under surname Schweitzer) *The Man Who Talked to a Tree,* illustrated by S. Shimin, Dutton, 1968.

Before You Came This Way, illustrated by Tom Bahti, Dutton, 1969.

Plink, Plink, Plink, illustrated by James Marshall, Houghton, 1971.

Coyote Cry, illustrated by S. Shimin, Lothrop, 1972.

When Clay Sings, illustrated by T. Bahti, Scribner, 1972.

Sometimes I Dance Mountains, illustrated by Ken Longtemps, photographs by Bill Sears, Scribner, 1973.

Everybody Needs a Rock, illustrated by Peter Parnall, Scribner, 1974.

They Put on Masks, illustrated by Jerry Ingram, Scribner, 1974.

The Desert Is Theirs, illustrated by P. Parnall, Scribner, 1975.

(Editor) *And It Is Still That Way: Legends Told by Arizona Indian Children,* illustrated by Lucy Jelinek, Scribner, 1976.

We Walk in Sandy Places, photographs by Marilyn Schweitzer, Scribner, 1976.

Hawk, I'm Your Brother, illustrated by P. Parnall, Scribner, 1976.

Guess Who My Favorite Person Is, illustrated by Robert Andrew Parker, Scribner, 1977.

Yes Is Better than No (for adults), illustrated by Mike Chiago, Scribner, 1977.

The Way to Start a Day, illustrated by P. Parnall, Scribner, 1978.

The Other Way to Listen, illustrated by P. Parnall, Scribner, 1978.

Your Own Best Secret Place, illustrated by P. Parnall, Scribner, 1979.

If You Are a Hunter of Fossils, illustrated by P. Parnall, Scribner, 1980.

Desert Voices, illustrated by P. Parnall, Scribner, 1981.

A God on Every Mountain Top: Stories of Southwest Indian Sacred Mountains, illustrated by Carol Brown, Scribner, 1981.

Moon Song, illustrated by Ronald Himler, Scribner, 1982.

The Best Town in the World, illustrated by R. Himler, Scribner, 1983.

I'm in Charge of Celebrations, illustrated by P. Parnall, Scribner, 1986.

Also contributor to *Redbook Magazine, McCall's,* and *Arizona Quarterly.*

ADAPTATIONS: *Hawk, I'm Your Brother; The Way to Start a Day;* and *The Other Way to Listen* have been adapted for video in English and Spanish versions by the Cheshire Corporation for its Southwest Series.

SIDELIGHTS: Born and raised in the American Southwest, Byrd Baylor has focused many of her writings on the region's landscape, peoples, and values. Her work reflects a familiarity with the area as well as her respect for the Southwest's unique culture, particularly that of the Native American. Her books of rhythmic prose poetry, written primarily for children, cover a wide range of themes—from exploring the life of prehistoric Indians through their art, to appreciating the environment and its flora and fauna, to realizing one's spiritual connection to nature. Throughout her writings, "Baylor celebrates the beauty of nature and her own feelings of rapport with it," assessed a reviewer for the *Bulletin of the Center for Children's Books.*

As a child, Baylor moved with her family to various locations in the Southwest—including Arizona, Texas, and Mexico—due to her father's work on ranches and in precious metal mines. Spending much of her time outdoors, she learned to value nature and became intrigued with the customs of Native Americans, including their rituals, folklore, and art. When she began her career as an author of children's books, Baylor fused her interests with prose to produce simple stories with important lessons. The alliance has yielded more than twenty-five books and has earned her numerous awards.

Baylor's first published book, *Amigo,* was issued in 1963, under the name Byrd Baylor Schweitzer. After three more books under the Schweitzer surname, she

Baylor's *The Desert Is Theirs* evokes the deep respect the "Desert People" of the Southwest hold for their environment. (Illustrated by Peter Parnall.)

began using the shortened version of her name with her fifth work, the popular *Before You Came This Way.* Released in 1969, the book uses Native American rock carvings, known as petroglyphs, to describe what life may have been like in prehistoric times. Baylor teamed with artist Tom Bahti to explain the significance of the drawings, which depict men, birds, animals, masked figures, and other designs, thereby introducing young readers to an ancient people and lifestyle. The book "treats the drawings for what they are," explained Euple L. Wilson in a review for *School Library Journal,* "the emotional expressions of a non-literate people." Generally well received by both critics and the public alike, *Before You Came This Way* was said to place readers "face to face with the minds and hearts of those people of long ago," according to the *New York Times Book Review*'s Gloria Levitas. Zena Sutherland in *Saturday Review* echoed that the story is "filled with a sense of wonder and quiet reverence, a vivid imagining."

The archeological study of prehistoric Indian life was again presented by Baylor in works such as 1972's *When Clay Sings* and 1974's *They Put on Masks.* The former work, a reteaming with illustrator Bahti, shows how ancient Indians, including the Anasazi, Hohokam, Mimbres, and Mogollon, recorded scenes from their everyday lives on their pottery. Revealing the meaning of the motifs painted on the earthenware, Baylor also details how some of the pottery was used and made. *When Clay Sings* received a Caldecott honorable mention and the prestigious Steck-Vaughn Award. *They Put*

on Masks, which discusses Indian and Eskimo ceremonial masks, also received the Catlin Peace Pipe Award as well as considerable critical attention.

Among Baylor's other works is *Everybody Needs a Rock,* which tells readers how to choose the rock that is right for them. The book also signified the beginning of a lengthy and successful collaboration between Baylor and illustrator Peter Parnall—an alliance that produced *The Desert Is Theirs,* Baylor's most critically acclaimed book to date, as well as several Caldecott honors. *Desert* investigates the relationship that desert dwellers have with their environment, pointing out the respect these inhabitants have for the land and its animals and resources. Baylor explains in the book that the desert's human inhabitants "say they *like* the land they live on so they treat it well—the way you'd treat an old friend. They sing it songs. They never hurt it. And the land knows." Critical response to the text and art was generally positive, with reviewers calling the work uncompromising, graceful, and striking. The duo, according to Mary M. Burns in *Horn Book,* has "brilliantly integrated myth, folklore, and factual description into a coherent whole."

Baylor continued to delve into humankind's oneness with nature, writing 1976's *Hawk, I'm Your Brother,* which also featured Parnall's artwork. Centering around a young boy's quest to experience the freedom of flying like a bird, the book follows the child as he captures and restrains a baby hawk, thinking that he can bond as its

In Baylor's *Hawk, I'm Your Brother,* a young boy who frees a captured hawk learns of the bonds between humans and animals. (Illustrated by Parnall.)

brother and be given the gift of flight. Baylor explains the youth's logic through her rhythmic prose: "And he even thought / that there might be / some special / magic / in a bird / that came from / Santos Mountain. // Somehow / he thought / he'd share / that / magic // and he'd *fly*. // They say / it used to / be / that way / when / we / knew how / to / talk / to birds // and how / to call / a bird's / wild spirit / down / into our own .... It seemed to him / he'd FLY— // if / a hawk / became / his / brother."

In time the boy realizes that his dream cannot be achieved as long as he denies another being its freedom. As he releases the hawk, a magical experience occurs— he mentally bonds with the creature, witnessing the gift of flight as he watches his "brother" soar through the sky. Elizabeth Martinez explained the story's moral in a review for *Interracial Books for Children Bulletin*: "No one can be truly free if others are not free, and we attain our own freedom by allowing others to be free." The critic also lauded Baylor for keeping the intrinsic identities of both the boy and the hawk intact.

Baylor's subsequent works have continued to be well regarded by both critics and children. Although she has completed more volumes featuring the culture of the American Southwest as a backdrop, she has also explored favorite things, important early morning attitudes, secret hiding places, and small-town life in books like *Guess Who My Favorite Person Is, The Way to Start a Day, Your Own Best Secret Place,* and *The Best Town in the World.* Her writings, particularly those that illuminate the sanctity of the natural wonders of the world, have endeared her to her young readers. While many critics laud her evocation of the mystic Native American spirit, they also praise her lyrical prose, believing that her text demands to be read aloud. "Baylor's sensitivity and eloquence are qualities that indelibly impress [her] readers," observed a *Publishers Weekly* reviewer.

WORKS CITED:

Baylor, Byrd, *The Desert Is Theirs,* illustrated by Peter Parnall, Scribner, 1975.
Baylor, Byrd, *Hawk, I'm Your Brother,* illustrated by Peter Parnall, Scribner, 1976.
Burns, Mary M., review of *The Desert Is Theirs, Horn Book,* February, 1976.
Levitas, Gloria, review of *Before You Came This Way, New York Times Book Review,* December 28, 1969.
Martinez, Elizabeth, review of *Hawk, I'm Your Brother, Interracial Books for Children Bulletin,* volume 7, number 6, 1976.
Review of *Moon Song, Publishers Weekly,* May 21, 1982, p. 76.
Sutherland, Zena, review of *Before You Came This Way, Saturday Review,* November 8, 1969.
Wilson, Euple L., review of *Before You Came This Way, School Library Journal,* December, 1969.
Review of *Your Own Best Secret Place, Bulletin of the Center for Children's Books,* January, 1980, p. 87.

FOR MORE INFORMATION SEE:

BOOKS

Children's Literature Review, Gale, Volume 3, 1978.

PERIODICALS

Booklist, September 15, 1981; November 1, 1986.
Bulletin of the Center for Children's Books, January, 1976; October, 1978; March, 1979.
Horn Book, April, 1964; June, 1976; February, 1984.
Instructor, August-September, 1972.
Junior Bookshelf, August, 1967; August, 1973.
Kirkus Reviews, September 15, 1969; October 15, 1973; April 15, 1974; August 1, 1974; June 15, 1981; July 15, 1981; May 1, 1991.
Kirkus Service, June 1, 1968.
New York Times Book Review, November 13, 1977.
Publishers Weekly, November 7, 1977.
School Library Journal, May, 1972; September, 1972; December, 1986.
Scientific American, December, 1969; December, 1972.*

—Sketch by Kathleen J. Edgar

*　　*　　*

BEINICKE, Steve 1956-

PERSONAL: Surname is pronounced "*by*-nick-a"; born February 25, 1956, in Toronto, Ontario, Canada; son of Manfred Wilhelm Kurt (a jeweler) and Ruth (an accountant; maiden name, Phuellendorfer) Beinicke. *Education:* Graduated from Ontario College of Art, 1978. *Politics:* None. *Religion:* None.

ADDRESSES: Home and office—50 Grant St., Toronto, Ontario, Canada M4M 2H5.

Andrew takes a midnight ride in Beinicke's animated illustration of *Andrew and the Wild Bikes.* (Written by Allen Morgan.)

CAREER: Free-lance designer/illustrator, 1978—; Myilolyn & Beinicke, Inc., partner, 1984-88. Involved with computer animation and interactive video presentations.

AWARDS, HONORS: Award from Art Directors Club of Toronto (design), 1983.

ILLUSTRATOR:

Joan Finnigan, *The Dog Who Wouldn't Be Left Behind,* Groundwood, 1989.
Allen Morgan, *Ellie and the Ivy,* Oxford, 1989.
A. Morgan, *Andrew and the Wild Bikes,* Annick, 1990.
Candace Savage, *Trash Attack,* Groundwood, 1990.
I'm Not Jenny, Groundwood, 1991.

WORK IN PROGRESS: Energy, for Groundwood.

SIDELIGHTS: Steve Beinicke told *SATA:* "The first film that I ever saw was *Pinocchio;* I was four years old."

*   *   *

BLACKLIN, Malcolm
See CHAMBERS, Aidan

*   *   *

BLADES, Ann 1947-

PERSONAL: Full name is Ann Sager Blades, born November 16, 1947, in Vancouver, British Columbia, Canada; daughter of Arthur Hazelton (an administrator) and Dorothy (a teacher; maiden name, Planche) Sager; married first husband (divorced); married David Morrison, 1984; children: two sons. *Education:* University of British Columbia, elementary teaching certificate, 1970; British Columbia Institute of Technology, R.N., 1974. *Hobbies and other interests:* Garage sales, gardening.

ADDRESSES: Home—2701 Crescent Dr., Surrey, British Columbia, Canada V4A 3J9. *Agent*—c/o Bella Pomer, 22 Shallmar Blvd., P.H. 2, Toronto, Ontario, Canada M5N 2Z8.

CAREER: Peace River North School District, Mile 18, British Columbia, elementary school teacher, 1967-68; Department of Indian Affairs and Northern Development, Tache, British Columbia, elementary school teacher, 1969; Surrey School District, Surrey, British Columbia, elementary school teacher, 1969-71; Vancouver General Hospital, Vancouver, British Columbia, part-time registered nurse, 1974-75; Mount St. Joseph Hospital, Vancouver, part-time registered nurse, 1975-80; artist, 1976—; author and illustrator of children's books.

EXHIBITIONS:

Some of Blades's illustrations have been exhibited at Vancouver Art Gallery, 1971; Biennale of Illustrations, Bratislava Czechoslovakia, 1977; Art Gallery of Ontario, 1977; Burnaby Art Gallery, 1978; Master Eagle

ANN BLADES

Gallery, New York, 1980; "Once upon a Time" exhibit, Vancouver Art Gallery, 1988; and Canada at Bologna, 1990.

Blades's paintings have been exhibited at Dunlop Art Gallery, 1982; and at Bau-Xi Galleries, Toronto, 1982, 1983, and 1985, and Vancouver, 1982, 1983, 1984, 1986, 1987, 1989, and 1991.

MEMBER: CANSCAIP.

AWARDS, HONORS: Book of the Year Award, Canadian Association of Children's Librarians (CALC), 1972, Best Illustrated Book Award runner-up, CALC, 1972, and Honour List, Austrian and German kinderbuchpreis, 1976, all for *Mary of Mile 18;* Amelia Frances Howard-Gibbon Illustrator's Award runner-up, CALC and Canadian Library Association, 1974, Best Children's Book Award, Child Study Association, 1977, and recommendation by National Conference of Christians and Jews: Books for Brotherhood, 1977, all for *A Boy of Tache;* grant from Canada Council, 1975; Children's Literature Award for Illustration (now called the Governor General's Award), Canada Council, and Amelia Frances Howard-Gibbon Illustrator's Award, both 1979, for *A Salmon for Simon;* Honourable Mention, Children's Literature Award for Illustration, Canada Council, 1981, for *Pettranella;* Amelia Frances Howard-Gibbon Illustrator's Award runner-up, 1985, and Elizabeth Mrazik-Cleaver Canadian Picture Book Award, Canadian Section of International Board on Books for Young People, 1986, both for *By the Sea: An Alphabet Book;* Canadian nominee for Hans Christian Andersen Award for Illustration, 1987.

WRITINGS:

FOR CHILDREN; SELF-ILLUSTRATED
Mary of Mile 18, Tundra Books, 1971.

A Boy of Tache, Tundra Books, 1973.
The Cottage at Crescent Beach, Magook Publishers, 1977.
By the Sea: An Alphabet Book, Kids Can Press, 1985.
Seasons Board Books, Lothrop, 1989.

ILLUSTRATOR

Michael Macklem, *Jacques the Woodcutter,* Oberon, 1977.
Betty Waterton, *A Salmon for Simon,* Douglas & McIntyre, 1978, Atheneum, 1980.
Margaret Laurence, *Six Darn Cows,* Lorimer, 1979.
Margaret Atwood and Joyce Barkhouse, *Anna's Pet,* Lorimer, 1980.
Waterton, *Pettranella,* Vanguard Press, 1980.
Jean Speare, *A Candle for Christmas,* Douglas & McIntyre, 1986, Macmillan, 1987.
Sue Ann Alderson, *Ida and the Wool Smugglers,* Macmillan, 1987.
The Singing Basket, edited by Kit Pearson, Camden House Publishing, 1990.
Ainslie Manson, *A Dog Came, Too,* Macmillan, 1992.

Also illustrator of the cover of *Canadian Books for Children: A Guide to Authors and Illustrators,* by Jon Stott and Raymond Jones, Harcourt (Toronto), 1988.

Some of Blades's works have been published in Germany, Austria, Sweden, Finland, Denmark, and Australia. Blades's manuscripts and illustrations for *By the Sea: An Alphabet Book, Mary of Mile 18,* and *A Boy of Tache* are housed at the National Library in Ottawa, Canada.

ADAPTATIONS: Mary of Mile 18 has been adapted into a filmstrip, distributed by Weston Woods Studios, Connecticut, 1978, and into a film of the same name, distributed by National Film Board of Canada, 1981; *A Salmon for Simon* has been adapted into a filmstrip, distributed by Weston Woods Studios, 1980.

WORK IN PROGRESS: Illustrations for the sequel to *Ida and the Wool Smugglers.*

SIDELIGHTS: Ann Blades is an award-winning author and illustrator who is best known for her simple, poignant tales of Canadian children. A self-taught artist, she illustrates her own works using rich, warm watercolors. Her style is unpolished, a technique many reviewers believe precisely captures the unpretentiousness of her writings. She centers her stories on basic themes—courage, for instance, or hope and family love. And sometimes she devotes an entire book to the depiction of a peaceful scene, such as a day spent lazily at the beach. But throughout her works she maintains a sense of optimism and simplicity, and as a result she creates books that reviewers continually praise as "beautiful" and "moving."

Blades began her professional career as an elementary school teacher in Mile 18, a small, remote farming community in northern British Columbia. There she discovered the need for children's books that focused on the rural lifestyles of her students. These children were accustomed to visiting an outhouse in sub-zero temperatures, for example, or living miles from their nearest neighbor; however, few books offered them anything other than stories set in typically urban surroundings. So Blades resolved to write a book of her own. First she taught herself to paint, and after deciding to model her story on one of her students, she completed what is perhaps her best-known work, *Mary of Mile 18.*

Winner of the 1972 Book of the Year Award from the Canadian Association of Children's Librarians, *Mary of Mile 18* tells the tale of Mary Fehr, a young, bespectacled girl who lives with her large, close-knit family in the backwoods of British Columbia. Life for the Fehr family is difficult; each member works to maintain the household, from Mary and her sister, who melt snow for washing and cooking, to her brother, who chops kindling for their wood-burning stove. The monotony of Mary's daily life is broken, though, when she finds a wolf-pup and quickly becomes attached to it. But her practical father forbids her to keep it. "'You know the rules,'" he tells her. "'Our animals must work for us or give us food.'" Although Mary protests, her father stands firm—until the pup proves his worth.

Mary of Mile 18 was well received by reviewers. Many critics praised Blades for her unadorned story line and for her colorful paintings that capture the oftentimes frigid northern Canadian countryside. "The simple text has an inner rhythm that supports full-page watercolours that are warm, still, unsentimental evocations of a bleak yet glowing northern scene," judged Sheila Egoff in the *Republic of Childhood.* Mary Rubio in *Canadian Children's Literature* found the book "plainly spoken" and "beautifully illustrated," while Callie Israel in *Profiles* decided that Blades "has succeeded in capturing the stark beauty of Canada's north." The reviewer added: "That the illustrations were done with a child's water paints on ordinary paper seems appropriate to the simple story."

Blades found inspiration for her next book, *A Boy of Tache,* while teaching at a Native American reservation in central British Columbia. Based on a real episode, the story revolves around Charlie, a Native American youth who is traveling to the trapping grounds with his grandparents, Za and Virginia. As the three progress on their journey, seventy-four-year-old Za falls ill with pneumonia, and Charlie must embark on a dangerous trek to summon help. Again reviewers praised Blades for her poignant narrative and also noted her ability to set the theme of Charlie's coming of age against his elderly grandfather's decline. "The story is remarkable because," noted Rubio, "while it operates on so many levels, it is at the same time so simple." Reviewers especially applauded Blades for her knowledge of Native American lifestyles and for her ability to evoke the Canadian terrain—the open skies, wooden cabins, and white birches—through her rich watercolors. "The illustrations show ... Blades' great talent as a landscape artist and as an interpreter of Indian life," decided Egoff.

Blades lived in the remote British Columbia community of Mile 18, where children faced hard work and a harsh environment. (Illustration from *Mary of Mile 18,* written and illustrated by Blades.)

During the late 1970s, Blades began illustrating works of other authors, most significantly, Betty Waterton's *Salmon for Simon.* Winner of the 1979 Canadian Children's Literature Award for Illustration, the story revolves around Simon, a young boy who desperately wishes to catch a fish with his new rod. He encounters little luck until an eagle flying overhead loses its hold on its prey—a salmon—and the fish falls to the ground. However, Simon finds himself so overcome with the fish's beauty, he cannot kill it. Instead he allows it to return to the sea. Many reviewers noted that Blades's illustrations for *Salmon* are unique; in one picture she draws the eagle thrillingly close, they note, with Simon appearing as a mere dot on the ground. In another, she paints the captured salmon as seen from Simon's eyes, as he gazes down at it. Using these techniques, Blades "causes the observer's viewpoint to alternate in an imaginative way," wrote Muriel Whitaker and Jetske Sybesma-Ironside in *Canadian Children's Literature.* The reviewers also declared that Blades's "illustrations complement this text ... superbly."

Blades's later books seem to concentrate more on her illustrations than her text, as evidenced by 1987's award-winning *By the Sea: An Alphabet Book.* At first glance, the work appears to be a typical "ABC" book— one word and illustration accompanying each letter. However, it actually depicts the adventures of a brother and sister as they spend a day at a beach near Vancouver, on the Pacific coast. Again using watercolors, Blades paints the various animals, people, and sights that the children encounter, including eagles, crabs, airplanes, kites, and sand castles. She also draws the children themselves engaged in a number of activities, ranging from eating ice cream, to wrapping themselves in beach towels, to tracing "X"s in the sand. Blades's "pictures do much more than teach the alphabet," assessed Celia Lottridge in *Quill and Quire.* "They show 26 aspects of a day at the beach in clear, pale colours that create the feeling of a cool breeze off the sea."

WORKS CITED:

Blades, Ann, *Mary of Mile 18,* self-illustrated, Bodley Head, 1971, p. 18.

Egoff, Sheila, "Illustration and Design" and "Picture-Books and Picture-Storybooks," *Republic of Childhood: A Critical Guide to Canadian Children's Literature in English,* 2nd edition, Oxford University Press, 1975, pp. 255-270, 271-291.

Israel, Callie, "Ann Blades," *Profiles,* edited by Irma McDonough, revised edition, Canadian Library Association, 1975, pp. 16-18.

Lottridge, Celia, review of *By the Sea: An Alphabet Book, Quill and Quire,* August, 1985, p. 37.

Rubio, Mary, "Pictorial and Narrative Realism," *Canadian Children's Literature: A Journal of Criticism and Review,* spring, 1975, pp. 77-79.

Whitaker, Muriel, and Jetske Sybesma-Ironside, review of *Six Darn Cows* and *A Salmon for Simon, Canadian Children's Literature: A Journal of Criticism and Review,* number 21, 1981, pp. 58-65.

FOR MORE INFORMATION SEE:

BOOKS

Children's Literature Review, Volume 15, Gale, 1988.
One Ocean Touching: Papers from the First Pacific Rim Conference on Children's Literature, edited by Sheila A. Egoff, Scarecrow, 1979.

PERIODICALS

Best Sellers, March, 1977.
Booklist, May 1, 1980.
Books in Canada, December, 1979.
Canadian Children's Literature: A Journal of Criticism and Review, numbers 39-40, 1985.
Children's Literature: Annual of the Modern Language Association Seminar on Children's Literature and the Children's Literature Association, volume 4, 1975.
In Review: Canadian Books for Children, spring, 1974.
Kirkus Reviews, February 15, 1977; May 1, 1980.
Maclean's, December 9, 1985.
School Library Journal, April, 1974; March, 1990.
World of Children's Books, number 1, 1978.

—*Sketch by Denise E. Kasinec*

*   *   *

BLOS, Joan W. 1928-

PERSONAL: Full name is Joan Winsor Blos; surname rhymes with "dose"; born December 9, 1928, in New York, NY; daughter of Max (a psychiatrist) and Charlotte (a teacher; maiden name, Biber) Winsor; married Peter Blos, Jr. (a psychoanalyst), in 1953; children: Stephen (deceased), Sarah. *Education:* Vassar College,

Joan W. Blos on a school visit, 1989.

B.A., 1949; City College (now of the City University of New York), M.A., 1956.

ADDRESSES: Agent—Curtis Brown Ltd., 10 Astor Place, New York, NY 10003.

CAREER: Jewish Board of Guardians, New York City, research assistant, 1949-50; City College (now of the City University of New York), New York City, assistant teacher of psychology, 1950-51; Yale University, Child Study Center, New Haven, CT, research assistant, 1951-53; Bank Street College of Education, New York City, associate editor in publications division, 1959-66, instructor in teacher education division, 1960-70; University of Michigan, Ann Arbor, research assistant and specialist in children's literature for the Department of Psychiatry, 1970-73, lecturer for School of Education, 1973-80; writer and lecturer, 1980—. Volunteer reviewer of children's books for the Connecticut Association of Mental Health and chairperson of children's Book Committee, 1954-56.

AWARDS, HONORS: John Newbery Medal from American Library Association, and American Book Award for children's hardcover fiction, both 1980, both for *A Gathering of Days: A New England Girl's Journal, 1830-32; A Gathering of Days* was also chosen as one of the

Best Books of the Year by *School Library Journal* and as an Ambassador Book by the English-Speaking Union.

WRITINGS:

FOR CHILDREN

In the City (reader), illustrated by Dan Dickas, Macmillan, 1964.

(With Betty Miles) *People Read* (reader), illustrated by Dan Dickas, Macmillan, 1964.

(With Miles) *Joe Finds a Way* (picture book), illustrated by Lee Ames, L. W. Singer, 1967.

"It's Spring," She Said (picture book), illustrated by Julie Maas, Knopf, 1968.

(With Miles) *Just Think!* (picture book), illustrated by Pat Grant Porter, Knopf, 1971.

A Gathering of Days: A New England Girl's Journal, 1830-32 (historical fiction), Scribner, 1979.

Martin's Hats (picture book), illustrated by Marc Simont, Morrow, 1984.

Brothers of the Heart: A Story of the Old Northwest, 1837-38 (historical fiction), Scribner, 1985.

Old Henry (picture book), illustrated by Stephen Gammell, Morrow, 1987.

The Grandpa Days (picture book), illustrated by Emily Arnold McCully, Simon & Schuster, 1989.

Lottie's Circus (picture book), illustrated by Irene Trivas, Morrow, 1989.

One Very Best Valentine's Day (picture book), illustrated by Emily Arnold McCully, Simon & Schuster, 1990.

The Heroine of the Titanic: A Tale Both True and Otherwise of the Life of Molly Brown, illustrated by Tennessee Dixon, Morrow, 1991.

A Seed, a Flower, a Minute, an Hour: A First Book of Transformations (picture book), illustrated by Hans Poppel, Simon & Schuster, 1992.

OTHER

Contributor of articles and reviews to periodicals, including *School Library Journal, New Outlook,* and *Merrill-Palmer Quarterly. Children's Literature in Education,* London, member of editorial board, 1973-77, U.S. editor, 1976-81.

Brothers of the Heart has been translated into Swedish and *Old Henry* into German, Dutch, and French.

ADAPTATIONS: Old Henry is available on cassette from National Library Service for the Blind and Physically Handicapped, 1987; *A Gathering of Days: A New England Girl's Journal, 1830-32,* is available on unabridged cassette from Random House and was read on "Books by Radio" over a University of Michigan radio station.

WORK IN PROGRESS: Adaptation of European folk tale, historical fiction for middle-grade readers, and a biographical picture book.

SIDELIGHTS: Joan Blos is an award-winning author of historical fiction for young people. She is also the author of several popular picture books, but she has earned the most recognition for *A Gathering of Days: A New England Girl's Journal, 1830-32,* about a young female growing up in nineteenth-century New Hampshire. Her interest in writing for children evolved after conducting graduate study in psychology, working in child development, and teaching children's literature. She also served as a volunteer reviewer of children's books beginning in 1954, and "from that time on," Blos was quoted by Betty Miles in *Horn Book,* "I never thought of other work, and I doubt that I ever will."

Born in 1928 in New York City, Blos was the only child of Max Winsor, a psychiatrist who helped juvenile delinquents, and Charlotte Winsor, a highly esteemed teacher of education. As a child, Blos was greatly encouraged to read. "My parents were both idealistic believers in the power of education and the educative process," the author related in *Something about the Author Autobiography Series (SAAS).* "We went to the library often in those years and both of my parents, as I recall, read aloud to me.... We read my favorites over and over again—some of them so often that I still know them nearly by heart." In addition, Blos began writing at an early age. "By the time I was three or four years old," Blos once told *Something about the Author*

(SATA), "my parents were writing down my 'poems' of which only one has survived."

At about the age of seven, Blos was enrolled in an experimental school at which her mother taught. Uniquely structured, the school not only strongly emphasized academics but stressed that children engage in all types of activities. Girls, for example, would work in carpentry, while boys were encouraged to take part in cooking classes. "My school experience was so different from that of my friends and contemporaries," Blos declared in *SAAS,* "that now ... it is almost hard to believe that we were going to school at the same time and in the same country.... My friends speak of punitive teachers. We respected ours...and we mostly called them by nicknames.... Friends recall how they would contrive to miss a day of school. For us the worst possible punishment was to be sent home from school."

During World War II Blos attended high school, where she nurtured her writing skills. One of her short stories earned publication in a national magazine, and she partook in writing her school's musical. Despite her penchant for English literature, Blos, upon attending college at Vassar, studied science and eventually became a physiology major. "If my newfound interest in physiology exerted a pull toward science, disappointment

Blos's Newbery Medal winner, *A Gathering of Days,* is the fictional journal of a teenaged girl growing up in nineteenth-century New Hampshire.

with courses in the English department seemed to push me away," Blos related in *SAAS*. "It was hard to respect myself, the faculty, or my fellow students when I regularly received *A*'s with but little preparation.... It came down to the fact that I was doing too well too easily in English and I didn't like knowing I was getting away with it. Besides, doesn't every doctor's daughter want, at one time or another, to be a doctor too?"

After graduating from Vassar, Blos worked as an assistant in a special school for young, disturbed children. Developing an interest in psychoanalytic theory, she enrolled in the master's program in psychology at New York's City College. She left the program to become a doctoral candidate at Yale University in New Haven, Connecticut, where she worked as a research assistant in the school's Child Study Center. At Yale, the author met Peter Blos, Jr., a medical student whom she married shortly thereafter.

"By the time we left New Haven three years later it had become clear that academic psychology and I were not a good match," Blos said in *SAAS*. Having worked with child patients and teaching student nurses in Yale's School of Nursing, Blos began to develop an affinity towards children's literature. "Suddenly," the author continued in *SAAS*, "there was a place where all I had learned about child development, all my interest in language, and all my love of books could at last come together."

The Bloses moved to New York City, where the author renewed her master's degree study and her husband completed his medical training. After the birth of their second child, Blos began working at Street College of Education, an institution dedicated to progressive education. There she taught language arts and children's literature and, as a member of the Publications Division, prepared numerous articles and book reviews and began to write for children. Her first two publications, both in collaboration with Betty Miles, were the primers *In the City* and *People Read*, both published in 1964. A few years later, Blos realized the publication of three more children's books, *"It's Spring," She Said*, *Just Think!*, and *Joe Finds a Way*, the last two also in collaboration with Miles.

Also around this time, Blos began to examine the history of an old farmhouse in New Hampshire that her husband's parents had bought in 1941. She visited libraries in New Hampshire and discovered that the house had been built in 1827. Also uncovering some interesting facts about the house's former owners, Blos was intrigued to find out more. She continued researching at New York City libraries. "Wonderful things, such as a collection of New Hampshire legends compiled in the mid-nineteenth century ... were to be found," Blos said in *SAAS*. "Memoirs and reminiscences, biographies and autobiographies became interesting for what they told of childhood in nineteenth-century New England. Novels and magazine stories gave further hints as to the sorts of things people cared about."

Her fascination with New England's history began as a hobby. Eventually, though, "I went on and on, filling notebooks...," Blos continued in *SAAS*. "It was quite a while before I began to think that I might have a book on my hands. Then it took me several more years before I was able to settle on the journal form." Before she could complete the book that would become *A Gathering of Days: A New England Girl's Journal, 1830-32*, the Bloses moved in 1970 to Ann Arbor, Michigan. For the next ten years, Blos worked at the University of Michigan, first at its Child Development Project and subsequently at the School of Education where she taught classes and seminars in children's literature with an emphasis on materials for the pre-reading child. She found time to continue research on New Hampshire's history at several Michigan libraries, and finally, in 1979, *A Gathering of Days* was published.

The story of fourteen-year-old Catherine Hall growing up in the early 1800s, *A Gathering of Days* relates the girl's inner-most thoughts as she matures. The experiences she records in her journal include how she offered assistance to a member of another race, dealt with the intrusion of a stepparent, and coped with the death of a close friend. Praised for its striking realism as well as its accurate representation of a historical time period, *A Gathering of Days* earned for its author a Newbery Medal, the highest honor in children's literature.

"It is an awesome thing to be told that you have made a distinguished contribution to children's literature," the author reflected in her acceptance speech for the award, as excerpted in *Top of the News*. "I learned that I had won the Newbery Medal late in January [of 1980]. The actual moment of notification ... was an event of transformative proportions, having all the trapping of magic, and not to be believed." As a result of her earning the prize, the author was catapulted into international stature and has been in high demand for speaking engagements. "Because I was a Newbery winner, what I had to say about children's literature was more interesting to more people!," Blos exclaimed in *SAAS*.

Since writing *A Gathering of Days*, the author has penned another work of historical fiction, *Brothers of the Heart: A Story of the Old Northwest, 1837-38*, about a young boy coming of age in nineteenth-century Michigan. She has also written successful picture books, including *Old Henry*, which tells of an eccentric man who antagonizes his neighbors by refusing to renovate his dilapidated house. Having dedicated much of her life to the field of children's literature, Blos will most likely continue to write books for young people. "What do books tell [children] about their world?," Blos commented to *SATA*. "What might I wish to say? 'Don't be scared and don't hang back,' my protagonist writes in *A Gathering of Days* as she ... reflects on her own long life. That pretty much sums it up."

WORKS CITED:

Blos, Joan W., *Something about the Author Autobiography Series,* Volume 11, Gale, 1991, pp. 51-68.

Blos, Joan W., "1980 Newbery Acceptance Speech," *Top of the News,* summer, 1980, pp. 393-96.

Miles, Betty, "Joan W. Blos," *Horn Book,* August, 1980, pp. 374-77.

Something about the Author, Volume 33, Gale, 1983, pp. 40-41.

FOR MORE INFORMATION SEE:

BOOKS

Children's Literature Review, Volume 18, Gale, 1989.

PERIODICALS

Detroit Free Press, February 1, 1981.
Detroit News, January 26, 1980; February 3, 1980.
Globe and Mail (Toronto), February 8, 1986.
Kirkus Reviews, January 15, 1980.
New York Times Book Review, March 23, 1980.
St. Louis Post-Dispatch, January 27, 1980.
Washington Post Book World, March 9, 1980.

*   *   *

BRESLOW, Susan 1951-

PERSONAL: Born February 9, 1951, in Mineola, NY; daughter of Irving (a jeweler) and Gwendolyn (a jeweler) Breslow. *Education:* Attended Northwestern University, 1968-70; State University of New York at Buffalo, B.A., 1972; Ohio State University, M.A., 1973.

ADDRESSES: Home—200 East Seventeenth St., New York, NY 10003.

CAREER: American Society for the Prevention of Cruelty to Animals, New York City, head of publications, 1981-83; *New York* (magazine), New York City, marketing director, 1983-91.

MEMBER: Advertising Women of New York, Mensa.

WRITINGS:

(With Sally Blakemore) *I Really Want a Dog,* illustrated by True Kelley, Dutton, 1990.

SIDELIGHTS: Susan Breslow told *SATA:* "When I was twelve, my family had to move and my mother decided to give our dog away because his care was an inconvenience to her. This broke my heart as I loved the dog most of all my family members. Years later, I adopted my own dog—and wrote this book for children who yearn for such a pet and will care for it."

*   *   *

BURGESS, Barbara Hood 1926-

PERSONAL: Born April 20, 1926, in Detroit, MI; daughter of Leland Doyle (an engineer) and Alma (a homemaker; maiden name, Westphal) Hood; married John Edgar Burgess (an appraiser), in June, 1947 (died

BARBARA HOOD BURGESS

in March, 1991); children: Lee, Christopher, Deborah Wagner, Eric. *Education:* Received bachelor's degree from Wayne State University, 1990. *Politics:* Independent. *Religion:* Protestant.

ADDRESSES: Home—9929 Auburndale, Livonia, MI 48150.

CAREER: Homemaker and writer. Past community activities include president of Parent-Teacher Association, coach of Little League Cheerleaders, and work for League of Women Voters.

MEMBER: Romance Writers of America.

AWARDS, HONORS: Judith Siegel Pearson Award, Wayne State University, 1983, for manuscript of a novel about Puritan dissenter Anne Hutchinson.

WRITINGS:

Oren Bell, Delacorte Press, 1991.

Past editor of *League of Women Voters Newsletter.*

WORK IN PROGRESS: A sequel to *Oren Bell;* further research for unpublished novel about Puritan dissenter Anne Hutchinson.

SIDELIGHTS: Barbara Hood Burgess told *SATA:* "I was born in Detroit, raised in Detroit. My father worked for Michigan Consolidated Gas Company in Detroit for all of his working life. I attended Cooley High School in the 1940s and graduated with a bachelor's degree from Wayne State University in 1990. My first job was downtown in the old Fidelity Building, across the street from the Penobscot Building. My happiest shopping was done at the downtown J. L. Hudson Company department store. The story of *Oren Bell* begins the year the downtown Hudson's store closed its doors forever. The store closing figures prominently in the plot.

"I was married forty-four years to my husband John, who died in 1991. He worked downtown in the Federal Building in Detroit as a reviewing appraiser for the U.S. Department of Housing and Urban Development. I have four grown children and six grandchildren. During the years that my children were growing up, my attempts at writing revolved around their activities. I wrote excellent Cub Scout and Boy Scout skits that took local prizes. I wrote religious education material for the National Association of Congregational Churches. I was twice Parent-Teacher Association president. I wrote rousing shows for school closings. I was editor for the *League of Women Voters Newsletter.* When I worked for money it was never a career, but a job to further some immediate goal or need.

"In the 1970s I was involved with a downtown neighborhood program at the First Congregational Church on Woodward Avenue. It was an every day summer job with side trips to the city park on Belle Isle and to museums. Neighborhood mothers were encouraged to help out. I admired these moms, who had pretty much the same aspirations for their kids as I did for mine. Why not? Neat kids brimming with energy and promise. Out of this experience came my plot and characters for *Oren Bell.*

"For the last couple of years I have not involved myself with working outside the home or community affairs. I was an honor student at Wayne State, but did not join the Honor Society. I am a paid-up member of Romance Writers of America, but I do not have a published romance to my credit. The editors at Dell have said they would like another Oren Bell book, so I am working on one. I still am inclined to take plot, action, and character ideas from my children. The house where I place the Bell family on Fourth Street and Hancock was the flat

my second son rented from the city when he was a Detroit policeman working from the Thirteenth Precinct. He is now an optometrist for a health maintenance organization in Detroit, and that has interesting possibilities. The idea for the *Oren Bell* sequel I am presently working on comes from my youngest son, who is a geologist working in groundwater for an environmental company. If there is a demand for more Oren stories when Oren and his twin sister reach eighteen years of age, they will be midshipmen at the Naval Academy in Annapolis, because I absorbed that adventure and tradition during the four years my oldest son was there. My daughter is a nurse in the delivery room at Hutzel Hospital in Detroit, and the thread of her experiences is worked into my stories. If my writing is nourished by the experiences of others more actively involved in the life of the city than myself, at least I am the voice of Oren.

"*Oren Bell* has received excellent reviews, but I am not sure anybody in Detroit has read it. A question I have been asked is: why does a white woman attempt to write a story about a black family? So far only my white friends have asked me this question. My goal was to write a story that children of all colors would find exciting and interesting."

FOR MORE INFORMATION SEE:

PERIODICALS

Bulletin of the Center for the Study of Children's Books, July, 1991.
Horn Book, March, 1991.
Kirkus Reviews, May 1, 1991.
Publishers Weekly, May 10, 1991.

*   *   *

BUXTON, Ralph
   See SILVERSTEIN, Alvin
   and SILVERSTEIN, Virginia B.

C

CALVERT, Patricia 1931-
(Peter J. Freeman)

PERSONAL: Born July 22, 1931, in Great Falls, MT; daughter of Edgar C. (a railroad worker) and Helen P. (a children's wear buyer; maiden name, Freeman) Dunlap; married George J. Calvert (in insurance business), January 27, 1951; children: Brianne L. Calvert Elias, Dana J. Calvert Halbert. *Education:* Winona State University, B.A., 1976, graduate study, 1976—. *Politics:* Liberal Democrat. *Religion:* Unitarian-Universalist. *Hobbies and other interests:* Reading, hiking, observing wildlife.

ADDRESSES: Home—Foxwood Farm, R.R. 2, P.O. Box 91, Chatfield, MN 55923. *Office*—Mayo Clinic, 200 Southwest First St., Rochester, MN 55901.

CAREER: St. Mary's Hospital, Great Falls, MT, laboratory clerk, 1948-49; clerk typist at General Motors Acceptance Corp., 1950-51; Mayo Clinic, Rochester, MN, cardiac laboratory technician, 1961-64, enzyme laboratory technician, 1964-70, senior editorial assistant in section of publications, 1970—; instructor, Institute of Children's Literature, 1987—.

MEMBER: American Medical Writers Association, Children's Reading Round Table, Society of Children's Book Writers, Society of Midland Authors.

AWARDS, HONORS: Best book award from American Library Association, juvenile fiction award from Society of Midland Authors, and juvenile award from Friends of American Writers, all 1980, all for *The Snowbird;* award for outstanding achievement in the arts from Young Women's Christian Association (YWCA), 1981, for *The Snowbird;* Mark Twain Award nomination from Missouri Association of School Libraries, 1985, for *The Money Creek Mare;* Maude Hart Lovelace Award nomination, 1985, for *The Stone Pony; Yesterday's Daughter* was named a best book for young adults by the American Library Association, 1986; William Allan White Award, 1987, for *Hadder MacColl; When Morn-*

PATRICIA CALVERT

ing Comes named one of "Best of 1990" by Society of School Librarians International, 1991.

WRITINGS:

(Contributor) Lyle L. Miller, editor, *Developing Reading Efficiency,* 4th edition, Burgess, 1980.
(Editor) *The Communicator's Handbook: Techniques and Technology,* Maupin House Publishing, 1990.

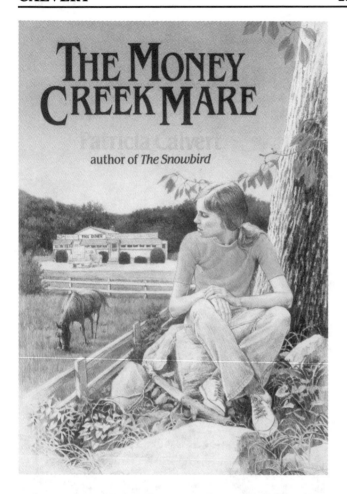

Calvert's *The Money Creek Mare* was nominated for the Mark Twain Award in 1985.

NOVELS FOR YOUNG ADULTS

The Snowbird, Scribner, 1980.
The Money Creek Mare, Scribner, 1981.
The Stone Pony, Scribner, 1982.
The Hour of the Wolf, Scribner, 1983.
Hadder MacColl, Scribner, 1985.
Yesterday's Daughter (Junior Literary Guild selection), Scribner, 1986.
Stranger, You and I, Scribner, 1987.
When Morning Comes, Macmillan, 1989.

Contributor, sometimes under the pseudonym Peter J. Freeman, of more than one hundred articles and stories to magazines, including *Highlights for Children, Grit, National Future Farmer, Friend, Junior Life,* and *Jack and Jill.*

SIDELIGHTS: Patricia Calvert was raised in rural Montana during the Great Depression. Her teenage parents, unable to find work, moved the family into an abandoned miner's shack in the country. "The cabin," Calvert tells *SATA,* "constructed nearly forty years before, was windowless; its puncheon floor had rotted away; rats and mice were its only inhabitants." Despite its rundown condition, the cabin was near creeks filled with trout and wild game was plentiful in the nearby countryside. The family was able to live off the land.

"The mountains that ringed the home where I grew up," Calvert recalls, "were known by such sonorous names as Thunder Mountain, Monument Peak, and Old Baldy; the brooks where I learned to fish were called Pilgrim Creek, Tenderfoot, Big Timber; the gold and silver mines that dotted the hillsides were labeled the Silver Bell, the Admiral Dewey, and the Gold Bug. It was a magic world for any child, one in which lodgepole pines grew like arrows toward a sky that seemed always blue. When I was older I had a sassy little horse named Redbird to ride, a collie named Bruno to keep me company, and a calico cat named Agamemnon to sleep at the foot of my bed."

But life in the country had drawbacks too. "It was an isolated life," Calvert remembers, "and two of the few recreations available to me and to my brother (who was my only playmate) were story-telling and reading. It was our good fortune to have a mother who was a lively story-teller; she was black-haired and green-eyed and had been raised in an Irish family of ten children—and she never tired of telling us sad and funny (and often outrageous!) tales about her own childhood."

At the age of ten, Calvert knew that she wanted to be a writer when she grew up. Two novels especially influenced her decision: *Call It Courage* by Armstrong Sperry and *The White Stag* by Kate Seredy. "Those books," she recalls, "embraced things that were important to me: each dealt with themes of honor and courage; each took place in the out-of-doors; each was written in an artful, elegant manner."

It was only years later that she was able to begin writing the books she wanted. After her children had grown and left home, Calvert and her husband moved to the country, living on a small farm they named Foxwood. "We turned our acres into a wildlife preserve where deer, fox, and raccoon could wander where they wished," she explains. In addition, Calvert created a place for herself on the farm. "I converted an old chicken coop into a place to write," she relates, "and when I did I returned to scenes from my childhood and to those half-forgotten tales told to me by my mother about her own childhood. I hoped that my first book, *The Snowbird,* would bring to young-adult readers some of the pleasure that came to me when I read *Call It Courage* and *The White Stag.* More than that, I hoped I could pass on to my readers my pet philosophy: that no matter how young one is, it is sometimes necessary to declare to the world *I am accountable.*" *The Snowbird* won awards from the American Library Association, the Society of Midland Authors, the Friends of American Writers, and the Young Women's Christian Association.

"I am everlastingly fascinated," Calvert states, "by that country from which we are all emigrants: the land of childhood—and that is the reason why my fiction is for (and about) children. When an acquaintance recently expressed to me the hope that, since I'd now had a couple of children's books published, I could write 'a real one' (that is, a novel for adults), I had to discourage him quickly. To write for and about children—and to write for and about the child in myself—is really all I intend to do."

FOR MORE INFORMATION SEE:

PERIODICALS

Bulletin of the Center for Children's Books, November, 1985; December, 1986; December, 1987.

*   *   *

CHAMBERS, Aidan 1934-
(Malcolm Blacklin)

PERSONAL: Born December 27, 1934, in Chester-le-Street, County Durham, England; son of George Kenneth Blacklin (a funeral director) and Margaret (Hancock) Chambers; married Nancy Harris Lockwood (former editor of *Children's Book News*), March 30, 1968. *Education:* Studied at Borough Road College, London, England, 1955-57.

ADDRESSES: Home and office—Lockwood, Station Rd., Woodchester, Stroud, Gloucestershire GL5 5EQ, England.

CAREER: Teacher of English and drama at various schools in England, 1957-68; full-time writer, 1968—. Cofounder and editorial publisher, Turton & Chambers, 1989—. Publisher and proprietor, Thimble Press; publisher, *Signal, Approaches to Children's Books,* and *Young Drama: The Magazine about Child and Youth Drama.* Tutor, Further Professional Studies Department, University of Bristol, 1970-82; visiting lecturer,

AIDAN CHAMBERS

Westminster College, Oxford, 1982—. Has produced children's plays for stage and written and presented several radio and television programs, including *Bookbox,* Radio Bristol, 1973-75, *Children and Books,* BBC Radio, 1976, *Ghosts,* Thames-TV, 1980, *Long, Short, and Tall Stories,* BBC-TV, 1981. *Military service:* Royal Navy, 1953-55.

MEMBER: Society of Authors, London Library.

AWARDS, HONORS: Highest honors, Children's Literature Association Conference, 1978, for article "The Reader in the Book"; Eleanor Farjeon Award, 1982; Best Book nomination, *Voice of Youth Advocates,* 1988.

WRITINGS:

JUVENILE; NOVELS

Cycle Smash, Heinemann, 1968.
Marle, Heinemann, 1968.
Breaktime, Bodley Head, 1978, Harper, 1979.
Seal Secret, Bodley Head, 1980, Harper, 1981.
Dance on My Grave, Bodley Head, 1982, Harper, 1983.
The Present Takers, Bodley Head, 1983, Harper, 1984.
Nik: Now I Know, Harper, 1987, published in England as *Now I Know,* Bodley Head, 1987.
The Toll Bridge, Bodley Head, 1992.

JUVENILE; EDITOR AND CONTRIBUTOR, EXCEPT WHERE INDICATED

(With wife, Nancy Chambers) *Ghosts,* Macmillan, 1969.
(With N. Chambers) *World Minus Zero: A SF Anthology,* Macmillan, 1971.
I Want to Get Out: Stories and Poems By Young Writers, Macmillan, 1971.
(With N. Chambers) *Hi-Ran-Ho: A Picture Book of Verse,* Longman, 1971.
(With N. Chambers) *In Time to Come: A SF Anthology,* Macmillan, 1973.
Fighters in the Sky, Macmillan, 1976.
Funny Folk: A Body of Comic Tales, Heinemann, 1976.
The Tenth [and] Eleventh Ghost Book, Barrie & Jenkins, two volumes, 1975-76, published in one volume as *The Bumper Book of Ghost Stories,* Pan Books, 1976.
Book of Cops and Robbers, Kestrel, 1977.
Men at War, Macmillan, 1977.
Escapers, Macmillan, 1978.
War at Sea, Macmillan, 1978.
(Under pseudonym Malcolm Blacklin) *Ghosts Four* (short stories), Macmillan, 1978.
Animal Fair, Heinemann, 1979.
Aidan Chambers' Book of Ghosts and Hauntings, Kestrel, 1980.
Fox Tricks (short stories), Heinemann, 1980.
Ghosts That Haunt You, Kestrel, 1980.
Loving You, Loving Me, Kestrel, 1980.
Ghost after Ghost, Kestrel, 1982.
Plays for Young People to Read and Perform, Thimble Press, 1982.
Out of Time: Stories of the Future, Bodley Head, 1984.
Shades of Dark, P. Hardy, 1984.

(With Jill Bennett) *Poetry for Children: A Signal Book-guide*, Thimble Press, 1984.
A Sporting Chance: Stories of Winning and Losing, Bodley Head, 1985.
(Compiler) *Shades of Dark*, Harper, 1986.
A Quiver of Ghosts, Bodley Head, 1987.
A Haunt of Ghosts, Harper, 1987.
Love All, Bodley Head, 1988.
On the Edge, Macmillan, 1990.

JUVENILE; PLAYS

Everyman's Everybody, produced in London, 1957.
Johnny Salter (produced in Stroud, Gloucester, 1965), Heinemann Educational, 1966.
The Car (produced in Stroud, 1966), Heinemann Educational, 1967.
The Chicken Run (produced in Stroud, 1967), Heinemann Educational, 1968.
The Dream Cage: A Comic Drama in Nine Dreams (produced in Stroud, 1981), Heinemann, 1982.

OTHER

The Reluctant Reader, Pergamon, 1969.
Mac and Lugs, Macmillan, 1971.
Haunted Houses, Pan Books, 1971.
Don't Forget Charlie and the Vase, Macmillan, 1971.
Ghosts Two (short stories), Macmillan, 1972.
More Haunted Houses, Pan Books, 1973.
Introducing Books to Children, Heinemann Educational, 1973, revised edition, Horn Book, 1983.
Great British Ghosts, Pan Books, 1974.
Great Ghosts of the World, Pan Books, 1974.
Snake River, Almqvist och Wiksell (Stockholm), 1975, Macmillan, 1977.
Book of Flyers and Flying, Kestrel Books, 1976.
Ghost Carnival: Stories of Ghosts in Their Haunts, Heinemann, 1977.
Booktalk: Occasional Writing on Children and Literature, Bodley Head, 1985, Harper, 1986.
The Reading Environment, Thimble Press, 1990.

Also author of television series *Ghosts*, 1980, and *Long, Short, and Tall Stories*, 1980-81. Contributor to *Winter's Tales for Children Four*, Macmillan. General editor, Macmillan "Topliners" series. Author of column, "Letter from England," *Horn Book*. Contributor to numerous periodicals, including *Times Educational Supplement*. Reviewer for *Children's Book News*.

SIDELIGHTS: Aidan Chambers—novelist, nonfiction writer, editor, critic, and dramatist—is widely known as an outspoken advocate of children's literature. Many of Chambers' writings highlight a recurring theme: that children should both be encouraged to read at an early age and allowed to develop their skills and reading preferences at an independent pace. Chambers firmly believes that children respond best to subjects that are of interest to them. To this end, he has compiled anthologies about a variety of subjects, including ghosts, crime, and aviation. Chambers' fiction, such as the novel *Dance on My Grave*, is noted for its honest depiction of adolescent emotions and sympathetic treatment of nontraditional young adult themes like homo-

sexuality. In an essay written for *Something about the Author Autobiography Series* (*SAAS*), Chambers explained that he wrote mostly about adolescence "because that is where I began. Because that is what I feel most comfortable doing. Because it is in adolescence that we face for the first time all the great questions of life and deal with them freshly. Because adolescence is about beginnings, not ends.... It's an old saying: writers choose the books they write; authors are chosen by the books they must write. For me, it isn't a question of choice."

Aidan Chambers was born one mile outside the small coal mining town of Chester-le-Street. Chambers spent most of his youth in the working-class neighborhood of Glen Terrace, where his father toiled as a finished woodworker. Because he was an only child, Chambers was very shy. His only friend was a little girl named Marion Rose who lived two doors away. "For some years, we were the only children who lived in the terrace, so we had the run of the place," Chambers wrote in his *SAAS* entry. "No one bothered us, and we did exactly as we pleased. If we were bored, we'd go 'seeing.' 'Let's go see Aunt Nelly,' we'd say, and scuttle off to number twenty.... Throughout my childhood, these were the safe houses of my extended family."

Because he lived so close to the coal mines, Chambers got a first-hand look at the harsh realities of mining life. He described for *SAAS* both the fascination and terror he associated with the pitmen: "Out of view at the head of the valley to my left was a coke factory, a huge, concrete affair from which oozed red-hot cinders in great vertical slabs like pus from a wound.... As I lay in the dark trying to get to sleep, for I never liked going to bed while my parents were still up, I could see through my back bedroom window the bobbing flashlights of pitmen as they walked to or from the mine along a path that skirted the top of the wood, imagined they were night spirits invading my territory, and was glad to be safe at home."

Chambers loved going to the movies. His most vivid movie-going image was the moment Judy Garland as Dorothy opened the black-and-white cottage door onto the dazzling colors of Oz in *The Wizard of Oz*. "'Going to the pictures' was the entertainment I looked forward to the most all through my childhood and youth," Chambers recalled for *SAAS*. "I loved the snug hiddenness of the dark cinema, the smell, the smoke-filled beam of light shining onto the screen ... the utterly absorbed attention of an audience captured by a film.... I'm sure the way I write stories, perhaps even the way I read them, owes more to those hundreds of hours spent watching movies than to anything else."

As a young boy, Chambers did not like school. He had difficulty making friends as well as grasping the purpose of certain tasks (such as learning the letters of the alphabet and the fundamentals of arithmetic). A succession of indifferent teachers did not help matters. It was not until Chambers developed a passion for reading that school became more tolerable. "One evening in what

A shy child who did not immediately like school, Chambers spent many pleasurable working holidays at this ancient family farm near the village of Middleton-One-Row.

must have been early 1944, I [looked] at a book I'd brought home.... Suddenly as I puzzled over the words on the page, I heard voices speaking in my head. The voices were coming from the printed words and were talking to each other and telling a story.... Not that I immediately became an avid reader; that happened later, but I did develop a liking for books themselves—the book as an object," Chambers noted in his essay.

After the war, Chambers' father took a job in the industrial town of Darlington. While Chambers was not happy about leaving his hometown, the move brought about one happy change—Darlington's school system was a good one, with attentive teachers and a challenging curriculum. Chambers was especially impressed by Jim Osborn, the head of the English department. With some prodding, Osborn convinced Chambers to join the debate and drama clubs. Chambers discovered that he loved public speaking and theatre. It was also about this time that Chambers realized that he wanted to become a fiction writer. He recalled for *SAAS:* "I wanted to write fiction. This impulse planted itself when I was fifteen, the night I finished D. H. Lawrence's *Sons and Lovers*.... Paul Morel's life seemed so like my own—the first time I experienced such a recognition—that I wished I could have written it."

Chambers did not have a lot of time to devote to his writing for the next few years. After he left school, he served two years of compulsory service in the armed

forces. Upon his release from the service, Chambers entered college, where he produced some plays and wrote his own. Partially due to his background in literature and drama, Chambers got a job teaching English at a boys' school upon graduation. "I arrived in Southend with just enough money to see me through to my first pay cheque, a suitcase of spare clothing, board and lodging arranged in a house near the school, and an exhilarating sense of an end and a beginning: an end to a constricted adolescence, to being a son supported by parents, ... a student required to pass exams, and the beginning of an independent life," Chambers noted in his *SAAS* entry.

Chambers enjoyed both his teaching position and living in Southend. He made a great many friends and rekindled his interest in religion. Chambers began attending Anglo-Catholic services on a regular basis. Over time, he was drawn to the idea of joining a monastery. After looking into various monastic orders, Chambers joined two brothers who were organizing a new type of order set up specifically to work with young people in the community. Chambers lived as a monk for the next seven years. While he enjoyed many aspects of the monastic life, however, Chambers still felt unfulfilled. Both his writing and work outside the monastery often brought him into conflict with the other brothers. After a great deal of thought, Chambers eventually decided to leave the order in order to devote himself full time to teaching and to writing fiction.

Both during and after leaving the order, Chambers served as the general editor for a young adult series at Macmillan Publishers. He also continued to write plays, novels, and reviews. After marrying Nancy Lockwood in 1967, Chambers quit teaching to devote himself full time to his writing. In 1969, the Chambers began publishing *Signal* magazine, a publication devoted to increasing the critical appreciation of children's literature. As the magazine gained circulation, Chambers' fiction writing took on a new voice. He told *SAAS:* "It happened like this. Having settled in ... my plan was to write another book of the kind I'd written before. But when I sat down to start, I realized that the prospect so bored me that I couldn't face it.... For days I sat and worried.... Finally, desperation took charge.... I grabbed a new notebook, a brand new pencil (I usually typed everything I wrote), sat myself in an easy chair (I usually sat at a desk), and told myself to write the first thing that came into my head and to go on until I told myself to stop."

The result was the novel *Breaktime*. Told in a mixture of narrative modes, *Breaktime* follows seventeen-year-old Ditto on an eye-opening school holiday. While working on the novel, Chambers was concerned that both the story's strong sexual emphasis and free-form narrative structure would hurt its chances for publication. Despite the author's initial misgivings, *Breaktime* was published and met with a generally favorable critical reaction. "With humor and wit, with ingenuity and candor, the author has offered one piece of one kind of truth in a spirit of technical and emotional investigation," remarked Margery Fisher in *Growing Point*. Richard Yates in the *New York Times Book Review* found Ditto to be "an appealing young man," so appealing that the nature of his quest for adventure is one that "any

number of readers can take to heart." A reviewer for *Horn Book* was equally laudatory, noting that Chambers "was interested in casting a teenage novel in a twentieth-century literary mode, and he has succeeded remarkably well.... In more ways than one ... this book is strong meat—for its intellectualism as well as for its realism."

Chambers also took stylistic and thematic chances with his novel *Dance on My Grave*. On one level the story behind a teenager's desecration of his friend's grave, *Dance on My Grave* also examines the complex love relationship between two male teens. Many critics found the book's format difficult to follow. "Chambers' style is often staccato, often introspective; this is not an easy book to read," pointed out Zena Sutherland in the *Bulletin of the Center for Children's Books*. She did see some strengths in the book, however, adding that "what should appeal to readers are the effective communication of deep and anguished feelings, the perceptive depiction of relationships, and the depth and consistency of characterization." A reviewer for *Growing Point,* likewise disturbed by certain stylistic inconsistencies such as a confusing narrative, nevertheless claimed that *Dance on My Grave* is "a book that makes its point through raucous good humor and implied feeling, through the sharp observation of a boy and his blundering apprehensions of the way others observe him. If teenage novels are to justify their existence, it will be by this kind of honest, particularized, personal writing."

Chambers continued taking risks with works such as *Now I Know* and *The Present Takers*. In his *SAAS* entry, Chambers admitted that his novels are actually a sequential body of work. He wrote: "This is how I think of it: I'm writing a portrait of a boy whose character is slowly emerging—is being created—as the books appear. *Breaktime* is largely to do with physical sensation—the life of the senses. *Dance on My Grave* is largely to do with the emotions—kinds of love, and our personal obsessions. *Now I Know* is largely about what people often call spiritual experience and about thought, and how they clash and blend and compliment each other."

According to Chambers, all of his novels are primarily concerned with how language defines individuals, language being the "god who makes us." Chambers takes a long time to write his fiction; sometimes it takes him years to fine-tune a novel or short story. Above all, Chambers views writing as a craft that demands great attention to detail. He continually struggles to find the right word or voice for his characters. "I have always found it a struggle to author books that matter to me," he wrote in his essay, adding that he does not "think of myself as successful and won't until I have written a book that satisfies me by matching in its objectified printed form the rich density of the imagined original. In this respect, nothing has changed since I was fifteen. I am also just as unsure of myself and as sure of failure ... still find reading both the best of pleasures and the best means of keeping some kind of grip on life."

Chambers and his wife Nancy outside Thimble Cottage, from which they took the name for their Thimble Press publishing company.

WORKS CITED:

Chambers, Aidan, *Something about the Author Autobiography Series,* Volume 12, Gale, 1991, pp. 37-55.
Contemporary Literary Criticism, Volume 35, Gale, 1985, pp. 97-101.
Fisher, Margery, review of *Breaktime, Growing Point,* November, 1978, pp. 3418-19.
Review of *Breaktime, Horn Book,* June, 1979.
Review of *Dance on My Grave, Growing Point,* July, 1982, p. 3928.
Sutherland, Zena, review of *Dance on My Grave, Bulletin of the Center for Children's Books,* June, 1983, p. 185.
Yates, Richard, "You Can and Can't Go Home Again," *New York Times Book Review,* April 29, 1979, p. 30.

FOR MORE INFORMATION SEE:

PERIODICALS

Bulletin of the Center for Children's Books, June, 1979; June, 1983; January, 1987.
Children's Literature in Education, autumn, 1978.
Horn Book, October, 1980; June, 1981; August, 1981; February, 1983.
Growing Point, November, 1983.
Junior Bookshelf, February, 1979; June, 1980; August, 1980; April, 1981; June, 1982.
Publishers Weekly, March 11, 1983; April 15, 1983.
School Library Journal, March, 1989.
Times Literary Supplement, March 25, 1977; December 2, 1977; December 1, 1978; July 18, 1980; July 23, 1982.

*   *   *

CHORAO, Kay 1936-

PERSONAL: Full name is Ann McKay Sproat Chorao; surname is pronounced "shoe-*row*"; born January 7, 1936, in Elkhart, IN; daughter of James McKay (a lawyer) and Elizabeth (Fleming) Sproat; married Ernesto A. K. Chorao (an artist), June 10, 1960; children: Jamie, Peter, Ian. *Education:* Wheaton College, B.A., 1958; graduate study at Chelsea School of Art, 1958-59; studied book illustration at School of Visual Arts, 1966-68.

ADDRESSES: Home—290 Riverside Dr., Apt. 12A, New York, NY 10025; (summer) Box 644, Jamesport, NY 11947.

CAREER: Artist; illustrator and writer of children's books. Free-lance art work includes educational filmstrips and a television commercial. *Exhibitions:* Montclair Museum, 1991-92; illustrations have appeared in several American Institute of Graphic Arts exhibitions.

AWARDS, HONORS: A Magic Eye for Ida was named one of the best books of the year by *School Library Journal,* 1973; certificate of excellence, American Institute of Graphic Arts, 1974, for *Ralph and the Queen's Bathtub;* American Library Association notable citation,

KAY CHORAO

Society of Illustrators Certificate of Merit, 1974, and Children's Book Showcase title, 1975, all for *Albert's Toothache;* Communicating with Children Award, 1976, for *Henrietta, the Wild Woman of Borneo;* Society of Illustrators Certificate of Merit, 1976, for *Clyde Monster;* Christopher Award, 1979, for *Chester Chipmunk's Thanksgiving,* and 1988, for *The Good-bye Book; Cathedral Mouse* was named one of the *New York Times* ten best books of the year, 1988; recipient of numerous other writing awards.

WRITINGS:

SELF-ILLUSTRATED; FOR CHILDREN

The Repair of Uncle Toe, Farrar, Straus, 1972.
A Magic Eye for Ida, Seabury, 1973.
Ralph and the Queen's Bathtub, Farrar, Straus, 1974.
Ida Makes a Movie, Seabury, 1974.
Maudie's Umbrella, Dutton, 1975.
Molly's Moe, Seabury, 1976.
Lester's Overnight, Dutton, 1977.
(Adapter) *The Baby's Lap Book* (nursery rhymes), Dutton, 1977, reprinted with color illustrations, 1990.
Molly's Lies, Seabury, 1979.
Oink and Pearl, Harper, 1981.
Kate's Car, Dutton, 1982.
Kate's Box, Dutton, 1982.
Kate's Quilt, Dutton, 1982.
Kate's Snowman, Dutton, 1982.
Lemon Moon, Holiday House, 1983.
(Compiler) *The Baby's Bedtime Book* (poems and rhymes), Dutton, 1984.
(Adapter) *The Baby's Story Book,* Dutton, 1985.
Ups and Downs with Oink and Pearl, Harper, 1985.
(Compiler) *The Baby's Good Morning Book* (poems and rhymes), Dutton, 1986.
George Told Kate, Dutton, 1987.

(Adapter) *The Child's Story Book* (fairy tales), Dutton, 1987.

Cathedral Mouse, Dutton, 1988.

The Cherry Pie Baby, Dutton, 1989.

(Adapter) *The Child's Fairy Tale Book,* Dutton, 1990.

(Compiler) *Baby's Christmas Treasury* (poems, stories, and songs), Random House, 1991.

Ida and Betty and the Secret Eggs, Clarion, 1991.

(Compiler) *Mother Goose Magic,* Dutton, 1992.

Annie and Cousin Precious, Dutton, in press.

ILLUSTRATOR

Judith Viorst, *My Mama Says There Aren't Any Zombies, Ghosts, Vampires, Creatures, Demons, Monsters, Fiends, Goblins, or Things,* Atheneum, 1973.

Madeline Edmonson, *The Witch's Egg* (Junior Literary Guild selection), Seabury, 1974.

Barbara Williams, *Albert's Toothache* (Junior Literary Guild selection), Dutton, 1974.

Williams, *Kevin's Grandma,* Dutton, 1975.

Winifred Rosen, *Henrietta, the Wild Woman of Borneo,* Four Winds, 1975.

Ann Schweninger, *The Hunt for Rabbit's Galosh,* Doubleday, 1976.

Williams, *Someday, Said Mitchell* (Junior Literary Guild selection), Dutton, 1976.

Daisy Wallace, editor, *Monster Poems,* Holiday House, 1976.

Robert Crowe, *Clyde Monster,* Dutton, 1976.

Marjorie Sharmat, *I'm Terrific,* Holiday House, 1977.

Jan Wahl, *Frankenstein's Dog* (also see below), Prentice-Hall, 1977.

Susan Pearson, *That's Enough for One Day, J.P.,* Dial, 1977.

Wahl, *Dracula's Cat* (also see below), Prentice-Hall, 1978.

Williams, *Chester Chipmunk's Thanksgiving,* Dutton, 1978.

Rosen, *Henrietta and the Day of the Iguana,* Four Winds, 1978.

Sharmat, *Thornton the Worrier,* Holiday House, 1978.

Norma Klein, *Visiting Pamela,* Dial, 1979.

A. E. Hoffman, *The Nutcracker,* Dutton, 1979.

Williams, *A Valentine for Cousin Archie,* Dutton, 1980.

Sharmat, *Sometimes Mama and Papa Fight,* Harper, 1980.

Crowe, *Tyler Toad and the Thunder,* Dutton, 1980.

Sharmat, *Grumley the Grouch,* Holiday House, 1980.

Rosen, *Henrietta and the Gong from Hong Kong,* Four Winds, 1981.

Steven Kroll, *Giant Journey,* Holiday House, 1981.

Barbara Joose, *The Thinking Place,* Pantheon, 1981.

Phyllis Naylor, *The Boy with the Helium Head,* Atheneum, 1982.

Joose, *Spiders in the Fruit Cellar,* Pantheon, 1983.

Charlotte Zolotow, *But Not Billy,* Harper, 1983.

Shirley Murphy, *Valentine for a Dragon,* Atheneum, 1984.

Maggie Davis, *Rickety Witch,* Holiday House, 1984.

Viorst, *The Good-bye Book,* Atheneum, 1988.

Lois Duncan, *Songs from Dreamland: Original Lullabies,* Random House, 1989.

Wahl, *Dracula's Cat and Frankenstein's Dog,* Simon & Schuster, 1990.

Riki Levinson, *Country Dawn to Dusk,* Dutton, 1992.

OTHER

Contributor of stories and essays to magazines.

ADAPTATIONS: The Baby's Lap Book, The Baby's Bedtime Book, The Baby's Story Book, and *The Baby's Good Morning Book* have been adapted as video cassettes and book/cassette packages.

SIDELIGHTS: An award-winning creator of children's books, Kay Chorao has illustrated a number of works by other authors as well. She is regarded as a skillful and imaginative illustrator whose drawings suitably express the accompanying text. In her own work, Chorao frequently uses gentle humor to address familiar childhood situations such as losing a toy, taking an overnight trip, or being caught in a lie. Populated by characters such as piglets, elephants, and whimsical monsters, Chorao's lighthearted picture books have widespread appeal.

As a child Chorao loved to draw; she remarked in *Books for Schools and Libraries* that "like most illustrators, I scribbled my drawings over every conceivable surface from the time I could hold a crayon. My earliest known picture was 'The Blue Fairy' scribbled in blue crayon on the underside of our breakfast room table." Chorao's penchant for drawing and painting was encouraged by the private school she attended in Cleveland, Ohio. The school's English department emphasized creative writing, a subject that Chorao also found enjoyable. Chorao pursued her interest in art at Wheaton College, where she received a bachelor's degree in art history. After graduation, she decided to enroll as an art student at the Chelsea School of Art in London, England.

At Chelsea the author and illustrator met her husband, Mozambique native and art student Ernesto Chorao. The couple married in 1960 and settled in New York City after living for a brief period in San Francisco, California. Between 1962 and 1968, the Choraos had three sons. While her children were still young, Chorao rekindled her childhood interest in writing. She penned several children's stories and, though she received many rejections, some were published in a children's magazine.

Bolstered by this encouragement, Chorao decided to study children's book illustration at night, hoping that she might illustrate her own work. She studied under Niels Bodecker and Edward Gorey, and with their help assembled a portfolio. Though editors often responded favorably to her work, none were willing to take a chance on publishing an unknown author. Chorao was persistent, however, and continually revised her portfolio. In the meantime, she did free-lance art and design projects. After about five years of publishers' rejections, Chorao's first book, *The Repair of Uncle Toe,* was published in 1972.

Chorao's illustrations depict everyday life as well as whimsical situations and characters. (Illustration from *Lemon Moon,* written and illustrated by Chorao.)

Since then Chorao has had many opportunities to express her talent. Apart from her own writings, she has successfully illustrated more than thirty books by other authors. She once explained her approach to *SATA:* "When I illustrate, I try to express the text as appropriately as possible. When I read *Albert's Toothache,* for example, I knew the illustrations had to be soft and big. That's how the text 'felt' to me. With *The Witch's Egg* they had to be crisper, black and feathery. With *Maudie's Umbrella,* there had to be a feeling of a soft scurrying mole's world. Her eyesight was terrible, so I thought it would be fun to have hidden faces in the gnarled trees, growing things, and everyday objects, which Maudie rushed blindly past. I suppose the point is to create a personal world within the world confined by those book covers!"

The worlds Chorao creates through her writings and illustrations sometimes are inspired by her children as well as memories of her own childhood. She once commented to *SATA:* "I like to think I write for my children, and sometimes I do. *Ralph and the Queen's Bathtub* was written with [my son] Peter in mind from the beginning. But usually I simply write what occurs to me and draw on my own feelings."

Chorao attributes her interest in writing and illustrating books for children to her long-standing love of art, her need to draw, and her fondness of children. Chorao once received a letter from a woman describing how special one of her books had become to a little girl. She noted in

Books for Schools and Libraries that "I don't pretend to be [a master artist] ... but it is very nice to know that my words and pictures have touched at least one tiny girl somewhere." In a *Horn Book* article she concluded: "I hope my drawings and those of many other illustrators offer new ways of seeing and arouse the curiosity of the young."

WORKS CITED:

Chorao, Kay, "Kay Chorao on Why Do I Illustrate (and Sometimes Write) for Kids," *Books for Schools and Libraries,* 1985.
Chorao, "A Delayed Reply: Illustration and the Imagination," *Horn Book,* August, 1979, pp. 463-69.
Something about the Author, Volume 8, Gale, 1976, pp. 24-26.

FOR MORE INFORMATION SEE:

PERIODICALS

Bulletin of the Center for Children's Books, September, 1977; September, 1979; March, 1984; December, 1985; June, 1987.
Horn Book, February, 1981; May/April, 1986; November/December, 1986.
Junior Literary Guild, September, 1976.
School Library Journal, November, 1985; December, 1986; May, 1990.

—Sketch by Michelle M. Motowski

CLARK, Emma Chichester 1955-

PERSONAL: Born October 15, 1955, in London, England; daughter of Robin Chichester Clark (a company director) and Jane Helen Goddard; married Lucas van Praag (a management consultant). *Education:* Chelsea School of Art, B.A. (with honors), 1978; Royal College of Art, M.A., 1983.

ADDRESSES: Home—47 Richford St., London W12 8BU, England. *Agent*—Laura Cecil, 17 Alwyne Villas, London N.1, England.

CAREER: Illustrator and author of children's books, 1983—. Visiting lecturer at Middlesex Polytechnic and City and Guilds School of Art, 1984-86.

MEMBER: Chelsea Arts Club.

AWARDS, HONORS: Mother Goose Award, 1988.

WRITINGS:

SELF-ILLUSTRATED CHILDREN'S BOOKS

Catch That Hat, Bodley Head, 1988, Little, Brown, 1990.
The Story of Horrible Hilda and Henry, Little, Brown, 1988.
Myrtle, Tertle, and Gertle, Bodley Head, 1989.
The Bouncing Dinosaur, Farrar, Strauss, 1990.
I Never Saw a Purple Cow, Little, Brown, 1991.

ILLUSTRATOR

Laura Cecil, compiler, *Listen to This,* Greenwillow, 1987.
L. Cecil, compiler, *Stuff and Nonsense,* Greenwillow, 1989.
Primrose Lockwood, *Cissy Lavender,* Little, Brown, 1989.
L. Cecil, compiler, *Boo! Stories to Make You Jump,* Greenwillow, 1990.
James Reeves, *Ragged Robin: Poetry from A to Z,* Little, Brown, 1990.
Margaret Mahy, *The Queen's Goat,* Dial, 1991.

WORK IN PROGRESS: Tea with Aunt Augusta, for Dial; illustrating Ben Frankel's *Tertius and Pliny,* for Harcourt.

FOR MORE INFORMATION SEE:

PERIODICALS

Times Literary Supplement, July 7-13, 1989.

*   *   *

CLIFTON, Lucille 1936-

PERSONAL: Full name is Thelma Lucille Clifton; born June 27, 1936, in Depew, NY; daughter of Samuel Louis, Sr. (a laborer) and Thelma (a laborer; maiden name, Moore) Sayles; married Fred James Clifton (an educator, writer, and artist), May 10, 1958 (died November 10, 1984); children: Sidney, Fredrica, Channing, Gillian, Graham, Alexia. *Education:* Attended Howard University, 1953-55, and Fredonia State Teachers College (now State University of New York College at Fredonia), 1955.

ADDRESSES: Agent—Marilyn Marlow, Curtis Brown Ltd., 10 Astor Pl., New York, NY 10003.

CAREER: New York State Division of Employment, Buffalo, claims clerk, 1958-60; U.S. Office of Education, Washington, DC, literature assistant for CAREL (Central Atlantic Regional Educational Laboratory), 1969-71; Coppin State College, Baltimore, MD, poet in residence, 1971-74; writer. Visiting writer, Columbia University School of the Arts; Jerry Moore Visiting Writer, George Washington University, 1982-83; University of California, Santa Cruz, professor of literature and creative writing, 1985—. Trustee, Enoch Pratt Free Library, Baltimore. Actor in first performance of James Baldwin's *The Amen Corner.*

MEMBER: International PEN, Authors League of America, Authors Guild.

AWARDS, HONORS: Discovery Award, New York YW-YMHA Poetry Center, 1969; *Good Times: Poems* cited as one of the year's ten best books by the *New York Times,* 1969; National Endowment for the Arts grants, 1970 and 1972; Jane Addams special recognition, 1978, for *Amifika;* Poet Laureate of the State of Maryland, 1979-82; Juniper Prize, 1980; Coretta Scott King Award, American Library Association, 1984, for *Everett Anderson's Goodbye.* Honorary degrees from University of Maryland and Towson State University.

WRITINGS:

CHILDREN'S FICTION

The Black BCs (alphabet poems), illustrations by Don Miller, Dutton, 1970.
All Us Come Cross the Water, illustrations by John Steptoe, Holt, 1973.
Don't You Remember?, illustrations by Evaline Ness, Dutton, 1973.
The Boy Who Didn't Believe in Spring, illustrations by Brinton Turkle, Dutton, 1973.
The Times They Used to Be, illustrations by Susan Jeschke, Holt, 1974.
My Brother Fine with Me, illustrations by Moneta Barnett, Holt, 1975.
Three Wishes, illustrations by Stephanie Douglas, Viking, 1976.
Amifika, illustrations by Thomas DiGrazia, Dutton, 1977.
The Lucky Stone, illustrations by Dale Payson, Delacorte, 1979.
My Friend Jacob, illustrations by T. DiGrazia, Dutton, 1980.
Sonora Beautiful, illustrations by Michael Garland, Dutton, 1981.
Ten Oxherding Pictures, illustrations by Lisa Bulawsky, Moving Parts Press, 1988.

LUCILLE CLIFTON

"EVERETT ANDERSON" SERIES; FOR CHILDREN

Some of the Days of Everett Anderson, illustrations by E. Ness, Holt, 1970.
Everett Anderson's Christmas Coming, illustrations by E. Ness, Holt, 1971.
Good, Says Jerome, illustrations by S. Douglas, Dutton, 1973.
Everett Anderson's Year, illustrations by Ann Grifalconi, Holt, 1974.
Everett Anderson's Friend, illustrations by A. Grifalconi, Holt, 1976.
Everett Anderson's 1 2 3, illustrations by A. Grifalconi, Holt, 1977.
Everett Anderson's Nine Month Long, illustrations by A. Grifalconi, Holt, 1978.
Everett Anderson's Goodbye, illustrations by A. Grifalconi, Holt, 1983.

VERSE

Good Times, Random House, 1969.
Good News about the Earth, Random House, 1972.
An Ordinary Woman, Random House, 1974.
Two-Headed Woman, University of Massachusetts Press, 1980.
Good Woman: Poems and a Memoir, 1969-1980, BOA Editions, 1987.
Next: New Poems, BOA Editions, 1987.

OTHER

Generations: A Memoir, Random House, 1976.
(Author of introduction) Christopher Bursk, *Places of Comfort, Places of Justice: Poems,* Humanities & Arts Press, 1987.

Contributor to *Free to Be . . . You and Me,* McGraw Hill, 1974; *Poetry of the Negro, 1746-1970,* Doubleday, 1970; *Selected from Twentieth-Century American Poetry: An Anthology,* Literacy Volunteers of New York City, 1991. Also contributor to *Free to Be a Family,* 1987, *Norton Anthology of Literature by Women, Coming into the Light,* and *Stealing the Language.* Contributor of fiction to *Negro Digest, Redbook, House and Garden,* and *Atlantic;* contributor of nonfiction to *Ms.* and *Essence.*

SIDELIGHTS: Great-great-granddaughter of a slave, poet and author of children's books Lucille Clifton was born in Depew, New York, near Buffalo, in 1936. Although her parents were poor and possessed little formal education, they raised her with a strong sense of family and taught her to prize the written word as well. Her father, who read to his children from the Bible but could write only his name, was a steel worker who would tell her tales of his Dahomean ancestors, especially his grandmother who had been kidnapped into slavery and whose daughter was the first black woman to be legally hanged in Virginia. Her mother was a laundress who found time to express her own thoughts in poetry that she then read to her children. At the age of sixteen, on a full scholarship from her church, Clifton became the first of her family to attend college. Never having been away from home before, she felt like a misfit at Howard University in Washington, D.C., and left after only two years, losing her scholarship by lack of study. In her autobiography, *Generations: A Memoir,* Clifton recounts the frustration of her family at the turn of events but also her resolve to become a writer: "And so I came home to a disappointed and confused Mama and a Daddy who was furious and defensive and sad. Feet of clay, he said to me. My idol got feet of clay. God sent you to college to show me that you got feet of clay. Daddy, I argued with him, I don't need that stuff. I'm going to write poems. I can do what I want to do! I'm from Dahomey women!"

Clifton continued her education at what was then Fredonia State Teachers College where she met her future husband, then a philosophy professor at nearby University of Buffalo, and became involved with a group of black intellectuals who encouraged each other's creative work. She graduated in 1955 but marriage and motherhood—six children in seven years—delayed the publication of her poems for nearly fifteen years. However, in 1969, her first book of verse, *Good Times,* was named one of the ten best books of the year by the *New York Times* and earned her the prestigious Discovery Award from the YW-YMHA Poetry Center in New York City. Ten years later, she was named Poet Laureate of the State of Maryland, where she lives with her family. She writes primarily about black, urban family life in a style that echoes black speech and music; and her work, which addresses children as effectively as it does adults, stresses strength through adversity. "Clifton's pride in being black and in being a woman helps her transform difficult circumstances into a qualified affirmation about the black urban world she portrays," states Ronald Baughman in his *Dictionary of Literary Biography* essay. "She perceives in her own African

The "Everett Anderson" series explores the fluctuations in a child's world—including the arrival of a new sibling. (Cover illustration from *Everett Anderson's Nine Month Long,* written by Clifton, illustrated by Ann Grifalconi.)

heritage models for courage and endurance that may find their counterparts in contemporary inner-city blacks."

Clifton's books for children are designed to help them understand their world. *The Boy Who Didn't Believe in Spring* tells of a young black boy's discovery of spring in an urban environment of concrete that obstructs but does not obliterate natural growth and the seasonal cycle of rebirth; and *My Friend Jacob* is a story about a black child who befriends his white adolescent neighbor who happens to be retarded. "Jacob is Sam's 'very very best friend' and all of his best qualities are appreciated by Sam," writes Zena Sutherland in *Bulletin of the Center for Children's Books,* "just as all of his limitations are accepted ... it is strong in the simplicity and warmth with which a handicapped person is loved rather than pitied, enjoyed rather than tolerated." Critics praise Clifton's characters for being accurately and positively drawn. And a contributor to *Reading Teacher* states that "in a matter-of-fact, low-keyed style, we discover how [Sam and Jacob] help one another grow and understand the world." Clifton's children's books also facilitate an understanding of black heritage specifically, which in turn fosters an important link with the past generally. Her *All Us Come Cross the Water,* for example, "in a very straight-forward way ... shows the relationship of Africa to Blacks in the U.S. without getting into a heavy rap about 'Pan-Africanism,'" states Judy Richardson in the *Journal of Negro Education,* adding that Clifton "seems able to get inside a little boy's head, and knows how to represent that on paper."

In addition to quickening an awareness of black heritage, Clifton's books for children frequently include an element of fantasy as well. Writing about *Three Wishes,* in which a young girl finds a lucky penny on New Year's Day and makes three wishes upon it, Christopher Lehmann-Haupt in the *New York Times Book Review* calls it "an urbanized version of the traditional tale in which the first wish reveals the power of the magic object ... the second wish is a mistake, and the third undoes the second." Lehmann-Haupt adds that "too few children's books for blacks justify their ethnicity, but this one is a winning blend of black English and bright illustration." And regarding *The Lucky Stone,* in which a lucky stone provides good fortune for all four generations of its owners, a contributor to *Interracial Books for Children Bulletin* states that "the concept of past and present is usually hard for children to grasp but this book puts the passing of time in a perspective that children can understand.... This book contains information on various aspects of Black culture—slavery, religion and extended family—all conveyed in a way that is both positive and accurate." Michele Slung writes in the *Washington Post Book World* that the book "is at once talisman and anthology: over the years it has gathered unto it story after story, episodes indicating its power, both as a charm and as a unit of oral tradition. Clifton has a knack for projecting strong positive values without seeming too goody-goody; her poet's ear is one fact in this, her sense of humor another."

While Clifton's books for children emphasize an understanding of the past, they also focus on the present. Her critically acclaimed series of books about Everett Anderson, for instance, explore the experiences of a young child's world in flux. The series begins with Everett at the age of six and follows the boy through several

Everett moves through the five stages of grief after the death of his father in Clifton's *Everett Anderson's Goodbye.* (Cover illustration by Ann Grifalconi.)

traumatic experiences, including the abandonment of the family by his father, his mother's eventual remarriage, the addition of a new baby to the family, and the death of his father. Writing about *Everett Anderson's Nine Month Long,* which concerns the anticipated birth of the family's newest member, a contributor to *Interracial Books for Children Bulletin,* who praises the book's "wonderful poetic style," adds that it "projects a warm, loving, understanding and supportive family." Joan W. Blos, who thinks that "the establishment of an active, effective, and supportive male figure is an important part of this story," adds in *School Library Journal,* "So is its tacit acknowledgement that, for the younger child, a mother's pregnancy means disturbing changes now as well as a sibling later." However, just as the birth of a sibling can cause upheaval in a child's world, so, too, can death. In *Everett Anderson's Goodbye,* Everett has difficulty moving through the five stages of grief: denial, anger, bargaining, depression, and acceptance.

"In everything she creates," writes Haki Madhubuti, formerly Don L. Lee, in *Black Women Writers (1950-1980): A Critical Evaluation,* "this Lucille Clifton, a writer of no ordinary substance, a singer of faultless ease and able storytelling, there is a message. No slogans or billboards, but words that are used refreshingly to build us, make us better, stronger, and whole. Words that defy the odds and in the end make us wiser." Calling Clifton a "Black cultural poet," Madhubuti adds, "We see in her work a clear transmission of values. It is these values that form the base of a developing consciousness of struggle." Although Clifton acknowledges a "responsibility as a black author," she maintains in an interview with Rudine Sims in *Language Arts,* "But first, I'm going to write books that tend to celebrate life. I'm about that. And I wish to have children see people like themselves in books."

WORKS CITED:

Baughman, Ronald, "Lucille Clifton," *Dictionary of Literary Biography,* Volume 5: *American Poets since World War II,* Gale, 1980, pp. 132-36.
Blos, Joan W., review of *Everett Anderson's Nine Month Long, School Library Journal,* February, 1979, pp. 39-40.
Clifton, Lucille, *Generations: A Memoir,* Random House, 1976.
Clifton, L., *Language Arts,* February, 1982, pp. 160-67.
Lehmann-Haupt, Christopher, review of *Three Wishes, New York Times Book Review,* December 20, 1976, p. C21.
Madhubuti, Haki, "Lucille Clifton: Warm Water, Greased Legs, and Dangerous Poetry," *Black Women Writers (1950-1980): A Critical Evaluation,* edited by Mari Evans, Doubleday-Anchor, 1984, pp. 150-60.
Review of *Everett Anderson's Nine Month Long, Interracial Books for Children Bulletin,* Volume 10, number 5, 1979, pp. 17-18.
Review of *The Lucky Stone, Interracial Books for Children Bulletin,* Volume 11, numbers 1 and 2, 1980, p. 28.

Review of *My Friend Jacob, Reading Teacher,* March, 1981, p. 735.
Richardson, Judy, review of *All Us Come Cross the Water, Journal of Negro Education,* summer, 1974, pp. 396-97.
Slung, Michele, review of *The Lucky Stone, Washington Post Book World,* February 10, 1980, p. 9.
Sutherland, Zena, review of *My Friend Jacob, Bulletin of the Center for Children's Books,* September, 1980, p. 4.

FOR MORE INFORMATION SEE:

BOOKS

Beckles, Frances N., *20 Black Women,* Gateway Press, 1978.
Children's Literature Review, Volume 5, Gale, 1983.
Contemporary Literary Criticism, Gale, Volume 19, 1981, Volume 66, 1991.
Dictionary of Literary Biography, Volume 41: *Afro-American Poets since 1955,* Gale, 1985.
Dreyer, Sharon Spredemann, *The Bookfinder: A Guide to Children's Literature about the Needs and Problems of Youth Aged 2-15,* Volume 1, American Guidance Service, 1977.

PERIODICALS

Children's Literature Association Quarterly, winter, 1989, pp. 174-78.
Christian Science Monitor, February 5, 1988, p. B3.
Ms., October, 1976.

—*Sketch by Sharon Malinowski*

*   *   *

COBB, Vicki 1938-

PERSONAL: Born August 19, 1938, in New York, NY; daughter of Benjamin Harold (a labor arbitrator) and Paula (Davis) Wolf; married Edward Scribner Cobb (a psychology professor), January 31, 1960 (divorced, 1983); children: Theodore Davis, Joshua Monroe. *Education:* Attended University of Wisconsin, 1954-57; Barnard College, B.A., 1958; Columbia University, M.A., 1960.

ADDRESSES: Home—910 Stuart Ave., Mamaroneck, NY 10453. *Office*— c/o J. B. Lippincott Co., 10 East 53rd St., New York, NY 10022.

CAREER: Scientific researcher in Rye, NY, at Sloan-Kettering Institute and Pfizer & Co., 1953-61; science teacher in high school in Rye, 1961-64; Teleprompter Corp., New York City, hostess and principal writer of television series, "The Science Game," beginning 1972; American Broadcasting Co., New York City, writer for "Good Morning America," 1976; Scott Publishing Co., public relations director, 1978-83; Pinwheel Publishers, vice-president; writer and lecturer.

MEMBER: Authors Guild, Authors League of America, Writers Guild, Society of Children's Book Writers.

The Secret Life of School Supplies

Vicki Cobb

Illustrated by Bill Morrison

Cobb suggests experiments and relates the history of such school supplies as paper, ink, and pencils in this unusual work of nonfiction. (Cover illustration by Bill Morrison.)

AWARDS, HONORS: Children's Science Book Award, New York Academy of Sciences, 1981, for *Bet You Can't! Science Impossibilities to Fool You;* Washington Irving Children's Book Choice Award for nonfiction, Westchester Library Association, 1984, for *The Secret Life of School Supplies;* Eva L. Gordon Award, American Nature Study Society, 1985.

WRITINGS:

JUVENILE NONFICTION

Logic, illustrated by Ellie Haines, F. Watts, 1969.
Cells: The Basic Structure of Life, illustrated by Leonard Dank, F. Watts, 1970.
Gases, illustrated by Haines, F. Watts, 1970.
Making Sense of Money, illustrated by Olivia H. H. Cole, Parents Magazine Press, 1971.
Science Experiments You Can Eat, illustrated by Peter Lippman, Lippincott, 1972.
Sense of Direction: Up, Down, and All Around, illustrated by Carol Nicklaus, Parents Magazine Press, 1972.
Heat, illustrated by Robert Byrd, F. Watts, 1973.
How the Doctor Knows You're Fine, illustrated by Anthony Ravielli, Lippincott, 1973.
The Long and Short of Measurement, illustrated by C. Nicklaus, Parents Magazine Press, 1973.
Arts and Crafts You Can Eat, illustrated by P. Lippman, Lippincott, 1974.
Supersuits, illustrated by P. Lippman, Lippincott, 1975.

Magic ... Naturally! Science Entertainments and Amusements, illustrated by Lance R. Miyamoto, Lippincott, 1979.
More Science Experiments You Can Eat, illustrated by Giulio Maestro, Lippincott, 1979.
Truth on Trial: The Story of Galileo Galilei, illustrated by George Ulrich, Coward, 1979.
(With Kathy Darling) *Bet You Can't! Science Impossibilities to Fool You,* illustrated by Martha Weston, Lothrop, 1980.
How to Really Fool Yourself: Illusions for All Your Senses, illustrated by Leslie Morrill, Lippincott, 1981.
Lots of Rot, illustrated by Brian Schatell, Lippincott, 1981.
The Secret Life of School Supplies, illustrated by Bill Morrison, Lippincott, 1981.
Fuzz Does It!, illustrated by B. Schatell, Lippincott, 1982.
The Secret Life of Hardware: A Science Experiment Book, illustrated by B. Morrison, Lippincott, 1982.
(With Darling) *Bet You Can! Science Possibilities to Fool You,* illustrated by Stella Ormai, Avon, 1983.
Gobs of Goo, Lippincott, 1983.
The Monsters Who Died: A Mystery about Dinosaurs, illustrated by Greg Wenzel, Coward, 1983.
Chemically Active! Experiments You Can Do at Home, illustrated by son, Theo Cobb, Lippincott, 1983.
The Scoop on Ice Cream, illustrated by G. Brian Karas, Little, Brown, 1985.
The Secret Life of Cosmetics: A Science Experiment Book, illustrated by T. Cobb, Lippincott, 1985.
Sneakers Meet Your Feet, illustrated by T. Cobb, Little, Brown, 1985.
Inspector Bodyguard Patrols the Land of U, illustrated by John Sanford, Simon & Schuster, 1986.
More Power to You!, illustrated by Bill Ogden, Little, Brown, 1986.
The Trip of a Drip, illustrated by Eliot Kreloff, Little, Brown, 1986.
Skyscraper Going Up! A Pop-Up Book, design and paper engineering by John Strejan, Crowell, 1987.
Getting Dressed, illustrated by Marylyn Hafner, Lippincott, 1988.
Keeping Clean, illustrated by M. Hafner, Lippincott, 1988.
Why Doesn't the Earth Fall Up? And Other Not Such Dumb Questions About Motion, Lodestar, 1988.
Why Can't You Unscramble an Egg? And Other Not Such Dumb Questions about Matter, illustrated by Ted Enik, Dutton, 1989.
This Place Is Cold!, illustrated by Barbara Lavallee, Walker, 1989.
This Place Is Dry!, illustrated by B. Lavallee, Walker, 1989.
This Place Is Wet, illustrated by B. Lavallee, Walker, 1989.
This Place Is High, illustrated by B. Lavallee, Walker, 1989.
For Your Own Protection: Stories Science Photos Tell, Lothrop, 1989.
Writing It Down, illustrated by M. Hafner, Lippincott, 1989.

Feeding Yourself, illustrated by M. Hafner, Lippincott, 1989.

Natural Wonders: Stories Science Photos Tell, Lothrop, 1990.

Why Doesn't the Sun Burn Out? And Other Not Such Dumb Questions about Energy, illustrated by T. Enik, Dutton, 1990.

This Place Is Lonely, illustrated by B. Lavallee, Walker, 1991.

Fun & Games: Stories Science Photos Tell, Lothrop, 1991.

This Place Is Crowded, Walker, 1992.

(With Darling) *Let There Be Optics! Amazing Experiments with Light,* illustrated by T. Cobb, Harper-Collins, 1993.

OTHER

Brave in the Attempt: The Special Olympics Experience (adult nonfiction; photographs by Rosemarie Hausherr), Pinwheel, 1983.

Also editor of *Biology Study Prints,* 1970, and author of *Scraps of Wraps,* 1988.

SIDELIGHTS: Vicki Cobb, author of science books for children, told *SATA:* "When you think about the great teachers who influenced you, who they were as human beings was at least as important as what they taught you. The passion and energy they brought to their teaching— their humanity—somehow touched their students. I believe that revealed humanity is the bridge to authentic and powerful communication, both oral and written. Students and readers learn best when they are moved— when feelings are associated with concepts. The feelings and personalities of top fiction writers are part of their 'voice' as storytellers. Personal voices are beginning to be heard in children's nonfiction, but such writing is a break with tradition. There is an underlying assumption that nonfiction gains authority by being dispassionate and straightforward, although the result may be dry and perhaps boring. But is the word from 'on high' any more than the word communicated with wit or enthusiasm? Why can't the real world be presented in lively prose as fictional worlds are? I consider myself to be a storyteller of the real world. It is my job to present that world in a manner that is engaging to my readers."

In an essay for *Something about the Author Autobiography Series* (*SAAS*), Cobb credited childhood experiences for her hands-on approach to science and her interest in books. "The importance of being a doer obviously came from my home," the author commented. "I painted and did woodwork with my father. I cooked and sewed and knitted with my mother. I had four years as an only child, four years as the sole apple of my parents' eyes before my sister Elly was born. All that exclusive adult attention helped me become a reader at age four. Reading became my most important form of entertainment." Another early influence on the author was her experience at "The Little Red School House," a private school in Greenwich Village. "At 'Little Red,' it was strongly believed that children learned by doing things," Cobb explained. "When we studied the Indians, we built

a tepee in the classroom and we ground corn to make cornmeal the way the Indians did. When we studied the early American colonists, we made candles and soap. We wrote stories and did arts-and-crafts projects. We wrote plays and performed them for each other." Cobb was also influenced by her experience as a counselor-in-training at Buck's Rock Work Camp, where campers and counselors designed and produced crafts for sale to the public. "In those days I was interested in being an artist," the author commented. "I created all kinds of designs for production.... No other camper or CIT had as many items in production as I. I loved thinking up products that the public might enjoy having and then creating them. My success this last summer, before entering college, played an important part in my becoming what I am today."

At age sixteen, under an early enrollment program for promising high school students, Cobb entered the University of Wisconsin. The author said that 1954, the first year of her college studies, was a time when "girls went to college to find husbands." While at Wisconsin, Cobb found that she liked the study of the sciences, and she also became engaged to a student from New York. She later transferred to Barnard College in Manhattan in order to stay with her fiance, but the engagement ended soon after the transfer. After graduating, the author worked for several years as a researcher testing anti-

Vicki Cobb demonstrates the fun of science to schoolchildren.

In *Natural Wonders: Stories Science Photos Tell,* Cobb describes how scientists—by using a red smoke screen—are able to see the wind.

cancer drugs on mice. During that time, she married Edward Cobb.

Two years after her marriage, the author became a junior high school teacher and discovered that she liked explaining basic concepts to her students. While pregnant with her first child, Cobb left her job and turned her attention to writing science texts. However, her first few manuscripts were not printed because the publishers with whom she had contracted went out of business. In 1969, *Logic* became Cobb's first published work. The author commented in *SAAS:* "In the process of producing a book, publishers send the typeset manuscript, called 'galley proofs,' to authors for final corrections before the book goes on press. The day I remember best was the day the galleys arrived and I first saw 'by Vicki Cobb' in type. I must have spent hours gazing at those three words. Suddenly, it was real. After five years, three unpublished books, and countless small writing jobs, I would finally be an author." However, Cobb's first books were parts of series in which authors' writing styles were strictly regulated. She declared, "When you write for a series, your job as author is to sound like all the other authors in the series. My editors made sure of it. When I look back on these early books now, I cringe.

The writing is so flat and dull! I'm glad these books are out of print."

Cobb has cited *Science Experiments You Can Eat,* published in 1972, as the first book in which she could be creative. Commenting on her research for the book, the author stated: "In the morning I got the boys off to day camp and then went prowling through the supermarket aisles looking for ideas. I tried out all kinds of experiments, which often failed. Nevertheless, my family was game about eating them." A *Scientific American* review called *Science Experiments You Can Eat* "a first-rate introduction to the sciences of matter for boys and girls old enough to work by themselves." At the time Cobb was working on *Science Experiments You Can Eat,* her husband was developing a problem with alcoholism, and they were divorced a few years later.

Some of Cobb's earlier books have occasionally been criticized for inaccuracies or oversimplifications. For example, an *Appraisal* reviewer found that *Heat* is "well conceived and planned, but carelessly executed in too many spots." The reviewer was particularly disturbed by Cobb's assertion that "dust particles increase the motion of the air, which causes the temperature to drop." Similarly, a contributor to *Horn Book* objected to

Cobb's statement in *Magic ... Naturally! Science Entertainments and Amusements* that the force of friction acting upon a sheet of paper could be reduced by increasing the speed of the paper. However, the *Horn Book* critic also stated, "the author has done something I like very much—making science fun." A more recent work, *Lots of Rot,* was judged by another *Appraisal* reviewer to be "a wonderful introduction to the subject of decay and the agents and condition that cause it." Cobb's writings have also won several awards, including the Children's Science Book Award in 1981 for *Bet You Can't! Science Impossibilities to Fool You,* and the Eva L. Gordon Award for children's literature in science in 1985.

In the early- and mid-1970s, Cobb worked as a writer for television programs. She stated, "When I was a child, I became a reader because it was the best form of entertainment. We didn't get a television until I was twelve. But my children were brought up on television. I was fascinated and sometimes appalled at the impact it had on them .... As a writer for children, the medium fascinated me. I thought it could be used to teach all kinds of things because there was no question that children learned from it." In 1972, Cobb wrote and hosted "The Science Game," featuring experiments that could be reproduced at home, for a cable television company in New York. In 1976, Cobb became a writer for "Good Morning America," a talk show of the American Broadcasting Corporation (ABC), but she lost her job when a new executive producer brought in his own staff. The author then resumed her writing of science books for children.

In addition to writing, the author now conducts science demonstrations based on her writings and she also holds science workshops for teachers. She asserted in her *SAAS* essay: "Doing in-service programs for teachers all over the country has made me think hard, again, about education. I am more firmly convinced than ever that the Little Red educational philosophy was right. I look back over my life and see that my fulfillment in my work comes from repeating the same kinds of activities I enjoyed as a child. I recall sixth grade as a magic year of self-discovery and discovery of the world around me. In some ways, I now recreate sixth grade for myself through my work. When I think of new ideas for books, I am recreating that summer at Buck's Rock when I was dreaming up products to sell to the public."

Commenting on her departure from the traditional approach to writing about science, Cobb told *SATA* that "traditional written treatment of information often requires that the reader have an agenda, such as a school assignment, before coming to the material. Thus, the reasons a reader wants access to information may have nothing to do with the intrinsic nature of the material or the reader's basic curiosity. When something is required reading, dry, impersonal writing is likely to stifle further inquiry, rather than nurture and support it. My books are a departure from the traditional. I've used a slightly irreverent tone—'science is not the mysterious process for eggheads it's cracked up to be.'" The author further

asserted: "If my books are among the first a child reads on a subject, I've done my job. I have failed if they are the last."

WORKS CITED:

Appraisal, fall, 1974; winter, 1982, p. 22.
Horn Book, April, 1977, p. 197.
Scientific American, December, 1972, p. 119.
Something about the Author Autobiography Series, Volume 6, Gale, 1988.

*   *   *

COXE, Molly 1959-

PERSONAL: Born November 6, 1959, in Atlanta, GA; daughter of Tench (an attorney) and Frankie (maiden name, Marbury) Coxe; married Craig Canine (a writer), June 16, 1984; children: Will, Frances. *Education:* Princeton University, B.A. (magna cum laude), 1981. *Hobbies and other interests:* Gardening, animals.

ADDRESSES: Agent—Marilyn Marlow, Curtis Brown Ltd., 10 Astor Place, New York, NY 10032.

CAREER: Walden School, New York City, preschool teacher, 1983-85; free-lance writer and illustrator, 1985—.

MOLLY COXE

Molly Coxe's bright watercolor illustrations complement Carolyn Otto's rhythmic read-aloud text.

WRITINGS:

SELF-ILLUSTRATED

Louella and the Yellow Balloon, Harper, 1988.
Whose Footprints? HarperCollins, 1990.

ILLUSTRATOR

Claudine G. Worths and Mary Bowman-Kruhm, *Where's My Other Sock? How to Get Organized and Drive Your Parents and Teachers Crazy,* Harper, 1989.

Carloyn Otto, *Ducks, Ducks, Ducks,* HarperCollins, 1991.
Franklyn Branley, *The Big Dipper,* HarperCollins, 1991.

WORK IN PROGRESS: Mop Top and Edie, HarperCollins, 1994.

SIDELIGHTS: Molly Coxe has written and illustrated several books for children. Her first work, *Louella and the Yellow Balloon,* is a self-illustrated book depicting an adventure at the circus. Young Louella Pig accidentally drops her yellow balloon and jumps into the circus ring to retrieve it. As her mother Patricia nervously looks on, Louella chases the balloon, coming face to face with each of the different performers, including clowns, magicians, and even a lion. According to critics, the book's double-page ink and watercolor illustrations will appeal to young children.

Coxe's 1990 self-illustrated work *Whose Footprints?* is the story of a mother and young daughter who follow animal tracks in the snow, leading them to the various animals that made them. The text, like a simple word game, employs a repetitive question-and-answer format. Reviewers noted that the brightly-colored watercolor and ink illustrations complement the text by creating a rustic setting and emphasizing the warm, playful relationship between mother and daughter. Critics found the work valuable as an introduction to animals and tracking.

Coxe told *SATA:* "My husband and I and our two young children live on a small farm in Iowa that has been in my husband's family for three generations. We have a large organic vegetable garden and orchard, and I spend lots of my time there in the spring and summer, planting, weeding, and harvesting. We also raise our own chickens and eggs. My studio is in the corner of an old, renovated schoolhouse on our property. I work there in the mornings and spend the rest of the day with my two children."

D

DESHPANDE, Chris 1950-

PERSONAL: Full name is Christine Lydia Deshpande; born July 9, 1950, in Bolton, Lancashire, England; daughter of Fred and Elena (Rambotski) Clare; married Pratap Deshpande (an education advisor), December 22, 1975 in England, then in his native country, India, August 29, 1976; children: Tara, Leela. *Education:* Trained as a teacher at Madeley College of Education, 1969-72. *Politics:* "Mainly concerned that individual and societal needs are met to increase both equality and justice (particularly race and sex equality)." *Religion:* None. *Hobbies and other interests:* Twentieth-century American literature, India (its history, cultures, and peoples), travel (particularly to sites of historical and archaeological interest), music of the 1960s and 1970s.

ADDRESSES: Agent—A. & C. Black Ltd., 35 Bedford Row, London WC1R 4JH, England.

CAREER: Teacher throughout the four to eighteen age range in Nottingham, London, and Birmingham, England, 1972—, currently head of the learning support department in a Birmingham 11-18 comprehensive school; author of children's nonfiction books, 1985—. Lecturer in schools and at conferences.

AWARDS, HONORS: Junior Education best children's multicultural books of 1985 citation, for *Diwali;* best multicultural children's book, Junior Education, 1988, for *Finger Foods.*

WRITINGS:

Diwali, photographs by Prodeepta Das, A. & C. Black, 1985.
Finger Foods, photographs by Das, A. & C. Black, 1988.
Five Stones and Knuckle Bones, photographs by Jenny Thomas, A. & C. Black, 1988.
Scrape, Rattle and Blow, photographs by Das, A. & C. Black, 1988.
Tea ("Threads" series), photographs by Das, A. & C. Black, 1989.
Bangles, Badges and Beads, A. & C. Black, 1990.

Silk ("Threads" series), photographs by Das, A. & C. Black, 1991.

WORK IN PROGRESS: Springing Tinderbox, an assembly book for primary schools, for A. & C. Black; an arts and crafts book looking at different celebrations and festivals from around the world, for A. & C. Black; and a book on foods focusing on the arts and crafts aspects, for A. & C. Black.

SIDELIGHTS: Chris Deshpande introduces children to such things as the Hindu Diwali festival, the processes of making tea and musical instruments, the feeling of being a "new comer," and playground games in her various works. The Hindu Festival of Light, Diwali, is described in Deshpande's 1985 work of the same title. The celebration, which is observed in Britain and the United States, is related through the eyes of two children, Sanjay and Tara, to draw together what happens in the home, the school, and the wider community. "Such a photogenic subject has resulted, through the skill of the photographer, in colourful and delightful illustrations," remarks a *Junior Bookshelf* contributor. "Learning something about other people's celebrations can only be helpful in understanding the different ways of thinking and behaving that become apparent in our multi-racial society," relates Jean Raynor in *Books for Your Children.* Books such as *Diwali* "can help very much."

In *Five Stones and Knuckle Bones,* published in 1988, Deshpande presents the common questions a child asks when they move and must enter a new school. Leela makes two friends in class, but the playground brings back her insecurities as she wanders from group to group of playing children looking for her new friends. Unable to find them, Leela sees some big footprints painted on the cement and begins to play alone. Soon, though, she finds herself leading a line of children in a game of Follow the Leader. At the end of the book, Deshpande includes a section which describes how to play the world-wide range of cultural games mentioned and a "Things to do" page. "The book is written in simple language with interesting real-life photographs which children find stimulating," relates Penny Thomas in *School Librarian.* "In all, a thoroughly enjoyable and interesting book."

Written for the "Threads" series, which examines such everyday products as bread and water, Deshpande's *Tea* describes how this beverage is grown and produced. The many varieties of tea are included as are legends about the drink and the different ways in which various countries and cultures serve it. The book explains how tea is produced and offers classroom activities for children parallel to the processes. "The text is clear and informative and illustrated by line drawings and colour photographs," comments a *Junior Bookshelf* contributor. And Stewart Scott remarks in *School Librarian:* "The illustrations and text complement each other very well.... Plenty of information, nicely presented. A delightful book."

Deshpande told *SATA:* "In all my books, I have tried to provide a positive projection of the values of a multicultural society, learning within the school curriculum, ideas for teachers to extend learning in curriculum areas (such as science) and about issues of equality and justice. Essentially, the books have been curriculum development projects for the children I have taught and represent the experience of my pupils. I have constructed each book in detail to provide pupils with experiential learning in the classroom (such as the tea making processes in *Tea*) to parallel what happens in the wider world. I have also visualized the purpose and composition of each photograph to convey the information, values and experience built into my teaching."

WORKS CITED:

Raynor, Jean, review of *Diwali, Books for Your Children,* autumn, 1986, p. 6.
Review of *Diwali, Junior Bookshelf,* February, 1986, p. 21.
Review of *Tea, Junior Bookshelf,* April, 1990, p. 83.
Scott, Stewart, review of *Tea, School Librarian,* May, 1990, p. 70.
Thomas, Penny, review of *Five Stones and Knuckle Bones, School Librarian,* November, 1988, p. 136.

FOR MORE INFORMATION SEE:

PERIODICALS

Books for Keeps, January, 1989, p. 10.
British Book News, Children's Books, March, 1986, p. 34.
Junior Bookshelf, October, 1988, p. 239; February, 1989, p. 20.
School Library Journal, August, 1986, p. 79.
Times Educational Supplement, March 21, 1986, p. 27; October 7, 1988, p. 60; November 8, 1991, p. 26.

* * *

DIAMOND, Donna 1950-

PERSONAL: Born October 19, 1950, in New York, NY; divorced. *Education:* Boston University, B.F.A.; attend-

This illustration for Esther Hautzig's *A Gift for Mama* is a self-portrait of Diamond with a younger family member.

ed School of Visual Arts and Tanglewood Summer Art Program.

CAREER: Writer and illustrator. *Exhibitions: The Boy Who Sang the Birds* was exhibited at the American Institute of Graphic Arts show, 1976; work shown in exhibit "The Fine Art of Children's Book Illustration," Port Washington (NY) Public Library, November, 1986.

AWARDS, HONORS: A Transfigured Heart was named Children's Choice book by International Reading Association/Children's Book Council, 1976; *The Boy Who Sang the Birds* was cited as one of fifty best books of the year by American Institute of Graphic Arts, 1976; *Beat the Turtle Drum* and *The Dark Princess* were both named Notable Books by the American Library Association, 1976; *Bridge to Terabithia* received the Newbery Award and the Lewis Carroll Shelf Award, both 1978, and the Blue Spruce Award, 1986; *A Gift for Mama* was named a Notable Book by the American Library Association, 1981; *Mustard* received the Irma Simonton Black Award, 1983.

Diamond's use of light and shadow in her black and white prints captures the mystery and emotion of the stories. (Illustration from *The Dream Book,* written by Olga Litowinsky.)

WRITINGS:

ILLUSTRATOR AND ADAPTER; FOR CHILDREN

The Seven Ravens: A Grimm's Fairy Tale, Viking, 1979.
(Adapter with Clive Barnes; sole illustrator) *Swan Lake,* Holiday House, 1980.
The Bremen Town Musicians: A Grimm's Fairy Tale, Delacorte, 1981.
The Pied Piper of Hamelin, Holiday House, 1981.
Rumpelstiltskin: A Grimm's Fairy Tale, Holiday House, 1983.

ILLUSTRATOR ONLY; FOR CHILDREN

Jane H. Yolen, *The Transfigured Heart,* Crowell, 1975.
Constance C. Greene, *Beat the Turtle Drum,* Viking, 1976.
John Weston, *The Boy Who Sang the Birds,* Scribner, 1976.
Andre Norton, *Red Hart Magic,* Crowell, 1976.
Daniel Curley, *Ann's Spring,* Crowell, 1977.

Katherine Paterson, *Bridge to Terabithia,* Crowell, 1977.
Richard Kennedy, *The Dark Princess,* Holiday House, 1978.
Olga Litowinsky and Bebe Willoughby, *The Dream Book,* Coward, 1978.
Elizabeth Winthrop, *Are You Sad, Mama?,* Harper, 1979.
Steven J. Myers, *The Enchanted Sticks,* Coward, 1979.
Esther R. Hautzig, *A Gift for Mama,* Viking, 1981.
Barbara Wersba, *The Crystal Child,* Harper, 1982.
Penny Pollock, *Keeping It Secret,* Putnam, 1982.
Charlotte Graeber, *Mustard,* Macmillan, 1982.
Eve Merriam, *If Only I Could Tell You: Poems for Young Lovers and Dreamers,* Knopf, 1983.
Isaac Bashevis Singer, *Joseph and Koza,* translated by the author and Elizabeth Shub, Hamilton, 1984.
Milton Meltzer, *Dorothea Lange: Life through the Camera,* Viking Kestrel, 1985.
Lois Duncan, *Horses of Dreamland,* Little, Brown, 1985.
Eth Clifford, *The Remembering Box,* Houghton, 1985.
Margaret Hodges, *The Arrow and the Lamp: The Story of Psyche,* Little, Brown, 1989.
Kathleen V. Kudlinski, *Helen Keller: A Light for the Blind,* Viking Kestrel, 1989.
Shirley Rousseau Murphy, *The Song of the Christmas Mouse,* HarperCollins, 1990.

SIDELIGHTS: Donna Diamond is best known for her unique illustrations for children's books. Her black and white prints, with their use of light and shadow, capture the mystery and emotion of the stories she has worked on, which range from traditional fairy tales, including several she has adapted herself, to a nonfiction book about American photographer Dorothea Lange.

Born in 1950 in New York City, Diamond was encouraged by her parents to pursue her interests in the arts, taking lessons in dance and music as well as art classes at the Museum of Modern Art. She later attended New York City's High School of Music and Art and went on to study art at Boston University. Diamond's decision to write and illustrate children's books grew out of her artistic interests and training. Diamond once told *SATA:* "I was always very attracted to children's books and I like to draw. But, at Boston University you couldn't major in drawing. It was painting or sculpture; I chose sculpture." When she graduated, Diamond moved back to New York where she was encouraged to pursue a career in drawing and began taking courses in illustration at the School of Visual Arts. After trying her hand at editorial illustration, Diamond approached a children's book editor. She later illustrated her first work, *The Transfigured Heart,* which was published in 1975. Since then, Diamond told *SATA,* her focus has remained on illustration: "I haven't done any sculpture since a year after I graduated. I've mostly been involved with drawing and printmaking."

Diamond's illustrations are sometimes inspired by her own experiences. For *A Gift for Mama* by well-known children's author Esther Hautzig, Diamond used her family as models and drew on her own Jewish heritage to create the illustrations for Hautzig's story of a young Jewish boy: "As a Jew, I was familiar with the traditions that Hautzig was referring to, and so I felt a special rapport with the story." Diamond has worked on books for many other authors, including Jane Yolen and Andre Norton, and appreciates stories that she has a personal interest in. As Diamond told *SATA*, though, some of her work has created a misleading stereotype about her preference in manuscripts: "In a manuscript I look for excuses to do pictures I would like to do. I'm happy that the things that I've been offered seem to relate to the things that I'm interested in. Until very recently I didn't know how to draw teeth so that none of the characters in my books smiled. So I think I got the reputation of being an illustrator of moody books. And so I got a lot of manuscripts about people who die and I think that was less about who I am and more about the fact that I didn't know how to draw teeth, so nobody ever smiled."

Diamond has also adapted the classic fairy tales *The Seven Ravens, The Bremen Town Musicians,* and *Rumpelstiltskin* from the versions by the Brothers Grimm. She once explained to *SATA* the difficulty in attempting to keep the original, often metaphoric and violent, images of the tales without using unnecessarily gruesome language: "For *The Seven Ravens* I gathered about two dozen different versions of the tale in English. And I got the German text. I don't speak German so I used a German dictionary. Then I sat down after reading all of this and tried to tell the story.... I agree [with author Bruno Bettelheim in *The Uses of Enchantment: The Meaning and Importance of Fairy Tales*] that ... the violence in traditional fairy tales should [not] be edited out for children.... I tried to be as faithful as I could to the original German text and to the most respected translations. So I didn't cut any sort of bloody scenes out, but I didn't think that I needed to use gory words."

Critics praised Diamond's illustrations of the Grimm tales. *School Library Journal* contributor Marjorie Lewis, in a review of *The Seven Ravens,* commented that Diamond's "misty black-and-white pencil drawings ... seem strangely lit by a heavenly light." Karla Kuskin in the *New York Times Book Review* agreed that the unusual light of the drawings suggest "many mysteries" but felt that such polished illustrations failed to capture the starkness of the tale. In *The Bremen Town Musicians,* Diamond attempted to imitate what she considers the personal tone and warmth of nineteenth-century illustrations, creating the pictures with tiny black dots, an old-style technique that "produce[s] the effect of a textured play of light and shadow," noted Patricia Dooley in *School Library Journal.*

Reviewers of *Rumpelstiltskin* were also impressed by the quality of light in Diamond's illustrations. Diane Gersoni Edelman in *New York Times Book Review* stated that "Miss Diamond's luminous, sophisticated pencil drawings are exquisitely wrought, with superbly subtle shading and light-dark gradations.... Yet they have a classic, frozen quality that, in some cases, may endear them more to adults than to the children reading the

Diamond's illustration for Charlotte Graeber's *Mustard* focuses on the emotions surrounding the illness and death of a beloved family pet.

story." In an interview for *SATA*, Diamond said of her illustrations in *Rumpelstiltskin:* "They're deliberate—on purpose—and I feel very good about them. (Rumpelstiltskin has a painful grimace—*with teeth*.)"

Drawing upon her interest in dance, Diamond has also adapted the Petr Ilich Tchaikovsky ballet *Swan Lake* into a children's story. Because there were no existing versions of the tale as a children's book, Diamond found *Swan Lake* more difficult than the Grimm tales to adapt; hours of listening to Tchaikovsky's music helped to inspire her adaptation of the book. Reviewers praised Diamond's *Swan Lake* as an effective rendering of the tale that was complemented by her illustrations. "This narrative version of *Swan Lake* has the tension and appeal of a classic fairy tale," wrote Janet French in *School Library Journal.*

Diamond once told *SATA* that her books begin as pictures in her mind. "I don't understand how people are writers. For me situations appear in my brain as pictures. I remember incidents visually, and the emotional implications of an incident suggest visual motifs—for me, all the triggers are visual. For writers, stories occur to them. Things put themselves together in terms of words. I don't know how that happens in their brains. And it also seems so lonely.... If I'm drawing a character, I'm trying to keep that character looking consistent. There has got to be a real person in front of me in order for me to get enough information. I'm not sure a writer needs that. Novels are unbelievable. I have no idea how they're made. It's like voodoo...."

Diamond places illustrators into two categories; she told *SATA* that there are some who "are illustrating a feeling in the story.... There are other illustrators I think [who] are 'thing' illustrators.... You never stop looking at the details of what they put in.... I think both kinds of drawings can be very detailed, in different ways. There are people I think [who] draw a very elaborate fog, and that's very detailed—but they don't necessarily have a lot of objects in that fog. I'm not an object illustrator. I'm more an illustrator of very specific fog ... and I feel compelled to make it convey the right emotion. So I do very specific fogginess."

WORKS CITED:

Dooley, Patricia, review of *The Bremen Town Musicians: A Grimm's Fairy Tale, School Library Journal,* April, 1981, p. 113.

Edelman, Diane Gersoni, review of *Rumpelstiltskin, New York Times Book Review,* January 29, 1984, p. 20.

French, Janet, review of *Swan Lake, School Library Journal,* May, 1980, p. 66.

Kuskin, Karla, review of *The Seven Ravens, New York Times Book Review,* April 22, 1979, p. 25.

Lewis, Marjorie, review of *The Seven Ravens, School Library Journal,* May, 1979, p. 51.

Something about the Author, Volume 35, Gale, 1984, pp. 84-90.

FOR MORE INFORMATION SEE:

BOOKS

Lee Klingman and others, compilers, *Illustrators of Children's Books: 1967-1976,* Horn Book, 1978.

PERIODICALS

New York Times Book Review, May 11, 1980, p. 24.

School Library Journal, April, 1981, p. 111; January, 1984, p. 64.

*   *   *

Dr. A
See SILVERSTEIN, Alvin and SILVERSTEIN, Virginia B.

E

EHLERT, Lois 1934-

PERSONAL: Full name is Lois Jane Ehlert; born November 9, 1934, in Beaver Dam, WI; daughter of Harry and Gladys (Grace) Ehlert; married John Reiss, 1967 (separated, 1977). *Education:* Graduated from Layton School of Art, 1957; University of Wisconsin, B.F.A., 1959.

CAREER: Writer and illustrator. Layton School of Art Junior School, Milwaukee, WI, teacher; John Higgs Studio, Milwaukee, layout and production assistant; Jacobs-Keelan Studio, Milwaukee, layout and design illustrator; free-lance illustrator and designer, 1962—. Has also designed toys and games for children, a series of basic art books, banners for libraries and public spaces, posters and brochures, and sets for the Moppet Players, a children's theater. *Exhibitions:* Work has been shown at the Creativity on Paper Show in New York, 1964; at Society of Illustrators shows, 1971, 1989, and 1990; and at the International Children's Book Exhibit in Bologna, Italy, 1979.

MEMBER: American Institute of Graphic Arts.

AWARDS, HONORS: Three gold medals for outstanding graphic art, a best of show citation, and fourteen merit awards, Art Directors Club of Milwaukee, 1961-69; five awards of excellence, five merit awards, one gold medal, and one bronze medal, Society of Communicating Arts of Milwaukee, 1970-72 and 1976; Graphic Arts awards, Printing Industries of America, 1980 and 1981, for posters for Manpower; Paul Revere Award for Graphic Excellence, Hal Leonard Publishing Corp., 1983; grant from National Endowment for the Arts/Wisconsin Arts Board, 1984; Design Award, Appleton Paper Co., 1985; grants from Wisconsin Arts Board, 1985 and 1987; Award of Excellence citations, Art Museum Association of America, 1985, 1986, and 1987; Best Children's Book citations, New York Public Library, 1987, for *Growing Vegetable Soup,* and 1989, for *Planting a Rainbow;* Pick of the Lists citations, American Booksellers, 1988, for *Planting a Rainbow,* and 1989, for *Color Zoo* and *Eating the Alphabet; Eating the Alphabet* was selected as one of the year's ten best books by *Parenting,* 1989; Caldecott Honor Book citation, American Library Association, 1989, for *Color Zoo; Growing Vegetable Soup* was placed on the Museum of Science and Industry book list of children's science books, 1989; *Planting a Rainbow* was placed on the John Burroughs list of nature books for young readers, 1989; Notable Children's Book citation, American Library Association, 1989, for *Chicka Chicka Boom Boom;* Wisconsin Library Association Citation of Merit, 1989; Outstanding Science Trade Book for Children citations, National Science Teachers Association, 1989, for *Planting a Rainbow,* and 1990, for *Color Farm;* John Cotton Dana Award, Summer Reading Program—State of Wisconsin, 1990; *Color Farm* and *Fish Eyes* were named best books by *Parenting,* 1990; *Boston Globe-Horn Book* Honor Award, 1990, for *Chicka Chicka Boom Boom; Parents' Choice* Honor awards for story book, 1990, for *Chicka Chicka Boom Boom* and *Fish Eyes; Parents' Choice* Award for paperback, 1990, for *Growing Vegetable Soup; Feathers for Lunch* was named one of *Redbook's* ten best picture books, 1990; *Fish Eyes* was named one of the ten best illustrated books of the year by the *New York Times,* 1990; Certificate of Merit, Graphics Arts Awards, 1990, for *Fish Eyes.*

WRITINGS:

SELF-ILLUSTRATED

Growing Vegetable Soup, Harcourt, 1987.
Planting a Rainbow, Harcourt, 1988.
Color Zoo, Lippincott, 1989.
Eating the Alphabet: Fruits and Vegetables from A to Z (Book-of-the-Month Club selection), Harcourt, 1989.
Color Farm, Lippincott, 1990.
Feathers for Lunch, Harcourt, 1990.
Fish Eyes: A Book You Can Count On, Harcourt, 1990.
Red Leaf, Yellow Leaf, Harcourt, 1991.
Circus, HarperCollins, 1992.

ILLUSTRATOR

Patricia M. Zens, *I Like Orange,* F. Watts, 1961.

Rectangle.

Oval.

Heart.

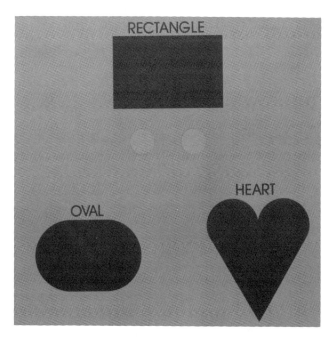

With the turn of a page, each cut-out shape of Ehlert's *Color Zoo* creates a colorful animal.

Edward Lear, *Limericks,* World Publishing, 1965.
Mary L. O'Neill, *What Is That Sound!,* Atheneum, 1966.
Mannis Charosh, *Mathematical Games for One or Two,* Crowell, 1972.
Andrea Di Noto, *The Great Flower Pie,* Bradbury, 1973.
Vicki Silvers, *Sing a Song of Sound,* Scroll Press, 1973.
Nina Sazer, *What Do You Think I Saw?: A Nonsense Number Book,* Pantheon, 1976.
Diane Wolkstein, *The Visit,* Knopf, 1977.
Jane J. Srivastava, *Number Families,* Crowell, 1979.
Richard L. Allington, *Shapes and Sizes,* Raintree Publishers, 1979.

Bill Martin, Jr., and John Archambault, *Chicka Chicka Boom Boom* (Book-of-the-Month Club selection), Simon & Schuster, 1989.
Gene Baer, *Thump, Thump, Rat-a-tat-tat,* Harper, 1989.

Also illustrator and designer of "Scribbler's" products for Western Publishing.

Works included in the Kerlan Collection at the University of Minnesota.

SIDELIGHTS: Lois Ehlert has used her talent as an illustrator to entertain and educate children for over twenty-five years. In the mid-1980s she began writing her own material to accompany her artwork and created books on subjects such as birds, flowers, and the alphabet. These books included pictures that featured bold colors and clear, crisp shapes. She wrote and illustrated *Color Zoo,* which was named a Caldecott Honor Book in 1989. A year later, her illustrations helped *Chicka Chicka Boom Boom,* written by Bill Martin, Jr., and John Archambault, win a *Boston Globe-Horn Book* Honor Award. In an article for *Horn Book* she discussed her attraction to picture books and described her work: "I didn't want to be gimmicky; I wanted to distill, to get the essence of what it was that was so exciting. I hope I'm still exploring that idea. I don't see any sense in creating books otherwise. I get a lot of joy out of it."

As a child, Ehlert received both the encouragement and the environment to develop an interest in art. Her mother, who liked to sew, supplied her with scraps of cloth, and her father gave her wood from his woodworking projects. They also provided her with a place to work by setting up a card table in a little room in their house. She spent a great deal of time at the table, both as a small child and through high school, working on projects that helped her to develop her talent. Finally she sent some of her work to the Layton School of Art and received a scholarship that allowed her to become a student there. After taking the table with her to Layton, she made it into a drawing table by placing a wooden bread board on top of it and then giving the board a slant by propping a tin can underneath it. The table has traveled with her during her career as an artist. "It's got holes drilled in it and ink slopped on it and cuts from razor blades," she noted in *Horn Book,* "but I still use it."

After graduating from art school in 1957, Ehlert did graphic design work and illustrated some children's books. She did not enjoy working on picture books, however, mainly because she couldn't approve the final color selections for her illustrations when her books went to the printer. In disappointment, she stopped working on picture books and concentrated on graphic design projects. But her friends eventually convinced her to go back to illustrating children's books. In *Horn Book* she acknowledged: "I began to see an emphasis on graphics in picture books, and I thought that the time might be right for my work. I could see that there was a lot more care being taken in the production of children's books."

After providing artwork for many children's books, Ehlert decided to try both writing and illustrating a book of her own. While working as a free-lance graphic designer, she created *Growing Vegetable Soup,* a book that combines pictures and words to show the steps involved in growing a vegetable garden. Then she wrote and illustrated *Planting a Rainbow,* which tells the story of a mother and a child who cultivate a flower garden. Both of these books show Ehlert's passion for using bold

colors. Andrea Barnet of the *New York Times Book Review* noted that Ehlert's "colors are tropical, electric and hot—the grape purples and sizzling pinks children tend to choose when they paint. Often she pairs complementary hues ... to startling effect, giving her illustrations a vibrant op-art feel, a visual shimmer that makes them jump off the page."

After achieving success with *Growing Vegetable Soup,* Ehlert took a class at the University of Wisconsin and found new ways to design books by using such eye-catching techniques as cutting holes in the pages and using different combinations of light and dark colors in the illustrations. She made use of methods that she learned in this class in *Color Zoo,* a book that introduces children to a wide range of colors and geometrical figures through the use of different-shaped holes cut in sturdy paper and placed on top of a design. Each new cut-out shape—circle, square, triangle—is decorated with the features of different animals which make readers think of the whole figure as a tiger, then a mouse, and then a fox. Ehlert repeats this routine with two more sets of shapes and ends *Color Zoo* with a summary of all of the shapes and colors used in the book.

Ehlert often uses a technique called collage that lets her move parts of her illustrations around before she has to decide exactly how they will finally look in her books. Using real models, she paints the colors of the objects that she wants to show people onto different pieces of watercolor paper. After the papers dry, she backs them with rubber cement and cuts different shapes out of them. Gradually, she puts the shapes together and paints the edges so that it looks like the illustration is all of a piece. In *Horn Book* she described how collage affected her mood when she worked on *Eating the Alphabet,* a book that introduces children to many different fruits and vegetables. "Once I got the paintings done, I made color photocopies of all the paintings, because the art was so fragile. If I had had to put everything in place all at once and permanently, I would have tightened up. In that book, in particular, I remained very loose—because I would literally do it over and over and over and over again, almost with gay abandon, knowing that I wasn't using expensive watercolor paper. If I made a major error, I knew that I wouldn't have to choose between living with it or starting over again."

For *Feathers for Lunch* Ehlert regularly used numerous pieces of paper to create collages that tell the story of a hungry cat at mealtime that chases after a dozen birds. A bell, worn around the cat's neck, alerts the birds of his presence. Ehlert's artwork is accompanied by a rhyming text, a list of the birds that are presented, and printed representations of their calls. In order to create a book that was both educational and attractive, she presents the birds in natural settings with flowers that are harmonious with the birds' actual colors. Since she wanted to make sure that her collages of the birds were the right colors and sizes, she checked them against the skins of birds kept at the Field Museum in Chicago.

Ehlert also wanted to make life-size pictures of the birds for the pages of *Feathers for Lunch,* but that meant that she also had to make a cat that was life-size. Instead of trying to make such a big book, Ehlert decided to show only parts of the cat on certain pages and to replace him entirely with the "JINGLE JINGLE" of his bell on others. Such practice is routine in Ehlert's books. "If I say something with words, I don't need to describe it with the art, and vice versa." she wrote in *Horn Book,* later noting, "I really use typography as just another design form, another element of the art."

In *Fish Eyes* Ehlert uses the patterns and shapes of sea creatures in order teach kids about arithmetic. Holes cut in the pages encourage youngsters to touch the book while they learn about numbers by counting fish. Ehlert also puts black type on blue pages, hoping that children will find the subtle, hidden text. She explained in *Horn Book:* "I purposely didn't want that design element to be dominant because I already had a dominant theme. So I worked on my layout, and then I stood in front of a full-length mirror to see how close I had to come to the mirror before I could read that second line. I wanted the type to be a surprise to a child discovering it. I try to work on a lot of different levels in every book. Some things are more successful than others." Ehlert's efforts were rewarded by Andrea Barnet of the *New York Times Book Review,* who wrote that *Fish Eyes* has "enough novelty to hold a child's interest, and enough complexity to sustain repeated readings."

Although Ehlert wants children to learn from her books, she doesn't think of herself as an educator. She admitted in *Horn Book* that "it's like being a grandmother in a way—setting down something that might, if I'm lucky, be remembered after I'm gone. And also to communicate what I think is important. Look for those birds! Plant a garden or a tree! They are very homely, ordinary subjects—yet spiritual."

WORKS CITED:

Barnet, Andrea, Review of *Fish Eyes, New York Times Book Review,* May 20, 1990, p. 40.
Ehlert, Lois, "The Artist at Work: Card Tables and Collage," *Horn Book,* November-December, 1991, p. 695.

FOR MORE INFORMATION SEE:

PERIODICALS

Horn Book, May-June, 1989; July-August, 1989.
Publishers Weekly, October 13, 1989.

—*Sketch by Mark F. Mikula*

F

FEELINGS, Tom 1933-

PERSONAL: Full name is Thomas Feelings; born May 19, 1933, in Brooklyn, NY; son of Samuel (a taxicab driver) and Anna (Nash) Feelings; married Muriel Grey (a schoolteacher and writer), February 18, 1968 (divorced, 1974); children: Zamani, Kamili. *Education:* Attended School of Visual Art, 1951-53 and 1957-60. *Hobbies and other interests:* Jazz and playing guitar.

ADDRESSES: Home—180 Wateree Ave., Columbia, SC 29205. *Office*—Department of Art, University of South Carolina, Columbia, SC 29208. *Agent*—Marie Brown, 625 Broadway, New York, NY 10012.

CAREER: Writer and illustrator. Free-lance illustrator, 1959—; Ghana Publishing Company, Ghana, illustrator for *African Review,* 1964-66; Government of Guyana, teacher of illustrators for Ministry of Education and head of children's book project, 1971-74; University of South Carolina, Columbia, associate professor of art, 1989—. Has worked as a free-lance illustrator for Ghana television programs and for newspapers and other businesses in Ghana. *Exhibitions:* Work has been presented at several institutions, including the Ghana Institute of Arts and Culture, Accra, Ghana; the Market Place Gallery, Harlem, NY; and Central Library, San Francisco, CA. *Military service:* U.S. Air Force, 1953-57, illustrator in Graphics Division in London, England; became airman first class.

AWARDS, HONORS: Certificate of Merit for exhibition, Society of Illustrators, 1961, 1962, 1967, and 1968; Nancy Bloch Memorial Award, Downtown Community School, 1968, and Lewis Carroll Shelf Award, 1970, both for *To Be a Slave; To Be a Slave* also received a Newbery Honor Book citation from the American Library Association, 1969; Caldecott Honor Book citations, American Library Association, 1972, for *Moja Means One,* and 1975, for *Jambo Means Hello;* Art Books for Children citations, Brooklyn Museum and Brooklyn Public Library, 1973, 1974, and 1975, for *Moja Means One; Boston Globe-Horn Book* Award, 1974, Art Books for Children citation, 1976, and

TOM FEELINGS

American Book Award nomination, 1981, for *Jambo Means Hello;* Woodward School annual book award, and Brooklyn Museum citation, both 1973, American Library Association notable book citation and placement on *Horn Book* honor list, all for *Black Pilgrimage;* School of Visual Art outstanding alumni achievement award, 1974; Children's Book Showcase award, Children's Book Council, 1977, for *From Slave to Abolitionist;* Coretta Scott King Book Award, American Library Association, 1979, for *Something on My Mind;* National Endowment for the Arts visual arts grant, 1982; Award of Excellence in children's book art and first place for literary children's book, both Multicultural Publishers

Exchange, 1991, for *Tommy Traveler in the World of Black History.*

WRITINGS:

SELF-ILLUSTRATED

Black Pilgrimage (autobiography), Lothrop, 1972.
Tommy Traveler in the World of Black History (adapted from his comic strip "Tommy Traveler in the World of Negro History" [also see below]), Writers & Readers, 1991.

Author of introduction and illustrator for *Now Sheba Sings the Song* (also see below), Dial, 1987. Also author and illustrator of the comic strip "Tommy Traveler in the World of Negro History," published in the *New York Age* (now defunct), c. 1958-59; and of a comic book on black Revolutionary War hero Crispus Attucks. Contributor of articles to *Black World* and *Horn Book.*

ILLUSTRATOR

Rolland Snellings, *Samory Toure,* Nommo Associates, 1963.
Letta Schatz, *Bola and the Oba's Drummers,* McGraw, 1967.
Eleanor Heady, compiler, *When the Stones Were Soft: East African Folktales,* Funk, 1968.
Robin McKown, *The Congo: River of Mystery,* McGraw, 1968.
Osmond Molarsky, *Song of the Empty Bottles,* Walck, 1968.
Julius Lester, editor, *To Be a Slave,* Dial, 1968.
Nancy Garfield, *The Tuesday Elephant,* Crowell, 1968.
Julius Lester, compiler, *Black Folktales,* Baron, 1969.
Ruskin Bond, *Panther's Moon,* Random House, 1969.
Rose Blue, *A Quiet Place,* F. Watts, 1969.
Kathleen Arnot, *Tales of Temba: Traditional African Stories,* Walck, 1969.
(With Marylyn Katzman) Jane Kerina, *African Crafts,* Lion Press, 1970.
Muriel Feelings, *Zamani Goes to Market,* Seabury, 1970.
Muriel Feelings, *Moja Means One: Swahili Counting Book,* Dial, 1971.
Muriel Feelings, *Jambo Means Hello: Swahili Alphabet Book,* Dial, 1974.
Lucille Schulberg Warner, adapter, *From Slave to Abolitionist: The Life of William Wells Brown,* Dial, 1976.
Nikki Grimes, *Something on My Mind,* Dial, 1978.
Joyce Carol Thomas, *Black Child,* Zamani Productions, 1981.
Eloise Greenfield, *Daydreamers,* Dial, 1981.
Maya Angelou, *Now Sheba Sings the Song,* Dial, 1987.
Talking with Artists, Bradbury, 1992.
The Middle Passage, Dial, in press.

Also illustrator for *We Are One,* 1972; works included in *On-the-Spot Drawings,* Watson-Guptill, 1976, *Flights of Color,* Ginn, 1982, and *Dreams and Decisions,* McMillan, 1983; contributor to periodicals, including *Cricket, Freedomways, Harper's, Liberator, Look,* and *Pageant.*

WORK IN PROGRESS: Illustrations for a poetry book for black teenagers, publication by Dial expected in 1992.

SIDELIGHTS: During his career as an author and illustrator Tom Feelings has tried to show the strength and beauty that black people possess despite the suffering and pain that they have experienced in countries such as America. "I strive to intensify the reality, to tell the truth about the past, even if it hurts now in the present," Feelings told *Horn Book.* "I magnify the beauty to show strength and dignity because I know the beauty is there." In his autobiography, *Black Pilgrimage,* Feelings tells how his quest to capture the black experience developed as he grew up in New York City, struggled to become established in his field, spent several years in Africa, and then returned to the United States to gain widespread praise as an illustrator of children's books.

Feelings spent his childhood in Bedford-Stuyvesant, a mostly black community in the Brooklyn area of New York City. With the help of a scholarship he went to the School for Visual Arts and studied cartooning, interrupting his education for four years to serve as an illustrator for the graphics division of the Air Force. When he returned to the school in 1957, he switched the focus of his studies to illustration. "Illustration had changed during the years when I was in the service," Feelings explained in *The Black Expatriates.* "It had become more concentrated on feeling than on realism and that made it more attractive to me. I remember once before I went into the service, I did a comic strip on lynching. The teacher didn't comment on it directly to me but told the class, 'You shouldn't get your personal feelings into a comic strip.' So when I returned to school I had decided that I was through with comic strips because what I was concerned about *was* my personal feelings and what *I* was doing."

Feelings' first printed work, a comic strip called "Tommy Traveler in the World of Negro History," showed how he thought he could use cartoons to express his feelings. Published in the late 1950s in the Harlem newspaper *New York Age,* the strip centered around a young man who looked through a doctor's book collection for information on famous blacks that was not available in public libraries. The comic was strongly rooted in Feelings' own childhood desire to learn about his people's history. In his autobiography Feelings notes: "Tommy read and, each time, fell asleep dreaming himself into the story he'd just read. Tommy was really me."

During the next several years Feelings walked the streets of Bedford-Stuyvesant with a pen and paper and drew the people and places of his community. Although he tried to establish himself as a free-lance artist, he was not very successful at selling his drawings to magazines and newspapers. "Even when illustrations of Black people were needed, the assignments generally went to white illustrators, who knew nothing of the Black images or experiences," he contends in *Black Pilgrimage.*

U uzuri means beauty

(oo· zoo·ree)   Beauty means different things in different parts
of Africa. In one it is a woman with a clean-
shaven head; in another it is a great crown of
braided hair.

After his 1964 trip to Africa, Feelings's style of illustration became brighter and more luminous to capture the glow of black pride. (From *Jambo Means Hello: Swahili Alphabet Book,* by Muriel Feelings, illustrated by Tom Feelings.)

"When I did get assignments they were usually stories about depressive situations."

In the early 1960s *Look* magazine sent Feelings to New Orleans for an article about black people in America. While on his assignment, he sensed that the children of the South were happier than those in the North. He notes in his autobiography that the children in the neighborhoods of New Orleans "seemed different from kids in Bed-Stuy. There was more warmth, openness and happiness in these faces." His desire to uncover and capture the same warmth and beauty in the faces of black people in Brooklyn increased his devotion to illustration. In his autobiography he proclaims, "I felt a driving responsibility to put it all on paper, because, as

far as I knew then, no one else was going to draw what I was living and feeling every day."

His drawings of the people of Bedford-Stuyvesant were often of children of his neighborhood. "I chose children as subjects because they had had less time to be exposed to the pain of being Black in a white country, and because they reflect the best in us before it is changed or corrupted," Feelings avers in *Black Pilgrimage.* He wrote more about working with children in *Horn Book:* "When I asked to draw them—and they never questioned that activity—and when they felt I liked them and saw their own beauty in my eyes, they gave it right back, and the drawings flowed. But the conditioning, the environment, and the experiences of the adults made it difficult for them to give that up. They would say, 'Wait.

This illustration from *Jambo Means Hello: Swahili Alphabet Book* is one of many Feelings created to provide black children with positive black images.

I want to fix my hair. Will you draw my nose smaller? Don't make my lips too large.' And I could feel the strain and pain of the present that was rooted in an aching past."

During this time Feelings traveled to the schools of Bedford-Stuyvesant and showed his drawings to black students. He hoped to inspire them to use their own ability to draw their surroundings. Some children, however, seemed less concerned with Feelings' talent, and more concerned with the amount of money that he made. In his autobiography the artist reveals, "I didn't want to project myself as a symbol of success to them. I was having a hard time, and was definitely not a success in this country's terms." In *Black Pilgrimage* Feelings also writes of a young girl who called his paintings

"ugly." Defending his work, Feelings said, "They're pretty little Black children, like you." The girl responded, "Ain't nothin' Black pretty."

This experience made Feelings decide that it was hopeless to try to convince black children of their worth on a classroom-by-classroom basis. He concluded that the attitudes of young black children, like those held by the students in Bedford-Stuyvesant, could only be changed when they had access to books that portrayed positive images of black people. He had no way to produce such books but still wanted to continue his work as an illustrator, portraying the strength and beauty of blacks in his drawings. He states in *Black Pilgrimage:* "I had to go someplace where Black children did not think themselves ugly. I had to go to the true source of Black people—Africa. In 1964, I left for Africa—where I did not have to compromise my identity, change my subject matter, or have it questioned."

Feelings traveled to Ghana, a country in Africa that had become independent from Great Britain in 1957. He was attracted, in part, by the presence of a printing press in a region of the country known as Tema. He had discovered that the Ghanaian government wanted to publish its own books and thought that he could use his skills as an illustrator to help the country as it developed. When he started drawing in the African environment, using Ghanaians as models, he immediately noticed a difference between Ghanaians and the majority of blacks who lived in Bedford-Stuyvesant. The Africans seemed to have a "glow in [their] faces," he recalls in *Black Pilgrimage*. "It was a glow that came from within, from a knowledge of self, a trust in life, or maybe from a feeling of being part of a majority in your own world. I had seen this same glow in the faces of very young Black children in America, the ones who hadn't yet found out that they were considered 'ugly.'"

His discovery of this glow and his exposure to new surroundings in Ghana caused him to change his artistic style. "My black-and-white paintings became brighter—the contrast glaring, a luminous glowing atmosphere of warm light set against and around dark skin," he explained in *Horn Book*. "When it came to color, I had to change my whole palette. In America my colors were muted, monochromatic, and somber. In Africa they became more vivid and alive, as though they had light radiating from within."

In the late 1960s changes in the Ghanaian government forced Feelings out of his job. He returned to the United States to discover that during his absence the social and political climate had changed so that the government now supported the publication of books geared toward minorities. Using techniques of working with color and light that he had developed in Africa, Feelings illustrated several books that he hoped would provide black children with positive black images and inspire them to use their talents in a similar manner to benefit other blacks. The majority of the books that he illustrated were written by whites, however, and Feelings began to wonder whether he was truly setting a proper example for black students.

Feelings began to collaborate on books that were written by fellow blacks. After providing illustrations for Julius Lester's *To Be a Slave,* he worked with Muriel Feelings, his wife at the time, to produce *Moja Means One* and *Jambo Means Hello.* The latter two books, designed to introduce children to the Swahili number system and the Swahili alphabet, received several important awards. Both of them were named Caldecott Honor Books, and *Jambo Means Hello* earned a *Boston Globe-Horn Book* Award and a nomination for the American Book Award. Their success relied partly on Feelings' illustrations, which affectionately portrayed daily life in East Africa. Reviewer Anita Silvey of *Horn*

Book acknowledged that *Jambo Means Hello* "has been engendered by an intense, personal vision of Africa—one that is warm, all-enveloping, quietly strong, and filled with love."

Providing illustrations for books about the black American experience was a particular challenge for Feelings. After returning to the United States in the mid-1960s, he used the bright colors that he had discovered in Africa while trying to paint pictures about slavery for a proposed book on the life of black educator Booker T. Washington. Such vibrant colors, he realized, would mislead his readers because they did not suggest how difficult life had been for the slaves. He later solved the problem when working on illustrations for *To Be a Slave.* In *Horn Book* he explained: "I was able to pull the two things together and use those dark, muted, somber images from my past work plus my personal feelings about my people—seen in the form of an underlined glow—and combine joy and sorrow appropriately in a meaningful, balanced way."

Since his work on *To Be a Slave,* Feelings has attempted to present both the joy and the sadness that characterize his people's experiences. In *Horn Book* Feelings described the way in which black artists, like himself, must try to capture the black experience in their work. "We celebrate life; we can take the pain; we have endured it," he declared. "We don't want our experience just stated or told to us in a flat way—not even our sorrow. It must move for us—up and down like the blues, flowing, flying, flourishing, like jazz. It must pulsate for us like a deep, heavy heartbeat, or glow with the uplifting, luminous energy of our spirituals. Whatever it is, it must always *sing for us.*"

WORKS CITED:

Dunbar, Ernest, editor, *The Black Expatriates,* Dutton, 1968.
Feelings, Tom, "The Artist at Work: Technique and the Artist's Vision," *Horn Book,* November/December, 1985, p. 685.
Feelings, Tom, *Black Pilgrimage,* Lothrop, 1972.
Silvey, Anita, Review of *Jambo Means Hello, Horn Book,* August, 1974, p. 367.

FOR MORE INFORMATION SEE:

BOOKS

Innocence and Experience: Essays and Conversations on Children's Literature, Lothrop, 1987.
The Multicolored Mirror, [Wisconsin], 1991.

PERIODICALS

The Advocate, winter, 1985.
Black World, August, 1971; November, 1972.
Book World, May 7, 1972.
Horn Book, August, 1972.

OTHER

Head and Heart (biographical film), New Images, 1976.

—*Sketch by Mark F. Mikula*

FRASIER, Debra 1953-

PERSONAL: Born April 3, 1953, in Vero Beach, FL; daughter of George (stepfather; in marine sales) and Mildred (an artist; maiden name, Carter) Bunnell; married James V. Henkel (an artist/photographer), March 17, 1991; children: Calla Virginia Frasier-Henkel. *Education:* Florida State University, B.S., 1976; attended Penland School of Crafts, 1976-81, and Humphrey Institute, University of Minnesota, 1988-89.

ADDRESSES: Home—45 Barton Ave., SE, Minneapolis, MN 55414. *Office*—Harcourt Brace Jovanovich, 1250 6th Ave., San Diego, CA 92101. *Agent*—Virginia Knowlton, Curtis Brown, Ltd., 10 Astor Pl., New York, NY 10003.

CAREER: Author and illustrator. Director of visual arts department for Project CAST, Tallahassee, FL, 1974-75; participant in various national "Artist-in-Education" programs, 1976—; artist in residence, Penland School, 1981-83; sculptor, projects for cities in the U.S., 1981-86; sculptor in residence, American Cultural Center and Cite des Arts, Paris, France, 1986-87; artist in residence, Department of Community Services, St. Paul, MN, 1989. Guest artist at University of Wisconsin, 1985. Lecturer at conferences and workshops. *Exhibitions:* Has exhibited her works in one-woman and group shows in the U.S. and Europe, including "Salmon Run" in Alaska, "Windwalk: A Wind/Poem Environment" in Minnesota and Pennsylvania, "Windwalls" in New York, "Windtent" and "Window" in North Carolina, and "Layered Windows" in Switzerland.

DEBRA FRASIER

MEMBER: Society of Children's Book Writers.

AWARDS, HONORS: National Endowment for the Arts project grant, 1980; Parents' Choice Illustrators Award and American Graphics Society honor list citation, both 1991, both for *On the Day You Were Born.*

WRITINGS:

FOR CHILDREN

On the Day You Were Born (self-illustrated), Harcourt, 1991.
(Illustrator) William Stafford, *The Animal That Drank Up Sound,* Harcourt, 1992.

ADAPTATIONS:

A Quest and *The Late Great American Picnic,* both by Dan Bailey Films, document two of Frasier's outdoor collaborative pageants.

OTHER

Frasier collaborated with In the Heart of the Beast Puppet and Mask Theatre in producing *On the Day Your Were Born,* which toured the United States in 1992. Frasier also designed a Braille edition of *On the Day You Were Born,* where each visual illustration has a tactile counterpart.

WORK IN PROGRESS: Writing and illustrating *Out of the Ocean,* a picture book about a young girl and loggerhead sea turtles; illustrating *A Measure of Space,* by Richard Lewis; developing books for adults and children using cut-paper collage with text.

SIDELIGHTS: Debra Frasier was born and raised in Vero Beach, Florida, where her family has lived since her great grandfather helped to lay out the streets in 1911. "Vero Beach faces the Atlantic Ocean," Frasier told *SATA,* "and I grew up looking out at the great curved line made where the ocean meets the sky. Summers were my favorite time and often my brother and I would crawl into bed with our bathing suits hidden under our pajamas so we did not have to waste time changing for the beach the following morning! Swimming and walking the beaches were our daytime pastimes, along with collecting shells, drawing with mangrove seeds, and building sand castles and forts out of driftwood. Around fourth grade I discovered books, and began reading with a passion. I remember keeping a flashlight under my pillow so I could creep into the bathroom to read at night."

"I loved art from the beginning," says Frasier. "My mother is an artist and she was always collecting shells and bits of surf worn glass to glue into collaged pictures. She also painted on driftwood and taught me how to paint canvas when I was about twelve." Frasier nurtured her love of art and eventually received her college degree in textiles. "I studied batik, an ancient wax resist process, with the idea of designing for interiors. But, upon graduation, I gave a final party that changed my life—I staged a giant puppet show in my backyard,

During a difficult pregnancy, Frasier wrote *On the Day You Were Born* to show her new child all the elements of the world that would welcome her when she arrived.

drafting all of my neighbors into an improvised version of the story of Persephone. I loved making the characters and figuring out the staging, and that led to years of building large, outdoor puppet pageants." Her outdoor pageants have integrated fabrics, words, and even wind; her sixty-foot puppets have danced on a North Carolina mountaintop, and an exhibit called "Windwalk" led viewers through an outdoor trail lined with thousands of strips of cloth blowing in the breeze, interspersed with quotes about the wind.

Frasier has devoted a great deal of time to introducing art to children in the classroom through various "Artist-in-Education" programs in Minneapolis and elsewhere. One of her programs, titled *Walk Around the World,* integrates art, storytelling, and academic material into a unified curriculum "where art plays a major part in the learning process rather than its usual minor role," she told *SATA.* Students are asked to use factual information *and* their imagination to understand how people in other countries live. The experience is "aimed at tolerance," Frasier told Mike Steele, a *Star Tribune: Newspaper of the Twin Cities* reviewer. "The geography, architecture, languages [we study] are different from [the children's] experience. Instead of being afraid of that, they learn to enjoy the differences."

A desire to explore the ways that children understand the world gave Frasier the idea of writing a book, but experiencing a difficult pregnancy provided the special motivation that she needed. "I hoped my baby would be born safe and sound, and, while I was hospitalized, I began the notes for the book, *On the Day You Were Born.* I wanted to write about all the things that would welcome my child if she could just get here. I started making notes of things that defied boundaries, that were everywhere and could be counted on to welcome all children. After my daughter was born, I began writing those notes into a manuscript. All of the illustrations were made with cut paper. I was influenced by the work of Matisse and the clear, clean shapes in Japanese textiles."

The best-selling *On the Day You Were Born* is "exceptionally simple and marvelously deep. It's simply a welcome to the world and to each reader's place in it," says Steele. The poetic text describes the welcome that the sun, the trees, the moon, and other natural forces extend to every newborn child. The illustrations are bold paper cutouts vividly portraying that welcome, and depict children of all colors dancing in the natural world. Michele Landsberg, writing in *Entertainment Weekly,* thinks that the award-winning book "will make each child feel linked to planet Earth in a thrillingly personal way."

WORKS CITED:

Landsberg, Michele, "Happy Birthdays," *Entertainment Weekly,* April 5, 1991, pp. 72-73.
Steele, Mike, "In Book and Play, Debra Frasier Celebrates Life," *Star Tribune: Newspaper of the Twin Cities,* March 17, 1991, pp. 1, 7F.

FOR MORE INFORMATION SEE:

PERIODICALS

Five Owls, March/April, 1991.
Publishers Weekly, February 15, 1991; March 22, 1991.
Reading Teacher, December, 1991.
St. Paul Pioneer Press, March 16, 1991.
School Library Journal, June, 1991.
Star Tribune: Newspaper of the Twin Cities, April 21, 1991.
Twin Cities Reader, March 20, 1991.

*   *   *

FREEMAN, Peter J.
See CALVERT, Patricia

G

GAFFNEY, Timothy R. 1951-

PERSONAL: Born April 12, 1951, in Dayton, OH; son of Elmer (a former Department of Defense employee) and Clara (a homemaker; maiden name, Stoddard) Gaffney; married Jean Buckle (a librarian), January 22, 1977; children: Kimberly, Christine, Mark, Matthew. *Education:* Ohio State University, B.A., 1974. *Politics:* Democrat. *Religion:* Presbyterian.

ADDRESSES: Home—Miamisburg, OH. *Office*—433 South Fifth St., Dayton, OH 45342.

CAREER: Piqua Daily Call, Piqua, OH, reporter, 1974-78; *Kettering-Oakwood Times,* Kettering, OH, reporter, 1978-79; *Dayton Daily News,* Dayton, OH, reporter, 1979—.

MEMBER: Dayton Newspaper Guild (executive board member).

WRITINGS:

Jerrold Petrofsky: Biomedical Pioneer, Children's Press, 1984.
Kennedy Space Center, Children's Press, 1985.
Chuck Yeager: First Man to Fly Faster Than Sound, Children's Press, 1986.
Edmund Hillary: First to Climb Mt. Everest, Children's Press, 1990.

Also contributor of articles to various adult and juvenile magazines.

SIDELIGHTS: Timothy R. Gaffney told *SATA:* "I have had a lifelong interest in writing. My interests in space and exploration were sparked by such books as *Have Spacesuit—Will Travel* by Robert Heinlein, everything by Arthur C. Clarke, the TV show *Sea Hunt,* and *The Silent World* by Jacques Cousteau. I enjoy the sounds that words make and the pictures they can evoke in one's mind.

"My interest in aviation was probably inevitable. I was born in Dayton, the home of the Wright Brothers, who invented the airplane and established the principles of flight. My mother and father worked at old Wright Field in the 1930s and 1940s, the Air Force's center for aeronautical research and development. My parents encouraged reading and I feasted on books about dinosaurs (*Lost World,* by Arthur Conan Doyle), adventure (*The Silent World,* by Cousteau, *Kon Tiki,* by [Thor] Heyerdahl), and space (the 'Tom Swift' series, all books by Heinlein and Clarke).

"I was good at writing but bad at math, so instead of becoming a scientist I became a newspaper reporter, which allowed me to write and draw a weekly paycheck. In 1985 I became the military affairs reporter for the *Dayton Daily News;* as a result, I have interviewed many aviation pioneers and astronauts. I have had unusual opportunities to fly in blimps, biplanes, bombers and fighters." According to Gaffney, himself a private pilot, this included a special opportunity: "At the Dayton Air Show in 1990, officials of the Soviet Union's Mikoyan design bureau granted my request to fly in one of the Soviet Union's most advanced fighters, the MiG-29." This made Gaffney the first newspaper reporter to fly in such an advanced Soviet jet.

*   *   *

GARNER, Alan 1934-

PERSONAL: Born on October 17, 1934, in Congleton, Cheshire, England; son of Colin and Marjorie Garner; married Ann Cook, 1956 (marriage dissolved); married Griselda Greaves, 1972; children: (first marriage) one son, two daughters; (second marriage) one son, one daughter. *Education:* Attended Magdalen College, Oxford. *Hobbies and other interests:* Archaeology and the history and folklore of Cheshire.

ADDRESSES: Home—"Toad Hall," Blackden-cum Goostrey, Cheshire CW4 8BY, England.

CAREER: Writer. *Military service:* Served two years in the Royal Artillery; became second lieutenant.

ALAN GARNER

AWARDS, HONORS: Carnegie Medal commendation, 1965, for *Elidor;* Carnegie Medal, 1967, and *Guardian* Award for children's fiction, 1968, both for *The Owl Service;* Lewis Carroll Shelf Award, 1970, for *The Weirdstone of Brisingamen;* selected as a highly commended author by the Hans Christian Andersen Awards committee of the International Board on Books for Young People, 1978; first prize, Chicago International Film Festival, 1981, for *Images;* Mother Goose Award, 1987, for *A Bag of Moonshine.*

WRITINGS:

FICTION

The Weirdstone of Brisingamen: A Tale of Alderley, Collins, 1960, published as *The Weirdstone: A Tale of Alderley,* F. Watts, 1961, revised edition, Penguin, 1963, Walck, 1969.
The Moon of Gomrath (sequel to *The Weirdstone of Brisingamen*), Collins, 1963, Walck, 1967.
Elidor (also see below), illustrations by Charles Keeping, Collins, 1965, Walck, 1967.
The Old Man of Mow, photographs by Roger Hill, Collins, 1966, Doubleday, 1970.
The Owl Service (also see below), Collins, 1967, Walck, 1968.
Red Shift (also see below), Macmillan, 1973.
The Breadhorse, illustrations by Albin Trowski, Collins, 1975.
Alan Garner's Fairy Tales of Gold (contains *The Golden Brothers, The Girl of the Golden Gate, The Three Golden Heads of the Well,* and *The Princess and the Golden Mane*), illustrations by M. Foreman, four

volumes, Collins, 1979, one-volume edition, Philomel, 1980.

"THE STONE BOOK" QUARTET

The Stone Book (also see below), etchings by Michael Foreman, Collins, 1976, Collins (New York), 1978.
Tom Fobble's Day (also see below), etchings by M. Foreman, Collins, 1977, Collins (New York), 1979.
Granny Reardun (also see below), etchings by M. Foreman, Collins, 1977, Collins & World, 1978.
The Aimer Gate (also see below), etchings by M. Foreman, Collins, 1978, Collins (New York), 1979.
The Stone Book Quartet (contains *The Stone Book, Granny Reardun, The Aimer Gate,* and *Tom Fobble's Day*), Collins, 1983, Dell, 1988.

PLAYS

Holly from the Bongs: A Nativity Play (music by William Mayne; produced in Goostrey, Cheshire, 1965; revised version with music by Gordon Grosse produced in Manchester, 1974), photographs by Roger Hill, Collins, 1966, revised version published in *Labrys 7,* (Frome, Somerset), 1981.
The Belly Bag, music by Richard Morris, produced in London, 1971.
Potter Thompson (music by G. Crosse; produced in London, 1975), Oxford University Press, 1975.
To Kill a King (televised, 1980), published in *Labrys 7,* 1981.
The Green Mist (dance drama), published in *Labrys 7,* 1981.

Also author of plays, *Lurga Lom,* 1980, and *Sally Water,* 1982. Also author of screenplays, including *Places and Things,* 1978, and *Images,* 1981. Also author of radio plays, including *Have You Met Our Tame Author?,* 1962; *Elidor,* 1962; *The Weirdstone of Brisingamen,* 1963; *Thor and the Giants,* 1965, revised, 1979; *Idun and the Apples of Life,* 1965, revised as *Loki and the Storm Giant,* 1979; *Baldur the Bright,* 1965, revised, 1979; *The Stone Book, Granny Reardun, Tom Fobble's Day,* and *The Aimer Gate,* all 1980. Author of television plays, including *The Owl Service,* 1969; *Lamaload,* 1978; *To Kill a King,* (*Leap in the Dark* series), 1980; *The Keeper,* 1982; and, with John Mackenzie, *Red Shift,* 1978.

OTHER

(Editor) *A Cavalcade of Goblins,* illustrations by Krystyna Turska, Walck, 1969, published in England as *The Hamish Hamilton Book of Goblins: An Anthology of Folklore,* Hamish Hamilton, 1969, also published as *A Book of Goblins,* Penguin, 1972.
(Compiler) *The Guizer: A Book of Fools,* Hamish Hamilton, 1975, Greenwillow, 1976.
The Lad of the Gad (folktales), Collins, 1980, Philomel Books, 1981.
Alan Garner's Book of British Fairy Tales (retellings), illustrations by Derek Collard, Collins, 1984, Delacorte, 1985.
Jack and the Beanstalk (retelling), Collins, 1985, illustrations by Julek Heller, Delacorte, 1992.

A Bag of Moonshine (folktales), illustrations by Patrick James Lynch, Delacorte, 1986.

Member of editorial board of "Detskaya Literatura," Moscow. Manuscripts collected at Brigham Young University, Provo, Utah.

WORK IN PROGRESS: Strandloper, a novel and screenplay.

SIDELIGHTS: Alan Garner is "undoubtedly the most gifted but perhaps the most problematical author writing for children in England today," states Justin Wintle in *The Pied Pipers: Interviews with the Influential Creators of Children's Literature.* Garner writes challenging, highly intellectual books that consistently function on multiple levels. In such works as *The Weirdstone of Brisingamen, Elidor,* and *The Owl Service,* Garner weaves ancient symbolism from Welsh folklore with modern stories about teenagers to create puzzling meditations about the nature of time and the imagination. Although his books are marketed to young readers, some critics maintain that they are difficult even for adults. Garner told Wintle that he writes for no specific age group, but that "most of the people who read my books are adults—whatever their age."

Garner sets nearly all his stories in the Cheshire countryside of England where he was born and has lived all his life. His childhood was far from normal. Afflicted variously by spinal and cerebral meningitis, diptheria, pleurisy, and pneumonia, Garner rarely attended school before he was eleven years old. For this reason, explained Garner to Wintle, "Childhood memory is difficult. I seem to have spent about six years alone in a room looking at a wall." When he did attend school, however, Garner received high marks and was also an excellent athlete.

Garner became the first in his family to receive formal schooling, finishing grammar school and going on to Oxford University. He specialized in Homeric archaeology at Oxford, but his distaste for the subject prompted him to explore British mythology, which became the foundation of his later books. Garner told Wintle that his education left him "unbalanced," for it distanced him immeasurably from his family even as it made him feel closer to the land on which they lived. He contended that the tension in the family between wanting him educated and accepting the results of that education led to a "traumatization within the family resulting in a total failure of communication, absolute social breakdown, collapse." For Garner, this conflict led to "rejecting living people and going to the dead—that is, those who are safe in parish records," a trend evidenced by his reliance on ancient archetypes to develop his fictional characters.

Garner left Oxford, which he once called "cloud cuckoo land," because he realized that formal study could only diminish his imaginative interaction with the myths and legends of his native land, and because he refused to commit himself to a study of Classics simply because others thought it was important. He told Wintle of the day he quit Oxford in the middle of a lecture on the Greek playwright Aeschylus. After the lecturer dismissed Garner's question about the meaning of a passage from the *Agammemnon* as having no relevance, he "got up, walked down the road, saw my tutor and said: 'I'm sorry. I'm going. Now. This afternoon.' He asked why. I said, 'I'm going to write.'"

Since leaving Oxford, Garner has devoted his life to writing. In the first few years he published no books and earned no money. Instead of giving up, he relied on public assistance to support him while he continued writing. Garner took two years to write *The Weirdstone of Brisingamen: A Tale of Alderley,* and followed it with a sequel, *The Moon of Gomrath,* three years later. The books describe the adventures of two Welsh children as they explore the otherworld of Fundindelve, meeting a wizard and involving themselves in often dangerous encounters with figures from ancient Celtic legend. Many critics now see these early works as a warm-up for Garner's later, more sophisticated work. Walter McVit-

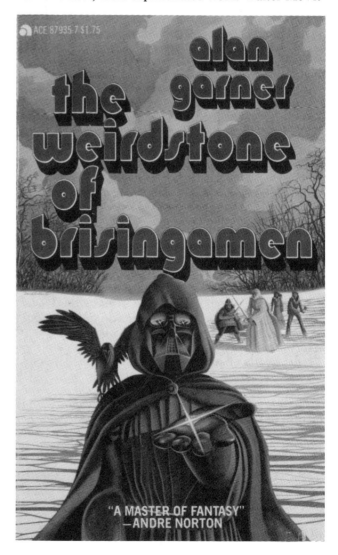

Two Welsh children encounter a wizard and figures from ancient Celtic legend in Garner's fantasy novel, *The Weirdstone of Brisingamen.*

Ancient models form the basis of many of Garner's fictional characters. (Cover illustration by George Adamson.)

ty calls Garner's first two books a "conventional beginning" in his *Twentieth-Century Children's Writers* sketch, and Frank Eyre notes in *British Children's Books in the Twentieth Century* that "although [the books] were warmly received when they were first published they are clearly prentice work and the author abandoned this vein when he moved on to stronger work."

Garner's third book, *Elidor*, further explores the unique mixture of myth and modern reality that distinguishes the author's work. In this novel, four Manchester children explore the backstreets of a derelict neighborhood and are quickly drawn into another world. Following the pattern of quest legends, they return from that world with four treasures and use them in a battle against the forces of evil. A *Times Literary Supplement* reviewer comments that "there emerges clearly the twin theme that while the primitive dark powers cannot be vanquished but only contained, there are also rich worlds upon which the mind can draw, beneficent forces which can be evoked, and which are in danger of being destroyed by modern ways of thinking and living." In

Elidor follows the pattern of traditional quest legends, but moves from the magical world of Elidor to modern British times. (Cover illustration by George Barr.)

The Marble in the Water, David Rees notes that in *Elidor,* myth "is a way of expressing certain fundamental truths about human behavior." Garner told Wintle that his use of myth is "a recycling of energy. Myth is a very condensed form of experience—it is very highly worked material. It has passed through unknown individual subconsciouses, until it has become almost pure energy. [Writing] is a way for me to tap that energy."

Garner's first book to receive wide critical acclaim was *The Owl Service,* winner of the Carnegie Medal and the *Guardian* Award for children's fiction. Eyre says that *The Owl Service* "stands head and shoulders above the average book written for children and is obviously the work of a genuinely creative artist." Noting that the book faced "formidable competition," John Rowe Townsend claims in his *A Sense of Story* that it was "the most remarkable single novel to appear on a children's list in the 1960s." In the book, a group of youngsters find themselves reenacting the tragic relationship of a trio of lovers who lived in the same Welsh valley centuries ago. As the story progresses, the complexities of clashing class and gender combine with the mounting certainty that history is doomed to repeat itself to produce a palpable sense of tension. Margery Fisher says in *Growing Point:* "Here is an attempt to fuse, actually to combine, the thrust and terror of human relationships as we know them and the mysterious, evasive, legendary loves and hates of Celtic folklore; not to compare or contrast but to force from the two together the power of pity and terror."

Critics thought *The Owl Service* was a challenging book; they found *Red Shift,* Garner's next book, nearly incomprehensible. The book contained three different stories taking place in different centuries and linked only by a Cheshire village, a nearby hill, and a Stone Age axe-head. Adding to the complexity was the fact that the book consisted entirely of dialogue. Without denying the difficulty of the book, McVitty suggests that Garner's works are a "counterpart" to the television programs and films that children are adept at understanding, "with emphasis on dialogue rather than narrative, with the abrupt tentativeness of ordinary discourse replacing the artificial conventions of literary speeches. With much of the rapid action, ideas, and words being unexplained, the reader is forced to concentrate and participate if he is to share in the experience and to extract meaning."

A *Times Literary Supplement* reviewer calls *Red Shift* "the most difficult book ever to be published on a children's list," and suggested that "it may prove impenetrable to most readers." Aidan Chambers speculates in *Horn Book* that "Garner has given up any pretense of writing for children and is now writing entirely to please himself and those mature, sophisticated, literate readers who care to study his work." However, Garner's continuing ability to write for children was made clear with the publication of *The Stone Book Quartet,* a collection of independent tales all centered on the same village in Cheshire. Chambers hails the first book in the series, *The Stone Book,* as "a dramatic contemplation of the deep truths of life through images entirely open to even quite young children's imaginations," calling its author "a rare artist greatly to be cherished." And McVitty finds Garner's books "absorbing experiences. In spite of all the critical agonising over them, they are basically simple stories which ... build up to an overwhelming climax on the very last page or two, leaving one thrilled yet stunned."

Garner avoids labelling himself a children's writer or an adult's writer, telling Wintle: "My writing is a totally selfish process that other people seem to find it worth spending money on. Although I do know that I came to it by a conscious elimination of the things I couldn't stand to do.... The only thing I was trained for was the arts, and therefore I had to be an artist. And the only art form I had any proficiency in was language. Therefore I had to write a book. It was as crude as that." Despite his belief that "adolescents read with greater application, intelligence and understanding than anyone else," Garner added that he never has written explicitly for children, only about them. And concerning the charac-

ters in his fiction, he informed Wintle: "They're me. The danger about the autobiographical question— which one is you?—is asking the question the wrong way round. Every one of them is autobiographical, some more than others of course. But I don't think I've ever written about anyone else."

WORKS CITED:

"Alan Garner: Thursday's Child Has Far to Go," *Times Literary Supplement,* November 30, 1967, p. 1134.

Chambers, Aidan, "Letter from England: Literary Crossword Puzzle ... or Masterpiece?," *Horn Book,* October, 1973, pp. 494-97.

Chambers, A., "Letter from England: A Matter of Balance," *Horn Book,* August, 1977, pp. 479-82.

Crouch, Marcus, "Magic Casements," *The Nesbit Tradition: The Children's Novel in England 1945-1970,* Ernest Benn Ltd., 1972, pp. 112-41.

Eyre, Frank, "Fiction for Children," *British Children's Books in the Twentieth Century,* Dutton, 1973, pp. 76-156.

Fisher, Margery, "Special Review: *The Owl Service,*" *Growing Point,* September, 1967, pp. 949-50.

McVitty, Walter, sketch of Alan Garner, *Twentieth-Century Children's Writers,* 3rd edition, St. James Press, 1989, pp. 376-77.

Rees, David, "Hanging in Their True Shapes: Alan Garner," *The Marble in the Water: Essays on Contemporary Writers of Fiction for Children and Young Adults,* Horn Book, 1980, pp. 56-67.

"To the Dark Tower," review of *Red Shift, Times Literary Supplement,* September 28, 1973, p. 1112.

Townsend, John Rowe, "Alan Garner," *A Sense of Story: Essays on Contemporary Writers for Children,* Lippincott, 1971, pp. 108-19.

Wintle, Justin, and Emma Fisher, interview with Alan Garner, *The Pied Pipers: Interviews with the Influential Creators of Children's Literature,* Paddington Press, 1975, pp. 221-35.

FOR MORE INFORMATION SEE:

BOOKS

Children's Literature Review, Volume 20, Gale, 1990, pp. 90-119.

Contemporary Literary Criticism, Volume 17, Gale, 1981, pp. 134-51.

Philip, Neil, *A Fine Anger: A Critical Introduction to the Work of Alan Garner,* Philomel, 1981.

PERIODICALS

Children's Book World, November 3, 1968.

Children's Literature in Education, March, 1974.

Christian Science Monitor, November 2, 1967.

Labrys 7, special Garner issue, (Frome, Somerset), 1981.

New York Times Book Review, October 28, 1973; July 22, 1979.

School Library Journal, November, 1986, p. 76.

Signal, September, 1978.

Times Educational Supplement, December 5, 1986, p. 25.

Times Literary Supplement, March 25, 1977; December 2, 1977; September 29, 1978; November 30, 1984; November 28, 1986, p. 1346.
Village Voice, December 25, 1978.
Washington Post Book World, July 8, 1979.

—*Sketch by Tom Pendergast*

*   *   *

GOBLE, Paul 1933-

PERSONAL: Born September 27, 1933, in Haslemere, Surrey, England; son of Robert John (a harpsichord maker) and Marion Elizabeth (a painter and musician; maiden name, Brown) Goble; married Dorothy Lee (author and industrial designer), 1960 (divorced 1978); married Janet A. Tiller, June 2, 1978; children: (first marriage) Richard, Julia; (second marriage) Robert George. *Education:* Central School of Arts and Crafts, London, England, Diploma (with honors), National Diploma in Design, 1959.

CAREER: Illustrator, author, painter. Free-lance industrial designer, 1960-68; Ravensbourne College of Art and Design, London, England, senior lecturer in three-dimensional design, 1968-77; illustrator and author of children's books, 1969—. Central School of Arts and Crafts, visiting lecturer, 1960-68. *Exhibitions:* Dahl Fine Art Museum, Rapid City, SD. *Military service:* British Army, 1951-53; served in Germany.

MEMBER: Society of Industrial Artists and Designers (fellow); Royal Society of Art (fellow).

AWARDS, HONORS: Horn Book Honor List, 1969, for *Red Hawk's Account of Custer's Last Battle;* American Library Association Notable Book award, 1970, for *Red Hawk's Account of Custer's Last Battle,* 1979, for *The*

PAUL GOBLE

Girl Who Loved Wild Horses, and 1984, for *Buffalo Woman;* Art Books for Children award, 1974, for *The Friendly Wolf,* and 1979, for *The Girl Who Loved Wild Horses;* Caldecott Medal, 1979, for *The Girl Who Loved Wild Horses;* Ambassador of Honor/Books Across the Sea award, English-Speaking Union, for *The Gift of the Sacred Dog, Star Boy,* and *Buffalo Woman; Star Boy* was a Library of Congress Children's Book of the Year and an International Youth Library Choice. Recipient of prizes in three industrial design competitions.

WRITINGS:

FOR CHILDREN; SELF-ILLUSTRATED

(With Dorothy Goble) *Red Hawk's Account of Custer's Last Battle,* Pantheon, 1969.
(With D. Goble) *Brave Eagle's Account of the Fetterman Fight, 21 December 1866,* Pantheon, 1972, published in England as *The Hundred in the Hands: Brave Eagle's Account of the Fetterman Fight, 21st December, 1866,* Macmillan, 1972.
(With D. Goble) *Lone Bull's Horse Raid,* Macmillan, 1973.
(With D. Goble) *The Friendly Wolf,* Bradbury, 1974, completely revised edition published as *Dream Wolf,* Bradbury, 1990.
The Girl Who Loved Wild Horses, Bradbury, 1978.
The Gift of the Sacred Dog, Bradbury, 1980.
Star Boy, Bradbury, 1980.
Buffalo Woman, Bradbury, 1984.
The Great Race of the Birds and Animals, Bradbury, 1985.
Death of the Iron Horse, Bradbury, 1987.
Her Seven Brothers, Bradbury, 1988.
Iktomi and the Boulder: A Plains Indian Story, Orchard Books, 1988.
Beyond the Ridge, Bradbury, 1989.
Iktomi and the Berries: A Plains Indian Story, Orchard Books, 1989.
Iktomi and the Buffalo Skull: A Plains Indian Story, Orchard Books, 1990.
Iktomi and the Ducks: A Plains Indian Story, Orchard Books, 1990.
I Sing for the Animals, Bradbury, 1991.

ILLUSTRATOR

Richard Erdoes, editor, *The Sound of Flutes and Other Indian Legends,* Pantheon, 1976.

ADAPTATIONS: Red Hawk's Account of Custer's Last Battle was read by Arthur S. Junaluska for a Caedmon Records release, 1972.

SIDELIGHTS: Paul Goble is one of the foremost interpreters of Native American folklore for young children through his retelling of Indian myths and legends. Coupled with the watercolor-and-ink illustrations reflecting his deep love of nature, Goble's stories introduce young readers to the Sioux, Blackfoot, and Cheyenne Indian cultures and preserve the tradition of Native American storytelling.

"I have been interested in everything Indian since I can remember," Goble said during his acceptance speech—published in *Horn Book*—for the 1979 Caldecott Medal awarded to him for *The Girl Who Loved Wild Horses.* "Before television days my mother read the complete works of [American naturalist writers Grey Owl and Ernest Thomas Seton] to my brother and me.... The world they wrote about was so different from the crowded island where I lived." As a young boy, Goble accompanied his family searching for stone-age flint instruments which can be found in certain locations within Britain. Goble pictured the people who made such tools as being similar in some ways to the American Indians who had captured his imagination. Throughout his youth, he collected pictures from magazines and books of everything he could find relating to the Indian people of the Great Plains.

One Christmas the young Goble received a gift, a copy of American artist and author George Catlin's book *Notes on the North American Indian,* which elevated his study of Indian lore to a more advanced level. He began compiling what has since become a comprehensive library of many noteworthy books on Native American culture. Two such books, *The Sacred Pipe* and *Black Elk Speaks,* both by the Lakota holy man Black Elk, aided Goble in determining his life's orientation. Goble has continued his interest in North American Indians and has successfully integrated this knowledge into both his personal philosophy and his unique style of illustration.

While continuing his independent study of the American Indians, Goble pursued a career in industrial design as both a teacher and designer. While his love of nature and Indian culture remained uppermost in his thoughts, he never saw it as a way to support his family. In the summer of 1959, after completing his degree at London's Central School of Arts and Crafts, Goble had the opportunity to tour Sioux and Crow Indian reservations in South Dakota and Montana. During his visit he was adopted into the Yakima and Sioux tribes and was given the name *Wakinyan Chikala,* or "Little Thunder," by Chief Edgar Red Cloud, a great grandson of a famous Sioux war chief.

As a teacher in England, Goble took the opportunity provided by extended breaks to make several summer trips to the United States, accompanied by his son, Richard. They would rent a car and, with a small tent and few belongings, spend the summer among the Sioux in South Dakota and their Crow Indian friends in Montana. "I was privileged to take part in ceremonies, to be present at their sacred Sun Dances," Goble said in his Caldecott Medal acceptance speech. "I have taken part in building the Sun Dance lodge and have helped to pitch tipis."

Although first confining his painting and writing to holidays while lecturing at Ravensbourne School, he changed to full-time author/illustrator in 1977, and made his new home in the Black Hills of South Dakota.

As an interpreter of Native American myths and legends of the Great Plains, Goble evaluates several different versions of the same story before writing the text for his books. "I try to go back to the oldest sources when researching a story," he told an interviewer in *Publishers Weekly,* explaining that it was only during the period 1890-1910 that many Indian stories were first recorded by ethnologists. Goble presents the traditional myths in the formal poetic style characteristic of Indian oral tradition. Many times songs or prayers relating to the subject are included, as well as bibliographies and informative notes on different aspects of Indian culture. The "Iktomi" (pronounced Eek-toe-me, a Lakota word for "spider") series of books encourages reader participation through italicized running commentary. Iktomi is a show-off and a trickster whose clever plans to avoid work constantly backfire with humorous consequences. Goble's insertions of periodic questions invite readers to participate directly in the traditional storytelling process and also help to demonstrate that tales about Iktomi are continually evolving and timeless in their appeal.

In all his books, Goble emphasizes the widespread Native American belief in the harmonious relationship between man and nature. Goble mentioned in his Caldecott Medal acceptance speech that he wrote *The Friendly Wolf* because he was concerned about the threatened extinction of Alaskan wolves by the practice of hunting such animals by helicopter. He believes that children have an inborn love for the natural world, which Indian myths help foster. Exposure only to the conventional worlds of cartoons and picture books, where bears are "cuddly", wolves and tomcats "vicious," and spiders and snakes "evil," blunt children's empathy for the world of nature. The belief that animals are deserving of man's respect and inspiration rather than their fear or ridicule is the theme of most Indian legends. Goble passes these legends on so that his readers can learn how other cultures viewed "the environment."

Goble's book *Death of the Iron Horse* is his attempt to dispel the "movie myth" that American Indians regularly destroyed railroad trains, robbing and murdering their helpless passengers. The story is based on the only substantiated account of a train wrecked by Indians: the Union Pacific freight train derailed by Cheyennes on August 7, 1867. Goble portrays the Indian attack as a justifiable defense of their camp by the encroaching "iron horse" and its "iron road." The looting of the train's cargo is seen as the just reward for a battle won. The story takes on an almost humorous element when the author shows the Indians gathering up small coins contained in the train's strongbox while throwing great quantities of "useless" paper money away, to be carried off by the prairie winds.

Death is a difficult subject for children to understand, and Goble's book *Beyond the Ridge* sensitively recounts some of the Indian beliefs. Mortality is only one of many stages within the "great circle of life" rather than something to be feared due to its threatening finality:

In an instant the herd was galloping away like the wind. She called to the horses to stop, but her voice was lost in the thunder. Nothing could stop them. She hugged her horse's neck with her fingers twisted into his mane. She clung on, afraid of falling under the drumming hooves.

Paul Goble's self-illustrated *The Girl Who Loved Wild Horses*, a Caldecott Medal book, introduces young readers to Native American culture through vivid pen-and-ink and watercolor illustrations and simple text.

"Dying is like climbing up a long and difficult slope towards a high, pine-covered ridge on the Great Plains. From the top we shall see, beyond the ridge, the Spirit World, the Land of Many Tipis, the place from which we came, and the place to which we shall return .... We shall live there without fatigue or sorrow or illness."

In his Caldecott Medal acceptance speech, Goble describes *The Girl Who Loved Wild Horses* as a synthesis of many legends which stress the Indian's rapport with his natural surroundings. Goble points out, "The Indian does not feel afraid or alone in the forests and prairies; he knows many stories about ancestors who turned into the seven stars of the Big Dipper and others who became the Pleiades .... Knowledge of this relationship with the universe gives [him] confidence. [He has] no thought to reorganize nature in a way other than that in which the Great Spirit made it."

Although Goble's style of writing has been criticized for being "a bit stiff" by a reviewer for the *Bulletin of the Center for Children's Books,* Eleanor K. MacDonald of *School Library Journal* credited Goble for his reserve, saying, "He resists the temptation to dramatize the tale, choosing instead the quiet, matter-of-fact voice of the traditional Indian storyteller." A restrained narrative is characteristic of Goble's work as is his stylized artwork. His illustrations contain many symbols from Indian culture, among which are the circle motif, signifying unity, and wavy lines which depict lightning bolts and power. His art is also greatly influenced by research into early paintings which Indian people did in ledger books obtained from the traders. In these books they recorded their tribal history with brightly-colored, two-dimensional pictures. In his books, Goble combines the spirit of these historic drawings with his knowledge of design and technique.

Goble's long-standing respect for the Indians of the Great Plains has not diminished over the years and he still lives in the Black Hills of South Dakota, one of the major contemporary chroniclers of Native American legends and myths. Through his writing and illustration he has helped to give people a greater understanding of other cultures, as well as giving American Indian children the encouragement to value their cultural heritage. "We're in need of differences," Goble told *Publishers Weekly,* "*and* to not be afraid of those differences."

Paul Goble commented: "My wife, Janet, and our son, Robert, make frequent visits to friends, and to ceremonies and powwows on various reservations in South Dakota and Montana. We have driven for miles and miles over the Northern Plains looking for the places of history, museums, and to find the birds and animals and flowers with which Indian people used to live. Janet and Robert see all these things, and later they see them again when I write and illustrate in my studio. I work at home. Janet, my best-beloved wife and true companion, is always kind and encouraging."

WORKS CITED:

Review of *The Gift of the Sacred Dog, Bulletin of the Center for Children's Books,* March, 1981, pp. 133-134.
Goble, Paul, *Beyond the Ridge,* Bradbury, 1989.
Goble, Paul, Caldecott Medal acceptance speech, delivered June 26, 1979, published in *Horn Book,* August, 1979, pp. 396-398.
Interview with Paul Goble, *Publishers Weekly,* February 26, 1988, p. 114.
Eleanor K. MacDonald, review of *Her Seven Brothers, School Library Journal,* June-July, 1988, p. 97.

FOR MORE INFORMATION SEE:

BOOKS

Children's Literature Review, Volume 21, Gale, 1990, pp. 123-138.
de Montreville, Doris, and Elizabeth D. Crawford, editors, *Fourth Book of Junior Authors and Illustrators,* H. W. Wilson, 1978.

PERIODICALS

American Indian Quarterly, spring, 1984, pp. 117-125.
Booklist, May 1, 1990, p. 1714; November 1, 1990, p. 523; February 1, 1991, p. 1129.
Bulletin of the Center for Children's Books, March, 1983; September, 1985; April, 1987; April, 1988; March, 1989.
Horn Book, December, 1972, pp. 605-606; February, 1977; December, 1978, pp. 631-632; August, 1979, pp. 399-401; February, 1981; May, 1989, p. 355.
Language Arts, December, 1984, pp. 867-873.
Los Angeles Times Book Review, June 4, 1989, p. 11; September 24, 1989, p. 12.
New York Times Book Review, November 9, 1970; September 24, 1972, p. 8; November 11, 1973, p. 8; November 22, 1987; December 10, 1989, p. 34; June 17, 1990, p. 21.
Publishers Weekly, February 23, 1990, p. 215.
Wilson Library Bulletin, September, 1984; November, 1988.

—*Sketch by Pamela L. Shelton*

*   *   *

GRINNELL, David
See WOLLHEIM, Donald A(llen)

*   *   *

GROVER, Wayne 1934-

PERSONAL: Born October 24, 1934, in Minneapolis, MN; son of Henry Percy (a machinist) and Dora (Dreon) Grover; married Ursula Seubert, June 12, 1956 (divorced, 1965); married Barbara Wiseman (a writer), December 21, 1970; children: Leigh Anne Musser, Sabrina Hamner, Christian Grover, Greg Grover. *Education:* University of Maryland, B.S.

ADDRESSES: Home and office—3282 Parade Place, Lantana, FL 33462.

WAYNE GROVER

CAREER: United States Air Force, air traffic controller at various locations around the world, 1954-76, became a master sergeant; journalist, 1978—. Hosted television program in Chicago, 1990-91. Palm Beach County Animal Care and Control Board, chairman, three years, currently member. Former chairman of Toastmasters Clubs.

AWARDS, HONORS: Named Top United States Air Force Journalist; received 27 military decorations.

WRITINGS:

Dolphin Adventure, Greenwillow Books, 1990.
Ali and the Golden Eagle, Greenwillow Books, 1992.

Contributor to newspapers, magazines, and tabloids.

WORK IN PROGRESS: Alone, the story of a POW left alive in Laos, his twenty-year confinement and escape to the West; *The World of Tabloid Journalism.*

SIDELIGHTS: Wayne Grover told *SATA:* "The most important aspect of life in 1991 is that there are too many humans taking too little care of our mother earth. The advent of the consumer-driven, throwaway society has resulted in the pollution of the entire planet on a scale never imagined. We as Americans evolved thinking science and technology could always stave off calamity, but we did not consider the emerging second and third world nations that could not and would not take the time and effort to protect the environment. Within the span of the twentieth century alone, we have pushed the planet to the brink of pollution saturation. Where diamonds and precious gems were once the minerals of the wealthy, we will see water become the most important mineral on earth.

"Our hope lies with our children and the world's children being educated and motivated to ensure not an ounce of material is wasted or disposed without recycling. There is no longer enough animal and fish species to allow mindless hunting by so called sportsmen and trophy fishers.

"The food chain is just one vicious weather cycle removed from disaster due to the ozone layer's ever thinning, allowing the UV rays to penetrate to the earth's crust and create droughts to spread famine.

"The good news is that we as a species can each and every one take a hand in stopping the destruction of our planet. From the individual to the top men in government, we can reverse this mindless laying waste of our ONLY home. I write my books and articles to let people know they can make a difference. They can work together to create a new world, dedicated to natural balance and returning to the earth what we take from it.

"ALL hunting must be stopped. We must manage our forests and waters until we return them to the pristine condition we found them in less than two hundred years ago.

"Man walked the planet for several million years, leaving nothing but his footprints. Within the space of a hundred years, we stand on the brink of planetary destruction. We can stop it ... TOGETHER."

H

HAMLEY, Dennis 1935-

PERSONAL: Full name is Dennis Charles Hamley; born October 14, 1935, in Crockham Hill, Kent, England; son of Charles Richard (a post office engineer) and Doris May (a homemaker and telephone operator; maiden name, Payne) Hamley; married Agnes Moylan (a nurse and administrator), August 5, 1965; children: Peter, Mary. *Education:* Jesus College, Cambridge, B.A., 1959, M.A., 1963; University of Bristol, P.G.C.E., 1960; University of Manchester, diploma in advanced studies in education, 1965; University of Leicester, Ph.D., 1980. *Politics:* "None, but left-wing slant." *Religion:* "None, but nominally Church of England." *Hobbies and other interests:* Music, railways, watching football, drama, camping, motoring.

ADDRESSES: Home—Hillside, 2 King's Rd., Hertfordshire SG13 7EY, England. *Office*—Education Department, County Hall, Hertfordshire SG13 8DF, England.

CAREER: English master at grammar and secondary modern schools in England, 1960-67; Milton Keynes College of Education, Bletchley, Buckinghamshire, England, lecturer, 1967-69, senior lecturer in English, 1969-78; Hertfordshire Local Education Authority, Hertfordshire, England, county advisor for English and drama, 1978—. Counselor and tutor for Open University, 1971-78. *Military service:* Royal Air Force, 1954-56.

MEMBER: National Association of Educational Inspectors and Advisors, Eastern Arts Association (literary panel, 1983-90), Society of Authors (chair of educational writers' group, 1979-83).

WRITINGS:

Three Towneley Plays (adapted into modern English), Heinemann, 1963.
Pageants of Despair (juvenile novel; also see below), S. G. Phillips, 1974.
(With Colin Field) *Fiction in the Middle School*, Batsford, 1975.
Very Far from Here (juvenile novel), Deutsch, 1976.

DENNIS HAMLEY

Landings (juvenile novel), Deutsch, 1979.
Pageants of Despair (radio play based on novel of the same title), British Broadcasting Corporation (BBC) Radio, 1979.
Court Jester (radio play), BBC Radio, 1979.
(Translator and adaptor) Gian Paolo Ceserani, *The Travels of Columbus,* Kestrel, 1979.
(Translator and adaptor) Ceserani, *Travels of Livingstone,* Kestrel, 1979.
(Translator and adaptor) Ceserani, *The Travels of Marco Polo,* Kestrel, 1980.
(Translator and adaptor) Ceserani, *The Travels of Captain Cook,* Kestrel, 1980.
The Shirt off a Hanged Man's Back (short stories), Deutsch, 1984.
The Fourth Plane at the Flypast (juvenile novel), Deutsch, 1985.
Haunted United (juvenile novel), Deutsch, 1986.

TIGGER AND FRIENDS

DENNIS HAMLEY

ILLUSTRATIONS BY
MEG RUTHERFORD

One of Hamley's favorite books, *Tigger and Friends,* is a true story of the author's three-legged cat. (Jacket illustration by Meg Rutherford.)

Dangleboots (juvenile novel), illustrated by Tony Ross, Deutsch, 1987.
Hare's Choice (first juvenile novel in trilogy), illustrated by Meg Rutherford, Deutsch, 1987.
Cat Watchers, illustrated by Kim Palmer, Basil Blackwell, 1988.
The Railway Passengers, illustrated by Palmer, Basil Blackwell, 1988.
Tigger and Friends, illustrated by Rutherford, Lothrop, 1989.
Blood Line, Deutsch, 1990.
Coded Signals, Deutsch, 1990.
The War and Freddy, illustrated by George Buchanan, Deutsch, 1991.

Contributor of short stories to numerous books, including *The Methuen Book of Sinister Stories,* edited by Jean Russell, Methuen, 1982; *Aliens,* edited by Bryan Newton, Collins, 1985; *An Oxford Book of Christmas Stories,* edited by Dennis Pepper, Oxford University Press, 1986; *Twisted Circuits,* edited by Mick Gowar, Century Hutchinson, 1987; *Mystery Tour,* edited by Gowar, Bodley Head, 1991. Contributor of articles to periodicals, including *English in Education.* Reviewer for *School Librarian* and *Times Educational Supplement.* Developer of *Julius Caesar: Study Guide and Cassette,* Argo Records, 1980.

WORK IN PROGRESS: Badger's Fate, illustrated by Meg Rutherford, the second novel in the *Hare's Choice* trilogy; the third novel in the *Hare's Choice* trilogy;

cowriting *Living Writers* series in three volumes, for Macmillan; working on a retelling of Carl Maria Friedrich Ernst von Weber's opera "Der Freishuetz," for a book of opera stories edited by Mick Gowar, for Bodley Head; writing and researching a longer novel set in the present day United Kingdom.

SIDELIGHTS: Dennis Hamley told *SATA:* "Though I always wanted to be a writer (and, indeed, had a book for schools published in the 1960s—a sort of false start), it was not until 1971 that I realized I was to be a children's writer. I carried around in my head for over a year the idea which was later to emerge as my first children's novel. On a hot July evening in 1971 I sat down at last to write it; my proper writing career dates from that evening. *Pageants of Despair* was published in the United Kingdom in 1974. It was then I decided I had to learn *how* to be a writer. My first book was a good idea badly presented. My next two books had less original ideas but were better done. Although I was learning to handle a plot, the writing only fitfully had the resonance I aimed at.

"The discipline of writing short stories helped to improve this. I believe firmly that novels are much easier to do than short stories. The self-imposed discipline of the short story has improved my novels (which are now much shorter!) no end.

"I started a collection of short stories to show myself I could do it. I owe the inspiration to my editor, Pam Royds, at Andre Deutsch. She looked at the rag-bag of bits I fondly believed was going to be my second novel, told me to go away and write again and that perhaps one bit of the rejected novel might make a story in a future collection of ghost stories.

"Five years later I started on the stories again. I used those first ideas from the failed novel to learn how to do it and laboriously pieced together two stories which seemed to work. I now found the other stories coming much easier; the resulting collection, *The Shirt off a Hanged Man's Back,* has always pleased me. Ghosts are useful devices for an author. Stories are basically all about the past affecting the present. Ghosts are good short-circuits for revealing the past. Look at the ghost of Hamlet's father—for me, the best ghost of all.

"One story for this collection proved too long. So I lengthened it even further to form the 1985 novel *The Fourth Plane at the Flypast,* in which the ghost bringing secrets from the past is a Royal Air Force (RAF) World War II Wellington bomber. I wrote this story while convalescing after a major heart operation—a triple bypass. Before I was taken, quickly and alarmingly, to the hospital for this, I had been asked to write a short story for a forthcoming collection for schools. I actually wrote it when I came home—a ghost story about a boy having a heart operation! I won't say that writing is purely therapeutic, but writing that story enabled me to understand what had happened to me and, I am sure, to recover quicker.

"The books of mine that mean most to me are *Tigger and Friends,* a true story about our own cats (as of 1991, three-legged Tigger is still with us, having just celebrated his 17th birthday) and *Hare's Choice.* Both were helped by Meg Rutherford's incomparable illustrations. The questions left at the end of *Hare's Choice* went on niggling away in my mind until eventually I saw a way to write a much darker sequel, *Badger's Fate,* and then embark on a joyful (partly!) end to the trilogy.

"In many ways, the trilogy is my educational statement about language and stories in schools, because I am only a part-time writer and work full-time in education as county English advisor for Hertfordshire. I also run a lot of courses in writing and writing workshops for teachers and children. Each year I organize a writing course for nine- to eleven-year-old children at a lovely big house in Bishop's Stortford called Pearse House, and also a two-day workshop for sixth-formers, writing stories and desk-top publishing them on the spot. The writing of children and young people is very important to me. Expression through writing is everybody's right and entitlement and I aim to develop it as much as I can.

"I write when I can (often early in the morning) in longhand and take the second or third draft to the word processor. I seldom plan ahead. I usually have a structure in my mind—a general situation map of where my characters ought to be at the end of the story—and let the story 'unfold.' I have two mottoes in this: How do I know what I think till I see what I say? and You only know what it is you want to write by writing it. It was many years before I realized this. I was taught at school to plan everything in detail before I wrote. I found this so difficult that I decided early on that in spite of my wishes I would *never* be a writer! One of the most interesting things I was asked to do accompanied the request for a short story of mine that was published in a textbook for schools. This was a 'writing diary,' where I carefully chronicled the actual process of writing the story as a day-by-day diary. I found a lot out about myself in doing this.

"I live in Hertford with my wife, who is Irish. My son is a scientist finishing his Ph.D. at Cambridge and soon embarking on a postdoctoral fellowship at the University of Pennsylvania. My daughter is working in publishing in Oxford. They have been my sharpest and most constructive critics.

"I was born in Kent in 1935 and from the ages of three to nine lived in southern England—throughout the second world war, which to me exists as a sort of childhood fantasy (as shown in my book *The War and Freddy*). I was born into a working class home with no history of education beyond the minimum. That I was able to go to grammar school and then Cambridge University was entirely due to the understanding and sacrifice of my parents and the great 'time of hope' brought about by the end of the war. It appalls and disgusts me that those values are being denigrated and scorned in the money-grubbing, collapsing mess that constitutes Western society today. Part, at least, of my

reason for writing children's books is to attempt to reverse this—while still looking the world in the face and at least *trying* to be realistic."

*   *   *

HASKINS, James 1941-
(Jim Haskins)

PERSONAL: Born September 19, 1941, in Montgomery, AL; son of Henry and Julia (Brown) Haskins. *Education:* Georgetown University, B.A., 1960; Alabama State University, B.S., 1962; University of New Mexico, M.A., 1963; graduate study at New School for Social Research, 1965-67, and Queens College of the City University of New York, 1967-68.

ADDRESSES: Home—325 West End Ave., Apt. 7D, New York, NY 10013. *Office*—Department of English, University of Florida, Gainesville, FL 32611.

CAREER: Smith Barney & Co., New York City, stock trader, 1963-65; New York City Board of Education, New York City, teacher, 1966-68; New School for Social Research, New York City, visiting lecturer, 1970-72; Staten Island Community College of the City University of New York, Staten Island, NY, associate professor, 1970-77; University of Florida, Gainsville, professor of English, 1977—. New York *Daily News,* reporter, 1963-64. Elisabeth Irwin High School, visiting lecturer, 1971-73; Indiana University/Purdue University—Indianapolis, visiting professor, 1973-76; College of New Rochelle, visiting professor, 1977. Union Mutual Life, Health and Accident Insurance, director, 1970-73. Member of board of advisors, Psi Systems, 1971-72; member of board of directors, Speedwell Services for Children, 1974-76. Member of Manhattan Community Board No. 9, 1972-73, academic council for the State University of New York, 1972-74, New York Urban League Manhattan Advisory Board, 1973-75, and National Education Advisory Committee and vice-director of Southeast Region of Statue of Liberty—Ellis Island Foundation, 1986. Consultant, Education Development Center, 1975—, Department of Health, Education and Welfare, 1977-79, National Research Council, 1979-80, and Grolier, Inc., 1979-82. Member of National Education Advisory Committee, Commission on the Bicentennial of the Constitution.

MEMBER: National Book Critics Circle, Authors League of America, Authors Guild, 100 Black Men, Phi Beta Kappa, Kappa Alpha Psi.

AWARDS, HONORS: Notable children's book in the field of social studies citations from *Social Education,* 1971, for *Revolutionaries: Agents of Change,* from *Social Studies,* 1972, for *Resistance: Profiles in Nonviolence,* and *Profiles in Black Power,* and 1973, for *A Piece of the Power: Four Black Mayors,* from National Council for the Social Studies-Children's Book Council book review committee, 1975, for *Fighting Shirley Chisholm,* and 1976, for *The Creoles of Color of New Orleans* and *The Picture Life of Malcolm X,* from Children's Book Council, 1978, for *The Life and Death of Martin Luther*

JAMES HASKINS

King, Jr.; World Book Year Book literature for children citiation, 1973, for *From Lew Alcindor to Kareem Abdul Jabbar;* Books of the Year citations, Child Study Association of America, 1974, for *Adam Clayton Powell* and *Street Gangs;* Books for Brotherhood bibliography citation, National Council of Christians and Jews book review committee, 1975, for *Adam Clayton Powell: Portrait of a Marching Black;* Spur Award finalist, Western Writers of America, 1975, for *The Creoles of Color of New Orleans;* Eighth Annual Coretta Scott King Award, and books chosen by children citation, Children's Book Council, both 1977, both for *The Story of Stevie Wonder;* Woodson Outstanding Merit Award, National Council for the Social Studies, 1980, for *James Van DerZee: The Picture-Takin' Man;* American Society of Composers, Authors and Publishers-Deems Taylor Award, 1980, for *Scott Joplin: The Man Who Made Ragtime;* Ambassador of Honor book, English-Speaking Union Books-Across-the-Sea, 1983, for *Bricktop;* Coretta Scott King honorable mention, 1984, for *Lena Horne;* American Library Association (ALA) best book for young adults citation, 1987, for *Black Music in America;* Alabama Library Association best juvenile work citation, 1987, for "Count Your Way" series; "Bicentennial Reading, Viewing, Listening for Young Americans" selections, ALA and National Endowment for the Humanities, for *Street Gangs: Yesterday and Today,* Ralph

Bunche: A Most Reluctant Hero, and *A Piece of the Power: Four Black Mayors.*

WRITINGS:

JUVENILE

Resistance: Profiles in Nonviolence, Doubleday, 1970.
Revolutionaries: Agents of Change, Lippincott, 1971.
The War and the Protest: Vietnam, Doubleday, 1971.
Religions, Lippincott, 1971.
Witchcraft, Mysticism and Magic in the Black World, Doubleday, 1974.
Street Gangs: Yesterday and Today, Hastings House, 1974.
Jobs in Business and Office, Lothrop, 1974.
The Creoles of Color of New Orleans, Crowell, 1975.
The Consumer Movement, F. Watts, 1975.
Who Are the Handicapped?, Doubleday, 1978.
(With J. M. Stifle) *The Quiet Revolution: The Struggle for the Rights of Disabled Americans,* Crowell, 1979.
The New Americans: Vietnamese Boat People, Enslow, 1980.
Black Theatre in America, Crowell, 1982.
The New Americans: Cuban Boat People, Enslow, 1982.
The Guardian Angels, Enslow, 1983.
(With David A. Walker) *Double Dutch,* Enslow, 1986.
Black Music in America: A History through Its People, Crowell, 1987.

Winner of the ASCAP Deems Taylor Award $6.95
"Authoritative...solid, sober, and informative."—*Library Journal*

SCOTT JOPLIN
The Man Who Made Ragtime

by James Haskins
with Kathleen Benson

Haskins's biography of ragtime musician Scott Joplin won an American Society of Composers, Authors, and Publishers Deems Taylor Award in 1980. (Cover illustration by Douglas Bergstreser.)

(With Kathleen Benson) *A Sixties Reader,* Viking, 1988.
(With Rosa Parks) *The Autobiography of Rosa Parks,* Dial, 1990.
Religions of the World, Hippocrene Books, 1991.

JUVENILE BIOGRAPHIES

From Lew Alcindor to Kareem Abdul Jabbar, Lothrop, 1972.
A Piece of the Power: Four Black Mayors, Dial, 1972.
Profiles in Black Power, Doubleday, 1972.
Deep Like the Rivers: A Biography of Langston Hughes, 1902-1967, Holt, 1973.
Adam Clayton Powell: Portrait of a Marching Black, Dial, 1974.
Babe Ruth and Hank Aaron: The Home Run Kings, Lothrop, 1974.
Fighting Shirley Chisholm, Dial, 1975.
The Picture Life of Malcolm X, F. Watts, 1975.
Dr. J: A Biography of Julius Irving, Doubleday, 1975.
Pele: A Biography, Doubleday, 1976.
The Story of Stevie Wonder, Doubleday, 1976.
Always Movin' On: The Life of Langston Hughes, F. Watts, 1976.
Barbara Jordan, Dial, 1977.

The Life and Death of Martin Luther King, Jr., Lothrop, 1977.
George McGinnis: Basketball Superstar, Hastings, 1978.
Bob McAdoo: Superstar, Lothrop, 1978.
Andrew Young: Man with a Mission, Lothrop, 1979.
I'm Gonna Make You Love Me: The Story of Diana Ross, Dial, 1980.
"Magic": A Biography of Earvin Johnson, Enslow, 1981.
Katherine Dunham, Coward-McCann, 1982.
Donna Summer, Atlantic Monthly Press, 1983.
About Michael Jackson, Enslow, 1985.
Diana Ross: Star Supreme, Viking, 1985.
Leaders of the Middle East, Enslow, 1988.
Corazon Aquino: Leader of the Philippines, Enslow, 1988.
The Magic Johnson Story, Enslow, 1988.
Shirley Temple Black: Actress to Ambassador, illustrations by Donna Ruff, Puffin Books, 1988.
Sports Great Magic Johnson, Enslow, 1989.

JUVENILE UNDER NAME JIM HASKINS

Jokes from Black Folks, Doubleday, 1973.
Ralph Bunche: A Most Reluctant Hero, Hawthorne, 1974.
Your Rights, Past and Present: A Guide for Young People, Hawthorne, 1975.
Teen-Age Alcoholism, Hawthorne, 1976.
The Long Struggle: The Story of American Labor, Westminster, 1976.
Real Estate Careers, F. Watts, 1978.
Gambling—Who Really Wins?, F. Watts, 1978.
James Van DerZee: The Picture Takin' Man, illustrations by Van DerZee, Dodd, Mead, 1979.
(With Pat Connolly) *The Child Abuse Help Book,* Addison Wesley, 1981.
Werewolves, Lothrop, 1982.
Sugar Ray Leonard, Lothrop, 1982.
(Editor) *The Filipino Nation,* three volumes, Grolier International, 1982.
(With Stifle) *Donna Summer: An Unauthorized Biography,* Little, Brown, 1983.
(With Benson) *Space Challenger: The Story of Guion Bluford, an Authorized Biography,* Carolrhoda Books, 1984.
Break Dancing, Lerner, 1985.
The Statue of Liberty: America's Proud Lady, Lerner, 1986.
Bill Cosby: America's Most Famous Father, Walker, 1988.
(With Helen Crothers) *Scatman: An Authorized Biography of Scatman Crothers,* Morrow, 1991.

JUVENILE UNDER NAME JIM HASKINS; "COUNT YOUR WAY" SERIES

Count Your Way through China, Carolrhoda Books, 1987.
... *through Japan,* Carolrhoda Books, 1987.
... *through Russia,* Carolrhoda Books, 1987.
... *through the Arab World,* Carolrhoda Books, 1987.
... *through Mexico,* illustrations by Helen Byers, Carolrhoda Books, 1989.
... *through Canada,* illustrations by Steve Michaels, Carolrhoda Books, 1989.

JAMES HASKINS

BLACK MUSIC IN AMERICA

A HISTORY THROUGH ITS PEOPLE

In *Black Music in America,* Haskins presents portraits of black musicians who were by turns thwarted and encouraged by the changing social climate from the early 1800s to the present.

... *through Africa,* illustrations by Barbara Knutson, Carolrhoda Books, 1989.
... *through Korea,* illustrations by Dennis Hockerman, Carolrhoda Books, 1989.
... *through Israel,* illustrations by Rick Hanson, Carolrhoda Books, 1990.
... *through India,* illustrations by Liz Brenner Dodson, Carolrhoda Books, 1990.
... *through Italy,* illustrations by Beth Wright, Carolrhoda Books, 1990.
... *through Germany,* illustrations by Byers, Carolrhoda Books, 1990.

ADULT NONFICTION UNDER NAME JIM HASKINS

Diary of a Harlem Schoolteacher, Grove, 1969, 2nd edition, Stein & Day, 1979.
(Editor) *Black Manifesto for Education,* Morrow, 1973.
(With Hugh F. Butts) *The Psychology of Black Language,* Barnes & Noble, 1973.
Snow Sculpture and Ice Carving, Macmillan, 1974.
The Cotton Club, Random House, 1977, 2nd edition, New American Library, 1984.
(With Benson and Ellen Inkelis) *The Great American Crazies,* Condor, 1977.

Voodoo and Hoodoo: Their Tradition and Craft as Revealed by Actual Practitioners, Stein & Day, 1978.
(With Benson) *The Stevie Wonder Scrapbook,* Grosset & Dunlap, 1978.
Richard Pryor, a Man and His Madness: A Biography, Beaufort Books, 1984.
Queen of the Blues: A Biography of Dinah Washington, Morrow, 1987.
Outward Dreams: Black Inventors and Their Inventions, Walker, 1991.

OTHER ADULT NONFICTION

Pinckney Benton Stewart Pitchback: A Biography, Macmillan, 1973.
A New Kind of Joy: The Story of the Special Olympics, Doubleday, 1976.
(With Kathleen Benson) *Scott Joplin: The Man Who Made Ragtime,* Doubleday, 1978.
(With Benson) *Lena: A Personal and Professional Biography of Lena Horne,* Stein & Day, 1983.
(With Benson) *Nat King Cole,* Stein & Day, 1984.
Mabel Mercer: A Life, Atheneum, 1988.
Winnie Mandela: Life of Struggle, Putnam, 1988.
Mr. Bojangles: The Biography of Bill Robinson, Morrow, 1988.
(With Lionel Hampton) *Hamp: An Autobiography* (with discography), Warner, 1989.
India under Indira and Rajiv Gandhi, Enslow, 1989.
Black Dance in America: A History through Its People, Crowell, 1990.

CONTRIBUTOR

Emily Mumford, *Understanding Human Behavior in Health and Illness,* Williams & Wilkins, 1977.
New York Kid's Catalog, Doubleday, 1979.
Notable American Women Supplement, Radcliffe College, 1979.
Jerry Brown, *Clearings in the Thicket: An Alabama Humanities Reader,* Mercer University Press, 1985.

Also contributor to *Author in the Kitchen* and to *Children and Books,* 4th edition, 1976. Contributor of articles and reviews to periodicals, including *American Visions, Now, Arizona English Bulletin, Rolling Stone, Children's Book Review Service, Western Journal of Black Studies, Elementary English, Amsterdam News, New York Times Book Review, Afro-Hawaii News,* and *Gainesville Sun.*

ADAPTATIONS: Diary of a Harlem Schoolteacher has been recorded by Recordings for the Blind; *The Cotton Club* inspired the 1984 film of the same name.

SIDELIGHTS: Teacher, lecturer, and author James Haskins has written biographies and histories that cover a wide range of subjects. For Haskins, realistic topics are much more engaging than fiction. "It has always seemed to me that truth is not just 'stranger than fiction,' but also more interesting," Haskins says in *Something about the Author Autobiography Series* (SAAS). "It seems to me that the more you know about the real world the better off you are, and since there is so much in the real world to talk about, you are better off concentrating on fact rather than fiction." Many of Haskins' works, especially his biographies of luminaries such as Magic Johnson and Shirley Chisholm and his histories of events such as the civil rights movement, are written specifically for young people. In an essay for the *Sixth Book of Junior Authors,* Haskins writes: "I feel that the young people of today will need to know more and more about the rest of the world when they grow up, and they may as well start early. My own experience, from childhood on, is that reading books is a nice way to find your own, private world and learn about the big world at the same time."

Haskin's first book grew out of his experiences teaching a Special Education class at Public School 92 in New York City. A social worker gave him a diary and suggested that he write down his thoughts about teaching disadvantaged students. Ronald Gross of the *New York Times Book Review* calls *Diary of a Harlem Schoolteacher* "plain, concrete, unemotional, and unliterary.... The book is like a weapon—cold, blunt, painful." The success of *Diary* impressed numerous publishers who approached Haskins about writing a series of books for young people. Haskins comments: "I knew exactly the kind of books I wanted to do—books about current events and books about important black people so that students could understand the larger world around them through books written on a level that they could understand."

With over eighty books to his credit, Haskins often uses his writing ability to support the causes he believes in, such as the renovations of the Statue of Liberty and Ellis Island. Ultimately, Haskins feels that the subjects he writes about are worthwhile and necessary. In his *SAAS* essay, Haskins notes: "When, some day, the missing second date after that '1941-' gets filled in, I will know that I not only have done something worthwhile in years between, but also that I had a good time doing it."

WORKS CITED:

Gross, Ronald, review of *Diary of a Harlem Schoolteacher, New York Times Book Review,* December 6, 1970.
Haskins, Jim, article in *Sixth Book of Junior Authors,* edited by Sally Holmes Holtze, Wilson, 1989, pp. 115-17.
Haskins, Jim, article in *Something about the Author Autobiography Series,* Volume 4, Gale, 1987, pp. 197-209.

FOR MORE INFORMATION SEE:

BOOKS

Brown, Jerry, *Clearings in the Thicket: An Alabama Humanities Reader,* Mercer University Press, 1985.
Children's Literature Review, Volume 3, Gale, 1978, pp. 63-69.

PERIODICALS

Bulletin of the Center for Children's Books, September, 1983; November, 1985; June, 1988.
Chicago Tribune Book World, April 13, 1986.

Los Angeles Times Book Review, July 24, 1983; March 11, 1984; January 20, 1985.
New York Times Book Review, February 8, 1970; May 7, 1972; May 5, 1974; August 4, 1974; November 20, 1977; September 23, 1979; October 7, 1979; January 20, 1980; March 4, 1984; May 17, 1987; September 13, 1987.
Times Literary Supplement, May 24, 1985.

* * *

HASKINS, Jim
See HASKINS, James

* * *

HEIDE, Florence Parry 1919-
(Alex B. Allen, Jamie McDonald)

PERSONAL: Surname is pronounced "*high*-dee"; born February 27, 1919, in Pittsburgh, PA; daughter of David W. (a banker) and Florence (an actress, columnist, and drama critic) Parry; married Donald C. Heide (an attorney), November 27, 1943; children: Christen, Roxanne, Judith, David, Parry. *Education:* Attended Wilson College; University of California, Los Angeles, B.A., 1939. *Politics:* Republican. *Religion:* Protestant.

FLORENCE PARRY HEIDE

Treehorn makes note of the fact that he is shrinking in Heide's *The Shrinking of Treehorn.* (Cover illustration by Edward Gorey.)

ADDRESSES: Home—6910 Third Ave., Kenosha, WI 53143. *Agent*—Curtis Brown, 10 Astor Pl., New York, NY 10003.

CAREER: Writer. Before World War II worked variously at Radio-Keith-Orpheum (RKO), and at advertising and public relations agencies, all New York City, and as public relations director of the Pittsburgh Playhouse, Pittsburgh, PA.

MEMBER: International Board on Books for Young People, American Society of Composers, Authors, and Publishers (ASCAP), Authors Guild, Authors League of America, Society of Children's Book Writers, Council for Wisconsin Writers, Children's Reading Round Table.

AWARDS, HONORS: Children's Book of the Year awards, Child Study Association of America, 1970, for *Sound of Sunshine, Sound of Rain,* and 1972, for *My Castle;* American Institute of Graphic Arts selection as one of the fifty best books of the year, 1971, American Institute of Graphic Arts Children's Book Show selection, 1971-72, *New York Times* Best Illustrated Children's Book citation, 1971, Children's Book Showcase selection, 1972, Judgendbuchpreis for best children's book in Germany, 1977, graphic arts prize from Bologna Book Fair, 1977, American Library Association notable book citation, and *School Library Journal* Best of the Best Books 1966-78 citation, 1978, all for *The Shrinking of Treehorn;* second prize for juvenile fiction from Council for Wisconsin Writers, and Golden Kite honor book, Society for Children's Book Writers, both 1976, both for *Growing Anyway Up;* Golden Archer Award, 1976; American Library Association notable book citation, 1978, for *Banana Twist,* 1981, for *Tree-*

horn's Treasure, and 1982, for *Time's Up!;* Litt.D. from Carthage College, 1979; Charlie May Simon Award, 1980, for *Banana Twist;* first prize from Council for Wisconsin Writers, 1982, for *Treehorn's Treasure;* honorable mention from Council for Wisconsin Writers, 1982, for *Time's Up!; The Day of Ahmed's Secret* was named an ALA Notable Book and Booklist Editors Choice, and a *School Library Journal* Best Book, all 1990; first prize from Council for Wisconsin Writers, 1990, and Charlotte Award, New York State, 1991, both for *The Day of Ahmed's Secret.*

WRITINGS:

FOR CHILDREN

Benjamin Budge and Barnaby Ball, illustrated by Sally Mathews, Four Winds Press, 1967.

(Under pseudonym Jamie McDonald, with Anne and Walter Theiss and others) *Hannibal,* illustrated by Anne and Walter Theiss, Funk, 1968.

Maximilian Becomes Famous, illustrated by Ed Renfro, McCall Publishing, 1970.

Alphabet Zoop, illustrated by Mathews, McCall Publishing, 1970.

Giants Are Very Brave People, illustrated by Charles Robinson, Parents' Magazine Press, 1970.

The Little One, illustrated by Ken Longtemps, Lion Press, 1970.

Sound of Sunshine, Sound of Rain, illustrated by Longtemps, Parents' Magazine Press, 1970.

The Key, illustrated by Ati Forberg, Atheneum, 1971.

Pulcifer's preference for reading over watching television is a matter of concern for his parents. (Cover illustration by Judy Glassner.)

tales for the PERFECT child

FLORENCE PARRY HEIDE
pictures by VICTORIA CHESS

In *Tales for the Perfect Child,* **Heide presents seven manipulative, willful, and deceitful children.** (Cover illustration by Victoria Chess.)

Look! Look! A Story Book, illustrated by Carol Nicklaus, McCall Publishing, 1971.
The Shrinking of Treehorn (Junior Literary Guild selection; also see below), illustrated by Edward Gorey, Holiday House, 1971.
Some Things Are Scary, Scholastic Book Services, 1971.
Who Needs Me?, illustrated by Mathews, Augsburg, 1971.
My Castle, illustrated by Symeon Shimin, McGraw, 1972.
(With brother, David Fisher Parry) *No Roads for the Wind* (textbook), Macmillan, 1974.
God and Me, illustrated by Ted Smith, Concordia, 1975.
When the Sad One Comes to Stay (novel), Lippincott, 1975.
You and Me, illustrated by Smith, Concordia, 1975.
Growing Anyway Up, Lippincott, 1975.
Banana Twist, Holiday House, 1978.
Changes, illustrated by Kathy Counts, Concordia, 1978.
Secret Dreamer, Secret Dreams, Lippincott, 1978.
Who Taught Me? Was It You, God?, illustrated by Terry Whittle, Concordia, 1978.
By the Time You Count to Ten, illustrated by Pam Erickson, Concordia, 1979.
Treehorn's Treasure (also see below), illustrated by Gorey, Holiday House, 1981.

The Problem with Pulcifer, illustrated by Judy Glasser, Lippincott, 1982.
The Wendy Puzzle (Junior Literary Guild selection), Holiday House, 1982.
Time's Up!, illustrated by Marylin Hafner, Holiday House, 1982.
Banana Blitz, Holiday House, 1983.
I Am, Concordia, 1983.
The Adventures of Treehorn (includes *The Shrinking of Treehorn* and *Treehorn's Treasure*), Dell, 1983.
Treehorn's Wish (also see below), Holiday House, 1984.
Time Flies!, illustrated by Hafner, Holiday House, 1984.
Tales for the Perfect Child, illustrated by Victoria Chess, Lothrop, 1985.
(With daughter, Judith Heide Gilliland) *The Day of Ahmed's Secret,* illustrated by Ted Lewin, Lothrop, 1990.
Grim and Ghastly Goings On (poems), illustrated by Chess, Lothrop, 1992.
(With J. H. Gilliland) *Sami and the Time of Troubles,* illustrated by Lewin, Clarion, 1992.
Treehorn Times Three (contains *The Shrinking of Treehorn, Treehorn's Treasure, and Treehorn's Wish*), Dell, 1992.
The Bigness Contest, illustrated by Victoria Chess, Little, Brown, in press.

WITH SYLVIA WORTH VAN CLIEF; FOR CHILDREN

Maximilian, illustrated by Renfro, Funk, 1967.
The Day It Snowed in Summer, illustrated by Longtemps, Funk, 1968.
How Big Am I?, illustrated by George Suyeoka, Follett, 1968.
It Never Is Dark, illustrated by Don Almquist, Follett, 1968.
Sebastian (includes songs by Sylvia W. Van Clief), illustrated by Betty Fraser, Funk, 1968.
That's What Friends Are For, illustrated by Brinton Turkle, Four Winds Press, 1968.
The New Neighbor, illustrated by Jerry Warshaw, Follett, 1970.
(Lyricist) *Songs to Sing about Things You Think About,* illustrated by Rosalie Schmidt, Day, 1971.
(Lyricist) *Christmas Bells and Snowflakes* (songbook), Southern Music Publishing, 1971.
(Lyricist) *Holidays! Holidays!* (songbook), Southern Music Publishing, 1971.
The Mystery of the Missing Suitcase, illustrated by Seymour Fleishman, Albert Whitman, 1972.
The Mystery of the Silver Tag, illustrated by Fleishman, Albert Whitman, 1972.
The Hidden Box Mystery, illustrated by Fleishman, Albert Whitman, 1973.
Mystery at MacAdoo Zoo, illustrated by Fleishman, Albert Whitman, 1973.
Mystery of the Whispering Voice, illustrated by Fleishman, Albert Whitman, 1974.
Who Can? (primer), Macmillan, 1974.
Lost and Found (primer), Macmillan, 1974.
Hats and Bears (primer), Macmillan, 1974.
Fables You Shouldn't Pay Any Attention To, illustrated by Chess, Lippincott, 1978.

WITH DAUGHTER, ROXANNE HEIDE; FOR CHILDREN

Lost! (textbook), Holt, 1973.

I See America Smiling (textbook), Holt, 1973.

Tell about Someone You Love (textbook), Macmillan, 1974.

Mystery of the Melting Snowman, illustrated by Fleishman, Albert Whitman, 1974.

Mystery of the Vanishing Visitor, illustrated by Fleishman, Albert Whitman, 1975.

Mystery of the Lonely Lantern, illustrated by Fleishman, Albert Whitman, 1976.

Mystery at Keyhole Carnival, illustrated by Fleishman, Albert Whitman, 1977.

Brillstone Break-In, illustrated by Joe Krush, Albert Whitman, 1977.

Mystery of the Midnight Message, illustrated by Fleishman, Albert Whitman, 1977.

Face at Brillstone Window, illustrated by Krush, Albert Whitman, 1978.

Fear at Brillstone, illustrated by Krush, Albert Whitman, 1978.

Mystery at Southport Cinema, illustrated by Fleishman, Albert Whitman, 1978.

I Love Every-People, illustrated by John Sandford, Concordia, 1978.

Body in the Brillstone Garage, illustrated by Krush, Albert Whitman, 1979.

Mystery of the Mummy Mask, illustrated by Fleishman, Albert Whitman, 1979.

Mystery of the Forgotten Island, illustrated by Fleishman, Albert Whitman, 1979.

A Monster Is Coming! A Monster Is Coming!, illustrated by Rachi Farrow, F. Watts, 1980.

Black Magic at Brillstone, illustrated by Krush, Albert Whitman, 1982.

Time Bomb at Brillstone, illustrated by Krush, Albert Whitman, 1982.

Mystery on Danger Road, illustrated by Fleishman, Albert Whitman, 1983.

Timothy Twinge, illustrated by Barbara Lehman, Lothrop, in press.

UNDER PSEUDONYM ALEX B. ALLEN; FOR CHILDREN

(With Van Clief) *Basketball Toss Up,* illustrated by Kevin Royt, Albert Whitman, 1972.

(With Van Clief) *No Place for Baseball,* illustrated by Royt, Albert Whitman, 1973.

(With son, David Heide) *Danger on Broken Arrow Trail,* illustrated by Michael Norman, Albert Whitman, 1974.

(With Van Clief) *Fifth Down,* illustrated by Dan Siculan, Albert Whitman, 1974.

(With D. Heide) *The Tennis Menace,* illustrated by Timothy Jones, Albert Whitman, 1975.

ADAPTATIONS: It Never Is Dark (filmstrip with cassette or record), BFA Educational Media, 1975; *Sound of Sunshine, Sound of Rain,* an animated short film, was produced by Filmfair in 1984 and nominated for an Academy Award from the Academy of Motion Picture Arts and Sciences.

SIDELIGHTS: A self-proclaimed "late-bloomer," Florence Parry Heide did not begin writing children's books until after her five children had started school. Once started, she quickly established a prolific and multi-award-winning career. Heide has written picture books, short stories, novels, religious books, mysteries, and poetry that range from slapstick humor to poignant drama. Well-known for her ability to find humor in parent-child struggles, Heide is often praised by critics for her whimsical imagination and her exuberant, if sometimes irreverent, wit. But despite her characteristically lighthearted tone, Heide has not hesitated to delve into painful subjects, such as self-absorbed parents, blindness, mental illness, and adolescent alienation. While many reviewers have praised Heide's ability to find the fun in most situations, others have applauded her strong characterizations and her keen perception of the colorful but often difficult and confusing life of a child.

Heide's account of her own childhood, like many of her books, is marked with a strong sense of love, hope, and comedy, as well as the insecurities involved in adapting to circumstances beyond her control. Her mother, a successful actress, gave up her career to marry and raise children. When Florence was not quite three years old, her father, a banker, died. Her mother, faced with the immediate need to support her family, left her two children temporarily with her parents, and moved to Pittsburgh, where she established a photography studio and became a regular columnist and drama critic for the *Pittsburgh Press.*

At her grandparents' large house, Heide became entrenched in the bustle of extended family life, with grandparents, aunts, uncles, and cousins always close at hand. There, she wrote in an essay for *Something about the Author Autobiography Series* (*SAAS*), she was "loved and indulged and spoiled," and "surrounded by strength and support and security." But she also developed a sense of inadequacy in comparison to others: her intelligent brother, her attractive cousin, and her dynamic, glamorous, and articulate mother, who visited every weekend. The young Florence resolved to focus on the one strength she knew she had—her sweet and loving disposition. "Recognizing instinctively early on that I was neither bright nor beautiful (the way a squirrel knows that it's a squirrel and not, for example, a dog or a bird)," she wrote in her autobiographical essay, "I tried to be neither, but went along cheerfully with what I did have. Cheerfully, that's the watchword."

When Heide's mother was financially able, she brought her children to live with her in Pittsburgh. Missing the constant companionship of the bustling home of her grandparents and competing for time with her mother's two demanding careers, Florence was initially lonely and shy. Her memories of life in Pittsburgh include the anxious moments of a very sensitive adolescent, as well as many good times with friends and family. But throughout her childhood, Heide maintained her belief in the power of a cheerful spirit, a strength she attributes largely to her mother, who so courageously faced the

Heide confronts some of the pain and alienation of childhood in her young adult novels such as *When the Sad One Comes to Stay*. (Jacket illustration by Kenneth Longtemps.)

unexpected disaster of her husband's death. The young girl's ability to confront difficult situations with a loving disposition and a sense of humor figures prominently in Heide's later writings.

After receiving her bachelor's degree in English at the University of California, Los Angeles, Heide worked for a few years in New York and Pittsburgh. She then met and married Donald Heide, and settled happily into family life. Heide commented, "Even as a child, I always knew what I wanted to be when I grew up—a mother. I'd meet the right person, I'd have children, I'd live happily ever after. And I did, and I am." The Heides had five children.

But as her children went off to school, Heide began to seek another vehicle for her energy. Her first attempt at a career was a joint venture into the hot fudge sauce business with her friend, Sylvia Van Clief. The two women began daily experiments with hot fudge recipes, but, since neither of them enjoyed kitchen work, the project was short-lived. Heide and Van Clief then turned to writing songs—Heide writing lyrics, Van Clief writing the music—but they could not find buyers for their work. When they began to write children's songs, however, they immediately found a market and Heide

settled upon what felt like a natural career: "Writing for children was an unexpected delight: I could reach my child-self (never long away or far from me) and I could reach the selves of other children like me.... Ideas flew into my head. I couldn't write fast enough to accommodate them. I wrote, and I wrote, and I wrote."

One of Heide's most popular and acclaimed works is the 1971 picture book *The Shrinking of Treehorn*. Treehorn is a very serious and competent boy who wakes up one morning to discover that he is shrinking. In dangling sleeves and dangerously long pants, he reports the strange phenomenon to his mother, father, principal, and teacher. The familiar adult reaction to children's announcements ("Think of that," his mother responds. "I just don't know why this cake isn't rising the way it should." "We don't shrink in this class," his teacher admonishes), are both funny and painful. The inflexible structure of the adult world is accentuated by illustrator Edward Gorey's two-dimensional, ordered, geometric line drawings, which interact as a "brilliant fugue with Heide's witty text," according to *Horn Book* contributor Gertrude Herman. The reviewer concluded that *The Shrinking of Treehorn* demonstrates the apparent adult dictum that "wonders may occur, but they are not allowed to disturb this universe." Two "Treehorn" sequels continue to juxtapose youthful wonder with the rigidity of adult order.

Noah, the main character in Heide's humorous books *Time's Up!* and *Time Flies,* has his hands full adapting to life in a new neighborhood and with a new brother or sister on the way. His mother, busy with her dissertation, leaves him to the care of his father, an efficiency fanatic who times him at his chores. With parents who seem to make life more difficult for him, Noah finds the strength within himself and in people around him to adapt to his circumstances. Parents are similarly unhelpful in Heide's 1982 book, *The Problem with Pulcifer,* in which a boy who prefers reading to television becomes a subject of concern among his parents, teachers, and a psychiatrist. "Heide pokes fun at television addicts, conformity, and certain adult-child relations in a very funny book that is written with acidulated exaggeration but that has a strong unstated message," a reviewer for the *Bulletin of the Center for Children's Books* summarized. But while adults are always in nominal control, the Pulcifers and Noahs of Heide's books are by no means powerless. In a playful spoof on the struggle between parents and children, Heide's 1985 collection of stories *Tales for the Perfect Child* presents a series of manipulative, willful, and often deceitful children who manage to get their own way in spite of their less calculating parents' authority.

Heide has written numerous books for adolescents that directly confront pain and alienation. In her first novel, *When the Sad One Comes to Stay,* Sara—a young girl whose ambitious and rather insensitive mother has taken her away from her home with her kindhearted father—receives comfort and friendship from an eccentric old woman named Crazy Maisie. When a choice must be made between her mother and Crazy Maisie,

Sara casts her lot with her mother—and with probable loneliness as well. Focusing on different manifestations of realities that are beyond one's control, Heide wrote her 1970 story about a blind boy, *Sound of Sunshine, Sound of Rain,* in order to help her readers understand what it would be like to be blind. In her 1978 book, *Secret Dreamer, Secret Dreams,* Heide explores the consciousness of a mentally handicapped young woman who cannot communicate with anyone. These works do not offer happy or resolved endings, but are commended by critics for their sensitive characterizations and realistic perspectives.

Among her many other works, Heide has written two mystery series: one featuring the Spotlight Detective Club, and the other set at Brillstone Apartments. Heide began writing mysteries in order to draw in reluctant readers with her easy, intriguing, and fast-paced plots. The first mysteries were written with her friend and partner, Sylvia Van Clief. When Van Clief died, Heide's daughter Roxanne collaborated with her mother on the mystery series and several other projects. One of Heide's sons, David, and her other daughter, Judith Gilliland, have also coauthored books with her.

With a close family and a successful writing career Heide says she has fulfilled her most cherished dreams, and she commented in *SAAS* that if she had to sum up her life in a word, that word would be "lucky." But Heide's works reveal that more than luck—and even more than hard work—is involved in establishing a happy life. The lesson she learned as a child—to take command of her own attitude and actions even when circumstances were beyond her control—resonates in the cheerful tone and the underlying messages of her books. Heide commented in *SAAS* that she wrote *When the Sad One Comes to Stay,* "because I wanted you younger readers (yes, you) to understand that although you may feel you have no choices, that the decisions are made for you by the GrownUps: where you live and who you live with, how late you stay up, where you go to school, whether you're rich or poor—everything's decided by THEM! All but the most important thing: what kind of person you're going to be. And this is a choice you make each day."

WORKS CITED:

Heide, Florence Parry, article in *Something about the Author Autobiography Series,* Volume 6, Gale, 1988, pp. 141-159.
Herman, Gertrude, "A Picture Is Worth Several Hundred Words," *Horn Book,* January, 1989, p. 104.
Review of *The Problem with Pulcifer, Bulletin of the Center for Children's Books,* October, 1982.
Review of *Time's Up!, Bulletin of the Center for Children's Books,* June, 1982.

FOR MORE INFORMATION SEE:

PERIODICALS

Bulletin of the Center for Children's Books, January, 1984; December, 1984; November, 1985.

Horn Book, April, 1976, p. 155; February, 1982, p. 42; December, 1990, p. 739.
New York Times Book Review, April 30, 1978, p. 46; March 5, 1972, p. 8; November 16, 1975, p. 52; October 18, 1981, p. 49; February 16, 1986, p. 22.
School Library Journal, January, 1985, p. 75; October, 1985, p. 155; August, 1990; December, 1990.

—*Sketch by Sonia Benson*

*　　*　　*

HEINLEIN, Robert A. 1907-1988
(Anson MacDonald, Lyle Monroe, John Riverside, Caleb Saunders, Simon York)

PERSONAL: Full name is Robert Anson Heinlein; surname rhymes with "fine line"; born July 7, 1907, in Butler, MO; died of heart failure, May 8, 1988, in Carmel, CA; cremated and ashes scattered at sea with military honors; son of Rex Ivar (an accountant) and Bam (Lyle) Heinlein; married Leslyn McDonald (divorced, 1947); married Virginia Doris Gerstenfeld, October 21, 1948. *Education:* Attended University of Missouri, 1925; U.S. Naval Academy, graduate, 1929; University of California, Los Angeles, graduate study (physics and math), 1934. *Hobbies and other interests:* Stone masonry and sculpture, figure skating, fencing, cats, ballistics, fiscal theory, and "an expert rifleman and pistol shot, both right- and left-handed."

CAREER: Writer. Commissioned ensign, U.S. Navy, 1929, became lieutenant (junior grade), retired because of physical disability, 1934; Shively & Sophie Lodes

ROBERT A. HEINLEIN

silver mine, Silver Plume, CO, owner, 1934-35; candidate for California State Assembly, 1938; also worked as a real estate agent during the 1930s; Naval Air Experimental Station, Philadelphia, PA, aviation engineer, 1942-45. James V. Forrestal Memorial Lecturer, U.S. Naval Academy, 1973. Guest commentator during Apollo lunar landing, Columbia Broadcasting System, 1969.

MEMBER: World Future Society, American Institute of Astronautics and Aeronautics, Authors Guild, Authors League of America, Navy League, Air Force Association, Air Power Council, Association of the Army of the United States, United States Naval Academy Alumni Association, Retired Officers Association, American Association for the Advancement of Science, National Rare Blood (donors) Club, American Association of Blood Banks, U.S. Naval Institute, California Arts Society, Minutemen of the *U.S.S. Lexington.*

AWARDS, HONORS: Guest of Honor, World Science Fiction Convention, 1941, 1961, and 1976; Hugo Award, World Science Fiction Convention, 1956, for *Double Star,* 1960, for *Starship Troopers,* 1962, for *Stranger in a Strange Land,* and 1967, for *The Moon Is a Harsh Mistress;* Boys' Clubs of America Best Liked Book Award, 1959; Sequoyah Children's Book Award of Oklahoma, Oklahoma Library Association, 1961, for *Have Space Suit—Will Travel;* named best all-time author, *Locus* magazine readers' poll, 1973 and 1975; Humanitarian of the Year Award, National Rare Blood Club, 1974; Nebula Grand Master Award, Science Fiction Writers of America, 1975; Council of Community Blood Centers Award, 1977; American Association of Blood Banks Award, 1977; Inkpot Award, 1977; L.H.D., Eastern Michigan University, 1977; Distinguished Public Service Medal, National Aeronautics and Space Administration (NASA), 1988 (posthumously awarded), "in recognition of his meritorious service to the nation and mankind in advocating and promoting the exploration of space"; the Rhysling Award of the Science Fiction Poetry Association is named after the character in Heinlein's story, "The Green Hills of Earth"; Tomorrow Starts Here Award, Delta Vee Society; numerous other awards for his work with blood drives.

WRITINGS:

SCIENCE FICTION NOVELS

Rocket Ship Galileo (juvenile; also see below), Scribner, 1947.
Beyond This Horizon (originally serialized under pseudonym Anson MacDonald in *Astounding Science Fiction,* 1942), Fantasy Press, 1948.
Space Cadet (juvenile), Scribner, 1948.
Red Planet (juvenile), Scribner, 1949, new paperback edition including previously unpublished passages, Del Rey, 1989.
Sixth Column, Gnome Press, 1949, published as *The Day after Tomorrow,* New American Library, 1951.

Farmer in the Sky (juvenile; originally serialized as "Satellite Scout" in *Boy's Life,* 1950), Scribner, 1950.
Waldo [and] *Magic, Inc.* (also see below), Doubleday, 1950, published as *Waldo: Genius in Orbit,* Avon, 1958.
Between Planets (juvenile; originally serialized as "Planets in Combat" in *Blue Book,* 1951), Scribner, 1951.
Universe, Dell, 1951, published as *Orphans of the Sky,* Gollancz, 1963, Putnam, 1964.
The Puppet Masters (also see below; originally serialized in *Galaxy Science Fiction,* 1951), Doubleday, 1951.
The Rolling Stones (juvenile; originally serialized as "Tramp Space Ship" in *Boy's Life,* 1952), Scribner, 1952, published in England as *Space Family Stone,* Gollancz, 1969.
Revolt in 2100, Shasta, 1953.
Starman Jones (juvenile), Scribner, 1953.
The Star Beast (juvenile; originally serialized as "The Star Lummox" in *Magazine of Fantasy and Science Fiction,* 1954), Scribner, 1954.
Tunnel in the Sky (juvenile), Scribner, 1955.
Double Star (originally serialized in *Astounding Science Fiction,* 1956), Doubleday, 1956.
Time for the Stars (juvenile), Scribner, 1956.
The Door into Summer (originally serialized in *Magazine of Fantasy and Science Fiction,* 1956), Doubleday, 1957.
Citizen of the Galaxy (juvenile; originally serialized in *Astounding Science Fiction,* 1957), Scribner, 1957.
Methuselah's Children (originally serialized in *Astounding Science Fiction,* 1941), revised version, Gnome Press, 1958.
Have Space Suit—Will Travel (juvenile; originally serialized in *Magazine of Fantasy and Science Fiction,* 1958), Scribner, 1958.
Starship Troopers (juvenile; originally serialized as "Starship Soldier" in *Magazine of Fantasy and Science Fiction,* 1959), Putnam, 1959.
Stranger in a Strange Land, Putnam, 1961, revised and uncut edition with preface by wife, Virginia Heinlein, 1990.
Podkayne of Mars: Her Life and Times (juvenile; originally serialized in *Worlds of If,* 1962 and 1963), Putnam, 1963.
Glory Road (originally serialized in *Magazine of Fantasy and Science Fiction,* 1963), Putnam, 1963.
Farnham's Freehold (originally serialized in *If,* 1964), Putnam, 1964.
Three by Heinlein (contains *The Puppet Masters, Waldo,* and *Magic, Inc.*), Doubleday, 1965, published in England as *A Heinlein Triad,* Gollancz, 1966.
A Robert Heinlein Omnibus, Sidgwick & Jackson, 1966.
The Moon Is a Harsh Mistress (originally serialized in *If,* 1965 and 1966), Putnam, 1966.
I Will Fear No Evil (originally serialized in *Galaxy,* 1970), Putnam, 1971.
Time Enough for Love: The Lives of Lazarus Long, Putnam, 1973.
The Notebooks of Lazarus Long (excerpts from *Time Enough for Love*), Putnam, 1978.
The Number of the Beast, Fawcett, 1980.
Friday, Holt, 1982.

Job: A Comedy of Justice, Ballantine, 1984.
The Cat Who Walks through Walls: A Comedy of Manners, Putnam, 1985.
To Sail beyond the Sunset: The Life and Loves of Maureen Johnson, Being the Memoirs of a Somewhat Irregular Lady, Putnam, 1987.

STORY COLLECTIONS

The Man Who Sold the Moon, Shasta, 1950.
The Green Hills of Earth, Shasta, 1951.
Assignment in Eternity, Fantasy Press, 1953.
The Menace from Earth, Gnome Press, 1959.
The Unpleasant Profession of Jonathan Hoag, Gnome Press, 1959, published as *6 x H,* Pyramid Publications, 1962.
The Worlds of Robert A. Heinlein, Ace Books, 1966.
The Past through Tomorrow: Future History Stories, Putnam, 1967.
The Best of Robert Heinlein, 1939-1959, two volumes, edited by Angus Wells, Sidgwick & Jackson, 1973.
Destination Moon, Gregg, 1979.
Expanded Universe: The New Worlds of Robert A. Heinlein, Ace Books, 1980.

SCREENPLAYS

(With Rip Van Ronkel and James O'Hanlon) *Destination Moon* (based on *Rocket Ship Galileo;* produced by George Pal/Eagle Lion, 1950), edited by David G. Hartwell, Gregg Press, 1979.
(With Jack Seaman) *Project Moonbase,* Galaxy Pictures/Lippert Productions, 1953.

Also author of scripts for television and radio programs.

OTHER

(Contributor) Lloyd Arthur Eshbach, editor, *Of Worlds Beyond: The Science of Science Fiction,* Fantasy Press, 1947.
(Author of preface) *Tomorrow, the Stars* (anthology), Doubleday, 1952.
(With others) *Famous Science Fiction Stories,* Random House, 1957.
(With others) *The Science Fiction Novel: Imagination and Social Criticism,* edited by Basil Davenport, Advent, 1959.
(Author of preface) Daniel O. Graham, *High Frontier: A Strategy for National Survival,* Pinnacle Books, 1983.
Grumbles from the Grave (correspondences), edited by V. Heinlein, Ballantine, 1989.
Robert A. Heinlein Requiem (collection of fiction and nonfiction), edited by Yoji Kondo, Tor Books, 1992.
Tramp Royale (travel), Putnam, 1992.

Also author of engineering report, *Test Procedures for Plastic Materials Intended for Structural and Semi-Structural Aircraft Uses,* 1944. Contributor to anthologies and to the *Encyclopaedia Britannica.* Contributor of over 150 short stories and articles, some under pseudonyms, to *Saturday Evening Post, Analog, Galaxy, Vertex, Astounding Science Fiction,* and other publications. A collection of Heinlein's manuscripts is kept at the University of California, Santa Cruz.

ADAPTATIONS: The television series *Tom Corbett: Space Cadet,* which aired from 1951-1956, was based on Heinlein's novel *Space Cadet;* television, radio, and film rights to many of Heinlein's works have been sold; a military simulation board game has been created based on *Starship Troopers.*

SIDELIGHTS: "The one author who has raised science fiction from the gutter of pulp space opera ... to the altitude of original and breathtaking concepts," Alfred Bester declared in *Publishers Weekly,* "is Robert A. Heinlein." Some critics and authors have compared Heinlein's importance as a science fiction writer to that of H. G. Wells, author of such classics as *The War of the Worlds* and *The Time Machine.* Writer Robert Silverberg, for example, wrote in a *Locus* obituary for Heinlein that like "no one else but H. G. Wells, he gave science fiction its definition." Silverberg later added that Heinlein "utterly transformed our notions of how to tell a science fiction story, and the transformation has been a permanent and irreversible one."

Heinlein gave credibility to science fiction by taking "the science in science fiction out of the realm of fantasy and bas[ing] his extrapolations on research then going on in the nation's laboratories," according to another *Locus* obituary by Frank Robinson. "And it was Heinlein who decided that science fiction stories would be more believable if believable people did all those unbelievable things." In his earlier books, these characters were mostly teenage boys living in high-tech civilizations of the future. But in later novels Heinlein became increasingly concerned with philosophical problems and his work came under fire from critics who felt that the author was using his novels merely as forums for preaching his personal ideas. "It will be remembered that after 1957," wrote *Dictionary of Literary Biography* contributor Joseph Patrouch, "Heinlein began to write about unpopular, conservative political causes ... and unpopular, liberal sexual causes." This made Heinlein an ever more controversial figure in the science fiction field during his later years.

"I was born in 1907 in Butler, Missouri," Heinlein once told *SATA,* "a small country town where my grandfather was a horse-and-buggy doctor who strongly influenced me. I have been influenced by my parents and six siblings and everything I have seen, touched, eaten, endured, heard, and read." Heinlein developed an interest in science fiction at an early age by reading the "Tom Swift and Frank Reade stories, later Jules Verne, H. G. Wells, Edgar Rice Burroughs, and *Argosy* magazine," according to Patrouch. But these stories were only a diversion at first. Originally, Heinlein wanted to follow his older brother's example and become an officer in the U.S. Navy. He graduated from the U.S. Naval Academy in 1929 and served first on the *U.S.S. Lexington* and then as a gunnery officer on a destroyer, the *Roper.* But tuberculosis forced him to retire in 1934—his disease later led him to do volunteer work for

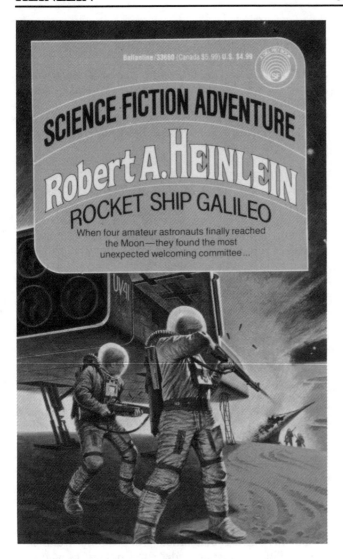

Published in 1947, *Rocket Ship Galileo* was Heinlein's first novel. (Cover illustration by Darrell Sweet.)

blood drives after a blood transfusion saved his life. Heinlein once revealed his disappointment at not being able to remain in the navy when he told Curt Suplee of the *Washington Post:* "I write stories for money. What I wanted to be was an admiral." After leaving the navy, Heinlein studied mathematics and physics at the University of California, Los Angeles, but his illness stopped him short again. He then tried unsuccessfully to sell real estate in Los Angeles before moving to Colorado, where he owned and operated a silver mine for a short time.

It was chance that guided Heinlein into his writing career. In need of money, he answered an add he happened to read in a science fiction magazine that offered fifty dollars for the best short story. Quickly writing a story entitled "Life-Line," Heinlein was so happy with the results that at first he tried to get his work published in *Collier's,* a more reputable mainstream magazine. When *Collier's* rejected his submission, the author sent "Life-Line" to *Astounding,* whose editor, John W. Campbell, Jr., paid seventy dollars for the story and published it in the August, 1939, issue.

Under the guidance of Campbell, whose magazine helped launch the careers of other famous science fiction writers like Isaac Asimov, L. Sprague de Camp, Fritz Leiber, and Theodore Sturgeon, Heinlein's short stories appeared regularly in *Astounding.* Sometimes they would be published so frequently that Campbell asked Heinlein to use pseudonyms to avoid having the author's byline appear more than once in any single issue.

Together, Heinlein's short stories formed a single vision. According to Patrouch, rather than writing escapist stories that had little to do with reality, Heinlein used his knowledge of science "to make the future believable, plausible, possible.... Heinlein's stories convinced a whole generation that man will really be able to do things he can only imagine now—and that generation grew up and sent Apollo to the moon." But Heinlein's new writing career was interrupted with the onset of World War II, during which he worked as an aviation engineer at the naval yard in Philadelphia. After the war he broke new ground for science fiction writers by becoming the first to be published in important mainstream fiction magazines like the *Saturday Evening Post.*

The next step for Heinlein was to expand his stories into novels. Although he had written two novel-length stories before the war, he had only published short stories up to that time. "When an editor assigned me the task of writing a juvenile novel," the author told *SATA,* "I entered the field with determination not to 'write down' to children." Most of his fiction written during the late 1940s and 1950s feature young main characters and are therefore considered juvenile novels, but some novels like *Between Planets* were originally published in serial form in adult magazines, "demonstrating that there is no clear demarcation of Heinlein's 'juvenile' fiction," argued H. Bruce Franklin in his *Robert A. Heinlein: America as Science Fiction.* Jack Williamson believed Heinlein succeeded in his writing goal, noting in *Robert A. Heinlein* that "Heinlein never writes down. His main characters are young, the plots move fast, and the style is limpidly clear; but he never insults the reader's intelligence."

In *Critical Encounters: Writers and Themes in Science Fiction,* David N. Samuelson described the nature of Heinlein's novels for young adults in general: "In a Heinlein juvenile, a young boy typically (one [main character] was a girl) grows to maturity, in the process of living through and effecting events projected into our next century, by means of making decisions that involve his intelligence and mold his character." Books like *Space Cadet, Farmer in the Sky, Starman Jones,* and *Tunnel in the Sky* have therefore been classified by critics as novels about the transition from childhood to adulthood. Franklin also discovered another type of progression in these novels. The "story of the conquest of space" is illustrated by how each succeeding Heinlein novel is set deeper and deeper in outer space: *Rocket Ship Galileo,* Heinlein's first novel, tells of a voyage to the moon; novels like *Farmer in the Sky* and *Red Planet*

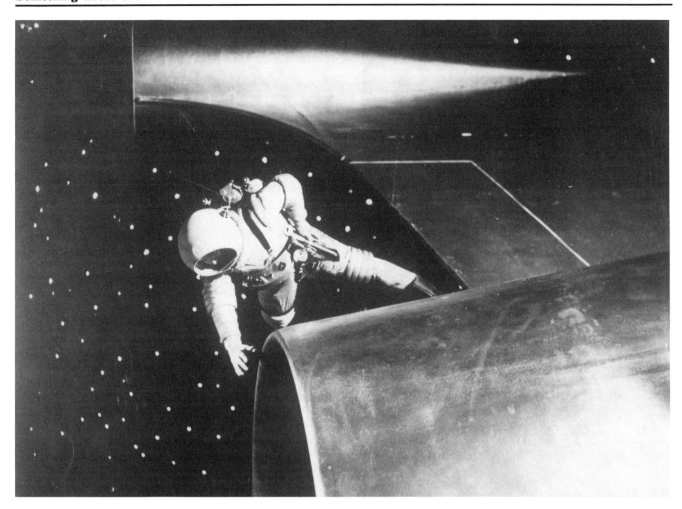

The story of a lunar voyage, the 1950 film *Destination Moon* was coauthored by Heinlein and based on his novel *Rocket Ship Galileo.*

are set in the solar system; and later juveniles like *Tunnel in the Sky* and *Have Space Suit—Will Travel* take readers to worlds across the galaxy. The author's optimism about mankind's ability to settle the galaxy appealed to many readers and critics, including Williamson, who remarked: "What I most admire about [his young adult books] is Heinlein's dogged faith in us and our destiny. No blind optimist, he is very much aware of evil days to come. His future worlds are often oppressively misruled, pinched by hunger, and wasted by war. Yet his heroes are always using science and reason to solve problems, to escape the prison of Earth, to seek and build better worlds."

Heinlein's popularity as a writer grew steadily during the 1950s when he entered the field of television and motion pictures. Some of his work produced during that time includes *Tom Corbett: Space Cadet*—a television adaptation of his novel, *Space Cadet*—and *Destination Moon,* for which he wrote the screenplay and served as technical adviser. *Destination Moon* was the first film to attempt to accurately describe what a flight to the Moon might be like. With his successes in all these endeavors, Heinlein became "the most diversified writer American science fiction had yet produced," according to Patrouch.

The author's career took a sharp turn in the late 1950s with *Starship Troopers.* Although similar to his earlier young adult novels in that it describes a young man's coming of age, it was the first book by Heinlein to speculate not on future scientific changes, but on future changes in society. The book was rejected by Scribner's—Heinlein's longtime publisher—and became controversial because of its strong militaristic message. More than novels like *Starman Jones,* which revealed early the influence of Heinlein's naval training, the message that "violence has been the greatest settler of issues in the history of the world" is clearly made in *Starship Troopers.* Some critics even charged that *Starship Troopers*—describing a society based on a military at constant war with spider-like aliens who live in a communist society—was a fascist novel. But *Extrapolation* contributor Dennis E. Showalter countered that the society Heinlein describes does not have the "common benchmarks of fascism. There is no indication of a ruling party, a secret police, a charismatic leader, or an official ideology."

Despite critical resistance, *Starship Troopers* marked the beginning of a new phase in Heinlein's writing. While he continued to write some straight science fiction novels, his interest in addressing issues about society and

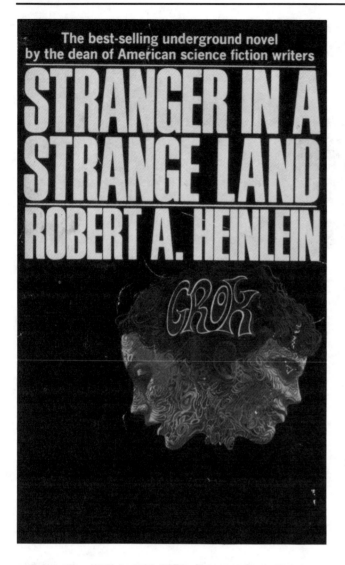

The best-selling underground novel by the dean of American science fiction writers

STRANGER IN A STRANGE LAND

ROBERT A. HEINLEIN

GROK

Originally published in 1961, *Stranger in a Strange Land* sold millions of copies and became the first science fiction book to appear on the *New York Times* bestseller list.

philosophy continued to grow. The author's next novel, *Stranger in a Strange Land,* was even more controversial than *Starship Troopers.* Considered a classic work of science fiction by many critics, *Stranger in a Strange Land* challenges traditional ideas about religion and sex. Heinlein speculated in his story what might happen if a man were raised by Martians to have a completely different philosophy of life and then was brought back to Earth. Valentine Michael Smith, the "Man from Mars," has learned to control objects around him and even the functions of his body with the powers of his mind, but it is his ideas about life after death and "grokking" that eventually establish a new religion on Earth, the Church of All Worlds. Grokking is a Martian word meaning "to understand something so completely that it becomes a part of you." Later in the novel, as Smith begins to understand more about human beings, his desire to become one with those around him leads him to participate in group sex and to encourage his growing number of followers to participate as well.

Little did Heinlein suspect the consequences that writing *Stranger in a Strange Land* would bring. On the positive side, the novel sold millions of copies and became the first science fiction book to appear on the *New York Times* bestseller list. But the book also created an intense cult following and inspired the founding of a real-life Church of All Worlds. Heinlein was harassed so much by his admirers that he had to build a fence around his home to keep fans out. He was dumbfounded by this reaction: "I was *not* giving answers [to religious questions]," *New York Times Book Review* contributor Richard E. Nichols quoted the author as saying. "I was trying to shake the reader loose from some preconceptions and induce him to think for himself, along new and fresh lines." "Only in a fictional sense does Heinlein defend the sexual attitudes in the novel," Patrouch cautioned; "that is, he tries to make them plausible in the context of his story. This is entirely different from saying that Heinlein [was] in favor of them."

Several critics guessed that timing was part of the reason for the success of *Stranger in a Strange Land,* which was published in 1961. The book "fit ... the mood of the time," commented Samuelson, "attacking human folly under several guises, especially in the person or persons of the Establishment: government, the military, organized religion." In the novels that followed *Stranger in a Strange Land* Heinlein continued to speculate about what sorts of changes humanity might go through in the future. Books like *The Moon Is a Harsh Mistress, I Will Fear No Evil,* and *Time Enough for Love: The Lives of Lazarus Long* all involve—to a greater or lesser degree—controversial ideas like group marriage and incest.

All these later works, claimed Robinson, also show a consistent philosophical concern "which one critic summarized as 'You can conquer death through love.' [Heinlein] was now writing about the two themes most important to an adult audience: Love and Death." This theme is embodied in the character of Lazarus Long, the immortal hero who appears in *Methuselah's Children, Time Enough for Love: The Lives of Lazarus Long, To Sail beyond the Sunset,* and *The Cat Who Walks through Walls: A Comedy of Manners.* In these and other later works, Heinlein tries to answer the question "What is the meaning of life?" It is an important question for Lazarus, whose gift of immortality would be meaningless without the answer. According to Patrouch, Heinlein concluded "that the reason for living is involvement in life," to love and enjoy life for its own sake.

A number of critics have complained that Heinlein's novels after *Starship Troopers* were not as good as his earlier juvenile novels. "In science-fiction circles it is a truism that the early Heinlein was a much better writer than the late Heinlein," according to *Los Angeles Times Book Review* contributor and fellow science fiction author Rudy Rucker. Part of the problem, Patrouch remarked, was that Heinlein's books became more and more like essays concerning Heinlein's opinions about life, and were only thinly veiled by plotting and characterization: "Much of his fiction since 1957 is in the form of a dialogue in which two figures sit down and discuss a topic." And Williamson felt that the juvenile novels "are cleanly constructed and deftly written, without the digressions and the preaching that often weaken the drama in [Heinlein's] later work."

The importance of Heinlein's influence on science fiction has not been denied by any of his reviewers, but, as Ivor A. Rogers observed in *Robert A. Heinlein,* "there is little consensus on what is his best work." Although Heinlein kept writing bestselling novels far into the 1980s, and his *Stranger in a Strange Land* remains the work for which he is most often remembered, it is his groundbreaking early work that has most changed the face of science fiction according to his critics. "He is 'historically' important as a pioneer in realistic and extrapolative science fiction," wrote Samuelson in *Voices for the Future: Essays on Major Science Fiction Writers,* "and as a representative writer whose craftsmanship and technical knowledge-ability were generally quite high."

At the time of Heinlein's death in 1988, he had won four Hugo Awards and the first Nebula Grand Master Award, and forty million copies of his books had been sold in thirty different languages. Through his writing, science fiction, like so many of Heinlein's heroes, had come of age. Fellow writer Isaac Asimov was quoted in a *Los Angeles Times* obituary as crediting Heinlein with "single-handedly ... lift[ing] science fiction to a new pitch of quality." In the same article, publisher Christine Schillig observed that Heinlein "was a 50-year influence on the genre.... He was one of the original writers who created from vision, what the future should be, what it might be." In *Grumbles from the Grave,* Heinlein's wife Virginia concluded, "I will leave it to others to evaluate the influence of Robert's work, but I have been told many times that he was 'The Father of Modern Science Fiction.' [His] books have been published in many languages, in many lands, and some of them seem to have been landmark stories."

WORKS CITED:

Bester, Alfred, "Robert Heinlein," *Publishers Weekly,* July 2, 1973, pp. 44-45.

Franklin, H. Bruce, *Robert A. Heinlein: America As Science Fiction,* Oxford University Press, 1980, pp. 73-124.

Heinlein, Robert A., *Grumbles from the Grave,* edited by Virginia Heinlein, Ballantine, 1989, pp. xi-xviii.

Los Angeles Times, May 10, 1988.

Nichols, Richard E., "The Biggest, Fattest Sacred Cows," *New York Times Book Review,* December 9, 1990, p. 13.

Patrouch, Joseph, "Robert A. Heinlein," *Dictionary of Literary Biography,* Volume 8: *Twentieth Century American Science Fiction Writers,* Gale, 1981, pp. 208-228.

Robinson, Frank, "Robert A. Heinlein Dies," *Locus,* June, 1988, pp. B, 78-81.

Rogers, Ivor A., "Robert Heinlein: Folklorist of Outer Space," *Robert A. Heinlein,* edited by Joseph D. Olander and Martin Harry Greenberg, Taplinger, 1978, pp. 222-239.

Rucker, Rudy, review of *Stranger in a Strange Land, Los Angeles Times Book Review,* December 23, 1990, p. 7.

Samuelson, David N., *Voices for the Future: Essays on Major Science Fiction Writers,* Volume 1, edited by Thomas D. Clareson, Bowling Green University, 1976, pp. 104-152.

Samuelson, David N., "'Stranger' in the Sixties: Model or Mirror?," *Critical Encounters: Writers and Themes in Science Fiction,* edited by Dick Riley, Ungar, 1978, pp. 144-175.

Showalter, Dennis E., "Heinlein's 'Starship Troopers': An Exercise in Rehabilitation," *Extrapolation,* May, 1975, pp. 113-124.

Silverberg, Robert, in an obituary in *Locus,* June, 1988, p. 82.

Suplee, Curt, *Washington Post,* September 5, 1984.

Williamson, Jack, "Youth Against Space: Heinlein's Juveniles Revisited," *Robert A. Heinlein,* edited by Joseph D. Olander and Martin Harry Greenberg, Taplinger, 1978, pp. 15-31.

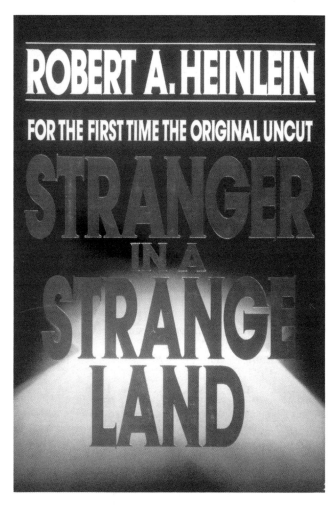

To commemorate the thirtieth anniversary of *Stranger in a Strange Land*'s original publication, Putnam released an uncut edition of this watershed work in 1991.

FOR MORE INFORMATION SEE:

BOOKS

Aldiss, Brian W., *Billion Year Spree: The True History of Science Fiction,* Doubleday, 1973, pp. 269-274.

Atheling, William, Jr., *The Issue at Hand,* Advent, 1964, pp. 68-79.

Atheling, William, Jr., *More Issues at Hand,* Advent, 1970, pp. 51-58.

Contemporary Literary Criticism, Gale, Volume 1, 1973, Volume 3, 1975, Volume 8, 1978, Volume 14, 1980, Volume 26, 1983, Volume 55, 1989.

Gunn, James, *Alternate Worlds: The Illustrated History of Science Fiction,* Prentice-Hall, 1975.

Gunn, James, *The Road to Science Fiction: From Heinlein to the Present,* New American Library, 1979.

Knight, Damon, *In Search of Wonder: Critical Essays on Science Fiction,* Advent, 1956, pp. 76-89.

Moskowitz, Sam, *Seekers of Tomorrow: Masters of Modern Science Fiction,* Ballantine, 1967, pp. 191-214.

Nicholls, Peter, *Robert A. Heinlein,* Scribner, 1982.

Panshin, Alexei, *Heinlein in Dimension: A Critical Analysis,* Advent, 1968.

Rose, Lois, and Stephen Rose, *The Shattered Ring: Science Fiction and the Quest for Meaning,* John Knox, 1970.

Scholes, Robert, and Eric S. Rabkin, *Science Fiction: History, Science, Vision,* Oxford University Press, 1977, pp. 52-58.

Slusser, George Edgar, *Robert A. Heinlein: Stranger in His Own Land,* Borgo, 1976.

Slusser, George Edgar, *The Classic Years of Robert A. Heinlein,* Borgo, 1977.

Wollheim, Donald A., *The Universe Makers: Science Fiction Today,* Harper, 1971, pp. 99-102.

PERIODICALS

American Mercury, October, 1960.
Analog, May, 1954; September, 1964.
Author and Journalist, January, 1963.
CEA Critic, March, 1968.
Chicago Tribune, August 6, 1961.
Chicago Tribune Book World, August 17, 1980; January 7, 1984.
Christian Science Monitor, November 7, 1957.
Detroit News, July 25, 1982.
Extrapolation, December, 1970; spring, 1979; fall, 1979; fall, 1982.
Galaxy, February, 1952; December, 1966.
Journal of Popular Culture, spring, 1972.
Los Angeles Times, December 19, 1985.
Los Angeles Times Book Review, June 20, 1982; October 21, 1984.
Magazine of Fantasy and Science Fiction, June, 1956; November, 1961; March, 1971; October, 1980.
Modern Fiction Studies, spring, 1986.
National Observer, November 16, 1970.
National Review, March 26, 1963; November 16, 1970; December 12, 1980.
New Statesman, July 30, 1965.
New Worlds, June, 1962.

New Yorker, July, 1974.
New York Herald Tribune Book Review, November 28, 1954; November 13, 1955; November 18, 1956; May 12, 1962.
New York Times, March 3, 1957; August 22, 1973.
New York Times Book Review, October 23, 1949; November 14, 1954; December 29, 1957; December 14, 1958; January 31, 1960; March 23, 1975; August 24, 1980; September 14, 1980; July 4, 1982; November 1984; December 22, 1985.
Observer, December 23, 1984.
Punch, August 25, 1965; November 22, 1967.
San Francisco Chronicle, November 8, 1959.
Saturday Review, November, 1958.
Science Fiction Review, November, 1970.
SF Commentary, May, 1976.
Spectator, June 3, 1966; July 3, 1977.
Speculation, August, 1969.
Times Literary Supplement, October 6, 1969; December 1, 1970; April 2, 1971; June 14, 1974.
Washington Post Book World, May 11, 1975; June 27, 1982.

OBITUARIES:

PERIODICALS

Chicago Tribune, May 11, 1988.
Detroit News, May 10, 1988.
New York Times, May 10, 1988.
Time, May 23, 1988.
Times (London), May 11, 1988.
Washington Post, May 10, 1988.

[Sketch verified by wife, Virginia Heinlein]

—Sketch by Kevin S. Hile

*   *   *

HEMMANT, Lynette 1938-

PERSONAL: Full name is Margaret Lynette Hemmant; born September 20, 1938, in London, England; daughter of Daniel Ground (a mining engineer and lawyer) and Margaret Joyce (a homemaker; maiden name, Pegler) Hemmant; married Jueri Evald Gabriel (a writer and literary agent), August 25, 1962. *Education:* St. Martin's School of Design, national diploma of design, 1958. *Politics:* "Center-leftish, sometimes center-rightish." *Religion:* None.

ADDRESSES: Home and office—38 Camberwell Grove, London SE5 8JA, England.

CAREER: Free-lance artist, painter, and illustrator. Worked variously in England in water softener sales and as a cook for the City of London Bankers, c. late 1950s. *Exhibitions:* Two one-person shows in Italy.

ILLUSTRATOR:

Alison Farthing, *The Hollyhock Race,* Chatto, Boyd & Oliver, 1969.
Rosemary Weir, *Summer of the Silent Hands,* Brockhampton Press, 1969.

LYNETTE HEMMANT

Mabel Esther Allan, *Christmas at Spindle Bottom*, Dent, 1970.

Jean Blathwayt, *Lucy's Brownie Road*, Brockhampton Press, 1970.

Suzanne Butler, *Starlight in Tourrone*, Chatto, Boyd & Oliver, 1970.

Geraldine Kay, *In the Park*, Macmillan, 1970.

Kay, *The Rainbow Shirt*, Macmillan, 1970.

Rosemary Manning, *The Rocking Horse*, Hamilton, 1970.

Ian Niall, *Wild Life of Field and Hedgeside*, Heinemann, 1970.

Niall, *Wild Life of Moor and Mountain*, Heinemann, 1970.

Pamela Rogers, *Fish and Chips*, Hamilton, 1970.

Paul Rowland, *A Piece of Wire: The Story of a Refugee Boy*, University of London Press, 1970.

Barbara Euphan Todd, *The Box in the Attic*, World's Work, 1970.

Blathwayt, *River in the Hills*, Epworth Press, 1971.

Dorothy Clewes, *Two Bad Boys*, Hamilton, 1971.

Barbara Cox, *Stop Thief!*, University of London Press, 1971.

L. A. Hill, reteller, *Hansel and Gretel* (based on the original fairy tale by Jacob and Wilhelm Grimm), Oxford University Press, 1971.

Hill, reteller, *The Happy Dragon* (based on the original story by Richard Wilson), Oxford University Press, 1971.

Peggy Miller, *Gold on Crow Mountain* (adapted from the television series), British Broadcasting Corporation, 1971.

Niall, *Wild Life of Wood and Spinney*, Heinemann, 1971.

Blathwayt, *Lucy's Last Brownie Challenge*, Brockhampton Press, 1972.

Frances Eagar, *The Little Sparrow*, Hamilton, 1972.

Terry Ingelby and Jenny Taylor, *Messy Malcolm*, World's Work, 1972.

Todd, *The Wand from France*, World's Work, 1972.

Leslie Dunkling, *The Battle of Newton Road*, Longman, 1973.

Eagar, *The Tin Mine*, Hamilton, 1973.

Daphne Ghose, *Bediga*, Lutterworth Press, 1973.

Godfrey Young, *Waiting for Cherry*, Hamilton, 1973.

Irene Byers, *Timothy and Tiptoes*, Brockhampton Press, 1974.

Freda Collins, *Pow-wow Stories*, Knight Books, 1974.

Eagar, *Midnight Patrol*, Hamilton, 1974.

Marie Hynds, *The Wishing Bottle*, Blackie, 1975.

G. F. Lamb, *More Good Stories*, four volumes, Wheaton, 1975, Volume 1: *The Three Donkeys, and Other Stories*, Volume 3: *Bertie the Bat, and Other Stories*. (Hemmant not associated with other volumes.)

R. H. Barham, *The Jackdaw of Rheims: An Ingoldsby Legend*, World's Work, 1976.

Byers, *Tiptoes Wins Through*, Hodder & Stoughton, 1976.

Helen Cresswell, *The Barge Children*, White Lion, 1976.

Charles Dickens, *A Christmas Carol*, World's Work, 1978.

Rachel Field, *Poems for Children*, World's Work, 1978.

Ingelby and Taylor, *Messy Malcolm's Birthday*, World's Work, 1978.

Edward Fitzgerald, translator, *The Rubaiyat of Omar Khayyam*, World's Work, 1979.

Jane Austen, *Pride and Prejudice*, World's Work, 1980.

Ingelby and Taylor, *Messy Malcolm's Dream*, World's Work, 1981.

Kemal E. Sakarya, editor, *The Obstinate Hodja* (short story collection), Trafalgar Square, 1990.

Dick King-Smith, *Ace: The Very Important Pig*, Crown, 1990.

King-Smith, *The Toby Man*, Crown, 1991.

Also illustrator of picture line books *The Farm, The Fun Fair, The Market, The River, The Street,* and *The Zoo,* all published in 1972, and of *The Holiday Bus,* 1976, and Usha Bahl's *Exams! Exams!,* Nelson. Illustrator of a set of stamps for one of the English-French channel islands and a set of twelve collectors' plates depicting the months of the year in the English countryside. Contributor of illustrations to children's magazine *Cricket.*

WORK IN PROGRESS: Paintings to be used as dust jackets for Dedalus, a publisher in England; ongoing landscapes and large garden paintings; etchings.

SIDELIGHTS: Lynette Hemmant told *SATA:* "I was born in London, England, just before World War II and immediately whisked off to South Wales, where we were hardly affected by the war. Half of the house we occupied there was a proper farmhouse with a vast old stone-flagged kitchen, a black kitchen range, and a great coming and going (it seemed to me) of people who spoke Welsh amongst themselves and taught me a sentence from time to time.

"I spent a few years of my childhood watching great heavy-hooved shire horses work the land and helping with haymaking and other traditional agricultural tasks, all of which left very strong impressions on me. I was packed off to boarding school at the age of nine but was 'rescued' by the need for the whole family to go to Brisbane, Australia, for three years because my father had a contract there. I managed to live a mostly unsupervised existence, rode lots of horses, and went to a normal school where I learned a little Australian history and not much else. At the same time, I was beginning to draw and paint seriously without realizing it.

"I came back to England overweight, badly missing the sun and sea and open spaces, and was soon squeezed back into boarding schools and conformity. But it wasn't totally successful—I was able to jump a year of school and begin art school one week short of my sixteenth birthday, just nine years after having announced that I was going to be 'an Artist.' Though so very young, I coped reasonably well with art school. I enjoyed it, worked very hard, and got a respectable grade for my finals. I was very aware of my lack of professional competence, though.

"Miraculously, jobs started to turn up and, with occasional temporary work to boost my finances, I got by. I married in 1962 and became a full-time illustrator, give or take an occasional portrait. Though I spent the next twenty-five years as an illustrator, I now earn most of my income and therefore spend most of my time as a painter. I was a voracious reader as a child but now find it difficult to find time to read enough, not just for information, but for important psychological input as well.

"Six years ago, after having lived with my husband for twenty years in the same house, fate sent us the gift of a decrepit Georgian house in southeast London. With a long garden and a wonderful view of a wedding cake gothic church and mature trees, it is difficult to believe that we are only three miles from the center of London. The house is an unending restoration job, but the garden is lovely, and I paint it often.

"As far as I'm concerned, the elusive thing we call 'Art' can be found between the covers of a book in the same way that it can emerge from formal fine arts craftsmanship. There are no rules, but most people tend to recognize it when they see it, quite often even when they don't have a particularly 'well-educated' visual sense. Rewards come to an artist when the work flows and people like it.

"Illustration at its best is a collusion between the author and the illustrator. The illustrator is the fairground 'barker,' calling the people to step inside and see the show. In a picture book, the illustrator dominates, aided by a short, concise text. In illustrated novels and other longer books, the author has set the stage, but the illustrator illuminates the characters and scene. For instance, Sir John Tenniel's illustrations for Lewis Carroll's *Alice in Wonderland* are so powerful that it is almost impossible to see Alice as anything other than that striped-stockinged, aproned little girl with her hair unsuccessfully confined by an 'Alice' band.

"What moved me out of full-time illustration was a combination of my wish to do my own thing—not to have to respond to a text—and to do it bigger. I had great encouragement and help from Italian painter Bruno Guaitamacchi, who pointed out the truth—that the energy that goes into those little illustrated images is the same as can be used for a much larger piece of work. He arranged my first one-person show in Italy, which made me realize that I was capable of broadening my horizons and using a larger brush.

"I enjoy my returns to illustration, and I wouldn't want to lose the ability to work in a restricted space. My years of research and practice have been useful in the production of large imaginative paintings. I do a lot of landscape painting on sight and paint still life in the studio. Most years I spend some time in Italy, often painting and drawing in Venice. I think my time there has been very useful. The contrast in Italian culture and temperament challenges my 'Northern Rational' mind. I have had two exhibitions, mainly of Venetian pictures, and I am collecting work towards another one.

"I think the best thing about being an artist is that one always has horizons. There is the feeling that there are no limits—that one *can* keep traveling. In this field, though, money is always hard earned. I am lucky never to have been forced to teach art in order to survive financially. Teaching is a vocation that is very demanding and should be taken up willingly. In addition, I have avoided having a family, because I know my limits: I could not have worked the hours I do and managed a complicated domestic life at the same time. Art isn't just a job; it's a life."

*   *   *

HENRY, Marguerite 1902-

PERSONAL: Born April 13, 1902, in Milwaukee, WI; daughter of Louis (owner of a publishing business) and Anna (Kaurup) Breithaupt; married Sidney Crocker Henry (a sales manager), May 5, 1923 (died in 1987). *Education:* Attended Milwaukee State Teachers College and University of Wisconsin—Milwaukee.

ADDRESSES: P.O. Box 385, Rancho Santa Fe, CA 92067.

CAREER: Writer.

AWARDS, HONORS: Newbery Honor Book, 1946, Junior Scholastic Gold Seal Award, and Award of the Friends of Literature, both 1948, all for *Justin Morgan Had a Horse;* Newbery Honor Book, 1948, and Lewis Carroll Shelf Award, 1961, both for *Misty of Chincoteague;* Newbery Medal, 1949, and Young Readers Choice Award, 1951, both for *King of the Wind;* Young Readers Choice Award, 1952, for *Sea Star: Orphan of*

Marguerite Henry and friends.

Chincoteague; William Allen White Award, 1956, for *Brighty of the Grand Canyon;* Sequoyah Children's Book Award, 1960, for *Black Gold,* and 1970, for *Mustang, Wild Spirit of the West;* Children's Reading Round Table Award, 1961; Society of Midland Authors Clara Ingram Judson Award, 1961, for *Gaudenzia: Pride of the Palio,* and 1973, for *San Domingo: The Medicine Hat Stallion;* Western Heritage Award, 1967, for *Mustang, Wild Spirit of the West;* Society of Midland Authors Award for *San Domingo: The Medicine Hat Stallion;* Literature for Children Award, Southern California Council, 1973, Kerlan Award, University of Minnesota, 1975; named Author of the Diamond Jubilee Year by Illinois Association of Teachers of English, 1982; honorary doctor of letters, Hamilton College, 1992.

WRITINGS:

FOR CHILDREN

Auno and Tauno: A Story of Finland, illustrated by Gladys Blackwood, Albert Whitman, 1940.

Dilly Dally Sally, illustrated by Blackwood, Saalfield, 1940.

Birds at Home, illustrated by Jacob Bates Abbott, Donohue, 1942, revised edition, Hubbard Press, 1972.

Geraldine Belinda (with verse by Henry and music by Russell E. Jupp), illustrated by Blackwood, Platt, 1942.

(With Barbara True) *Their First Igloo on Baffin Island,* illustrated by Blackwood, Albert Whitman, 1943.

A Boy and a Dog, illustrated by Diana Thorne and Ottilie Foy, Follett, 1944.

The Little Fellow (Junior Literary Guild selection), illustrated by Thorne, Winston, 1945, revised edition, illustrated by Rich Rudish, Rand McNally, 1975.

Robert Fulton: Boy Craftsman, illustrated by Lawrence Dresser, Bobbs-Merrill, 1945.

Misty, the Wonder Pony, by Misty, Herself, illustrated by Clare McKinley, Rand McNally, 1956.

Gaudenzia: Pride of the Palio, illustrated by Lynd Ward, Rand McNally, 1960, published as *The Wildest Horse Race in the World,* 1976, published in England as *Palio: The Wildest Horse Race in the World,* Fontana, 1976.

Mustang: Wild Spirit of the West, illustrated by Robert Lougheed, Rand McNally, 1966.

Dear Readers and Riders, Rand McNally, 1969.

(Editor) *Stories from around the World,* illustrated by Krystyna Stasiak, Hubbard Press, 1971.

San Domingo: The Medicine Hat Stallion, illustrated by Lougheed, Rand McNally, 1972, published as *Peter Lundy and the Medicine Hat Stallion,* 1976.

Dear Marguerite Henry, Rand McNally, 1978.

The Illustrated Marguerite Henry: With Wesley Dennis, Robert Lougheed, Lynd Ward, and Rich Rudish, Rand McNally, 1980.

Our First Pony, illustrated by Rudish, Rand McNally, 1984.

Misty's Twilight, Macmillan, 1992.

ILLUSTRATED BY WESLEY DENNIS; FOR CHILDREN

Justin Morgan Had a Horse, Follett, 1945, revised edition, Rand McNally, 1954.

Misty of Chincoteague (Junior Literary Guild selection), Rand McNally, 1947, excerpts published as *The Auction, The Big Race, The Capture, Going Home, The Storm,* and *The Whirlpool,* all Checkerboard Press, 1987.

Benjamin West and His Cat Grimalkin, Bobbs-Merrill, 1947.

Always Reddy, McGraw, 1947.

King of the Wind, Rand McNally, 1948, excerpts published as *A Colt Is Born,* illustrated by Stephen Moore, *An Innkeeper's Horse* and *The Rescue of Sham,* illustrated by Cindy Spenser, *Battle of the Stallions,* illustrated by Steven James Petruccio, *The Sultan's Gift,* and *Sire of Champions,* all Checkerboard Press, 1988.

Little-or-Nothing from Nottingham, McGraw, 1949.

Sea Star: Orphan of Chincoteague, Rand McNally, 1949.

Born to Trot, Rand McNally, 1950, excerpts published as *One Man's Horse,* 1977.

Album of Horses (Junior Literary Guild selection), Rand McNally, 1951, reissued, 1979, shortened version published as *Portfolio of Horses,* 1952, published as *Portfolio of Horse Paintings,* 1964.

Brighty of the Grand Canyon (Junior Literary Guild selection), Rand McNally, 1953.

Wagging Tails: An Album of Dogs, Rand McNally, 1955, published as *An Album of Dogs,* 1970.

With books such as *Brighty of the Grand Canyon*, Henry has carved out a reputation as one of the era's best authors of children's animal stories. (Cover illustration by Wesley Dennis.)

Cinnabar: The One O'Clock Fox, Rand McNally, 1956.
Black Gold, Rand McNally, 1957.
Muley-Ears, Nobody's Dog (Junior Literary Guild selection), Rand McNally, 1959.
All about Horses, Random House, 1962, revised edition, photographs by Walter D. Osborne, 1967.
Five O'Clock Charlie, Rand McNally, 1962.
Stormy, Misty's Foal, Rand McNally, 1963.
White Stallion of Lipizza, Rand McNally, 1964.
A Pictorial Life Story of Misty, Rand McNally, 1976.
Marguerite Henry's Misty Treasury: The Complete Misty, Sea Star, and Stormy, Rand McNally, 1982.

"PICTURED GEOGRAPHIES" SERIES; ILLUSTRATED BY KURT WIESE

Alaska in Story and Pictures, Albert Whitman, 1941, 2nd edition, 1942.
Argentina in Story and Pictures, Albert Whitman, 1941, 2nd edition, 1942.
Brazil in Story and Pictures, Albert Whitman, 1941, 2nd edition, 1942.
Canada in Story and Pictures, Albert Whitman, 1941, 2nd edition, 1942.

Chile in Story and Pictures, Albert Whitman, 1941, 2nd edition, 1942.
Mexico in Story and Pictures, Albert Whitman, 1941, 2nd edition, 1942.
Panama in Story and Pictures, Albert Whitman, 1941, 2nd edition, 1942.
West Indies in Story and Pictures, Albert Whitman, 1941, 2nd edition, 1942.
Australia in Story and Pictures, Albert Whitman, 1946.
The Bahamas in Story and Pictures, Albert Whitman, 1946.
Bermuda in Story and Pictures, Albert Whitman, 1946.
British Honduras in Story and Pictures, Albert Whitman, 1946.
Dominican Republic in Story and Pictures, Albert Whitman, 1946.
Hawaii in Story and Pictures, Albert Whitman, 1946.
New Zealand in Story and Pictures, Albert Whitman, 1946.
Virgin Islands in Story and Pictures, Albert Whitman, 1946.

OTHER

Contributor to *World Book Encyclopedia.* Contributor to magazines, including *Delineator, Forum, Nations' Business, Reader's Digest,* and *Saturday Evening Post.*

Henry's manuscripts are held in the Kerlan Collection at University of Minnesota, Minneapolis.

ADAPTATIONS:

Misty (feature film based on *Misty of Chincoteague*), Twentieth Century-Fox, 1961.
Brighty of the Grand Canyon (feature film), Feature Film Corp., 1967.
Justin Morgan Had a Horse, Walt Disney Productions, 1972.
Peter Lundy and the Medicine Hat Stallion (television movie; based on *San Domingo: The Medicine Hat Stallion*), National Broadcasting Company, Inc., 1977.
Story of a Book, Pied Piper Productions, 1980.
King of the Wind, HTV (London), 1990.

Misty of Chincoteague, Justin Morgan Had a Horse, and *King of the Wind* were also adapted as filmstrips.

SIDELIGHTS: Best known for her many books about horses, Marguerite Henry has delighted young readers with stories about animals, people, and places for more than forty years. Miriam E. Wilt, writing in *Elementary English* in 1954, acknowledged that "today many of us believe her to be the best author of children's horse stories in this era, perhaps of all time." In the years following that assessment Henry has maintained her stature. She has won the prestigious Newbery Medal and numerous other honors, and her works have earned praise from a long line of critics. Frequently based on true stories, Henry's books are commended for their accuracy as well as for their way of making history come alive. Fleshed-out characters, realistic plotting, and an honest, well-informed, and nonhumanized treatment of animals are also considered virtues of her work. Assert-

A pregnant Misty—the wild pony immortalized in *Misty of Chincoteague*—welcomes Henry back to Chincoteague Island by doing a favorite trick. (From Henry's *A Pictorial Life Story of Misty.*)

ed Wilt, Henry's are among "the most beautiful and worthwhile books ever published for children."

One of Henry's first stories to win acclaim was *Justin Morgan Had a Horse,* which was named a Newbery Honor Book. Set in the late eighteenth century, it describes the beginnings of the Morgan breed of horses in rural Vermont, focusing on a few of the people associated with the breed's founding sire. With this book Henry began a long and successful partnership with artist Wesley Dennis, who illustrated some of her most popular works. Henry herself initiated the collaboration. When she finished writing *Justin Morgan* she searched library books for the right illustrator for it. As she recounted in her *Something about the Author Autobiography Series* (*SAAS*) essay, Henry "fell wildly in love with *Flip,* a first book with pictures and text by Wesley Dennis." She sent a copy of *Justin Morgan* to Dennis, and when they met he immediately told her, "I'm dying to do the book and I don't care whether I get paid for it or not." The pair's working relationship was characterized by their uncanny ability to think along the same lines. In an article for *Young Wings,* Henry recalled one incident: "In doing the Appaloosa chapter for *Album of Horses,* I started with a buffalo hunt.... And just as I was mailing my chapter to Wesley, the postmistress handed me a note from him. 'I'm doing a

buffalo hunt for the Appaloosa chapter,' it said. 'Okay?'" Noted Henry, "This happens again and again, book after book."

Misty of Chincoteague, the second Henry-Dennis effort, has become one of Henry's most enduring books. Set off the coast of Virginia on Chincoteague Island, whose residents hold an annual roundup and sale of wild horses from nearby Assateague Island, it follows the efforts of two children, Paul and Maureen Beebe, to buy and raise a wild pony of their own. The horse they set their hearts on is the Phantom, a mysterious mare who has avoided capture for two years. In Paul's first year as a "roundup man" the Phantom is finally caught, however, for she is slowed by her newborn foal. Henry based the story closely on real people and ponies of Chincoteague. With Dennis she attended Pony Penning Day, and there she first saw the tiny foal who became the heroine of her story. Henry even kept the filly at her Illinois home for a few years during and after the writing of the novel, eventually sending Misty back to the Beebe ranch to be bred.

The success of *Misty of Chincoteague* made the little pony a celebrity. Misty was invited to a conference of the American Library Association, and a movie was made about her life. On the day she left Illinois to return

Henry won the coveted Newbery Medal for *King of the Wind,* a story about a small Arabian stallion who became a foundation sire of thoroughbreds. (Cover illustration by Wesley Dennis.)

to Chincoteague, reporters from local papers, wire services, and national magazines came to see her off. When Misty's first colt needed a name, thousands of children wrote Henry with their suggestions. Recognizing the lasting appeal of novel and horse, Wilt suggested that "for those of us who first met Marguerite Henry in *Misty of Chincoteague,* probably none of her books will ever take its place in our hearts." The critic called *Misty* "one of the finest horse stories ever written," and she praised "the fine sense of values, the feeling of drama, [and] the deft characterization" of the book. Writing in a 1967 *Elementary English* article, Norine Odland remarked that "the ponies of Chincoteague are no 'once upon a time' story for thousands of boys and girls. Misty and the Beebe family are special friends of the readers." *Misty* was Henry's second Newbery Honor Book and the winner of a Lewis Carroll Shelf Award—judged worthy to stand next to such classics of children's literature as Carroll's "Alice in Wonderland" stories.

The year after publishing *Misty,* Henry published *King of the Wind,* another work illustrated by Dennis, which resulted from a story the artist told Henry. Dennis had heard details about an Arabian stallion of the early eighteenth century who was abused and neglected for years, yet who eventually became one of the three founding sires of Thoroughbred racehorses. Henry was

enthralled, despite concerns voiced by her family and publishers. Relatives confronted her about the amount of research she would have to do for a story that began in Morocco, moved on to France, and ended in England. Her editors worried because none of the three main characters—the stallion, the loyal Moroccan stableboy who tended him throughout his life, and a cat—could speak, and the settings would be very foreign to American readers. In her *SAAS* essay, Henry remembered telling the doubters, "'I don't want to do anything but let the seed of the story grow.'" She added: "And grow it did, at a breathtaking pace. Aware now of the warnings, we could make doubly sure that our characters ... showed their feelings in a universal language. Wesley, with his strong action paintings, jumped all the hurdles without fault, and I, with my reams of research, covered the course in tandem with him. When *King of the Wind* won the Newbery Medal we were both in shock."

In her Newbery Medal acceptance paper, published in *Horn Book,* Henry recalled beginning to work on *King of the Wind:* "With great excitement I began to probe and pry into the life of this famous stallion who had rubbed shoulders with sultans and kings, with cooks and carters. Here were no burned-out cinders of history. Here were live coals showering their sparks over Morocco, France, England." Pinning up pictures in her study of the real people and places involved in the novel, Henry immersed herself in her subject, soon finding that "it was the present that grew dim and the long ago that became real!"

Henry's book, judged accurate in all major details, also became a gripping adventure story. Through the eyes of Agba, the Moroccan stableboy, Henry described the omen-filled birth of the stallion, whom Agba named Sham. She recounted how Sham was sent as a gift to the young king of France, was starved on the journey, and was ultimately made a cart horse in Paris. From hand to brutal hand she traced Sham's path to England's earl of Godolphin, who finally accepted the stallion when a colt Sham sired without the earl's consent grew up to outrun all the other colts his age at the stable. With this book, asserted a *New York Herald Tribune Weekly Book Review* critic, Henry "stirs the reader's imagination, holds his interest, makes him laugh a little and cry a little—satisfies him."

In subsequent works Henry explored other equine worlds and non-equine worlds with the same dedicated research and the same insight into human and animal characters. Summing up the various elements of Henry's work, *Dictionary of Literary Biography* contributor Rebecca Lukens wrote: "Henry's books bring to life legends of the origins of great horses, traditions of the past, historical events, carefully recorded facts about breeds and generations of horses. Her imagination gleams through the portrayal of the characters and their conflicts. Few animal stories can surpass Henry's in suspense.... When examined as fiction, the novels are engrossing; when seen in the light of the history they present, they are enlightening; and when read for their insight into human and animal natures, they are highly satisfying."

WORKS CITED:

"Castaways: 'King of the Wind,'" *New York Herald Tribune Weekly Book Review,* November 14, 1948, p. 18.

Henry, Marguerite, "Marguerite Henry," *Something about the Author Autobiography Series,* Volume 7, Gale, 1989, pp. 91-108.

Henry, Marguerite, "Newbery Acceptance Paper," *Horn Book,* January-February, 1950, pp. 9-17.

Henry, Marguerite, "What I Know about Wesley Dennis," *Young Wings,* January, 1952, pp. 8 and 14.

Lukens, Rebecca, "Marguerite Henry," *Dictionary of Literary Biography,* Volume 22: *American Writers for Children, 1900-1960,* Gale, 1983, pp. 217-22.

Wilt, Miriam E., "In Marguerite Henry—The Thread That Runs So True," *Elementary English,* November, 1954, pp. 387-95.

FOR MORE INFORMATION SEE:

BOOKS

Children's Literature Review, Volume 4, Gale, 1982, pp. 104-16.

Twentieth-Century Children's Writers, third edition, St. James Press, 1989, pp. 443-44.

PERIODICALS

Elementary English, January, 1967, pp. 7-11.

Horn Book, January-February, 1950, pp. 18-24; February, 1965.

New York Times Book Review, January 15, 1967, p. 28.

Times Literary Supplement, December 9, 1965, p. 1134.

—*Sketch by Polly A. Vedder*

*   *   *

HENTOFF, Nat 1925-

PERSONAL: Full name is Nathan Irving Hentoff; born June 10, 1925, in Boston, MA; son of Simon (a salesman) and Lena (Katzenberg) Hentoff; married Miriam Sargent, 1950 (divorced, 1950); married Trudi Bernstein, September 2, 1954 (divorced August, 1959); married Margot Goodman, August 15, 1959; children: (second marriage) Jessica, Miranda; (third marriage) Nicholas, Thomas. *Education:* Northeastern University, B.A. (with highest honors), 1946; graduate study at Harvard University, 1946, and Sorbonne, 1950.

*ADDRESSES: Home—*37 West 12th St., New York, NY 10011. *Office—* Village Voice, 842 Broadway, New York, NY 10003.

CAREER: WMEX (radio station), Boston, MA, writer, producer, and announcer, 1944-53; *Downbeat,* New York City, associate editor, 1953-57; *Village Voice,* New York City, columnist, 1957—; *New Yorker,* New York City, staff writer, 1960—; *Washington Post,* Washington, DC, columnist, 1984—. Reviewer for several magazines, including, *New York Herald Tribune Book*

Week, Peace News, and *Reporter.* Adjunct associate professor, New York University; member of faculty, New School of Social Research. Lecturer at schools and colleges.

MEMBER: Authors League of America, American Civil Liberties Union (board member), American Federation of Television and Radio Artists, Reporters Committee for Freedom of the Press (steering committee), PEN (Freedom to Write Committee), New York Civil Liberties Union.

AWARDS, HONORS: Children's Spring Book Festival Award, *New York Herald Tribune,* and Nancy Bloch Award, both 1965, Woodward Park School Award, 1966, all for *Jazz Country;* Golden Archer Award, 1980, for *This School Is Driving Me Crazy;* Hugh M. Hefner First Amendment Award, Deadline Club, 1981, for *The First Freedom: The Tumultuous History of Free Speech in America;* Cranberry Award List, Acton Public Library, 1983, for *The Day They Came to Arrest the Book.*

WRITINGS:

YOUNG ADULT FICTION

Jazz Country, Harper, 1965.

I'm Really Dragged but Nothing Gets Me Down, Simon and Schuster, 1971.

In the Country of Ourselves, Simon and Schuster, 1971.

This School Is Driving Me Crazy, Delacorte, 1976.

Does This School Have Capital Punishment?, Delacorte, 1981.

The Day They Came to Arrest the Book, Delacorte, 1982.

YOUNG ADULT NONFICTION

Journey into Jazz, illustrations by David Stone Martin, Coward McCann, 1968.

The First Freedom: The Tumultuous History of Free Speech in America, Delacorte, 1980.

American Heroes: In and Out of School, Delacorte, 1987.

NOVELS

Call the Keeper, Viking, 1966.

Onwards!, Simon and Schuster, 1967.

Blues for Charlie Darwin, Morrow, 1982.

The Man from Internal Affairs, Mysterious Press, 1985.

OTHER

(Editor with Nat Shapiro) *Hear Me Talking to Ya: The Story of Jazz by the Men Who Made It,* Rinehart, 1955.

(Editor with Shapiro) *The Jazz Makers,* Rinehart, 1957.

(Editor with Albert McCarthy) *Jazz: New Perspectives on the History of Jazz by Twelve of the World's Foremost Jazz Critics and Scholars,* Rinehart, 1959.

Peace Agitator: The Story of A. J. Muste, Macmillan, 1963.

The New Equality, Viking, 1964.

Our Children Are Dying, Viking, 1966.

(Editor) *The Essays of A. J. Muste,* Bobbs-Merrill, 1967.

A Doctor among the Addicts, Rand McNally, 1967.

Nat Hentoff in his office at the *Village Voice*.

A Political Life: The Education of John V. Lindsay, Knopf, 1969.

(Author of introduction) *The London Novels of Colin MacInnes,* Farrar, Straus, 1969.

(Editor and author of introduction) *Black Anti-Semitism and Jewish Racism,* Schocken, 1970.

(With others) *State Secrets: Police Surveillance in America,* Holt, 1973.

The Jazz Life, Da Capo Press, 1975.

Jazz Is, Random House, 1976.

Does Anybody Give a Damn?: Nat Hentoff on Education, Knopf, 1977.

(Editor with Shapiro) *The Jazz Makers: Essays on the Greats of Jazz,* Da Capo Press, 1979.

(Author of introduction) Pauline Rivelli, editor, *Giants of Black Music,* Da Capo Press, 1980.

(Author of introduction) Max Gordon, *Live at the Village Vanguard,* Da Capo Press, 1982.

(With Tim Keefe and Howard Levine) *The 1984 Calendar: An American History,* Point Blank Press, 1983.

(Author of introduction) Frederick Ramsey, editor, *Jazzmen,* Limelight Editions, 1985.

Boston Boy (memoir), Knopf, 1986.

(Author of introduction) K. Abe, editor, *Jazz Giants,* Watson-Guptill Publications, 1988.

John Cardinal O'Connor: At the Storm Center of a Changing American Church, Scribner, 1988.

SIDELIGHTS: Nat Hentoff is an established jazz critic, author of novels for young people, and respected civil rights advocate. He traces his enthusiasm for writing to childhood interests. "I sometimes wonder," he wrote in

American Libraries, "if I would know more by now if I had simply stayed in the library during [my school years] and not gone to school at all." The freedom of the public library contrasted with the routines of public schooling, where required readings left little time for independent study. In the library, Hentoff felt both mature and powerful, because it was up to him to choose the books he read. "I never ceased marveling at the continual surprises that came with my first library card," he commented in *American Libraries,* "the library was—and still is—a place where one can find and keep on finding one's own surprises." Hentoff's love of learning convinced him to pursue a writing career.

In an essay for *Contemporary Authors Autobiography Series (CAAS),* Hentoff recalled an interview during which he was asked to cite the key influences on his life and work. "No one had ever asked me that before," Hentoff remarked. "But without a pause, I knew, and gave, the answer: Being Jewish. Jazz. The First Amendment." In his numerous writings, Hentoff has portrayed jazz from the musician's point of view, spoken against racism and anti-Semitism, and assembled a history of free speech in America for young readers. Despite his wide-ranging interests, Hentoff sees a fundamental similarity between his ethnicity, his taste for jazz, and his criticism of authority: each contributes to his exclusion from "conventional" American society.

Hentoff's parents were Russian-Jewish immigrants who settled in Roxbury, a traditionally Jewish neighborhood of Boston. During the 1930s and early 1940s, a mood of anti-Semitism swept the country. "There were pamphlets, broadsides, newspapers that spread the inciteful word that Jews were simultaneously in the highest ranks of international communism while also being capitalist bloodsuckers who were draining the very life out of working people," Hentoff recalled in *CAAS.* This prejudice gave rise to persecution; encounters between Jews and anti-Semites often resulted in violence. The obvious conflict between the promise of the "melting pot" and abundant American racism made Hentoff question authority. "I was an outsider," he noted. "I thought like an outsider; and therefore I learned to be continually skeptical of what insiders with power said they believed." Hentoff further remarked: "As I grew older, the knowledge of what it feels like to be an outcast led me to learn empathy with others of the excluded—blacks, women, homosexuals, and in time, Arab-Americans, Hispanics, [and] Catholics.... Over the years I have written primarily about people on the margins."

In addition to his initial perception of himself as an outsider, Hentoff was significantly influenced by another ideological aspect of his Jewish community. As a boy Hentoff was taught that the strength of the Jewish neighborhood resided in a Jewish idea of social justice, or fairness. "I constantly heard that to be just is to be Jewish, and to be unjust is un-Jewish," he explained in *CAAS.* "Where I lived [they] believed in the perfectibility of man and therefore of society. Accordingly, they believed justice.... was a realistic possibility, let alone necessity, in any new world worth making."

At age ten Hentoff began commuting daily from Roxbury to attend the prestigious Boston Latin School. "Under the purple-and-white flag of Boston Latin School," wrote Hentoff in his memoir, *Boston Boy,* "we were all united—the Irish, the Italians, the Jews, the Greeks, the Scots, the Armenians, the relatively few Yankees ... and the far fewer blacks." Despite the student body's ethnic diversity, the teachers "paid no attention to where we came from, to whether our parents worked in grocery stores or were State Street bankers. The only thing that counted was whether you were willing to do the work, the incessant work, it took to stay in Boston Latin."

During his travels to and from Boston Latin, Hentoff was introduced to jazz. He first heard jazz music over a loud speaker outside a downtown record store. Hentoff was immediately captivated by "a fierce wailing of brass and reeds, a surging, pulsing cry that made me cry out too." Boston was home to many of the great jazz musicians of the period, and Hentoff quickly learned where he could find these men playing their passionate, "dangerous" music. He hid the jazz magazine *Downbeat* in his geography book during the day; on weekends, he sneaked out to hear his favorite musicians play in bars and clubs throughout the city. Hentoff reminisced in *Boston Boy:* "Acting as if I had no reason to ask what the minimum age was, and already needing a shave practically every day, I went to Sunday jam sessions in downtown Boston at the Ken Club. A dark, sleazy joint,

but on those afternoons it was transformed into a glorious battlefield, a tournament of giants, horn-playing giants."

Upon graduating from Boston Latin, Hentoff entered Northeastern University, where he worked as a staff writer on the *Northeastern News,* a student-run newspaper. At the beginning of his junior year, Hentoff was named editor of the paper. Under his direction, student reporters began to investigate corruption in city government. A struggle emerged between the university administration and the student journalists when Hentoff outlined a controversial story on the university trustees. The president got word of Hentoff's plan and gave the editorial staff a choice: back off the story or resign. Rather than sacrifice their right to publish the truth, the entire staff quit the paper. "At that point," Hentoff remarked in *Boston Boy,* "I became passionately interested in freedom of the press."

Upon graduating from Northeastern, Hentoff took a job hosting a regular jazz program at WMEX in Boston. He combined live interviews with musical programming, and held face-to-face conversations with some of his boyhood heroes, including saxophonist Charlie Parker

Originally a jazz critic, Hentoff was coaxed into writing young adult fiction—such as *Does This School Have Capital Punishment?*—by an editor at Harper & Row.

An outspoken civil rights advocate, Hentoff focuses on the issue of censorship in a public school in *The Day They Came to Arrest the Book.*

and composer Duke Ellington. While he worked at the radio station, Hentoff learned to respect the lifestyle of the jazz performer, which usually included working in crowded, smoky, and often hostile, nightclubs, where both pay and job security were scant. Despite these conditions, Hentoff found that the best jazz musicians had devoted themselves to maintaining the purity of their art.

In the early 1950s Hentoff began writing a review column for *Downbeat.* Although considered a controversial critic, Hentoff and his opinions quickly gained recognition in the jazz world. In 1953, he was invited to New York City to become the editor of *Downbeat.* During his years with *Downbeat,* Hentoff was "utterly immersed in the jazz-world—reviewing musicians in clubs every night, writing [about jazz] during the day and all through the weekends." He added in *CAAS:* "It was a glorious period. The giants of jazz were still jousting and surprising their audiences and themselves.... When I was a boy I romanticized jazz creators. By the time I was working for *Downbeat* I knew their flaws as well as their strengths, but I continued to admire the honesty and courage of their art."

Hentoff was released by *Downbeat* in 1957. "I was fired," he claimed in *CAAS,* "because I had been

agitating for some time for someone black to be hired in the New York office. Here we were ... profiting from an essentially black American music, but no blacks were on staff." After his release, Hentoff found free lance work difficult to come by because he was stereotyped as a jazz critic. He wrote occasional music reviews for literary magazines but wasn't publishing regularly enough to earn a living. Despite the financial risk involved, Hentoff eventually decided to break away from jazz writing. After his experiences with *Downbeat* management and the *Northeastern News,* he saw injustice all around him, and he longed to write social criticism regularly.

In 1958 Hentoff was given a column at a small weekly paper in New York's Greenwich Village called the *Village Voice.* The paper's finances were so unsure that Hentoff agreed to work without pay on the sole condition that he never be asked to write about jazz. The paper's circulation increased rapidly, and Hentoff was able to escape the jazz-writer stereotype by writing on such topics as civil liberties, education, politics, corporal punishment, and the supreme court.

In 1960, the Harper and Row publishing company asked Hentoff if he would try writing a book for young adults. Hentoff refused at first, feeling that a younger audience would limit him unfairly in matters of subject and style. He was persuaded to attempt the book when Ursula Nordstrom, the head of Harper and Row's young readers division, convinced him that there were plenty of young readers who would invest their time in a challenging book. Nordstrom left Hentoff free to employ an adult vocabulary and plot. The result was *Jazz Country,* a novel which juxtaposed the lifestyles of a young white musician trying to break into the jazz scene and the older, accomplished black musicians to whom he looks for guidance. The novel detailed the hard work that accompanies success and introduced young readers to a world of disciplined musical creativity. "I wanted to show all kids how rich and deep this music is," Hentoff said in *CAAS.*

Hentoff has also focused on civil liberties in his young adult fiction. In *The Day They Came to Arrest the Book,* he dealt with the issue of censorship in public schools. When a black student's father is offended by the characterization of a fugitive slave in Mark Twain's *Huckleberry Finn,* the schoolboard attempts to have the book removed from the school library. The school librarian and some vocal students defend the book, which is eventually returned to circulate freely. Reviewers have noticed that the characters who favor the banning of *Huckleberry Finn* are represented by reasonable arguments, despite their political defeat.

Although critics generally applaud the lessons of books such as *The Day They Came to Arrest the Book,* Hentoff has been criticized for reducing his characters to mere representatives of ideology who do not hold the reader's interest as "real" people. Hentoff, however, is primarily concerned with the presentation of social and political dialogue through fiction. In his opinion, far too many children are forced to accept doctrine in place of making reasoned, personal decisions. "Children need to learn to think for themselves," he remarked in *CAAS.* Toward that end, Hentoff wrote *The First Freedom: The Tumultuous History of Free Speech in America,* a concise work which outlines historical interpretations of the First Amendment. It is particularly important to Hentoff that all young people in America know how fundamental, and just how fragile, their rights to free speech and expression are. "Of all my obsessions," Hentoff stated in *Boston Boy,* "this is the strongest .... If children do not get the sense that the Constitution, very much including the Bill of Rights, actually belongs to them, they will grow up indifferent to their own—and other's—liberties and rights. And if enough of the citizenry are careless in these matters, those liberties and rights will be suicidally lost."

WORKS CITED:

Hentoff, Nat, *Contemporary Authors Autobiography Series,* Volume 6, Gale, 1988, p. 165-74.
Hentoff, N., *Boston Boy,* Knopf, 1986.
Hentoff, N., "The Saturday Library Matinee," *American Libraries,* April, 1976.

FOR MORE INFORMATION SEE:

BOOKS

Arbuthnot, May Hill and Zena Sutherland, *Children and Books,* 4th edition, Scott, Foresman, 1972.
Children's Literature Review, Volume 1, Gale, 1976, p. 107-109.
de Montreville, Doris and Donna Hill, editors, *Third Book of Junior Authors,* H. W. Wilson, 1972, p. 124.
Twentieth-Century Children's Authors, St. Martin's Press, 1978.

PERIODICALS

Harper's, November, 1966; April, 1966, p. 81ff.
Horn Book, December, 1972, p. 578; August, 1981, p. 432ff.
Los Angeles Times, April 13, 1980.
Nation, November 14, 1966.
Negro Digest, June, 1965; March, 1967.
Negro History Bulletin, March, 1971.
Newsweek, December 21, 1964; September 5, 1966; September 15, 1969.
New Yorker, September 17, 1966.
New York Times, May 23, 1968; September 11, 1969; March 21, 1980.
New York Times Book Review, April 27, 1986, p. 34.
Saturday Review, September 19, 1970, p. 74ff; May 22, 1971, p. 60ff; July 21, 1979, p. 22ff.
School Library Journal, March, 1988, p. 114ff.
Spectator, April 7, 1967.
Time, August 12, 1966; October 11, 1968, p. 109.
Times Educational Supplement, January 20, 1978.
Times Literary Supplement, May 19, 1966, p. 442.
Village Voice, November 24, 1966; July 18, 1968; May 23, 1977.
Wilson Library Bulletin, November, 1968, p. 261ff; May, 1974, p. 742ff.*

HIGHWATER, Jamake 1942(?)- (J Marks, J Marks-Highwater)

PERSONAL: Full name is Jamake Mamake Highwater; given name is pronounced "ja-*mah*-ka"; actual birthdate and location unknown, though many sources say February 14, 1942(?), in Montana; son of Jamie (a rodeo clown and movie stuntman) and Amana (Bonneville) Highwater; adopted at or about age of seven by Alexander and Marcia Marks. *Education:* Attended a community college and a university in California.

ADDRESSES: Office—Native Lands Foundation, Little River Farm, Rt. 97, Hampton, CT 06247. *Agent*—Alfred Hart, Fox Chase Agency, Ledger Bldg., Philadelphia, PA 19106.

CAREER: Writer. Choreographer in San Francisco, CA, beginning in 1954; Contemporary Center, San Francisco, founder of modern dance troupe, 1950s and 1960s; lecturer at various universities in United States and Canada, 1970s; senior editor, Fodor's travel guides, 1971-75; New York University, New York City, graduate lecturer at School of Continuing Education, 1982; Columbia University, Graduate School of Architecture, New York City, adjunct assistant professor, 1984, visiting scholar, 1985; writer. Writer and host of television shows for Public Broadcasting Service (PBS), 1977, *Indian America* for WHET-TV, New York City, 1982, and of the documentaries *The Primal Mind,* PBS, 1985, and *Native Land,* PBS, 1986; guest on television shows, including *Six Great Ideas* and *Red, White, and Black: Ethnic Dance in America,* both for PBS, 1982. Comoderator and organizer of "Indian America: Past, Present and Future," Aspen Institute's art festivals and seminars, 1982-83; general director of Native Arts Festival, Rice University, 1986; general director of "Festival Mythos: A Celebration of Multicultural Myth-

JAMAKE HIGHWATER

ologies in the Arts," Philadelphia, 1991. Member of President Carter's art task force, Commission on Mental Health, 1977-78; member of task force on the individual artist, New York State Arts Council, 1981-82; board member, American Poetry Center, 1990—; member of national advisory panel, PEN Fellowships in the Arts, 1990—; founding president of Native Lands Foundation; founding member and past president of American Indian Community House, New York City; member of National Support Committee of the Native American Rights Fund; nominator for awards in the visual arts for the Rockefeller Foundation and the National Endowment for the Humanities.

MEMBER: PEN American Center (executive board, 1984-86), American Federation of Television and Radio Artists, Authors Guild, Dramatists Guild, Business Music, Inc.

AWARDS, HONORS: Honorary Citizen of Oklahoma, 1977; Newbery Honor Award, 1978, *Boston Globe/Horn Book* Award, and Best Book for Young Adults award from American Library Association, 1978, all for *Anpao: An American Indian Odyssey;* named Piitai Sahkomaapii, or "Eagle Son," by Blood Band of Blackfeet Nation of Alberta, Canada, 1979, for achievements on behalf of Indian culture; Jane Addams Peace Award, 1979, for *Many Smokes, Many Moons;* Best Book for Young Adults award from *School Library Journal,* 1980, for *The Sun, He Dies;* Anisfield-Wolf Award from the Cleveland Foundation, 1981, and citation as one of three hundred books chosen by the American Publishers Association to represent America at the Moscow International Book Fair, both for *Song from the Earth;* Virginia McCormick Scully Literary Award, 1982, for *The Primal Mind;* Notable Children's Book award, Best Books for Young Adults award from American Library Association, and citation as one of the best books of 1984 from *School Library Journal,* all 1984, all for *Legend Days;* honorary doctor of fine arts, Minneapolis College of Art and Design, 1986; Best Book for Young Adults award from American Library Association, 1986, for *Legend Days* and *The Ceremony of Innocence;* best film of the year, National Educational Film Festival, 1986, and ACE Award, National Cable Television Association, 1990, both for *The Primal Mind.*

WRITINGS:

(Under pseudonym J Marks) *Rock and Other Four Letter Words: Music of the Electric Generation,* Bantam, 1968.
(Editor under name J Marks-Highwater, with Eugene Fodor) *Europe under Twenty-Five: A Young Person's Guide,* Fodor's, 1971.
(Under pseudonym J Marks) *Mick Jagger: The Singer Not the Song,* Curtis Books, 1973, published under name J Marks-Highwater as *Mick Jagger,* Popular Library, 1974.
Fodor's Indian America, McKay, 1975.
Song from the Earth: American Indian Painting (Literary Book Club Selection), Little, Brown, 1976.

Ritual of the Wind: North American Indian Ceremonies, Music, and Dances, Viking, 1977.
Anpao: An American Indian Odyssey, Lippincott, 1977.
Journey to the Sky: A Novel about the True Adventures of Two Men in Search of the Lost Maya Kingdom, Crowell, 1978.
Many Smokes, Many Moons: A Chronology of American Indian History through Indian Art, Lippincott, 1978.
Dance: Rituals of Experience, A & W Publishers, 1978.
Masterpieces of American Indian Painting, two folios, limited and signed edition, Folio/Bell Editions, 1979-83.
The Sun, He Dies: A Novel about the End of the Aztec World, Lippincott, 1980.
The Sweet Grass Lives On: Fifty Contemporary North American Indian Artists, Harper, 1981.
The Primal Mind: Vision and Reality in Indian America (also see below), Harper, 1981.
Moonsong Lullaby (poems), Morrow, 1981.
Eyes of Darkness (novel), Morrow, 1983.
Arts of the Indian Americas: Leaves from the Sacred Tree, Harper, 1983.
Words in the Blood: Contemporary Indian Writers of North and South America, Meridian, 1984.
Legend Days (first book of "Ghost Horse" cycle), Harper, 1984.
The Ceremony of Innocence (second book of "Ghost Horse" cycle), Harper, 1984.
The Primal Mind (television script; broadcast by PBS, 1985), Cinema Guild, 1985.
I Wear the Morning Star (third book of "Ghost Horse" cycle), Harper, 1986.
Native Land: Nomads of the Dawn (television script; also see below; broadcast by PBS, 1986), Cinema Guild, 1986.
Native Land: Sagas of American Civilizations (based on PBS program), Little, Brown, 1986.
Shadow Show: An Autobiographical Insinuation, Alfred Van der Marck, 1986.
Myth and Sexuality, New American Library, 1990.
Songs for the Seasons (poems), Morrow, in press.
The World of 1492: "The Americas," Holt, in press.
Blood Fire (tentative title; fourth book of "Ghost Horse" cycle), Grove, in press.

AUTHOR OF INTRODUCTION

Bear's Heart, Lippincott, 1976.
Charles Eastman, *Indian Boyhood,* Rio Grande Press, 1976.
One Hundred Years of American Indian Painting, Oklahoma Museum of Art, 1977.
Master Pueblo Potters, ACA Galleries, 1980.

OTHER

Music critic and contributor to *New Grove Dictionary of American Music.* Contributor of articles and critiques to literary journals, including *New York Times, Chicago Tribune, Archaeology, Commonweal, Esquire, Dance Magazine, Saturday Review,* and *American Book Review.* Contributing editor, *Stereo Review,* 1972-79, *Indian Trader,* 1977-80, *New York Arts Journal,* 1978-86, and *Native Arts/West,* 1980-81; classical music editor,

Highwater describes his first novel, *Anpao*, with its blend of old and new Indian myth, as a "river of memory of a people." (Cover illustration by Fritz Scholder.)

Soho Weekly News, 1975-79, and *Christian Science Monitor*.

ADAPTATIONS: Anpao: An American Indian Odyssey was adapted into a sound recording, Folkways Records, 1978.

WORK IN PROGRESS: Athletes of the Gods: The Ritual Life of Sport; I Took the Fire: A Memoir; The Magic Ring, a novel; *Beyond the Looking Glass: 22 Meditations on Myth and Metaphor in the Arts.*

SIDELIGHTS: Jamake Highwater is a leading commentator on American Indian culture. A descendent of Blackfeet and Cherokee Indians, Highwater has received numerous accolades for exploring Indian myths, tales, and rituals in works of fiction and nonfiction. "Highwater's work is so important!," renowned mythologist Joseph Campbell once declared. "He has touched upon so many central themes of world mythology with both aesthetic and intellectual insight." Though Highwater's writings hold appeal for all age groups, he has been especially popular among young adults. "I value young readers," Highwater wrote in *Contemporary Authors, Autobiography Series* (*CAAS*). "But I cherish them as readers and not as children, because I strongly reject the

notion that writers create good books for specific, 'target audiences.'" Highwater's approach has won him a broad readership and several literary awards, including the prestigious Newbery Honor Award, which he received in 1978 for his first novel, *Anpao: An American Indian Odyssey.* In addition to *Anpao,* Highwater has written several other novels and nonfiction works on Indian life, art, dance, and history.

Highwater's success as an adult came after experiencing a troubled childhood. Because his natural parents were too poor and unstable to care for him, Highwater was placed in an orphanage while they were still alive. When he was adopted by Alexander and Marcia Marks, a California Anglo family, they insisted on keeping secret many of the details of his early life. Carl R. Shirley quoted Highwater in *Dictionary of Literary Biography Yearbook: 1985:* "I was adopted between the age of six and ten when adoption was a highly secretive matter—to such an extent that the state in which I was adopted permanently sealed all records of my birth and adoption. I have no original birth certificate. Since my adoption as a child I was put in the position of keeping my origins secret at my foster family's insistence. It is often difficult to know the difference between what I personally remember and what I was told." According to his autobiographical statement in *Children's Literature Review,* Highwater knows only that he "was born in the early forties and was raised in northern Montana and southern Alberta, Canada."

Though Highwater experienced some difficulties with his foster family, he at least could rely on getting the necessities of life—food, shelter, clothing, and education. He also gained a new set of siblings, and the youngest daughter became his close friend. They shared a love of music, dance, and books. She had a wonderful sense of humor and would do all sorts of things to make them laugh. In his *CAAS* entry Highwater described the significance of his relationship with her. "For many years this youngest of my sisters was the single most important person in my life. My love for her and my need for her were so massive that they were painful. Then, one day, not very long after I had become her brother, she went away. Her marriage and departure from our home devastated me. I took my resentment out on everyone . . . . Today I can joke about the old breach between us, but at the time it seemed like ultimate abandonment. Even during that debacle, I doggedly persisted in my affection for my sister. She was the only person whose approval I sought. It took me years to recognize that as a child without a history or life of my own, I had wanted to live out my existence through my sister's life."

In addition to his sister, Highwater had two other early positive influences. The first were the Dorrs, neighbors who gave Highwater a key to their house so he could come in when he was locked out of his foster family's house. While there Highwater would listen to classical music, read novels, and dance around the living room. He would also go there on Sunday mornings to listen to gospel music on the radio. The other positive influence was a teacher named Alta Black, who helped him through his troubles at school. "I was not liked, and so I took no delight in living," Highwater recollected in *CAAS*. "I didn't have a single friend or a moment of happiness in school, until a social studies teacher, named Alta Black, made me feel as if she cared about me. Once I felt her approval, I did anything to keep her good opinion of me. And the effort to please her gave me the motivation to become one of the most accomplished students in school.... And it was also Alta Black who gave me an old Royal portable typewriter and an instruction book, telling me that one night she had dreamed that I was going to be a writer."

During junior high and high school Alta Black continued to help Highwater with his schoolwork. After graduating he wanted to go on to college, but financing his education was a problem. During the 1950s there were few scholarships available and no guaranteed student loans. At first he attended a small, affordable community college, but he left when he realized he was not being challenged intellectually. Next he tried a major state university that required Reserve Officers Training Corps (ROTC) training, but this arrangement soon ended after Highwater decided he "absolutely could not endure this bristling, militant, and macho bullshit that was supposed to make a man out of me," he explained in *CAAS*. He further noted, "I did what I had to do, and eventually I managed to get the education I wanted. Under the circumstances, however, I always decline to make formal mention of my education in resumes and entries in various biographical directories. Even when I was appointed a lecturer at New York University and an [adjunct] assistant professor at Columbia University, I was hired without providing educational data."

At the beginning of his writing career Highwater felt himself to be part of both the Indian and Anglo cultures. His Indian heritage, however, exerted a greater influence on him after 1969, the year Indians took over Alcatraz island and claimed ownership. He reflected on the impact of the incident in *Something about the Author:* "With the Alcatraz takeover I was fired with a sense of visibility and courage as an Indian person. It was in 1969 that I began work on my first 'Indian' book which would bear my name, Jamake Highwater. It was called *Indian America: A Cultural and Travel Guide.*" Since 1969 Highwater has focused much of his writing on Indian ideas, some of which he explained to Sarah Crichton in a *Publishers Weekly* interview: "To the Indian mentality, dead people walk and things go backward and forward in time, and these are absolutely real and vivid ideas to my head.... And more than that, the Indian world is one of the few worlds where human identity is not a major issue. In this society, you're not permitted any kind of personal transformation. In ours, it is expected. We can even change gender if we want."

Highwater's first novel, *Anpao,* tells the story of an Indian boy's entrance into adulthood. At the beginning Anpao meets a beautiful girl named Ko-ko-mik-e-is who

refuses all offers of marriage until she meets Anpao. She says she will marry him if he can get permission from the Sun. This prompts Anpao to begin his journey. He travels with his brother Oapna, who says everything in reverse. Oapna dies during their travels, but by the story's end Anpao sees that Oapna is actually the contrary side of his own personality. Anpao gains experience and wisdom as he travels the earth and encounters a variety of creatures, eventually obtaining permission from the Sun to marry Ko-ko-mik-e-is. Highwater says at the end of the book in "The Storyteller's Farewell" that the novel is a combination of old and new Indian legends. "But old or new, the stories have no known authors. They exist as the river of memory of a people, surging with their images and their rich meanings from one place to another, from one generation to the next—the tellers and the told so intermingled in time and space that no one can separate them."

Anpao was a literary success, winning the Newbery Honor Award in 1978. Although critical response to *Anpao* was largely favorable, Jane Yolen claimed in the *New York Times Book Review* that the book read more like a series of Indian tales rather than as a coherent novel. Still, Yolen affirmed: "I applaud Highwater's effort. His retelling of the tales is fluid and in many

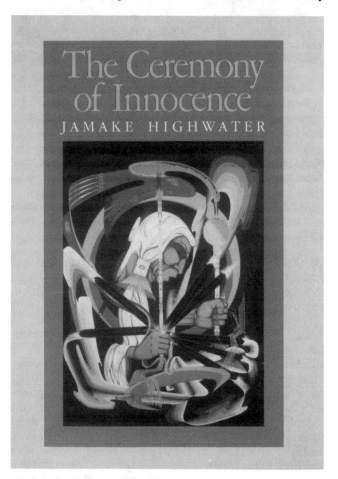

The Ceremony of Innocence is the second novel in Highwater's award-winning "Ghost Horse" quartet. (Cover illustration by Blackbear Bosin.)

In this third "Ghost Horse" novel, the youthful hardships and dreams of a main character named Sitko reflect Highwater's own childhood. (Cover illustration by David P. Bradley.)

instances compelling. The book cries to be read aloud." In addition, *Washington Post Book World* contributor Virginia Haviland praised "the author's gift for using the poetic, dignified language required of tellers of great epics." Haviland concluded that the novel is an "enduring book" that holds appeal for all age groups. Shirley expressed a similar sentiment: "The fact that *Anpao* won the Newbery Award and thus has frequently been characterized as a children's work has probably prevented many adults from savoring the richness of its language and the magic of its story. It is a fine novel that can be enjoyed by all readers."

During the 1970s Highwater began writing extensively on Indian history and art. Some of the nonfiction books he produced include *Song from the Earth: American Indian Painting,* which traces the increasing interest in Indian art from the nineteenth century to the 1960s and features interviews with nine contemporary Indian artists; *Ritual of the Wind: North American Indian Ceremonies, Music, and Dances,* which contains Highwater's descriptions of Indian rituals; and *Many Smokes, Many Moons: A Chronology of American Indian History through Indian Art,* a book that focuses

on Indian art from 3500 B.C. to modern day and details some of the destructive effects whites have had on Indians over the centuries. In his interview with Jane B. Katz, published in *This Song Remembers: Self-Portraits of Native Americans in the Arts,* Highwater reflected on the close connection between Indians and art. "For the Indian, art is not reserved for a leisure class, as it is in Anglo society. It is part of our fundamental way of thinking. We are an aesthetic people. Most primal people are. We represent a constant chord that's been resounding ever since man began.... This idea of life as art is part of being Indian. It's not quaint or curious or charming. It's fundamental, like plowing a field. There's great beauty in plowing a field."

In 1980 Highwater published *The Sun, He Dies: A Novel about the End of the Aztec World,* which some have called his best work. Before writing this historical novel, Highwater conducted extensive background research. The narrator of the story is Nanautzin, an Aztec Indian who becomes the spokesperson of Montezuma, the Aztec leader. Through Nanautzin the reader is able to gain insight into the development and destruction of the Aztecs, whose history covered more than two thousand years before Hernando Cortes destroyed it in six. Kurt Vonnegut, Jr., who is quoted by Shirley, called *The Sun, He Dies* a "historical novel of a very high order ... a stunning revelation to all who have never before glimpsed the history of this hemisphere through a Native American's eyes." Not all reviews were favorable—some thought Nanautzin was not fully developed—yet John Adams commented in *School Library Journal* that although the story is not new, "never has it been told with the eloquent, progressively angry Indian voice Highwater has created."

Highwater continued his prolific output during the 1980s, writing nonfiction works, novels, a book of poems entitled *Moonsong Lullaby,* and television scripts for the Public Broadcasting Service, including *The Primal Mind* and *Native Land.* One of the most notable works to come out of this period is the "Ghost Horse" cycle. This award-winning quartet of novels consists of *Legend Days,* 1984, *The Ceremony of Innocence,* 1984, *I Wear the Morning Star,* 1986, and a novel in progress, tentatively titled *Blood Fire.* The cycle contains several autobiographical elements. Like Highwater, Sitko—a main character who first appears in *The Ceremony of Innocence*—had a mother of French and Indian ancestry who married a rodeo clown and movie stuntman. Sitko's similarly unstable home life resulted in placement in a foster home, and he faced a constant struggle to maintain his Indian vision.

Many reviewers find considerable merit in Highwater's works. Nellvena Duncan Eutsler averred in *Dictionary of Literary Biography* that "Jamake Highwater's metaphors are meaningful; his symbols are vivid; his imagery is awe-inspiring. Highwater creates for the reader an awareness of the earth and its wonders." Shirley also holds a high opinion of Highwater, calling him "a storyteller whose tales of Native Americans are splendid stylistic re-creations of the oral literature of his ances-

Like Highwater, Yesa, the protagonist in *Eyes of Darkness,* is divided by his ties to two very different cultures. (Cover illustration by David Montiel.)

tors. His novels ... stand as successful examples of modern efforts to capture the Indian legender's voice that has endured the centuries—the songs, the recitals of history, the tales and chants passed from storyteller to storyteller, from generation to generation."

Highwater commented on his interests: "I have focused upon the rituals and myths that make the ineffable momentarily visible in art and in religion. I have never been much concerned with the great currents of prosaic facts that some of us mistake for history. I have always preferred the night and the shadow side of existence, because I believe that the unknown is knowable and that the real effort of the artist is to describe the fragile place where the inner and outer worlds meet. My dear friend, the late Joseph Campbell, often complained that people confuse the meal with the menu and end up munching on cardboard. I have devoted my career to the meal, and I have left the menu to others."

WORKS CITED:

Adams, John, review of *The Sun, He Dies* in *School Library Journal,* October, 1980, p. 167.
Brochure on Jamake Highwater, produced by the Native Land Foundation.

Children's Literature Review, Volume 17, Gale, 1989, pp. 19-32.
Crichton, Sarah, "PW Interviews: Jamake Highwater," *Publishers Weekly,* November 6, 1978, pp. 6-8.
Eutsler, Nellvena Duncan, "Jamake Highwater," *Dictionary of Literary Biography,* Volume 52: *American Writers for Children since 1960,* Gale, 1986, pp. 185-92.
Haviland, Virginia, "Tales of the Tribes," *Washington Post Book World,* February 12, 1978, p. G4.
Highwater, Jamake, "The Storyteller's Farewell," in *Anpao: An American Indian Odyssey,* Lippincott, 1977.
Highwater, Jamake, "I Took the Fire," *Contemporary Authors, Autobiography Series,* Volume 7, Gale, 1988, pp. 69-83.
Katz, Jane B., editor, *This Song Remembers: Self-Portraits of Native Americans in the Arts,* Houghton, 1980, pp. 171-77.
Shirley, Carl R., "Jamake Highwater," *Dictionary of Literary Biography Yearbook: 1985,* Gale, 1986, pp. 359-366.
Something about the Author, Volume 32, Gale, 1983, pp. 92-96.
Yolen, Jane, review of *Anpao* in *New York Times Book Review,* February 5, 1978, p. 26.

FOR MORE INFORMATION SEE:

BOOKS

Contemporary Literary Criticism, Volume 12, Gale, 1980.

PERIODICALS

America, September 26, 1981.
American Indian Journal, July, 1980.
Booklist, March 1, 1986.
Catholic Library World, December, 1977.
Horn Book, February, 1978; June, 1984.
Interracial Books for Children Bulletin, Volume 16, number 8, 1985.
Language Arts, February, 1978.
Los Angeles Times Book Review, October 18, 1981.
New York Times Book Review, December 4, 1977; July 17, 1980.
Publishers Weekly, June 25, 1973; November 6, 1978; November 12, 1982.
San Francisco Review of Books, April, 1978.
Village Voice, May 3, 1983.
Voice of Youth Advocates, August, 1985.
Washington Post, August 5, 1980.
Washington Post Book World, December 7, 1986.

—*Sketch by James F. Kamp*

* * *

HOBAN, Lillian

PERSONAL: Former surname, Aberman; born in Philadelphia, PA; children: Phoebe, Abrom, Esme, Julia. *Education:* Attended Philadelphia Museum School of Art, 1942-44.

Arthur's Christmas Cookies, published in 1972, is the first book that Lillian Hoban wrote and illustrated by herself.

ADDRESSES: Home—Connecticut.

CAREER: Illustrator of books for children. Has also worked as a modern dance instructor in New York and Connecticut, and danced professionally on television during the 1950s.

AWARDS, HONORS: Boys Club Award, 1968, for *Charlie the Tramp* (written by Russell Hoban); Lewis Carroll Shelf Award and Christopher Award, Children's Book Category, both 1972, both for *Emmet Otter's Jug-Band Christmas* (written by R. Hoban).

WRITINGS:

SELF-ILLUSTRATED

(With Russell Hoban) *London Men and English Men,* Harper, 1962.
(With R. Hoban) *Some Snow Said Hello,* Harper, 1963.
(With R. Hoban) *Save My Place,* Norton, 1967.
Arthur's Christmas Cookies, Harper, 1972.
The Sugar Snow Spring, Harper, 1973.
Arthur's Honey Bear, Harper, 1974.
Arthur's Pen Pal, Harper, 1976.
Mr. Pig and Sonny Too, Harper, 1977.
Stick-in-the-Mud Turtle, Greenwillow, 1977.
I Met a Traveller, Harper, 1977.

Arthur's Prize Reader, Harper, 1978.
Turtle Spring, Greenwillow, 1978.
Harry's Song, Greenwillow, 1980.
Mr. Pig and Family, Harper, 1980.
Arthur's Funny Money, Harper, 1981.
No, No, Sammy Crow, Greenwillow, 1981.
It's Really Christmas, Greenwillow, 1982.
(With daughter Phoebe Hoban) *Ready ... Set ... Robot!,* Harper, 1982.
(With P. Hoban) *The Laziest Robot in Zone One,* Harper, 1983.
Arthur's Halloween Costume, Harper, 1984.
Grandparents' Houses, Greenwillow, 1984.
Arthur's Loose Tooth, Harper, 1985.
The Case of the Two Masked Robbers, Harper, 1985.
Silly Tilly and the Easter Bunny, Harper, 1987.
Silly Tilly's Thanksgiving Dinner, Harper, 1990.
Arthur's Great Big Valentine, Harper, 1991.
Arthur's Camp-Out, Harper, 1992.

ILLUSTRATOR

R. Hoban, *Herman the Loser,* Harper, 1961.
R. Hoban, *The Song in My Drum,* Harper, 1961.
R. Hoban, *The Sorely Trying Day,* Harper, 1964.
R. Hoban, *Nothing to Do,* Harper, 1964.
R. Hoban, *Bread and Jam for Frances,* Harper, 1964.
R. Hoban, *A Baby Sister for Frances,* Harper, 1964.
Robert P. Smith, *When I Am Big,* Harper, 1965.

In *It's Really Christmas,* Hoban tells the story of a field mouse, born in a box of tinsel, who eagerly awaits his first Christmas. (Illustration by Hoban.)

Pencil drawings, like this one from Johanna Hurwitz's *Nora and Mrs. Mind-Your-Own Business,* are among Hoban's favorite illustrating techniques.

R. Hoban, *What Happened When Jack and Daisy Tried to Fool with the Tooth Fairies,* Scholastic Book Services, 1965.

R. Hoban, *The Story of Hester Mouse Who Became a Writer and Saved Most of Her Sisters and Brothers and Some of Her Aunts and Uncles from the Owl,* Norton, 1965.

R. Hoban, *Tom and the Two Handles,* Harper, 1965.

Felice Holman, *Victoria's Castle,* Norton, 1966.

Carl Memling, *A Gift-Bear for the King,* Dutton, 1966.

Mitchell F. Jayne, *The Forest in the Wind,* Bobbs-Merrill, 1966.

R. Hoban, *The Little Brute Family,* Macmillan, 1966.

R. Hoban, *Goodnight* (verse), Norton, 1966.

R. Hoban, *Henry and the Monstrous Din,* Harper, 1966.

Miriam Cohen, *Will I Have a Friend?,* Macmillan, 1967.

R. Hoban, *Charlie the Tramp* (book and record), Four Winds, 1967, Scholastic Book Services, 1970.

R. Hoban, *The Mouse and His Child* (novel), Harper, 1967.

R. Hoban, *The Stone Doll of Sister Brute,* Macmillan, 1968.

R. Hoban, *A Birthday for Frances,* Harper, 1968.

R. Hoban, *The Pedaling Man, and Other Poems,* Norton, 1968.

R. Hoban, *Ugly Bird,* Macmillan, 1969.

Jan Wahl, *A Wolf of My Own,* Macmillan, 1969.

R. Hoban, *Harvey's Hideout,* Parents' Magazine Press, 1969.

R. Hoban, *The Mole Family's Christmas,* Parents' Magazine Press, 1969.

R. Hoban, *Best Friends for Frances,* Harper, 1969.

Aileen T. Fisher, *In One Door and Out the Other: A Book of Poems,* Crowell, 1969.

R. Hoban, *A Bargain for Frances,* Harper, 1970.

Alma M. Whitney, *Just Awful,* Addison-Wesley, 1971.

Ellen Parsons, *Rainy Day Together,* Harper, 1971.

Meindert De Jong, *The Easter Cat,* Macmillan, 1971.

R. Hoban, *Emmet Otter's Jug-Band Christmas,* Parents' Magazine Press, 1971.

M. Cohen, *Best Friends,* Macmillan, 1971.

R. Hoban, *Egg Thoughts, and Other Frances Songs,* Harper, 1972.

M. Cohen, *The New Teacher,* Macmillan, 1972.

Marjorie Weinman Sharmat, *Sophie and Gussie,* Macmillan, 1973.

M. Cohen, *Tough Jim,* Macmillan, 1974.

William Cole, *What's Good for a Three-Year-Old?,* Holt, 1974.

Crescent Dragonwagon, *Strawberry Dress Escape,* Scribner, 1975.

Johanna Hurwitz, *Busybody Nora,* Morrow, 1976.

Janet Schulman, *The Big Hello,* Greenwillow, 1976.

Diane Wolkstein, *Squirrel's Song: A Hopi Indian Tale,* Knopf, 1976.

M. Cohen, *"Bee My Valentine!,"* Greenwillow, 1978.

T. Zagone, *No Nap for Me,* Dutton, 1978.

Sue Alexander, *Seymour the Prince,* Pantheon, 1979.

M. Cohen, *Lost in the Museum,* Greenwillow, 1979.

Judy Delton, *The New Girl at School,* Dutton, 1979.

Paula Kurzband Feder, *Where Does the Teacher Live?,* Dutton, 1979.

Ron Roy, *Awful Thursday,* Pantheon, 1979.

J. Schulman, *The Great Big Dummy,* Greenwillow, 1979.

M. W. Sharmat, *Say Hello, Vanessa,* Holiday House, 1979.

Nancy Willard, *Papa's Panda,* Harcourt, 1979.

M. Cohen, *First Grade Takes a Test,* Greenwillow, 1980.

M. Cohen, *No Good in Art,* Greenwillow, 1980.

J. Hurwitz, *Superduper Teddy,* Puffin, 1980.

Dorotha Ruthstrom, *The Big Kite Contest,* Pantheon, 1980.

M. Cohen, *Jim Meets the Thing,* Greenwillow, 1981.

Berniece Rabe, *The Balancing Girl,* Dutton, 1981.

M. Cohen, *So What?,* Greenwillow, 1982.

M. Cohen, *See You Tomorrow, Charles,* Greenwillow, 1983.

J. Delton, *I'm Telling You Now,* Dutton, 1983.

J. Hurwitz, *Rip-Roaring Russell,* Morrow, 1983.

M. Cohen, *Jim's Dog Muffins,* Greenwillow, 1984.

James Howe, *The Day the Teacher Went Bananas,* Dutton, 1984.

M. W. Sharmat, *The Story of Bentley Beaver,* Harper, 1984.

M. Cohen, *Liar, Liar, Pants on Fire!,* Greenwillow, 1985.

M. Cohen, *Starring First Grade,* Greenwillow, 1985.

M. W. Sharmat, *Attila the Angry,* Holiday House, 1985.

J. Hurwitz, *Russell Rides Again,* Morrow, 1985.

Elizabeth Winthrop, *Tough Eddie,* Dutton, 1985.

Ellen A. Switzer, *Lily Boop,* Crown, 1986.

M. Cohen, *Don't Eat Too Much Turkey!,* Greenwillow, 1987.

M. Cohen, *When Will I Read?,* Dell, 1987.

M. Cohen, *It's George!,* Greenwillow, 1988.

Julia Hoban, *Amy Loves the Sun,* Harper, 1988.

J. Hoban, *Amy Loves the Wind,* Harper, 1988.

J. Wahl, *Tales of Fuzzy Mouse: Six Cozy Stories for Bedtime,* Western, 1988.

J. Hurwitz, *Russell and Elisa,* Morrow, 1989.

J. Hurwitz, *Russell Sprouts,* Puffin, 1989.

J. Hoban, *Amy Loves the Rain,* Harper, 1989.

J. Hoban, *Amy Loves the Snow,* Harper, 1989.

J. Hoban, *Quick Chick,* Dutton, 1989.

M. Cohen, *See You in Second Grade,* Greenwillow, 1989.

M. Cohen, *The Real Skin Rubber Monster Mask,* Greenwillow, 1990.

Tony Johnston, *I'm Gonna Tell Mama I Want an Iguana* (poems), Putnam, 1990.

Shulamith Levey Oppenheim, *Waiting for Noah,* Harper, 1990.

Kristy Parker, *My Dad the Magnificent,* Dutton, 1990.

Meindert DeJong, *The Easter Cat,* Macmillan, 1991.

J. Hurwitz, *New Neighbors for Nora,* Morrow, 1991.

J. Hurwitz, *Nora and Mrs. Mind-Your-Own-Business,* Morrow, 1991.

J. Hurwitz, *"E" Is for Elisa,* Morrow, 1991.

T. Johnston, *Little Bear Sleeping,* Putnam, 1991.

Louise Borden, *Caps, Hats, Socks, and Mittens: A Book about the Four Seasons,* Scholastic, 1992.

ADAPTATIONS: Filmstrips entitled the *Frances Series* have been distributed by BFA Educational Media, and *Will I Have a Friend?,* by Macmillan in 1974.

SIDELIGHTS: Lillian Hoban, author and illustrator of books for children, spent much of her own childhood drawing and reading. Coming from a family of readers and museum-goers, she haunted the various neighborhood libraries and realized at an early age that she wanted to become an illustrator of children's books. She received a classical education at the Philadelphia High School for Girls and was awarded a scholarship to the Philadelphia Museum School of Art. Music and dance have played an important part in her life, but writing and illustrating books for children has remained a lifelong pursuit. Although she used pencil to illustrate several of the Frances books, a popular series about a little badger, she also likes to use a pen and ink wash for her drawings. Hoban finds comfort and contentment in drawing and painting, and her illustrations have graced the work of numerous other children's writers in addition to her own.

FOR MORE INFORMATION SEE:

BOOKS

Kingman, Lee, and others, compilers, *Illustrators of Children's Books: 1957-1966,* Horn Book, 1968.

I

IMPEY, Rose

PERSONAL: Born June 7, 1947, in Northwich, England; daughter of William Hall and Ella McVinnie; married Graham Impey; children: Rachel, Charlotte. *Education:* Attended Northumberland College of Education.

ADDRESSES: Home—38 Wanlip Rd., Syston, Leicester LE7 8PA, England.

CAREER: Has been employed as a bank clerk, primary school teacher in Leicester, and reader for a publishing company.

AWARDS, HONORS: Who's a Clever Girl, Then?, 1986, was included in the National Book League's list of Children's Books of the Year, as were *The Girls' Gang,* 1987, *A Letter to Father Christmas, Desperate for a Dog,* and *Scare Yourself to Sleep,* all 1989, and *The Ankle Grabber,* 1990; *Who's a Clever Girl, Then?* was named to Public Lending Right list of one hundred most-borrowed books, 1987; *Desperate for a Dog* was named to the short list of the Smarties Prize for Children's Books, Book Trust (England); Sheffield Children's Book Award, Sheffield Library Services, 1991, for *Joe's Cafe;* Prix Versele de litterature enfantine, Belgian Ligue des Familles, 1991, for French version of *Scare Yourself to Sleep.*

WRITINGS:

(Reteller) *The Ladybird Book of Fairy Tales,* illustrated by John Dyke and others, Ladybird, 1980.
(Reteller) *The Pied Piper of Hamelin,* illustrated by Richard Hook, Ladybird, 1985.
Who's a Clever Girl, Then?, illustrated by Andre Amstutz, Heinemann, 1985, published as *Who's a Bright Girl,* Barron's, 1989.
The Girl's Gang, illustrated by Glenys Ambrus, Heinemann, 1986.
The Not-So-Clever Genie, illustrated by Amstutz, Heinemann, 1987.

ROSE IMPEY

A Letter to Father Christmas, illustrated by Sue Porter, Orchard Books, 1988, published as *A Letter to Santa Claus,* Delacorte, 1989.
Desperate for a Dog, illustrated by Jolyne Knox, Dutton, 1988.
Houdini Dog, illustrated by Knox, Black, 1988.
Teddy's Story, illustrated by Porter, Heinemann, 1988.
Rabbit's Story, illustrated by Porter, Little Mammoth, 1988.
Be tu fhein an nighean, Acair, 1989.
You Herman, Me Mary!, illustrated by Amstutz, Heinemann, 1989.
Instant Sisters, Orchard, 1989, Macdonald & Co., 1990.

Revenge of the Rabbit, illustrated by Amstutz, Orchard Books, 1990.

(With Maureen Galvani) *My Mom and Our Dad,* Viking Kestrel, 1990.

(With Knox) *No-Name Dog,* Dutton, 1990.

Who's Afraid Now?, Longman/British Broadcasting Corporation (BBC) Books, 1991.

Trouble with the Tucker Twins, Viking, 1990.

Joe's Cafe, illustrated by Porter, Orchard Books/Little, Brown, 1991.

(With Porter) *Magical Tales from Toyland,* Treasure, 1991.

First Class, Orchard Books, 1992.

"THE BADDIES" SERIES

Baked Bean Queen, illustrated by Porter, Heinemann, 1986.

The Demon Kevin, illustrated by Porter, Heinemann, 1986.

Tough Teddy, illustrated by Porter, Heinemann, 1986.

The Bedtime Beast, illustrated by Porter, Heinemann, 1987.

The Little Smasher, illustrated by Porter, Heinemann, 1987.

The Toothbrush Monster, illustrated by Porter, Heinemann, 1987.

"CREEPIES" SERIES

The Flat Man, illustrated by Moira Kemp, Barron's, 1988.

Scare Yourself to Sleep, illustrated by Kemp, Barron's, 1988.

Jumble Joan, illustrated by Kemp, Barron's, 1989.

The Ankle Grabber, illustrated by Kemp, Barron's, 1989.

OTHER

Who's a Clever Girl, Then? has been translated into Welsh.

ADAPTATIONS: Who's Afraid Now? has been made into a cassette.

SIDELIGHTS: Rose Impey told *SATA:* "I left grammar school at sixteen feeling I had no talent for anything other than enjoying myself and having a good time. After some pretty dreadful career advice I ended up working in a bank! Banks are not places where people generally enjoy themselves and have a good time. I was soon terribly depressed and knew I had to get out—even if that meant going back to school for a while. I then trained as a primary teacher which suited me better than banking but still wasn't entirely right for me.

"I loved *reading* to classes and would have been happy spending the whole day doing that (in fact I sometimes did) and this is clearly where the desire to write began. I still spend a lot of time visiting schools, reading my work to children and when I am writing I have a strong sense of audience. I identify far more easily with storytellers than authors and I think this is evident in the way I write.

"Although I don't always write realistic stories much of my material comes from real life, either from my time as a teacher, or from my own family life. What I think I do well is to see the humour potential in a seemingly small event or anecdote and exaggerate it and elaborate on it until it makes a story. One of the most familiar cries in my household is, 'Oh mum, you do exaggerate.' And I do, but that's okay. If it makes a good story anything goes.

"The first story I wrote, 'Who's a Clever Girl, Then?' was contrived when one of my daughters asked for help on a story for a school assignment. I outlined a plot to her: A little girl, on her way to school, gets kidnapped by a gang of pirates. They want her to do the housework while they go off having adventures. But because she's a clever little girl she tricks the pirates and ends up captain of the ship. 'What do you think of that?' I asked triumphant. 'Rubbish,' she replied. 'Honestly, Mum. That wouldn't make a story.' I could hardly ignore the challenge so I wrote it to prove her wrong. The story was accepted immediately and I've just kept on writing ever since.

"I'm frequently asked why I write so much about girls, don't I like boys? Well, of course I do. But the fact is I am a girl, or I was; I have two sisters, two daughters, and most of my friends are female. Girls are what I know about; it isn't surprising I choose to write about what I know best.

"I've written a number of scary stories which are very popular with children but have met with some resistance from adults. My view is that those adults who are made uncomfortable by scary stories are the ones who as children were either unable to or prevented from working through their own childhood fears. Unfortunately, because of this they go on to make it hard for their own children to work on theirs. I'm a great believer in working through things. I think that may well be why I'm a writer."

J

JACOBS, Judy 1952-

PERSONAL: Born April 2, 1952, in St. Louis, MO; daughter of Charles C. (a physician) and Lois Louise (a nurse; maiden name, Long) Jacobs; married Mihaly Kun (an engineer), February 1, 1982; children: Joshua Jacobs Kun, Jeremy Jacobs Kun. *Education:* DePauw University, B.A., 1974. *Politics:* Democrat. *Religion:* "Raised a Lutheran."

ADDRESSES: Home—3545 Kempton Way, Oakland, CA 94611. *Office*—49 Stevenson St., San Francisco, CA 94105.

CAREER: Worked in traffic management for import companies in San Francisco, CA, 1974-79; free-lance correspondent based in Hong Kong, 1979-80; Cathay Pacific Airways, Hong Kong, magazine editor, 1982-83;

Judy Jacobs and Southeast Asian friends

112

OAG Travel Magazines, San Francisco, senior editor, 1984—; writer.

MEMBER: Society of Children's Book Writers.

WRITINGS:

Indonesia: A Nation of Islands (nonfiction for children), Dillon, 1990.

Contributor of numerous articles to periodicals.

SIDELIGHTS: Judy Jacobs' Indonesia: A Nation of Islands gives a simple yet in-depth look at Indonesian geography, history, and culture. Readers learn about everyday life and customs, including popular sports and foods. Aimed at middle-graders, Indonesia is considered an appealing and informative resource.

Jacobs told SATA: "When I was a child I had wild dreams. While my friends were planning to be fire fighters, nurses, and locomotive engineers, my dream was to be an adventurer. I was going to trek through the Borneo jungle, ride a camel across the Sahara desert, sail the South China Sea, and visit every country in the world.

"A great deal of my free time was spent ordering and reading the brochures that national and state tourist offices send to prospective visitors. My stamp collection also taught me a lot about the world.

"I was a voracious reader and consumed every book available about other countries, their legends, and cultures. Another favorite was mysteries, which often involved creaky old houses with secret passages. Books were not my entire life, however. My two brothers, my sister, and I would explore the woods in back of our house, look for tadpoles in the creek, play softball and tetherball, and sled down the hill in the winter.

"Meanwhile, I continued my study of other countries and my interest in children around the world. In high school, I devoured the works of Pearl Buck and developed a passionate interest in East Asia. My interest led to a year of study in Tokyo during my college days. I lived with a Japanese family and totally absorbed myself in the life of the neighborhood.

"I intended to be a college professor but took a one-year break after finishing my undergraduate studies to work for an import company in San Francisco. My future was changed forever when my college friend, Phijit, invited me to spend the summer with his family in Bangkok, Thailand. From there I explored Southeast Asia for nearly six months.

"Now I knew what I wanted to do. I wanted to travel. In order to really understand a place, you must be there, not just read books about it. My extended summer in Southeast Asia became a lifelong obsession, and now, more than fifteen years later, I have returned to Asia more than fifteen times and spent nearly two years discovering the area as a roving free-lance correspon-

dent. I gave up my idea of an ivory tower for a suitcase, passport, and computer. What began as a side job to pay for my travels has become a full-time career.

"The birth of my first child and a renewed interest in Dr. Seuss, Goodnight Moon, and Curious George encouraged me to take off in new directions. Because most of my knowledge centers on Asia, I decided to write about that part of the world for younger readers. I chose the middle grades, when children begin to show an acute interest in the world around them.

"Many studies have shown that Americans are geographically illiterate and that geography is one of the least popular subjects in school. I hope to help rectify this by writing interesting books about Asian cultures. A knowledge of Asia will become essential in the coming years, as the region's countries become more important economically and politically."

*   *   *

JAQUES, Faith 1923-

PERSONAL: Surname pronounced "Jakes"; born December 13, 1923, in Leicester, England; daughter of Maurice Thompson (a businessman) and Gladys Jaques. Education: Attended Central School of Art, London, England, 1946-48.

ADDRESSES: Home and office—16 Hillcrest, 51 Ladbroke Grove, London W11 3AX, England.

CAREER: Free-lance illustrator of magazines, books, postage stamps, film and television work, advertising, wallpaper, ceramics, and greeting cards, 1948—. Illustrator for Folio Society Books, 1949, and Reader's Digest Educational Books, beginning 1960; illustrator of dust jackets and covers for publishers, including BBC School Publications, 1953-73, Cape, Heinemann, Methuen, and Penguin Books. Visiting lecturer, Guildford School of Art, England, 1950-54, and Hornsey College of Art, London, England, 1958-64. Exhibitions: The Workshop Gallery, London, 1972 and 1976; Nicholas Hill Gallery, London, 1975; Chichester Gallery, Sussex, England, 1976; Piccadilly Gallery, London, 1977. Military service: Women's Royal Naval Service, 1941-45; became petty officer.

MEMBER: Association of Illustrators, Society of Authors.

AWARDS, HONORS: Tilly's House was selected one of the best illustrated books of 1979 by New York Review of Books, and among the ten most popular books in an international exhibition in Tokyo, Japan, 1979.

WRITINGS:

SELF-ILLUSTRATED

Drawing in Pen and Ink, Studio Vista, 1964.
Tilly's House, Atheneum, 1979.
Tilly's Rescue, Heinemann, 1980, Atheneum, 1981.
Frank and Polly Muir's Big Dipper, Heinemann, 1981.

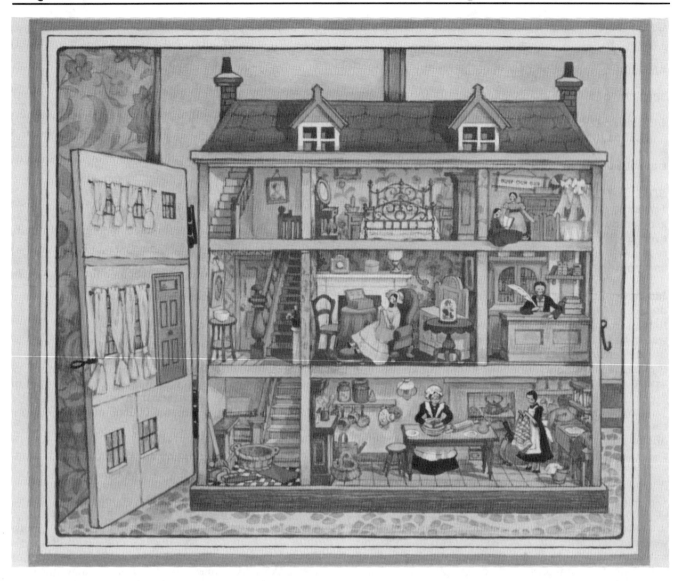

Faith Jaques's self-illustrated *Tilly's House* is the story of Tilly, an overworked doll house kitchen maid.

Little Grey Rabbit's House, Philomel, 1982.
Kidnap in Willowbank Wood (picture book), Heinemann, 1982.
Our Village Shop, Philomel, 1983.
The Christmas Party: A Model Book, Philomel, 1986.

ILLUSTRATOR

Cinderella and Goldilocks, Adprint, 1950.
Louisa May Alcott, *Little Women,* Contact Publications, 1950.
The Saturday Book 13, Hutchinson, 1953.
The Saturday Book 14, Hutchinson, 1954.
The Farmyard, Adprint, 1954.
Dorothy Wellesley, *Rhymes for Middle Years,* James Barrie, 1954.
The Saturday Book 15, Hutchinson, 1955.
Bambi, Adprint, 1956.
Miss Honeybun's Hat, University of London Press, 1956.
The Saturday Book 16, Hutchinson, 1956.
Sir Lancelot, Adprint, 1957.
The Twelve Days of Christmas, Hugh Evelyn, 1957.

Jo Manton, *A Portrait of Bach,* Abelard, 1957.
Sir Walter Scott, *Ivanhoe,* abridged edition, Ginn & Co., 1958.
James Reeves, editor, *A Golden Land,* Constable, 1958.
Rene Guillot, *The White Shadow,* Oxford University Press, 1959.
Gaskell, *Lois the Witch,* Methuen, 1960.
The Book of Knowledge, Amalgamated Press, 1960.
A Dog for Richard, University of London Press, 1960.
Aili Konyinnen, *Kirsti Comes Home,* Methuen, 1961.
Clive Gammon, *The Fisherman's Bedside Book,* Heinemann, 1961.
Josephine Kamm, *Mrs. Pankhurst,* Methuen, 1961.
A Child's Book of Composers, Novello, 1962.
Children's Cookery Book, Longmans, Green, 1962.
Eric Mathieson, *Jumbo the Elephant,* Hamish Hamilton, 1963, published as *The True Story of Jumbo the Elephant,* Coward, 1964.
The Road Book, Reader's Digest Association, 1966.
The Hugh Evelyn History of Costume, Hugh Evelyn, Volume 1: *A.D. 1800-1900,* 1966, Volume 2: *1660-*

1800, 1967, Volume 3: *1500-1600,* 1968, Volume 4: *B.C.-A.D. 1500,* 1970.

Anthology, Odhams Press, 1967.

Dorothy Richardson, *Pilgrimage,* four volumes, Dent, 1967.

Guidebooks, Volume 1: *Balmoral,* Volume 2: *Sandringham,* Her Majesty's Stationary Office, 1967.

Henry Treece, *The Windswept City,* Meredith, 1967.

Kamm, *Joseph Paxton,* Methuen, 1967.

Roald Dahl, *Charlie and the Chocolate Factory,* Allen & Unwin, 1967.

Ivan Turgenev, *The Torrents of Spring,* Folio, 1967.

Samuel Butler, *The Way of All Flesh,* Heron Books, 1967.

Henry James, *The Turn of the Screw,* abridged edition, Longman Books, 1967.

R. D. Blackmore, *Lorna Doone,* Heron Books, 1968.

Robert Louis Stevenson, *Treasure Island,* Heron Books, 1968.

Mary Treadgold, *The Humbugs,* Methuen, 1968.

Anthony Trollope, *The Small House at Allington,* Heron Books, 1968.

Georgina Infield, *A Seasoning of Menus,* Heinemann, 1969.

Ursula Moray Williams, *Mog,* Allen & Unwin, 1969.

Customs and Festivals, Collins, 1969.

Charles Dickens, *The Magic Fish-Bone* (picture book), Chatto & Windus, 1969, Harvey House, 1970.

Williams, *Johnny Golightly and His Crocodile* (picture book), Chatto & Windus, 1970, Harvey House, 1971.

Erick Houghton, *The Mouse and the Magician* (picture book), Lippincott, 1970.

Monica Dickens, *The Great Fire,* Kaye & Ward, 1970.

Edith Nesbit, *The Island of the Nine Whirlpools,* Kaye & Ward, 1970.

John Cunliffe, *The Giant Who Stole the World* (picture book), Deutsch, 1971.

Arthur Ransome, *Old Peter's Russian Tales,* Thomas Nelson, 1971, Puffin Books, 1974.

C. Dickens, *David Copperfield,* American Educational Publications, 1971.

Gillian Avery, *A Likely Lad,* Collins, 1971.

Philippa Pearce, *What the Neighbours Did and Other Stories,* Longman Young Books, 1972, Crowell, 1973.

Jane Austen, *Persuasion,* abridged version, Longman Books, 1972.

Margaret Crush, *A First Look at Costume,* C. A. Watts, 1972.

Williams, *A Picnic with the Aunts* (picture book), Chatto & Windus, 1972.

Cunliffe, *The Giant Who Swallowed the Wind* (picture book), Deutsch, 1972.

Charlotte Morrow, *The Glory House,* Chatto & Windus, 1972.

Natalie Savage Carlson, *The Half Sisters,* Blackie & Son, 1972.

Margaret Howell, *The Lonely Dragon,* Longman, 1972.

Sheila Glen Bishop, *Joe and the Caterpillar,* Heinemann, 1973.

Nina Bawden, *Carrie's War,* Lippincott, 1973.

Margery Fisher, editor, *Journeys,* Brockhampton Press, 1973.

Robert Newton Peck, *A Day No Pigs Would Die,* Knopf, 1973.

Cunliffe, *The King's Birthday Cake* (picture book), Deutsch, 1973.

Kathleen Lines, editor, *The Faber Book of Greek Legends,* Faber, 1973.

Dahl, *Charlie and the Great Glass Elevator,* Allen & Unwin, 1973, Puffin Books, 1975.

Hilary Seton, *Beyond the Blue Hills,* Heinemann, 1973.

Seton, *A Lion in the Garden,* Heinemann, 1974.

A Peck of Pepper, Chatto & Windus, 1974.

Leon Garfield, *Smith,* abridged edition, Longman Educational, 1974.

Great British Short Stories, Reader's Digest Association, 1974.

Elizabeth Yandell, *Henry,* Bodley Head, 1974.

Maurice Duggan, *Falter Tom and the Water Boy,* Kestrel, 1974.

John Rae, *The Golden Crucifix,* Brockhampton Press, 1974.

George Eliot, *The Mill on the Floss,* Collins, 1974.

Margery Sharp, *The Magical Cockatoo,* Heinemann, 1974.

Williams, *Grandpapa's Folly and the Woodworm-Bookworm* (picture book), Chatto & Windus, 1974.

Helen Cresswell, *Lizzie Dripping Again,* BBC Publications, 1974.

Lizzie Dripping by the Sea, BBC Publications, 1974.

Rae, *The Treasure of Westminster Abbey,* Brockhampton Press, 1975.

Nesbit, *The Old Nursery Stories,* Hodder & Stoughton, 1975.

Barbara Willard, editor, *Field and Forest,* Destrel, 1975.

Houghton, *A Giant Can Do Anything* (picture book), Deutsch, 1975.

Rae, *Christmas Is Coming,* Brockhampton Press, 1976.

Sharp, *Bernard the Brave,* Heinemann, 1976.

Andrew Lang, *The Red Fairy Book,* Viking, 1976.

Alison Uttley, *A Traveller in Time,* Puffin Books, 1977.

Avery, *Mouldy's Orphan,* Collins, 1978.

Gwen Grant, *Private—Keep Out!,* Heinemann, 1978.

Uttley, *Tales of Little Grey Rabbit,* Heinemann, 1980.

M. M. Kaye, *The Ordinary Princess,* Puffin Books, 1980.

Allan Ahlberg, *Mr. Buzz the Beeman,* Puffin Books, 1981.

Ahlberg, *Mr. Tick the Teacher,* Puffin Books, 1981.

Nesbit, *The Railway Children,* Puffin Choice, 1983.

Grant, *One Way Only,* Heinemann, 1984.

Uttley, *Tales of Little Brown Mouse,* Heinemann, 1984.

Arthur Ransome, *The War of the Birds and the Beasts,* J. Cape, 1984.

John Masefield, *The Box of Delights; or, When the Wolves Were Running,* Heinemann, 1984.

Willis Hall and Mary Hoffman, *The Return of the Antelope,* Heinemann, 1985.

Pat Thomson, *Good Girl, Granny* (picture book), Gollancz, 1987.

Zena Sutherland, *The Orchard Book of Nursery Rhymes,* Orchard Books, 1990.

Tilly leaves the doll house to seek a home of her own. (Illustration by Jaques.)

ILLUSTRATOR; "THE APPRENTICES" SERIES; BY LEON GARFIELD

Moss and Blister, Heinemann, 1976.
The Cloak, Heinemann, 1976.
The Valentine, Heinemann, 1977.
Labour in Vain, Heinemann, 1977.
The Fool, Heinemann, 1977.
Rosy Starling, Heinemann, 1977.
The Dumb Cake, Heinemann, 1977.
Tom Titmarch's Devil, Heinemann, 1977.
The Filthy Beast, Heinemann, 1978.
The Enemy, Heinemann, 1978.

OTHER

Also illustrator of several books published by Adprint, 1951-54. Contributor of articles to *Artist* and *Bookseller*, and of illustrations for stories and articles in *Cricket*, 1974-87.

ADAPTATIONS: Tilly's House was adapted as a filmstrip by Westonwood in 1982.

SIDELIGHTS: One of England's most prominent illustrators of children's books, Faith Jaques has visually recreated the characters and scenes of adult and juvenile fiction by such important authors as Margery Sharp, Edith Nesbit, Robert Louis Stevenson, Roald Dahl, Henry James, Jane Austen, and Charles Dickens. Jaques is particular about which books she works on because, as she once explained to *Something about the Author* (*SATA*), "the quality of the writing matters very much and I like to feel the book will stand the test of time." Although the majority of her art work has been for books by other authors, Jaques has also illustrated several of her own books, including the successful *Tilly's House* and *Tilly's Rescue*, which concern the adventures of a tiny wooden doll and her friend, Edward the teddy bear.

"I was born in Leicester," Jaques recalls for *SATA*, "a rather dull town then, in the midlands. After the war came I left it as soon as I was old enough (seventeen) to join the WRNS (Women's Royal Naval Service), hoping I'd be posted to the coast, as I love the sea. As it turned out I was sent to Oxford, very fortunately, as I was able to take part in university life to a certain extent. Most of all I was stunned by the beauty of the colleges and their gardens—coming from an industrial town it had never occurred to me that one could live in beautiful surroundings. So my adolescent years, though not without the usual problems, were spent in a very congenial place, with ready access to books, good conversation, theatre and music, museums and art classes. So Oxford had an important effect on me.

"I was demobbed in December, 1945, and started at the Central School of Art, London, in January, 1946, on a tiny ex-service grant ... lasting for four terms only. So my entire art school training was very short, but I made up for it by working about eighteen hours a day. I had to get any commissions I could while still a student, so I worked in every sort of illustration then and for the next fifteen years—newspapers, books, magazines, advertising, postage stamps, filmstrips, wall papers, pottery, textiles, etc. Only [by the time I was in my 40s was I] able to concentrate on book illustration, which is what I wanted to do ever since I was a child. I have also sold several illustrations to the British Museum, have work in various private collections, and did the four 1978 Christmas stamps on the theme of carol-singing (Great Britain issue)."

As a child, Jaques loved to read books by Victorian writers like Charles Dickens and William Makepeace Thackeray, so she was influenced by the illustrators who did wood and steel engravings for these books. "I still love this sort of illustration because it accomplished so much in the way of mood and scene-setting, is capable of great subtlety, and never dominates the text. My favorite illustrator of all time is a Frenchman called Grandville; he is not as well-known in England as he ought to be, but in my view he was the precursor of the sort of illustration which in the late nineteenth century became known as 'typically English.'" In her own illustrations, Jaques researches her subjects thoroughly and tries to achieve the same sense of realism that these nineteenth century models did.

For Jaques, her love of reading and illustrating led naturally to writing books of her own. "I've come late to writing," she once commented, "but have spent a lifetime as a voracious reader. I've illustrated more than a hundred books, the majority for children, but including classics for adults. It teaches one a lot about writing: the illustrator has to read the text over and over again to find each author's 'flavor' and try to interpret it. I often think book illustrators are more widely read than any other group of people." She explained that her work as an illustrator took too much of her time for her to compose texts of her own. "At last, though, I managed to produce *Tilly's House, Tilly's Rescue,* and the anthologized story, 'Tilly's Day Out.' The Tilly books have done very well, and have been published in several countries.

"There are a few problems in illustrating your own text. You have to fight back a desire to bring in scenes that would make good pictures but are irrelevant to the story, and you may have to illustrate a scene that is dull visually, but in *words* necessary. My interest will always be toward fantasy of one kind or another, so with luck I hope to find the pictures as interesting as the texts. Devising characters is what appeals to me, both in writing and illustrating."

WORKS CITED:

Something about the Author, Volume 21, Gale, 1980, pp. 81-84.

FOR MORE INFORMATION SEE:

BOOKS

Jaques, Robin, *Illustrators at Work,* Studio Vista, 1965.

PERIODICALS

Growing Point, January, 1980; September, 1981.
Guardian, February 10, 1975.
Mother, September, 1975.
New York Times Book Review, December 30, 1979, p. 19.
Publishers Weekly, July 16, 1979, p. 70; January 9, 1981, p. 73.
School Library Journal, February, 1980, p. 46; October, 1981, p. 155.
Times Educational Supplement, November 23, 1979; December 26, 1980.
Times Literary Supplement, November 25, 1983.
Washington Post Book World, December 13, 1981, p. 13.*

—*Sketch by Kevin S. Hile*

*   *   *

JAUSS, Anne Marie 1902(?)-1991

OBITUARY NOTICE—See index for *SATA* sketch: Born February 3, 1902 (some sources say 1907), in Munich, Germany; immigrated to United States, 1946; died September 13, 1991, in Milford, NJ. Artist and author. Jauss was the author and illustrator of numerous children's books, including *Under a Green Roof* and *The Pasture.* Jauss moved to Lisbon, Portugal, in 1942 to escape war-torn Germany, working as a painter, illustrator, and potter before immigrating to the United States. Her illustrations appear in various works, including Peter Lum's *The Stars in Our Heaven,* Mary Phillips's *Dragonflies and Damselflies,* and Alfred Duggan's *The Falcon and the Dove.*

OBITUARIES AND OTHER SOURCES:

BOOKS

The Writers Directory, 1990-1992, 9th edition, St. James Press, 1990.

PERIODICALS

New York Times, September 15, 1991, p. 38.
Washington Post, September 21, 1991, p. B4.

JOHNSON, Angela 1961-

PERSONAL: Born June 18, 1961, in Tuskegee, AL; daughter of Arthur (an autoworker) and Truzetta (an accountant; maiden name, Hall) Johnson. *Education:* Attended Kent State University. *Politics:* Democrat. *Religion:* None.

ADDRESSES: Home—Kent, OH. *Office*—c/o Orchard Books, 387 Park Ave. S., New York, NY 10016.

CAREER: Volunteers in Service to America (VISTA), Ravenna, OH, child development worker, 1981-82; freelance writer of children's books, 1989—.

MEMBER: Authors Guild, Authors League of America.

AWARDS, HONORS: Tell Me a Story, Mama was selected one of the best books of the year, *School Library Journal,* 1989; Ezra Jack Keats Award, United States Board on Books for Young People, Coretta Scott King Book Award, the American Library Association Social Responsibilities Round Table, both 1990, both for *When I Am Old with You.*

WRITINGS:

Tell Me a Story, Mama, illustrated by David Soman, Orchard Books, 1989.
Do Like Kyla, illustrated by James Ransome, Orchard Books, 1990.
When I Am Old with You, illustrated by Soman, Orchard Books, 1990.
One of Three, illustrated by Soman, Orchard Books, 1991.

WORK IN PROGRESS: Stories for adolescents.

SIDELIGHTS: Angela Johnson told *SATA:* "I don't believe the magic of listening to Wilma Mitchell read us stories after lunch will ever be repeated for me. Book people came to life. They sat beside me in Maple Grove School. That is when I knew. I asked for a diary that year and have not stopped writing. My family, especially my grandfather and father, are storytellers and those spoken words sit beside me too.

"In high school I wrote punk poetry that went with my razor blade necklace. At that point in my life my writing was personal and angry. I didn't want anyone to like it. I didn't want to be in the school literary magazine, or to be praised for something that I really didn't want understood. Of course, ten years later, I hope that my writing is universal and speaks to everyone who reads it. I still have the necklace, though."

*   *   *

JOHNSON, Dolores 1949-

PERSONAL: Born in New Britain, CT, February, 1949; daughter of Louis and Cornelia Johnson. *Education:* Boston University, B.F.A., 1971.

ADDRESSES: Home and office—127 North Eucalyptus Ave., No. 10, Inglewood, CA 90301. *Agent*—Kendra Marcus, Book Stop, 67 Meadow View Rd., Orinda, CA 94563.

CAREER: Author and illustrator. Worked in advertising, Los Angeles, CA, 1974-88. Tutor, Library Adult Reading Project. *Exhibitions:* "African-American Children's Authors and Illustrators" (group show), California Afro-American Museum, Los Angeles, summer, 1990; "From Freedom to Chains," San Diego Children's Museum, February, 1991; group exhibit, San Diego Museum of African American Art, spring, 1991; "Through Sisters' Eyes: Children's Books Illustrated by African American Women Artists," November 4, 1991-April 24, 1992; "The Paths to Freedom," San Diego Children's Museum, February, 1992.

MEMBER: Society of Children's Book Writers.

WRITINGS:

SELF-ILLUSTRATED

What Will Mommy Do When I'm at School?, Macmillan, 1990.
What Kind of Baby-Sitter Is This?, Macmillan, 1991.
The Best Bug to Be, Macmillan, 1992.
Your Dad Was Just Like You, Macmillan, 1992.

ILLUSTRATOR

Beth P. Wilson, *Jenny,* Macmillan, 1990.
Ella Jenkins, *Who Fed the Chickens?,* Scott-Foresman, 1992.

SIDELIGHTS: Dolores Johnson writes, "When I was young, I knew I could draw, but I didn't think I was an artist. You see, I had an artist living in the house with me, my older brother Billy, and I knew I wasn't in his league. Billy ate, slept, and drank art. He spent all of his time drawing and painting. In turn, I had many more divergent interests—I took piano lessons, I liked to sew and knit, and I loved to read.

"While my brother was still in high school he took art courses at the local university. When he graduated from art school he immediately found a job as an artist. I went to art school also, but upon graduating I floundered about. I moved from the East Coast to the West Coast. I found work as a part-time production artist in a Los Angeles television station. In 1977, I got a job in the art department of a mail order company, Sunset House, and worked there as a Production Manager for four years. As a production manager, I worked with artists, salesmen, and printers to make the products in our catalog look their best. When I left Sunset House, I worked as a production manager at various advertising agencies, but I was somewhat unhappy because my work was not very creative. I decided to spend more time making art, so every night I came home from work and spent my spare time making pottery, stained glass windows, and eventually painting in oils and water colors. A friend happened to see some of my writings and my paintings and suggested that I might consider

DOLORES JOHNSON

creating children's books. This idea was a brand new concept to me.

"I hadn't come from what I would call a story-telling family (Dad did not sit me on his knee to tell me stories about Great Aunt Minnie), nor did I have a lot of picture books around me as a child. But I did feel children's books would be a perfect outlet for my artwork and my writing. Also, I love children and I love books. I started taking courses in children's book writing and illustration. I wrote, drew pictures, and submitted manuscripts to publishers for five years before I was finally awarded a contract to illustrate *Jenny,* a book of poetry by Beth P. Wilson.

"I welcome the opportunity to write and illustrate books because it is a wonderful means to communicate with the most important segment of our society—the children. I like to write about the basic issues that are critical to the typical child's life: leaving home for school

for the first time, being left with a babysitter, coming home to an empty house, performing in a school play, etc. It's been a thousand years since I felt these fears personally, but I can still remember the intensity of experience brought about by these chapters in my life. Perhaps, through my writing and artwork, I can help a young child find comfort, maybe even a laugh, and hopefully a solution to some of the problems that trouble them.

"I love children's books. There are books written by certain authors or illustrated by certain artists that I have enjoyed again and again, even as an adult. I realize that I, as an artist, have a tremendous responsibility to the children who read my books. I hope that they might find as much pleasure reading my books as I have writing them.

"And, by the way, my brother is still a very good artist."

K

KEEPING, Charles 1924-1988

PERSONAL: Full name is Charles William James Keeping; born September 22, 1924, in Lambeth, London, England; died May 16, 1988; son of Charles (a professional boxer, under name Charles Clark, and newspaperman) and Eliza Ann (Trodd) Keeping; married Renate Meyer (an artist and illustrator), September 20, 1952; children: Jonathan, Vicki, Sean, Frank. *Education:* Polytechnic of Central London, London, England, National Diploma in Design, 1952. *Politics:* "Individualist." *Religion:* None. *Hobbies and other interests:* Walking, good conversation over a pint of beer in a pub, modern jazz, folksinging.

ADDRESSES: Home—16 Church Rd., Shortlands, Bromley BR2 0HP, England. *Office*—Camberwell School of Art and Crafts, London, England. *Agent*—B.L. Kearley Ltd., 59 George St., London W1, England.

CAREER: Apprenticed to printing trade, 1938; after war service, worked as engineer and rent collector before starting full-time art studies in 1949; Polytechnic of Central London, London, England, visiting lecturer in lithography, 1956-63; Croydon College of Art, Croydon, England, visiting lecturer in lithography, 1963-78; Camberwell School of Art and Crafts, London, visiting lecturer in print making, 1979-88. Book illustrator, advertising artist, and designer of wall murals, posters, and book jackets. *Exhibitions:* Lithographs exhibited in London, Italy, Australia, and United States, including International Exhibition of Lithography at Cincinnati, 1958; prints in many collections, including the Victoria and Albert Museum, London. *Military service:* Royal Navy, telegraphist, 1942-46.

MEMBER: Society of Industrial Artists.

AWARDS, HONORS: Carnegie Medal commendation, Library Association, 1957, for *The Silver Branch,* 1958, for *Warrior Scarlet,* 1963, for *The Latchkey Children,* 1965, for *Elidor,* 1967, for *The Dream Time,* and 1978, for *A Kind of Wild Justice;* Spring Book Festival older

CHARLES KEEPING

honor, *New York Herald Tribune,* 1958, for *The Silver Branch,* and 1962, for *Dawn Wind;* Carnegie Medal, Library Association, 1959, for *The Lantern Bearers,* and 1970, for *The God beneath the Sea;* International Board on Books for Young People (IBBY) honor list, 1960, for *Warrior Scarlet;* Certificate of Merit, Library Association, for *Shaun and the Cart-Horse,* and 1970, for *The God beneath the Sea;* Certificate of Merit, Leipzig Book Fair, for *Black Dolly: The Story of a Junk Cart Pony;* Kate Greenaway Medal, Library Association, 1967, for *Charley, Charlotte and the Golden Canary,* and 1981, for *The Highwayman,* honor, 1969, for *Joseph's Yard,* commendation, 1970, for *The God beneath the Sea,* and 1974, for *The Railway Passage;* W. H. Smith Illustration

Award, Victoria and Albert Museum, 1972, for *Tinker, Tailor: Folk Song Tales,* and 1977, for *The Wildman;* Biennale of Illustrations Bratislava honorable mention, 1973, for *The Spider's Web,* and golden apple, 1975, for *The Railway Passage;* Hans Christian Andersen highly commended illustrator award, IBBY, 1974; Kurt Maschler Award runner-up, 1985, for *The Wedding Ghost.*

WRITINGS:

SELF-ILLUSTRATED CHILDREN'S BOOKS

Shaun and the Cart-Horse, F. Watts, 1966.
Molly o' the Moors: The Story of a Pony, World Publishing, 1966, published in England as *Black Dolly: The Story of a Junk Cart Pony,* Brockhampton Press, 1966.
Charley, Charlotte and the Golden Canary, F. Watts, 1967.
Alfie Finds the Other Side of the World, F. Watts, 1968, published in England as *Alfie and the Ferryboat,* Oxford University Press, 1968.
(Compiler) *Tinker, Tailor: Folk Song Tales,* Brockhampton Press, 1968.
(Reteller) *The Christmas Story, as Told on "Play School,"* British Broadcasting Corporation, 1968, published in the United States as *The Christmas Story,* F. Watts, 1969.
Joseph's Yard, Oxford University Press, 1969, F. Watts, 1970.
Through the Window, F. Watts, 1970.
The Garden Shed, Oxford University Press, 1971.
The Spider's Web, Oxford University Press, 1972.
Richard, Oxford University Press, 1973.
The Nanny Goat and the Fierce Dog, Abelard, 1973, S. G. Phillips, 1974.
(Compiler of words and music) *Cockney Ding Dong,* Kestrel Books, 1973.
The Railway Passage, Oxford University Press, 1974.
Wasteground Circus, Oxford University Press, 1975.
Inter-City, Oxford University Press, 1977.
Miss Emily and the Bird of Make-Believe, Hutchinson, 1978.
River, Oxford University Press, 1978.
Willie's Fire-Engine, Oxford University Press, 1980.
(Reteller, with Kevin Crossley-Holland) *Beowulf,* Oxford University Press, 1982.
Sammy Streetsinger, Oxford University Press (Oxford), 1984, Oxford University Press (New York), 1987.
(Compiler) *Charles Keeping's Book of Classic Ghost Stories,* Peter Bedrick, 1986.
(Compiler) *Charles Keeping's Classic Tales of the Macabre,* Peter Bedrick, 1987.
Adam and Paradise Island, Oxford University Press, 1989.

Adapted *Joseph's Yard* and *Through the Window* for television.

ILLUSTRATOR

Nicholas Stuart Gray, *Over the Hills to Fabylon,* Oxford University Press, 1954, Hawthorn, 1970.
Rosemary Sutcliff, *The Silver Branch,* Oxford University Press, 1957, Walck, 1959.

Sutcliff, *Warrior Scarlet,* Walck, 1958.
John Stewart Murphy, *Bridges,* Oxford University Press, 1958.
Murphy, *Ships,* Oxford University Press, 1959.
Sutcliff, *The Lantern-Bearers,* Walck, 1959.
Sutcliff, *Knight's Fee,* Walck, 1960.
Murphy, *Roads,* Oxford University Press, 1960.
Ira Nesdale, *Riverbend Bricky,* Blackie, 1960.
Kathleen Fidler, *Tales of Pirates and Castaways,* Lutterworth, 1960.
Fidler, *Tales of the West Country,* Lutterworth, 1961.
Charles Kingsley, *The Heroes,* Hutchinson, 1961.
Mitchell Dawson, *The Queen of Trent,* Abelard, 1961.
Sir Henry Rider Haggard, *King Solomon's Mines,* Blackie, 1961.
Sutcliff, *Dawn Wind,* Oxford University Press, 1961, Walck, 1962.
Murphy, *Canals,* Oxford University Press, 1961.
Sutcliff, reteller, *Dragon Slayer,* Bodley Head, 1961, published as *Beowulf,* Dutton, 1962, published as *Dragon Slayer: The Story of Beowulf,* Macmillan, 1980.
Ruth Chandler, *Three Trumpets,* Abelard, 1962.
Kenneth Grahame, *The Golden Age* [and] *Dream Days,* Bodley Head, 1962, Dufour, 1965.
Barbara Leonie Picard, *Lost John,* Oxford University Press, 1962, Criterion, 1963.
Murphy, *Dams,* Oxford University Press, 1963.
Clare Compton, *Harriet and the Cherry Pie,* Bodley Head, 1963.
E. M. Almedingen, *The Knights of the Golden Table,* Bodley Head, 1963, Lippincott, 1964.
Philip Rush, *The Castle and the Harp,* Collins, 1963.
Paul Berna, *Flood Warning,* Pantheon, 1963.
Eric Allen, *The Latchkey Children,* Oxford University Press, 1963.
Wilkie Collins, *The Moonstone,* Oxford University Press, 1963.
Mollie Hunter, *Patrick Kentigern Keenan,* Blackie & Son, 1963, published as *The Smartest Man in Ireland,* Funk, 1965.
James Holding, *The King's Contest and Other North African Tales,* Abelard, 1964.
Henry Treece, *The Children's Crusade,* Longmans, 1964.
Nesdale, *Bricky and the Hobo,* Blackie, 1964.
Murphy, *Railways,* Oxford University Press, 1964.
Treece, *The Last of the Vikings,* Brockhampton Press, 1964, published as *The Last Viking,* Pantheon, 1966.
Elizabeth Grove, *Whitsun Warpath,* Jonathan Cape, 1964.
Jacoba Tadema-Sporry, *The Story of Egypt,* translated by Elsa Hammond, Thomas Nelson, 1964.
Hunter, *The Kelpie's Pearls,* Blackie & Son, 1964, Funk, 1966.
Almedingen, *The Treasure of Seigfried,* Bodley Head, 1964, Lippincott, 1965.
Treece, *Horned Helmet,* Puffin, 1965.
Murphy, *Wells,* Oxford University Press, 1965.
Gray, *The Apple Stone,* Dobson, 1965, Hawthorn, 1969.
Alan Garner, *Elidor,* Collins, 1965.

Henry Daniel-Rops, *The Life of Our Lord,* Hawthorn, 1965.

Sutcliff, *The Mark of the Horse Lord,* Walck, 1965.

Sutcliff, *Heroes and History,* Putnam, 1965.

Treece, *Splintered Sword,* Brockhampton Press, 1965, Duell, Sloan & Pearce, 1966.

John Reginald Milsome, *Damien the Leper's Friend,* Burns & Oates, 1965.

Kevin Crossley-Holland, *King Horn,* Macmillan (London), 1965, Dutton, 1966.

Walter Macken, *Island of the Great Yellow Ox,* Macmillan (London), 1966.

Richard Potts, *An Owl for His Birthday,* Lutterworth, 1966.

Erich Maria Remarque, *All Quiet on the Western Front,* translation by A. W. Wheen, Folio Society, 1966.

Eric and Nancy Protter, editors and adapters, *Celtic Folk and Fairy Tales,* Duell, Sloan and Pearce, 1966.

Holding, *The Sky-Eater and Other South Sea Tales,* Abelard, 1966.

Edna Walker Chandler, *With Books on Her Head,* Meredith Press, 1967.

Geoffrey Trease, *Bent Is the Bow,* Nelson, 1967.

Trease, *The Red Towers of Granada,* Vanguard Press, 1967.

James Reeves, *The Cold Flame,* Hamish Hamilton, 1967, Meredith, 1969.

Treece, *Swords from the North,* Pantheon, 1967.

Gray, *Mainly in Moonlight: Ten Stories of Sorcery and the Supernatural,* Meredith Press, 1967.

Treece, *The Dream Time,* Brockhampton Press, 1967, Hawthorn, 1968.

Gray, *Grimbold's Other World,* Meredith Press, 1968.

W. Somerset Maugham, *The Mixture as Before,* Heron, 1968.

Kenneth McLeish, *The Story of Aeneas,* Longmans, 1968.

Potts, *The Haunted Mine,* Lutterworth, 1968.

Reeves, compiler, *An Anthology of Free Verse,* Basil Blackwell, 1968.

Macken, *The Flight of the Doves,* Macmillan, 1968.

Holding, *Poko and the Golden Demon,* Abelard, 1968.

(With Swiethlan Kraczyna) Kenneth Cavander, *The 'Iliad' and 'Odyssey' of Homer: Radio Plays,* British Broadcasting Corporation, 1969.

Aldous Huxley, *After Many a Summer,* Heron, 1969.

Nevil Shute, *Ruined City* [and] *Landfall: A Channel Story,* Heron, 1969.

Margaret Jessy Miller, editor, *Knights, Beasts and Wonders: Tales and Legends from Mediaeval Britain,* David White, 1969.

Roger Lancelyn Green, reteller, *The Tale of Ancient Israel,* Dent, 1969, Dutton, 1970.

Robert Elliot Rogerson, *Enjoy Reading!,* edited by Rogerson and C. M. Smith, W. & R. Chambers, Book 4, 1970, Book 5, 1971.

John Watts, *Early Encounters: An Introductory Stage,* Longmans, 1970.

Lee Cooper, *Five Fables from France,* Abelard, 1970.

Leon Garfield and Edward Blishen, *The God beneath the Sea,* Kestrel Books, 1970, Pantheon, 1971.

Nigel Grimshaw, *The Angry Valley,* Longman, 1970.

Pamela L. Travers, *Friend Monkey,* Harcourt, 1971.

William Cole, compiler, *The Poet's Tales: A New Book of Story Poems,* World Publishing, 1971.

Fedor Dostoyevski, *The Idiot,* Folio Society, 1971.

Mary Shura Craig, *The Valley of the Frost Giants,* Lothrop, 1971.

Treece, *The Invaders: Three Stories,* Crowell, 1972.

Robert Newman, *The Twelve Labors of Hercules,* Crowell, 1972.

Roger Squire, reteller, *Wizards and Wampum: Legends of the Iroquois,* Abelard, 1972.

Garfield and Blishen, *The Golden Shadow,* Kestrel Books, 1972, Pantheon, 1973.

Ursula Synge, *Weland: Smith of the Gods,* Bodley Head, 1972, S. G. Phillips, 1973.

Montague Rhodes James, *Ghost Stories of M. R. James,* selected by Nigel Kneale, Folio Society, 1973.

Ian Serraillier, *I'll Tell You a Tale: A Collection of Poems and Ballads,* Longman, 1973.

Sutcliff, *The Capricorn Bracelet,* Oxford University Press, 1973.

Cooper, *The Strange Feathery Beast, and Other French Fables,* Carousel, 1973.

Helen L. Hoke, *Weirdies: A Horrifying Concatenation of the Super-Sur-Real or Almost or Not-Quite Real,* F. Watts (London), 1973, published as *Weirdies, Weirdies, Weirdies: A Horrifying Concatenation of the Super-Sur-Real or Almost Not-Quite Real,* F. Watts (New York), 1975.

Daphne du Maurier, *The Birds, and Other Stories,* abridged and simplified by Lewis Jones, Longman, 1973.

Hoke, *Monsters, Monsters, Monsters,* F. Watts, 1974.

Forbes Stuart, reteller, *The Magic Horns: Folk Tales from Africa,* Abelard, 1974, Addison-Wesley, 1976.

Travers, *About the Sleeping Beauty,* McGraw, 1975.

Marian Lines, *Tower Blocks: Poems of the City,* F. Watts, 1975.

Bernard Ashley, *Terry on the Fence,* Oxford University Press, 1975, S. G. Phillips, 1977.

Robert Swindells, *When Darkness Comes,* Morrow, 1975.

David Kossoff, *The Little Book of Sylvanus (died 41 A.D.),* St. Martin's, 1975.

Sutcliff, *Blood Feud,* Oxford University Press, 1976, Dutton, 1977.

Potts, *A Boy and His Bike,* Dobson, 1976.

Crossley-Holland, *The Wildman,* Deutsch, 1976.

Horace Walpole, *The Castle of Otranto: A Gothic Story,* Folio Society, 1976.

Victor Hugo, *Les Miserables,* translation by Norman Denny, Folio Press, 1976.

Rene Guillot, *Tipiti, the Robin,* translated by Gwen Marsh, [and] *Pascal and the Lioness,* illustrated by Barry Wilkinson, translated and adapted by Christina Holyoak, Bodley Head, 1976.

Hoke, compiler, *Haunts, Haunts, Haunts,* F. Watts, 1977, published as *Spectres, Spooks and Shuddery Shades,* 1977.

Ashley, *A Kind of Wild Justice,* S. G. Phillips, 1979.

Stuart, *The Mermaids' Revenge: Folk Tales from Britain and Ireland,* Abelard, 1979.

Leonard Clark, *The Tale of Prince Igor,* Dobson, 1979.

Author-illustrator Charles Keeping used somber browns and grays to portray this one-man band before his colorful rise to fame in _Sammy Streetsinger_.

Nina Bawden, _The Robbers,_ Gollancz, 1979.

Charles Causley, editor, _The Batsford Book of Stories in Verse for Children,_ Batsford, 1979.

Tony Drake, _Breakback Alley,_ Collins, 1979.

Ashley, _Break in the Sun: A Novel,_ S. G. Phillips, 1980.

Alfred Noyes, _The Highwayman,_ Oxford University Press, 1981.

(With Derek Collard and Jeroo Roy) John Bailey, McLeish, and David Spearman, retellers, _Gods and Men: Myths and Legends from the World's Religions,_ Oxford University Press, 1981.

Charles Dickens, _The Posthumous Papers of the Pickwick Club,_ Folio Society, 1981.

Dickens, _Great Expectations,_ Folio Society, 1981.

Dickens, _Our Mutual Friend,_ Folio Society, 1982.

Rudyard Kipling, _The Beginning of the Armadilloes,_ Macmillan, 1982, Peter Bedrick, 1983.

Dickens, _The Mystery of Edwin Drood,_ edited by Arthur J. Cox, Folio Society, 1982.

Dickens, _Hard Times,_ Folio Society, 1983.

Dickens, _The Personal History of David Copperfield,_ Folio Society, 1983.

Causley, compiler, _The Sun Dancing: Christian Verse,_ Puffin, 1984.

Kipling, _Rikki-Tikki-Tavi and Other Animal Stories,_ Macmillan, 1984.

Garfield, _The Wedding Ghost,_ Oxford University Press, 1985.

Alfred Tennyson, _The Lady of Shalott,_ Oxford University Press, 1985.

Dickens, _The Life and Adventures of Nicholas Nickleby,_ Folio Society, 1986.

Edgar Allan Poe, _Two Tales,_ Chimaera Press, 1986.

Neil Philip, reteller, _The Tale of Sir Gawain,_ Philomel Books, 1987.

Causley, _Jack the Treacle Eater and Other Poems,_ Macmillan, 1987.

Bram Stoker, _Dracula,_ Blackie, 1988.

Mary Shelley, _Frankenstein,_ Blackie, 1988.

Anna Sewell, _Black Beauty,_ Gollancz, 1989.

Also illustrator of Ted Kavanagh's _Man Must Measure,_ 1955; Martha Freudenberger and Magda Kelber's _Heute Morgen,_ 2 and 3, 1956-57; Guthrie Foote's _Merrily on High,_ 1959; Joseph Conrad's _The Shadow-Line_ [and] _Within the Tides,_ 1962; Frank Knight's _They Told Mr. Hakluyt,_ 1964; Emily Bronte's _Wuthering Heights,_ 1964; Joan Tate's _Jenny,_ 1964, _The Next-Doors,_ 1964, and _Mrs. Jenny,_ 1966; Lace Kendall's _The Rain Boat,_ 1965; Denys Thompson and R. J. Harris's _Your English,_ 1965; Harold Keith's _Komantcia,_ 1966; Murphy's _Harbours and Docks,_ 1967; Marie Butts's _Champion of Charlemagne,_ 1967; Frederic Westcott's _Bach,_ 1967; Hunter's _Thomas and the Warlock,_ 1967; H. G. Wells's _Mr. Britling Sees It Through,_ 1969; Huxley's _Time Must Have a Stop,_ 1969; Shute's _On the Beach,_ 1970; Potts's _The Story of Tod;_ Maugham's _Of Human Bondage;_ and Robert Louis Stevenson's _Stumpy, Dr. Jekyll and Mr. Hyde, The Wrecker, New Arabian Nights,_ and _More New Arabian Nights._

ADAPTATIONS: Charley, Charlotte and the Golden Canary, Alfie Finds the Other Side of the World, and _Through the Window_ were adapted for filmstrips by Weston Woods.

SIDELIGHTS: Charles Keeping portrayed the London scene and its many mysteries in his own children's books as well as in those he illustrated for other authors. His books grew out of settings, conversations, and events he observed both during his childhood and during his long walks through the city of London as an adult. In these works, Keeping "learned the trick of making his text a foil for the pictures and pared his words increasingly so as to convey more and more of his information visually," asserted Anne Carter in _Twentieth-Century Children's Writers._ Keeping's bold and sometimes formidable drawings were done in either somber browns and blacks or bright splashy colors, and "when in tune with a writer" he produced illustrations that "could add another dimension to a book," related M. S. Crouch in _Junior Bookshelf._ Keeping "was undoubtedly one of the outstanding figures of his time," concluded Carter.

Born in the borough of Lambeth, Keeping spent much of his childhood in the small fenced-in backyard behind his house. There was a stable yard next door that Keeping often looked at through the fence, this view gradually becoming his world. "I used to look through the cracks in the fence, so I was always looking at this isolated situation or image moving across," recalled Keeping in his interview with Cornelia Jones and Olivia R. Way for _British Children's Authors._ "I started to create stories around these things so that the horse, the people, the chickens, the dogs, all became sort of symbols." Keeping continued writing these stories until his father died and they moved. He maintained in his

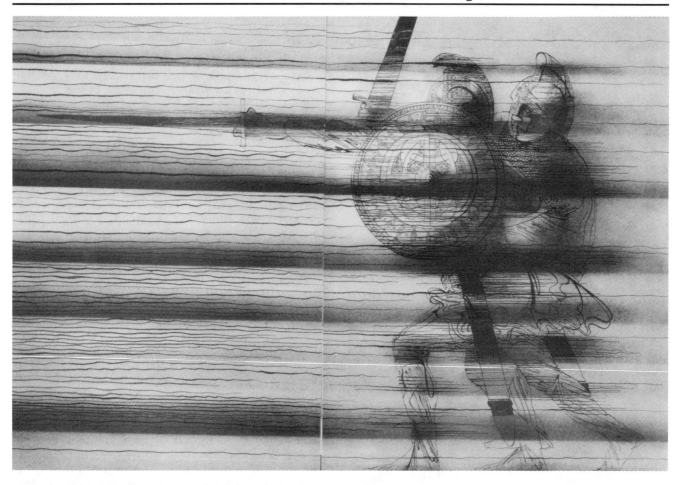

Keeping uses sharp lines and deep shadows in his interpretive portrayal of the warriors in *Beowulf*.

interview: "Certainly these early impressions were the strongest I experienced. They were so strong that I never thought of anything else than writing about them and drawing them."

Keeping's mother was unable to keep both children in school after his father's death, so he began working and was apprenticed to the printing trade at the age of fourteen. After serving four years in the Royal Navy, he went back to school part-time, working as a gas meter collector in North Paddington. "You know," he remarked in his interview, "a lot came out of that. I went in everybody's houses, saw the way people live. It was all in the poor parts of London, mostly North Paddington and Kilburn and North Kensington, which is the poor area of Kensington and almost like ghettos. I never stopped drawing." In 1949, Keeping finally got a grant so he could go to school full-time. But upon graduating, he found that it was almost impossible to sell paintings and that lithographs brought in little money, so he began illustrating books almost immediately.

The first book Keeping did was for an American publisher who thought his drawings were "a bit way-out." In 1956, however, Oxford University Press took him on and he began illustrating steadily. Keeping's first self-illustrated work grew out of childhood memories of the stable yard that was next to his house. "As I said before, horses are a symbolic thing," he related in his

interview. "I'd always wanted to do something about a horse, but I've got an absolute dislike of humanizing animals. I can't bear animals to talk.... I believe there's so much fantasy in real life that we don't need to do this.... But I always wanted to use the real story of a horse." Keeping had an idea, but he believed he needed a real animal in his living environment to write the story. He bought a donkey first, but it was so mean—biting and kicking—that he had to sell it. He next purchased an old black Welsh pony from the local junk man and his story slowly evolved into *Molly o' the Moors.*

Similarly, when Keeping was writing *Charley, Charlotte and the Golden Canary* he had a canary in a cage by the window. Unlike many of his earlier works, which were filled with dark and drab images, this one is full of vibrant, splashy colors. Keeping said in his interview that he believed "these bright colors came about for many reasons. One of them is, I think, that the city is full of brilliant color. This is not natural color, it is artificial color. You know, the whole tempo of the city is like—oh, like a jazz band, isn't it? It has this fantastic flashing-on of neon lights and things like this, and it has a sort of jarring quality of noise. Now we can't create noise. We can't have a book that makes a noise, so you see I often use color, again, in a symbolic way."

When it came to illustrating the works of other authors, Keeping saw it as a difficult task unless he really liked the story he was doing. "To do it well," he commented in his interview, "I think that you must first of all take the story and really feel for that story, but not necessarily will it be the way the author himself felt about it." So, Keeping always illustrated a book from his perspective, from the way he felt about it. Among those he illustrated are a number of Rosemary Sutcliff's historical novels. Keeping "recognised the strength and grandeur of her writing and matched them with his own sinewy, spiky drawings," explained Crouch. He also did a number of Henry Treece's "tough, sometimes heartless stories, all of which he illustrated conscientiously, but this author's last and most enigmatic book *The Dream Time* called forth some of his most memorable designs, hauntingly tender as well as strong," added Crouch.

During the course of his career, Keeping's "capacity for work was phenomenal. He met each new challenge with enormous creative energy," pointed out Crouch, adding: "No illustrator in this century has worked harder.... He established an individual style at the beginning of his career and stayed faithful to it." As far as this style is concerned, Keeping claimed in his interview: "I don't think I ever set out to write a conscious story or ever will, but the thing is that the story evolves from ideas. If people want me just to write a story, some clever story that's going to please them, they'll have to look for someone else, because I just present them with ideas.... It's exactly the same with the drawings, in that the drawings evoke just what I feel about something. I don't think this is so bad, because what are we all giving if not what we are? How boring it would be if we all gave the same thing."

WORKS CITED:

Carter, Anne, essay in *Twentieth-Century Children's Writers,* 3rd edition, edited by Tracy Chevalier, St. James Press, 1989, pp. 511-513.
Crouch, M. S., "Makers of Images," *Junior Bookshelf,* August, 1988, pp. 173-75.
Jones, Cornelia, and Olivia R. Way, *British Children's Authors: Interviews at Home,* American Library Association, 1976, pp. 101-113.

FOR MORE INFORMATION SEE:

PERIODICALS

Horn Book, April, 1981, p. 181.
Junior Bookshelf, December, 1984, p. 245; December, 1986, p. 235; August, 1989, p. 158.
Publishers Weekly, May 20, 1988, p. 94.
School Library Journal, January, 1981, p. 51.
Times Educational Supplement, May 27, 1983, p. 29; November 27, 1987, p. 47.
Times Literary Supplement, September 19, 1980, p. 1028; November 30, 1984, p. 1379; July 7, 1989, p. 757.
Voice of Youth Advocates, June, 1988, p. 84.
Washington Post Book World, December 27, 1987, p. 8.

OBITUARIES:

PERIODICALS

School Library Journal, August, 1988.
Times (London), May 20, 1988.*

*   *   *

KEITH, Carlton
See ROBERTSON, Keith (Carlton)

*   *   *

KNIGHT, Hilary 1926-

PERSONAL: Born November 1, 1926, in Hempstead, Long Island, NY; son of Clayton (an artist and writer) and Katharine (an artist and writer; maiden name, Sturges) Knight. *Education:* Attended Art Students League, New York, NY.

ADDRESSES: Home—300 East 51st St., New York, NY 10022.

CAREER: Author, illustrator, and designer. Began art career after his drawings were published in *House and Garden* and *Mademoiselle.* Has designed theater posters for numerous Broadway plays, including *Sugar Babies, Half a Sixpence, Irene,* and *Mike.* Artwork has been included in the seventh annual exhibition of "The Original Art: Celebrating the Fine Art of Children's Book Illustration," at the Major Eagle Gallery.

HILARY KNIGHT

When Knight drew his first picture of Eloise, author Kay Thompson said she recognized her feisty, six-year-old character immediately. (Illustration from *Eloise,* written by Thompson, illustrated by Knight.)

WRITINGS:

ALL SELF-ILLUSTRATED

ABC, Golden Press, 1961.

Angels and Berries and Candy Canes (also see below), Harper, 1963.

A Christmas Stocking Story (also see below), Harper, 1963.

A Firefly in a Fir Tree (also see below), Harper, 1963.

(With Clement Clarke Moore) *Christmas Nutshell Library* (contains Knight's *Angels and Berries and Candy Canes, A Christmas Stocking Story, A Firefly in a Fir Tree,* and Moore's *The Night before Christmas*), Harper, 1963.

Where's Wallace?, Harper, 1964.

Sylvia, the Sloth: A Round-about Story, Harper, 1969.

The Circus Is Coming, Western Publishing/Golden Press, 1978.

Hilary Knight's the Owl and the Pussy-Cat (based on poem by Edward Lear), Aladdin Books, 1983.

ILLUSTRATOR

Kay Thompson, *Eloise,* Simon & Schuster, 1955.

Patrick Gordon Campbell, *Short Trot with a Cultured Mind through Some Experiences of a Humorous Nature,* Simon & Schuster, 1955.

Jan Henry, *Tiger's Chance,* Harcourt, 1957.

Betty Bard MacDonald, *Hello, Mrs. Piggle-Wiggle,* Lippincott, 1957.

MacDonald, *Mrs. Piggle-Wiggle,* Lippincott, 1957.

MacDonald, *Mrs. Piggle-Wiggle's Magic,* Lippincott, 1957.

Thompson, *Eloise in Paris,* Simon & Schuster, 1957.

Wonderful World of Aunt Tuddy, Random House, 1958.

Dorothea W. Blair, *Roger: A Most Unusual Rabbit,* Lippincott, 1958.

Thompson, *Eloise at Christmas Times,* Random House, 1958.

Thompson, *Eloise in Moscow,* Simon & Schuster, 1959.

Evelyn Gendel, *Tortoise and Turtle,* Simon & Schuster, 1960.

Cecil Maiden, *Beginning with Mrs. McBee,* Vanguard, 1960.

Hilary Knight's Mother Goose, Golden Press, 1962.

Maiden, *Speaking of Mrs. McCluskie,* Vanguard, 1962.

Margaret Stone Zilboorg, *Jeremiah Octopus,* Golden Press, 1962.

Genel, *Tortoise and Turtle Abroad,* Simon & Schuster, 1963.

Marie Le Prince De Beaumont, *Beauty and the Beast,* Macmillan, 1963.

Clement Clarke Moore, *The Night before Christmas,* Harper, 1963.

Charles Dickens, *Captain Boldheart* [and] *The Magic Fishbone,* Macmillan, 1964.

Ogden Nash, *The Animal Garden: A Story,* M. Evans, 1965.

Charlotte Zolotow, *When I Have a Little Girl,* Harper, 1965.

Zolotow, *When I Have a Little Boy,* Harper, 1967.

Judith Viorst, *Sunday Morning: A Story,* Harper, 1968.

Margaret Fishback, *A Child's Book of Natural History,* Platt & Munk, 1969.

Patricia M. Scarry, *The Jeremy Mouse Book,* American Heritage Press, 1969.

Nathaniel Benchley, *Feldman Fieldmouse: A Fable,* Harper, 1971.

Duncan Emrich, editor, *The Book Wishes and Wishmaking,* American Heritage Press, 1971.

Janice Udry, *Angie,* Harper, 1971.

Adelaide Holl, *Most-of-the-Time Maxie: A Story,* Xerox Family Education Services, 1974.

Robert Kraus, *I'm a Monkey,* Windmill Books, 1975.

Marilyn Sachs, *Matt's Mitt,* Doubleday, 1975.

Steven Kroll, *That Makes Me Mad!,* Pantheon, 1976.

Lucille Ogle and Tina Thoburn, *The Golden Picture Dictionary: A Beginning Dictionary of More than 2500 Words,* Western Publishing, 1976.

Six Impossible Things before Breakfast, A-W, 1977.

Night Light Calendar 1977, Windmill, 1977.

Cinderella, Random House, 1979.

Alice Bach, *Warren Weasel's Worse than Measles,* Harper, 1980.

Stephanie Calmenson, compiler, *Never Take a Pig to Lunch; and Other Funny Poems about Animals,* Doubleday, 1982.

Peg Bracken, *The Compleat I Hate to Cook Book,* Harcourt, 1986, revised edition, 1979.

Ellen Weiss, *Telephone Time: A First Book of Telephone Do's and Don'ts,* Random House, 1986.

Val Schaffner, *Algonquin Cat,* Carol Publishing Group, 1987.

Natalie Standiford, *The Best Little Monkeys in the World,* Random House, 1987.

Hilary Knight's the Twelve Days of Christmas, Macmillan, 1987.

Kraus, *Screamy Mimi,* Simon & Schuster, 1987.

Lee Bennett Hopkins, editor, *Side by Side: Poems to Read Together,* Simon & Schuster, 1988.

Narcissa G. Chamberlain, *The Omelette Book,* David R. Godine, 1990.

Hopkins, compiler, *Happy Birthday,* Simon & Schuster, 1991.

Nancy Robinson, *Ten Tall Soldiers,* Holt, 1991.

SIDELIGHTS: Hilary Knight is a well-respected author and multi-talented illustrator with a world-wide reputation of creating unique and delightful characters in both words and pictures. Reviewers, such as a critic for *Bulletin of the Center of Children's Books,* have called his creations "ebullient and imaginative."

Very prolific and hardworking, Knight has written and illustrated nine books for children, illustrated nearly fifty other books for both children and adults, breathed new life into a number of classic folktales with his illustrations, as well as designed theater posters promoting several very popular Broadway plays.

Although he has illustrated nearly fifty books written by such famous children's authors as Betty MacDonald, Charlotte Zolotow, and Judith Viorst, Knight is probably most identified as the illustrator of Kay Thompson's enormously popular *Eloise* books. A long time favorite character of children and adolescents, Eloise is a feisty 6-year-old girl who lives in one of New York City's classic hotels, The Plaza, with her English nanny, her dog, and her turtle. In Thompson's original book, *Eloise,* and her three follow-up stories, *Eloise in Paris, Eloise at Christmas Time,* and *Eloise in Moscow,* Knight has charmed readers with Eloise's delightful antics and funny adventures.

In a *McCall's* interview with Cynthia Lindsay, Kay Thompson discussed her search for an illustrator for her idea of *Eloise* and shared her first impression of Knight: "A Princetonian young man, shy, gentle and soft-spoken, came in. He seemed terribly impressed with me, which naturally impressed me terribly with him. I noticed his hands, which were slim and artistic, and thought that was a step in the right direction. So I wrote twelve lines on a piece of paper and handed it to him. 'I'm going to write this book,' I said. 'I'll leave this with you. If you're interested, get in touch with me.' Then I spoke a few words of Eloisiana and left."

Thompson continued: "That Christmas I received a card from Knight. It was an interesting, beautifully executed and highly stylized picture of an angel and Santa Claus, streaking through the sky on a Christmas tree. On the end of the tree, grinning a lovely grin, her wild hair standing on end, was Eloise. It was immediate recognition on my part. There she was. In person. I knew at once Hilary Knight had to illustrate the book."

In a review of *Eloise,* a writer for *Books of Wonder News* noted: "Knight's two-color drawings bring Eloise to life better than words alone ever could. You and your favorite youngster can follow her high-speed travels up and down the elevator...through formal dining rooms...across the lobby...up the stars—zigzagging merrily across the page as she goes."

Reviewers and readers have wondered for years who was Knight's inspiration for his vision of Thompson's Eloise. While many people guessed a number of famous children, including the late Judy Garland's now famous daughter Liza Minnelli, Knight remarked to *New York* that his inspiration for the character was really a family acquaintance. "Her look—her little face—was based on a friend of my parents," Knight told Edith Newhall, "a friendly woman named Eloise Davison who was a food writer for the *Herald Tribune.* She was in her fifties

Eloise lives in New York City's Plaza Hotel, a grand setting for her adventures and antics. (Illustration from *Eloise,* written by Thompson, illustrated by Knight.)

when I knew her, so I imagined what she looked like as a little girl."

Knight and Thompson's Eloise character is so solidly linked with The Plaza Hotel that Knight was Plaza manager Ivana Trump's obvious choice to design a day care-type suite in the hotel where guests could leave their children. Demonstrating his versatility, Knight also created children's menus sprinkled with drawings of Eloise for the Plaza restaurants.

Knight has traveled extensively and in 1966, Knight spent a great deal of time visiting Rome, Moscow, and Paris, as well as many other European cities.

WORKS CITED:

Lindsay, Cynthia, "*McCall's* Visits Kay Thompson," *McCall's,* January, 1975.

Newhall, Edith, "Hilary of the Plaza," *New York,* January 16, 1989, p. 22.
Review of *Eloise, Books of Wonder News,* November, 1988.
Review of *Hilary Knight's The Owl and the Pussy-cat, Bulletin of the Center for Children's Books,* April, 1984.

FOR MORE INFORMATION SEE:

PERIODICALS

American Artist, March, 1963.
New York Herald, November 12, 1961.
New York Times Book Review, November 12, 1961.
Saturday Review, October 17, 1964.*

*   *   *

KNIGHT, Kathryn Lasky
   See LASKY, Kathryn

L

LASKY, Kathryn 1944-
(Kathryn Lasky Knight)

PERSONAL: Born June 24, 1944, in Indianapolis, IN; daughter of Marven (a wine bottler) and Hortense (a social worker) Lasky; married Christopher Knight (a photographer and filmmaker), May 30, 1971; children: Maxwell, Meribah. *Education:* University of Michigan, B.A., 1966; Wheelock College, M.A., 1977.

ADDRESSES: Home—7 Scott St., Cambridge, MA 02138. *Agent*—Jed Mattes, 175 West 73rd St., New York, NY.

CAREER: Writer.

AWARDS, HONORS: Boston Globe-Horn Book Award, 1981, for *The Weaver's Gift;* American Library Association (ALA) notable book citations, 1981, for *The Night Journey* and *The Weaver's Gift,* 1984, for *Sugaring Time,* and 1985, for *Puppeteer;* National Jewish Book Award, Jewish Welfare Board Book Council, and Sydney Taylor Book Award, Association of Jewish Libraries, both 1982, both for *The Night Journey;* ALA best books for young adults citations, 1983, for *Beyond the Divide,* 1984, for *Prank,* and 1986, for *Pageant; New York Times* notable book citation, 1983, for *Beyond the Divide;* Newbery Honor Book, ALA, 1984, for *Sugaring Time; Washington Post*/Children's Book Guild Nonfiction Award, 1986, for body of work; "Youth-to-Youth Books: A List for Imagination and Survival" citation, Pratt Library's Young Adult Advisory Board, 1988, for *The Bone Wars.*

WRITINGS:

JUVENILE BOOKS

Agatha's Alphabet, Rand McNally, 1975.
I Have Four Names for My Grandfather, illustrated with photographs by husband, Christopher Knight, Little, Brown, 1976.
Tugboats Never Sleep, illustrated with photographs by Knight, Little, Brown, 1977.

KATHRYN LASKY

Tall Ships, illustrated with photographs by Knight, Scribner, 1978.
My Island Grandma, Warne, 1979.
The Weaver's Gift, illustrated with photographs by Knight, Warne, 1981.
The Night Journey, illustrated by Trina Schart Hyman, Warne, 1981.
Dollmaker: The Eyelight and the Shadow, illustrated with photographs by Knight, Scribner, 1981.
Jem's Island, Scribner, 1982.
Sugaring Time, illustrated with photographs by Knight, Macmillan, 1983.
Beyond the Divide, Macmillan, 1983.

Lasky and her husband, Christopher Knight, recorded the entire process of turning sap into maple syrup in *Sugaring Time.*

A Baby for Max (in the words of son, Maxwell B. Knight), illustrated with photographs by Knight, Scribner, 1984.

Prank, Macmillan, 1984.

Home Free, Macmillan, 1985.

Puppeteer, illustrated with photographs by Knight, Macmillan, 1985.

Pageant, Four Winds Press, 1986.

Sea Swan, illustrated by Catherine Stock, Macmillan, 1988.

The Bone Wars, Morrow, 1988.

Traces of Life: The Origins of Humankind, illustrated by Whitney Powell, Morrow, 1989.

Dinosaur Dig, illustrated with photographs by Knight, Morrow, 1990.

Fourth of July Bear, illustrated by Helen Cogancherry, Morrow, 1991.

Double Trouble Squared, Harcourt, 1991.

ADULT BOOKS UNDER NAME KATHRYN LASKY KNIGHT

Atlantic Circle, illustrated with photographs by Knight, Norton, 1985.

Trace Elements, Norton, 1986.

The Widow of Oz, Norton, 1989.

Mortal Words, Simon & Schuster, 1990.

Mumbo Jumbo, Simon & Schuster, 1991.

OTHER

Contributor to periodicals, including *Sail* and *Horn Book.*

ADAPTATIONS: Sugaring Time was adapted as a filmstrip by Random House, 1986, for audio cassette, 1986, and for videocassette, 1988.

SIDELIGHTS: Kathryn Lasky is a versatile writer best known for her nonfiction juvenile works and her young adult novels. Her informational books, many of which contain photographs by her husband Christopher Knight, often focus on traditional crafts, such as doll-making and weaving. Through her descriptions of these arts, Lasky imparts feelings of both respect and wonder for the skill of the craftsmen who practice them. Lasky's novels similarly focus on traditional themes and feature

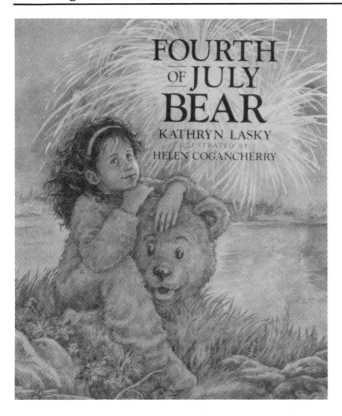

Lasky's *Fourth of July Bear* was inspired by her family's summers in Maine. (Cover illustration by Helen Cogancherry.)

strong-willed protagonists who are frequently challenged or inspired by ethnic, historical, or religious elements. Picture books for young children are also among Lasky's many works, as are adult books written under her married name. She is often praised for her use of vibrant imagery and her ability to capture moods and facts in eloquent, clear language.

While growing up, Lasky recalls that she "was always thinking up stories—whether I wrote them down or not didn't seem to matter. I was a compulsive story maker." These early stories were extremely private, and she shared them with no one. And although she always wanted to be a writer, Lasky saw the profession as lacking in authenticity. "It was enjoyable, not reliable, and you were your own boss. This all seemed funny," she explains. "It was only when I began to share my writing with my parents (and much later my husband) and sensed their responsiveness that I began to think that it was o.k. to want to be a writer."

Since then, Lasky has had a variety of books published, among them a number of nonfiction books which celebrate such crafts as weaving, dollmaking, and puppetry. *The Weaver's Gift* follows the process by which wool is sheared from sheep and transformed into finished products, such as a child's blanket. The seven brief chapters are illustrated with photographs by Lasky's husband and provide a "description that evokes the sights, sounds and textures of a homey, ancient art," points out Patricia Homer in *School Library Journal.* In

Dollmaker: The Eyelight and the Shadow and *Puppeteer,* Lasky offers similar examinations of artists and their crafts. She describes the steps involved in the creation of dolls and puppets while simultaneously presenting character traits of their creators. Lasky "gets inside the dollmaker's craft to such an extent that not only is each step beautifully detailed, but the dollmaker's anxieties and concerns over her creation are expressed as well," observes Homer in her review of *Dollmaker.* And Zena Sutherland asserts in the *Bulletin of the Center for Children's Books* that *Puppeteer* describes the skill and "theatrical flair that go into creating a polished and dramatic illusion in a form of the performing arts that has always been especially popular with children."

In other nonfiction books, Lasky takes part in the activity being described. For her 1983 *Sugaring Time,* she and her husband visited the Laceys' Vermont farm and recorded the entire process of turning sap into maple syrup, from the tapping of the trees to the cleanup months later. "In vivid, clear, and at times even mouth-watering prose the author explains the steps involved in making maple syrup," explains Karen Jameyson in *Horn Book.* Lasky's "perspective on the value of all living things, the seasons, work, and tradition provides a warm and satisfying framework for this presentation of information," concludes *Language Arts* contributor Alice Naylor.

Lasky collected research for her 1990 *Dinosaur Dig* in a similar fashion by taking her family to Montana to participate in a fossil dig. Led by paleontologist Keith Rigby, the Laskys and five other families learned the strenuous and elaborate aspects involved in such a dig, many of which Lasky describes in her book. "Lasky's writing literally covers new ground on the dinosaur frontier as she takes readers along through the hot Montana sun to share the excitement of uncovering bones that have lain unseen for millions of years," comments Cathryn A. Camper in *School Library Journal.* And Barbara Bottner notes in the *Los Angeles Times Book Review* that *Dinosaur Dig* "leaves one covered with sand, with dirt under his nails, bugs in his face and dryness in his mouth, but reawakens a powerful, currently underrated awe for nature and our Earth's history."

History is also a major element in Lasky's novels. *The Night Journey,* published in 1981, shifts back and forth between Nana Sashie's description of her Jewish family's dangerous escape from Czarist Russia, and the present realities of her great-granddaughter Rachel's secure and comfortable life. Thirteen-year-old Rachel spends a portion of her afternoons keeping Nana Sashie company, and it is during the course of these visits that Rachel is told the story of the escape. "The structure of the narrative underlines this sense of continuity and the book is full of images which echo across time and back into Jewish history," describes Peter Kennerley in the *School Librarian.* Ilene Cooper praises Lasky's mixture of the past and present in *Booklist,* claiming: "Just as Rachel must wait to hear the whole adventure, the reader too is tantalized, eager to hear more. The story has so many aspects that each person will come away with his own idea of what makes this book memorable."

Continuing her examination of history and the uncovering of fossils, Lasky presents the late action-filled 1800s in *The Bone Wars*. The Badlands of Montana provide the setting for this story of discovery in which scientific teams from Harvard, Yale, and Cambridge compete to unearth the most fossils to take back to their respective schools. Thad Longsworth, an orphan hired as a scout for the Harvard team, develops a friendship with Julian DeMott, the son of an aspiring British paleontologist. The two boys experience a number of adventures involving both Indians and other white men. Upon observing the greediness and betrayal taking place around them, the boys eventually decide to conduct their own dig and donate whatever they find to a museum for all to see. "The details Lasky uses to describe both the monotony and the thrill of excavation work are excellent, the historical background rich, the sense of adventure keen and the characterizations intriguing, but perhaps not so developed as they might be," remarks Kem Knapp Sawyer in the *Washington Post Book World*. And Yvonne A. Frey concludes in *School Library Journal:* "This is poetically written historical fiction that will give young adult readers a real sense of a complex period of our history."

Although many of Lasky's works are based on fact, she is more captivated with the ambiguous and hazy aspect of her subjects. "I have a fascination with the inexact and the unexplainable," she relates in *Horn Book.* "I try to do as little explaining as possible, but I try to present my subject in some way so it will not lose what I have found to be or suspect to be its sacred dimension. I seem to seek a nonfactual kind of truth that focuses on certain aesthetic and psychological realities. Facts are quite cheap, but real stories are rare and expensive." She adds that her books are "not concerned with messages, and I really do not care if readers remember a single fact. What I do hope is that they come away with a sense of joy—indeed celebration—about something they have sensed of the world in which they live."

WORKS CITED:

Bottner, Barbara, "Gifts That Traverse Afar," *Los Angeles Times Book Review,* March 25, 1990, p. 8.

Camper, Cathryn A., review of *Dinosaur Dig, School Library Journal,* May, 1990, p. 98.

Cooper, Ilene, review of *The Night Journey, Booklist,* November 15, 1981, pp. 439-40.

Frey, Yvonne A., review of *The Bone Wars, School Library Journal,* November, 1988, p. 126.

Homer, Patricia, review of *The Weaver's Gift, School Library Journal,* March, 1981, p. 147.

Homer, review of *Dollmaker: The Eyelight and the Shadow, School Library Journal,* March, 1982, pp. 148-49.

Jameyson, Karen, review of *Sugaring Time, Horn Book,* June, 1983, p. 323.

Kennerley, Peter, review of *The Night Journey, School Librarian,* June, 1983, p. 144.

Lasky, Kathryn, "Reflections on Nonfiction," *Horn Book,* September-October, 1985, pp. 527-32.

Naylor, Alice, review of *Sugaring Time, Language Arts,* September, 1984, p. 543.

Sawyer, Kem Knapp, "When Bad Things Happen," *Washington Post Book World,* December 25, 1988, p. 13.

Sutherland, Zena, review of *Puppeteer, Bulletin of the Center for Children's Books,* July-August, 1985, pp. 209-10.

FOR MORE INFORMATION SEE:

BOOKS

Children's Literature Review, Volume 11, Gale, 1986, pp. 112-22.

PERIODICALS

Appraisal: Science Books for Young People, winter, 1984, pp. 34-35.

Best Sellers, September, 1984, pp. 234-35.

Bulletin of the Center for Children's Books, May, 1979, p. 157; July-August, 1979, p. 194; January, 1982; June, 1983, p. 192; July-August, 1983, p. 213; May, 1984, p. 168; July-August, 1984, p. 208; July-August, 1985; February, 1986, p. 112; November, 1986.

English Journal, January, 1984, pp. 87-89.

Horn Book, April, 1982, pp. 166-67; February, 1983, p. 45.

Interracial Books for Children Bulletin, Volume 12, numbers 4, 5, 1981, p. 38; Volume 16, number 1, 1985, pp. 7-8.

Kirkus Reviews, July 1, 1976, p. 728; July 15, 1977, p. 729; February 1, 1979, p. 130; April 1, 1979, p. 385; March 1, 1981, p. 286; February 1, 1982, p. 136; February 15, 1982, p. 204; November 1, 1985, p. 1198; February 15, 1991, p. 255.

Language Arts, January, 1984, pp. 70-71; February, 1984, p. 183; March, 1985, pp. 287-88.

New York Times Book Review, March 18, 1979, p. 26; March 13, 1983, p. 29; August 21, 1983, p. 26; December 18, 1988, p. 30; June 24, 1990, p. 28.

Publishers Weekly, January 10, 1986, p. 84; February 8, 1991, pp. 56-57.

School Library Journal, November, 1976, p. 48; March, 1979, p. 141; January, 1982, p. 79; February, 1983, p. 78; October, 1984, p. 149; August, 1985, p. 67.

Times Educational Supplement, November 19, 1982, p. 36.

Voice of Youth Advocates, February, 1989, p. 286.

Washington Post Book World, July 8, 1990, p. 10.

—*Sketch by Susan M. Reicha*

*   *   *

LEVY, Elizabeth 1942-

PERSONAL: Born April 4, 1942, in Buffalo, NY; daughter of Elmer Irving and Mildred (Kirschenbaum) Levy; married George R. Vickers (a professor of sociology), January 26, 1979. *Education:* Brown University,

ELIZABETH LEVY

B.A. (magna cum laude), 1964; Columbia University, M.A.T., 1968.

ADDRESSES: Agent—Elaine Markson Literary Agency, Inc., 44 Greenwich Ave., New York, NY 10011.

CAREER: Writer, 1971—. American Broadcasting Co., New York City, editor and researcher in news department, 1964-66; Macmillan Publishing Co., Inc., New York City, assistant editor, 1967-69; New York Public Library, New York City, writer in public relations, 1969; JPM Associates (urban affairs consultants), New York City, staff writer, 1970-71.

MEMBER: Authors Guild, Authors League of America, Mystery Writers of America, PEN.

AWARDS, HONORS: Struggle and Lose, Struggle and Win: The United Mineworkers Story was named outstanding book of the year by the *New York Times*, 1977.

WRITINGS:

NONFICTION

The People Lobby: The SST Story, Delacorte, 1973.
Lawyers for the People, Knopf, 1974.
By-Lines: Profiles in Investigative Journalism, Four Winds Press, 1975.
(With cousin, Robie H. Harris) *Before You Were Three: How You Began to Walk, Talk, Explore, and Have*

Feelings (Book-of-the-Month Club alternate selection), Delacorte, 1977.
(With Mara Miller) *Doctors for the People: Profiles of Six Who Serve*, Knopf, 1977.
(With Tad Richards) *Struggle and Lose, Struggle and Win: The United Mineworkers Story*, Four Winds Press, 1977.
(With Earl Hammond and Liz Hammond) *Our Animal Kingdom*, Delacorte, 1977.
If You Lived When They Signed the Constitution (Book-of-the-Month Club selection), Scholastic Inc., 1987.

JUVENILE FICTION

Nice Little Girls, Delacorte, 1974.
Lizzie Lies a Lot (also see below), Dell, 1976.
Frankenstein Moved in on the Fourth Floor (*My Weekly Reader* Book Club selection), Harper, 1979.
The Tryouts, Four Winds Press, 1979.
Running Out of Time, Knopf, 1980.
Running Out of Magic with Houdini, Knopf, 1981.
Dracula Is a Pain in the Neck, Harper, 1983.
The Shadow Nose, Morrow, 1983.
The Computer That Said Steal Me, Four Winds Press, 1983.
Cold as Ice, Morrow, 1988.
Keep Ms. Sugarman in the Fourth Grade, Harper, 1992.

YOUNG ADULT FICTION

Come Out Smiling, Delacorte, 1981.
Double Standard, Avon, 1984.
The Dani Trap, Morrow, 1984.
Night of Nights, Ballantine, 1984.
All Shook Up, Scholastic Inc., 1986.

"SOMETHING QUEER" MYSTERY SERIES

Something Queer Is Going On (*My Weekly Reader* Book Club selection), Delacorte, 1973.
Something Queer at the Ballpark (Junior Literary Guild selection), Delacorte, 1975.
Something Queer at the Library (Xerox Book Club selection), Delacorte, 1977.
Something Queer on Vacation, Delacorte, 1980.
Something Queer at the Haunted School (*My Weekly Reader* Book Club selection), Delacorte, 1982.
Something Queer at the Lemonade Stand, Delacorte, 1982.
Something Queer in Rock 'n' Roll, Delacorte, 1987.

"JODY AND JAKE MYSTERY" SERIES

The Case of the Frightened Rock Star, Pocket Books, 1980.
The Case of the Counterfeit Race Horse, Pocket Books, 1980.
The Case of the Fired-Up Gang, Pocket Books, 1981.
The Case of the Wild River Ride, Pocket Books, 1981.

"FAT ALBERT AND THE COSBY KIDS" SERIES

The Shuttered Window, Dell, 1981.
Mister Big Time, Dell, 1981.
Take Two, They're Small, Dell, 1981.
Spare the Rod, Dell, 1981.
Mom or Pop, Dell, 1981.
The Runt, Dell, 1981.

"MAGIC MYSTERIES" SERIES

The Case of the Gobbling Squash, Simon & Schuster, 1988.

The Case of the Mind-Reading Mommies, Simon & Schuster, 1989.

The Case of the Tattletale Heart, Simon & Schuster, 1990.

The Case of the Dummy with Cold Eyes, Simon & Schuster, 1991.

"THE GYMNASTS" SERIES

The Beginners, Scholastic Inc., 1988.
First Meet, Scholastic Inc., 1988.
Nobody's Perfect, Scholastic Inc., 1988.
The Winner, Scholastic Inc., 1989.
The Trouble with Elizabeth, Scholastic Inc., 1989.
Bad Break, Scholastic Inc., 1989.
Tumbling Ghosts, Scholastic Inc., 1989.
Captain of the Team, Scholastic Inc., 1989.
Crush on the Coach, Scholastic Inc., 1990.
Boys in the Gym, Scholastic Inc., 1990.
Mystery at the Meet, Scholastic Inc., 1990.
Out of Control, Scholastic Inc., 1990.
First Date, Scholastic Inc., 1990.
World Class Gymnast, Scholastic Inc., 1990.
Nasty Competition, Scholastic Inc., 1991.
Fear of Falling, Scholastic Inc., 1991.
The New Coach, Scholastic Inc., 1991.
Tough at the Top, Scholastic Inc., 1991.
The Gymnast Gift, Scholastic Inc., 1991.

PLAYS

(Co-author) *Croon* (one-act), first produced in New York City, at Performing Garage, March 28, 1976.

(Co-author) *Never Waste a Virgin* (two-act), first produced in New York City at Wonderhorse Theatre, December 3, 1977.

Lizzie Lies a Lot (based on her novel of the same title), first produced by the Cutting Edge, 1978.

OTHER

Marco Polo: The Historic Adventure Based on the Television Spectacular, Random House, 1982.

Father Murphy's First Miracle (based on the television series *Father Murphy*), Random House, 1983.

Return of the Jedi (based on the film of the same title), Random House, 1983.

The Bride (based on the film of the same title), Random House, 1985.

SIDELIGHTS: Elizabeth Levy's books range from fiction to nonfiction and from juvenile stories to young adult novels. Her stories also range from mysteries for young readers to young adult problem novels to novelizations of screenplays. As Levy once explained to *SATA,* "As a child I read all the time and omniverously. I read everything from *Nancy Drew* to *War and Peace.* My mother recalls coming into my room when I was twelve years old and finding *Winnie-the-Pooh, War and Peace, Peyton Place,* and a *Nancy Drew* mystery scattered on my bed. My eclectic reading habits haven't changed much since then, which accounts in part for the variety of books I write."

Two brothers suspect that their strange new neighbor is really Frankenstein in Levy's *Frankenstein Moved in on the Fourth Floor.* (Cover illustration by Mordicai Gerstein.)

Levy's books based on the *Fat Albert and the Cosby Kids* cartoon characters have proven popular with young readers. This series covers such issues as honesty, facing the death of a loved one, drugs, stealing, and child abuse. Speaking of the *Fat Albert* books, Barbara Karlin writes in the *Los Angeles Times Book Review:* "Despite jargon, despite the shouting quality of capitalized sentences, these books succeed because they fill a need."

Lizzie Lies a Lot confronts the issue of honesty when a young girl realizes that her lies threaten a friendship. Lizzie has told her parents lies to make them think she is a good dancer in school. And she has told her friend Sara lies to entertain her. But Lizzie tires of telling lies and she realizes that she must change. *Lizzie Lies a Lot,* Levy explained to *SATA,* "is the most autobiographical of my books. I did lie a lot as a child, and I can distinctly remember what it felt like when I knew I was lying and no one else did. Like Lizzie in my novel, I told my mother I had been asked to perform in a school assembly and I kept up that lie for months.

"Oddly enough, my first published work was a lie. When I was in third grade, a newspaper published my poem

'When I Grow Up I Want to Be a Nurse All Dressed in White.' I didn't want to be a nurse. If I wanted to be anything, I wanted to be a writer, but the idea of being a writer seemed a fantasy. I grew up without any concrete ambitions, but with an entire card catalog of fantasies."

Although Levy draws upon her childhood for many of her plots, she also bases her books on what interests her today. "When I write for children," she told *SATA*, "I am really writing about things that seem funny or interesting to me now. I don't think writing a good book for children is very different from writing one for teenagers or adults. The emotions we have as children are in many ways as complex as those we have as adults. The best children's writers know this and are not tempted to oversimplify.

"I think about my own childhood a lot, and when I write about a certain age I have very vivid memories of what it felt like then. I think that memories from childhood are like dreams. It's not important to remember all of them, but what you do remember is important."

The characters in Levy's "The Gymnasts" series have become particularly special to her in the course of writing over twenty books of their adventures. "They've certainly been a major part of my life these last three years," she explains. "I've found that writing a series so intensely is a very vivid experience. The characters take on their own life, and actually kept me company. I took a lot of comfort and joy from my gymnasts. They were good friends to each other, and good friends to me through some family illnesses. I've spoken to other authors of series and they agree. Writing a series of twenty-two books with the same characters is similar to creating a make-believe group of 'best friends' who move in with you, driving your family nuts, but giving you a lot of comfort."

Among Levy's most popular books have been the "Something Queer" mystery series for younger readers, featuring the girl sleuths Gwen and Jill. The two girls solve puzzling mysteries at school and in their neighborhood. In *Something Queer at the Haunted School*, they track down what may be a real ghost. In *Something Queer on Vacation*, they discover who has been knocking down sandcastles at the beach. Among the series most engaging aspects, a reviewer for the *Bulletin of the Center for Children's Books* believes, are a "light style, active girl detectives, humor, and a gratifying solution to the mystery."

Levy finds that she takes a different approach when she writes a mystery. "I find writing mysteries," she told *SATA*, "very different from writing novels. The great pleasure of writing a mystery is that I know how the book will end. Before I begin a mystery, I have to figure out who did it and why. I know that by the end of the book my detectives will expose the character. Usually I do not know the path my detectives will take to make this discovery. I have to go back and on the second and third drafts I must change significant parts of the book to lay clues that develop towards the end of the book.

"However, the end is always in place. I think that is why we like mysteries. People who don't read mysteries can never understand how I can read them at night before I go to sleep. 'Don't they keep you up?' friends ask. I find mysteries comforting. I read them when I'm tired or upset. Unless the writer is a cheat, I know the book will have a satisfactory ending. The bad will be punished and the characters I like will survive to live in another book. I only like mystery 'series.'

"Novels are completely different. Usually I write a novel about a conflict that I remember from my own childhood or something that I have experienced recently but believe that I also experienced when I was younger. I believe that the gift of a novel is to let others know that they are not alone, and that our secrets are usually far more shameful if kept hidden than if allowed out in the open. In most of my books, friendship is important. My friends are a huge part of my life, without them I would be bereft, and in my books I try to celebrate the healing power of friendship."

WORKS CITED:

Karlin, Barbara, review of "Fat Albert" books, *Los Angeles Times Book Review*, May 31, 1981.
Review of *Something Queer in Rock 'n' Roll, Bulletin of the Center for Children's Books*, December, 1987.
Something about the Author, Volume 31, Gale, 1983, pp. 115-118.

FOR MORE INFORMATION SEE:

BOOKS

Fifth Book of Junior Authors and Illustrators, H. W. Wilson, 1983, pp.193-195.

PERIODICALS

Bulletin of the Center for Children's Books, May, 1983; October, 1983; March, 1984; November, 1984.
New York Times Book Review, April 26, 1981; April 25, 1982.
Washington Post Book World, May 9, 1982; November 6, 1983.

*   *   *

LEWIS, J. Patrick 1942-

PERSONAL: Born May 5, 1942, in Gary, IN; son of Leo J. and Mary (Cambruzzi) Lewis; married Judith Weaver, August 29, 1964 (divorced, 1983); children: Beth, Matthew, Leigh Ann. *Education:* St. Joseph's College, Rensselaer, IN, B.A., 1964; Indiana University—Bloomington, M.A., 1965; Ohio State University, Ph.D., 1974. *Religion:* None.

ADDRESSES: Home—481 Foxtrail Circle E., Westerville, OH 43081. *Office*— Otterbein College, Westerville, OH 43081. *Agent*—Joanna Lewis Cole, 532 West 114th St., New York, NY 10025.

CAREER: Otterbein College, Westerville, OH, professor of economics, 1974—.

J. PATRICK LEWIS

AWARDS, HONORS: The Tsar and the Amazing Cow was named children's book of the year by Ohioana Library Association, 1989; individual artist grant in adult poetry, Ohio Arts Council, 1991.

WRITINGS:

The Tsar and the Amazing Cow, illustrated by Friso Henstra, Dial Books for Young Readers, 1988.
The Hippopotamusn't, illustrated by Victoria Chess, Dial Books for Young Readers, 1990.
Two-legged, Four-legged, No-legged Rhymes, illustrated by Pamela Paparone, Knopf, 1991.
Earth Verses and Water Rhymes, illustrated by Robert Sabuda, Atheneum, 1991.
The Moonbows of Mr. B. Bones, illustrated by Dirk Zimmer, Knopf, 1992.
The Fat-Cats at Sea, Knopf, in press.

Contributor of reviews to periodicals, including *Nation, Chicago Tribune,* and *San Francisco Chronicle;* contributor of articles and reviews to professional journals.

WORK IN PROGRESS: Commissioned by Children's Book Council to write the 1992 National Book Week poem; *Christmas of the Reddle Moon* and *Ridicholas Nicholas Duck and Other Animal Poems,* both for Dial Books for Young Readers, publication expected in 1994; poetry.

SIDELIGHTS: J. Patrick Lewis told *SATA:* "The great ghosts of Edward Lear, Lewis Carroll, A. A. Milne, Walter de la Mare, and others rattle around my house. They're all the inspiration that a poet for children could wish for. I've been very lucky, too, for the constant friendship, generosity, and criticism of Myra Cohn Livingston, one of America's finest children's poet/anthologists."

LONG, Kim 1949-

PERSONAL: Born March 22, 1949, in Bloomington, IN; son of Robert Irving (a psychologist) and Thelma (an occupational therapist; maiden name, Miron) Long. *Education:* Wesleyan University, B.A., 1971.

ADDRESSES: Office—1447 Ogden, Denver, CO 80218.

CAREER: Free-lance graphic artist in Berkeley, CA, 1972-74; high school teacher of art and design in Palo Alto, CA, 1974-76; Scandia Die Co., Albuquerque, NM, printer and die designer, 1976-78; automotive mechanic in Albuquerque, 1977; political consultant and campaign manager in Albuquerque, 1978; writer, 1979—. Production manager of *The Daily Planet Almanac,* 1975-86. Worked variously in home remodeling, in a factory, and as a book illustrator.

WRITINGS:

(With Terry Reim) *Kicking the Bucket,* Morrow, 1985, reprinted as *Fatal Facts,* Crown, 1986.
(With Terry Reim) *The Daily Planet Vacation Almanac,* World Almanac, 1986.
The Trout Almanac: Rocky Mountain Region, Johnson Books, 1987.
The Moon Book: The Meaning of the Methodical Movements of the Magnificent Mysterious Moon and Other Interesting Facts, Johnson Books, 1988.
The Astronaut Training Book for Kids, Dutton, 1989.

Author of column distributed by North America Syndicate, 1986-87. Contributor to *The Old Farmer's Almanac* and *Consumer's Almanac,* and to periodicals, including *Spy, Longevity,* and a Japanese magazine.

KIM LONG

ANNUAL PUBLICATIONS

(Editor with Terry Reim) *The Daily Planet Almanac,* editions published by John Muir, And/Or Books, Planet Publications, Avon, and Running Press, 1976-87.

The Moon Calendar, Johnson Books, 1982—.

(Editor with Terry Reim) *Predictions 1984,* Putnam, 1984, subsequent editions published as *The American Forecaster Almanac,* Running Press, 1985-90, Johnson Books, 1991—.

WORK IN PROGRESS: Field Trips and Educational Destinations for Students, Contests, Prizes, and Awards for Students, and *The Almanac of Anniversaries,* all for ABC-CLIO; on-going research for *The American Forecaster Almanac.*

SIDELIGHTS: Kim Long told *SATA:* "Writing has always been a natural function for me. I have always found it easy to put down what I am observing, studying, or thinking on paper. The problem with writing has been that it was such an automatic process that I was in my thirties before I realized that it could be a useful way to make a living. Before writing as a career, I tried graphic art, illustration, automotive mechanics, home remodeling, factory work, teaching, and lots of part-time work. Writing was an important part of my school years, but it just seemed like a simple skill that helped get papers done on time. In various jobs, writing was also instrumental in getting things done. At one time, I helped design and illustrate books, but even when I contributed articles and did other writing assignments, I thought of this as a distraction from my 'real' career of graphic art.

"I soon realized that I was writing more than drawing or designing, and enjoying it more. Most of what I did as an illustrator and designer was work with other people's ideas. As a writer, I took my own ideas and made them do useful things such as describe astronomical events, how to fish, or understand the history of coffee. Before long, writing was the only thing I did, and through this craft, I discovered how to make a living.

"In 1983 one of my writing projects became a book: *The American Forecaster Almanac.* In order to write about a subject, I had to know as much as possible about it; before a writer begins to write, he or she must be a researcher. The research skills that I developed turned out to be as useful as writing, and often, just as enjoyable. As a child, spending time in the library had always been one of my most enjoyable pastimes, especially as we never had a television at home and reading was an important part of my daily activities. As an adult, libraries are where I do most of my research work, looking for information about different subjects. This information is used in *The American Forecaster Almanac,* my major ongoing writing project. Because this annual book covers upcoming changes in society, I am now known as a forcaster as well as a writer. Learning about different things that are undergoing change— from collecting baseball cards to designing new lids for medicine bottles—also gives me ideas for other books and articles. I write articles about American trends for a Japanese magazine, some American magazines, and occasionally newspapers. Book ideas can also come from this research. *The Astronaut Training Book for Kids,* for instance, was originally inspired by trends in education—to improve math and science teaching— and career goals of children; in the mid-1980s, most children wanted to become astronauts when they grew up."

* * *

LORD, Beman 1924-1991

OBITUARY NOTICE—See index for *SATA* sketch: Born November 22, 1924, in Delaware County, NY; died June 10, 1991, in London, England. Publishing executive and author. Lord, the author of numerous sports-oriented children's books, was vice-president and director of institutional sales at Charles Scribner's Sons from 1970 to 1985. In the early 1950s he served as the head of the *New York Times* and Children's Book Council "Reading Is Fun Exhibit." Lord's publications include *The Trouble with Francis, Quarterback's Aim, Rough Ice,* and *Shrimp's Soccer Goal.*

OBITUARIES AND OTHER SOURCES:

BOOKS

Authors of Books for Young People, 3rd edition, Scarecrow, 1990.

PERIODICALS

School Library Journal, August, 1991, p. 21.

M

MacDONALD, Anson
See HEINLEIN, Robert A.

* * *

MacKINNON, Bernie 1957-

PERSONAL: Born July 17, 1957, in Antigonish, Nova Scotia, Canada. *Education:* University of Maine at Orono, B.A., 1979.

ADDRESSES: Home—536 Cumberland Ave., No. 2, Portland, ME 04101.

CAREER: Writer of young adult fiction.

AWARDS, HONORS: American Library Association best book for young adult citations, 1984 and 1986, both for *The Meantime.*

WRITINGS:

The Meantime, Houghton, 1984.
Song for a Shadow, Houghton, 1991.

SIDELIGHTS: Bernie MacKinnon told *SATA:* "My two novels, *The Meantime* and *Song for a Shadow,* differ widely in background and in dynamics between the characters. Yet they are connected in ways that aren't necessarily obvious. Both depict the fires of adolescence, when a person's spirit and nerve endings meet life's central conflicts, point-blank and for the first time. The stories present young characters facing their personal and cultural baggage, trying to take a stand and declare themselves as individuals. Pressures beyond the characters' control touch off internal crises. Seventeen-year-old Luke Parrish, a black high school senior in *The Meantime,* has to face harassment in a white suburban community, keeping his integrity in one piece while not caving in to hate and fear. In *Song for a Shadow,* eighteen-year-old guitarist Aaron Webb must deal with the legacy of his parents—his father, a rock 'n' roll legend whose fame makes Aaron feel stifled, and his mother, a sixties flower child now hospitalized for depression. In hindsight I see that while writing these

BERNIE MacKINNON

novels I was drawing upon a major fixation of mine—the historical roots of our problems,and the lonely peculiar ways in which these legacies affect us, complicating the already tough question of how best to use our lives.

"At the heart of *The Meantime* is my concern with how violence and prejudice affect most people, and with finding that cut-off point where fear turns to cruelty, conformity and callousness. The idea for the story occurred to me when I saw a documentary about a formerly all-white suburb in Ohio where black families were being harassed. This triggered memories I had of Hartford, Connecticut, in the late 1960s, when the schools were being integrated.

"The spark for *Song for a Shadow* occurred when I read a magazine interview with one of the world's most famous rock stars, a man whose life exemplified the rock 'n' roll myth. He mentioned his son in the interview, and I wondered what it might be like to be that boy. How did he see things? What inner battles did he face, owing to his inheritance? This connected with my interest in the generational tug-of-war—the way in which each generation rebels against the previous one, rejecting or de-emphasizing some of their parents' values while stressing new ones. What I find most compelling is the distinct price that generations pay, collectively and as individuals, for choices made. Each one believes it hits closest to the truth about life, but time always brings this into question.

"*The Meantime* is a highly compressed story, covering only twelve days in which Luke faces verbal knives and the threat of physical violence at his high school. During this he wonders whether Oscar McBride, the history teacher whom he admires, will be able to effectively challenge the threat and whether he himself can take a stand. He witnesses the impact of this viciousness on his family and schoolmates. But while the story raises more than one question about youth, race and personal values, it has a single main source of tension.

"The time frame of *Song for a Shadow,* by contrast, is nearly three months. Locale and cultural context are different, and there are several intense focal points: Aaron's unresolved conflicts with his parents; his frustrated need to declare himself as a person, while maintaining an anonymity to separate himself from his father's fame; the adjustment of his prematurely jaded nature to the small-town life of Fox Hill, Maine; his relationship with the Fergusons, the family who more-or-less adopt him; his love for Gail, the Ferguson's daughter; his job at the corner grocery store of Gail's father, Jerry; his hopes for success with the garage band of Gail's brother, Doug; and finally, his deeper dilemma over the limits of human nature. Still, despite their greatly differing backgrounds, Luke and Aaron would understand and like each other if they ever met up."

FOR MORE INFORMATION SEE:

PERIODICALS

ALAN Review, fall, 1991.
Booklist, October 15, 1988; January 1, 1985; March 15, 1991.
Book Report, September/October, 1991.
Bulletin of the Center for Children's Books, January, 1985.
Horn Book, June, 1991.
Publishers Weekly, February 8, 1991.
School Library Journal, April, 1985.
Voice of Youth Advocates, June, 1991.

*   *   *

MAGGIO, Rosalie 1943-

PERSONAL: Born November 8, 1943, in Victoria, TX; daughter of Paul J. (a dentist) and Irene (a homemaker; maiden name, Nash) Maggio; married David Koskenmaki (a research scientist), December 2, 1968; children: Liz, Katie, Matt. *Education:* College of St. Catherine,

ROSALIE MAGGIO

B.A., 1966; Universite de Nancy, certificates, 1966. *Politics:* Democrat. *Religion:* Roman Catholic.

ADDRESSES: Home—1297 Summit Ave., St. Paul, MN 55105.

CAREER: Translator, editor, and writer.

MEMBER: Society of Children's Book Writers, The Loft.

AWARDS, HONORS: Corecipient, Northwind Story Hour contest, The Loft, 1985; Abigail Award, Abigail Quigley McCarthy Center for Women's Research, Resources, and Scholarship, 1988, for *The Nonsexist Word Finder: A Dictionary of Gender-Free Usage;* magazine merit award for outstanding work in nonfiction, Society of Children's Book Writers, 1988, for story "Daredevil Marie"; winner, *Highlights for Children* fiction contest, 1990, for "Harley and Me"; recipient, Jerome, Dayton Hudson, General Mills Foundation Literature Travel Award, 1990; winner in informational category of Minnesota Book Award, 1991, for *How to Say It: Words, Phrases, Sentences, and Paragraphs for Every Occasion.*

WRITINGS:

The Travels of Soc, American Guidance Service, 1985.
The Nonsexist Word Finder: A Dictionary of Gender-Free Usage, Oryx, 1987.

*How to Say It: Words, Phrases, Sentences, and Para-
   graphs for Every Occasion,* Prentice-Hall, 1990.
The Music Box Christmas, Morrow Junior Books, 1990.
(With Marcel Cordier) *Marie Marvingt: La Femme d'un
   siecle,* Les Editions Pierron, 1991.
*The Dictionary of Bias-Free Usage: A Guide to Nondis-
   criminatory Language,* Oryx, 1991, Beacon Press,
   1992.
The Beacon Book of Quotations by Women, Beacon
   Press, 1992.

Contributor of articles and short stories to periodicals,
including *Cricket Magazine, Highlights for Children,
Jack and Jill, Children's Playmate, Young American,*
and *Women's Sports and Fitness.*

WORK IN PROGRESS: A series of mysteries for ages
nine to twelve set in a 1950s orphanage; research on
orphans and orphanages.

SIDELIGHTS: Rosalie Maggio told *SATA:* "Although I
write books for adults too, the writing I have the most
fun with is for young people—mostly because of the
freedom and excitement that come with making and
living in different worlds. We all have to get along in the
real world with whatever families, talents, looks, and
possessions we might have. But I love being able to walk
through the door to another world by opening a book or
by writing that first sentence. I can do things in my
books that I can't do in the real world. For example, my
children wouldn't let me name our rabbit Primrose
because they didn't like the name. So guess what I called
the rabbit in *The Music Box Christmas?* Primrose, of
course!

"I am deeply concerned about the sexism, racism,
handicappism, and other kinds of discrimination in our
lives. There is even something called adultism, which
means that some adults act as though young people
don't have anything worthwhile to offer the world and
as though their thoughts and feeling don't really count.
One of the things I've done about this is to write a book
that helps people replace discriminatory words with
unbiased words.

"Another thing that I think is important is for writers of
children's books to develop strong, well-rounded characters who can become real for readers. When we read a
really good book about a character of the opposite sex,
or of another race, or from another country, or with a
disability we don't have, it's very hard after that to
stereotype that sex, race, or disability. Once we laugh
and cry with characters, share their thoughts and
adventures, hold our breath for them, we develop an
understanding and sympathy for people different from
ourselves. The world needs this."

*   *   *

MAHY, Margaret 1936-

PERSONAL: Born March 21, 1936, in Whakatane, New
Zealand; daughter of Frances George (a builder) and
May (a teacher; maiden name, Penlington) Mahy;

MARGARET MAHY

children: Penelope Helen, Bridget Frances. *Education:*
University of New Zealand, B.A., 1958. *Politics:* "Anar-
chist." *Religion:* "Humanist." *Hobbies and other interests:* Reading, gardening.

ADDRESSES: Home—R.D. 1, Lyttelton, New Zealand.
Agent—Vanessa Hamilton, The Summer House, Wood-
end, West Stoke Chichester, West Sussex, PO18 9BP
England.

CAREER: Writer. Petone Public Library, Petone, New
Zealand, assistant librarian, 1958-59; School Library
Service, Christchurch, New Zealand, librarian in charge,
1967-76; Canterbury Public Library, Christchurch, children's librarian, 1976-80. Writer in residence, Canterbury University, 1984, and Western Australian College
of Advanced Education, 1985.

MEMBER: New Zealand Library Association.

AWARDS, HONORS: Esther Glenn Medals, New Zea-
land Library Association, 1969, for *A Lion in the
Meadow,* 1973, for *The First Margaret Mahy Story
Book,* and 1983, for *The Haunting;* Een Zilveren Griffel,
1978; *School Library Journal* Best Book citation, 1982,
for *The Haunting;* Carnegie Medals, British Library
Association, 1982, for *The Haunting,* 1986, for *The
Changeover: A Supernatural Romance,* and 1987 for
Memory; 1984 Notable Children's Book citation, Asso-
ciation for Library Service to Children (ALSC), Chil-

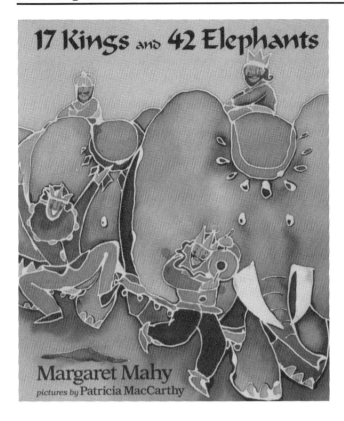

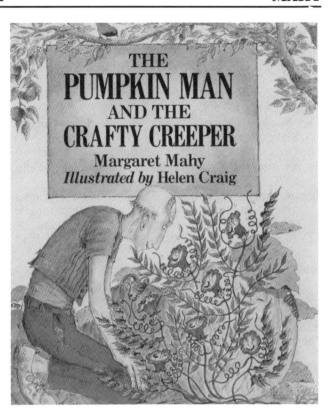

17 Kings and 42 Elephants is an award-winning combination of Mahy's rhythmic, tongue-twisting poetry and Patricia MacCarthy's colorful batik illustrations.

Mahy often explores magical possibilities in her junior books—such as the bossy talking pumpkin vine in *The Pumpkin Man and the Crafty Creeper.* (Cover illustration by Helen Craig.)

dren's Book of the Year citation, and Best Books for Young Adults award, American Library Association (ALA), all 1986, for *The Changeover;* Honor List citation, *Horn Book,* 1985, for *The Changeover,* and 1987, for *The Catalogue of the Universe; 17 Kings and 42 Elephants* was named one of the year's ten best illustrated books in 1987 by the *New York Times Book Review;* Best Books of 1987 citation, ALA Young Adult Services Division, for *The Tricksters,* and Best Books of 1989 citation for *Memory;* Society of School Libraries International Book award (Language Arts, Science and Social Studies category), and *Boston Globe/Horn Book* award, both 1988, for *Memory;* May Hill Arbuthnot Lecturer, ALSC, 1989.

WRITINGS:

PICTURE BOOKS

A Lion in the Meadow (verse; also see below), illustrated by Jenny Williams, F. Watts, 1969.
A Dragon of an Ordinary Family, illustrated by Helen Oxenbury, F. Watts, 1969.
Pillycock's Shop, illustrated by Carol Barker, F. Watts, 1969.
The Procession, illustrated by Charles Mozley, F. Watts, 1969.
Mrs. Discombobulous, illustrated by Jan Brychta, F. Watts, 1969.
The Little Witch, illustrated by Mozely, F. Watts, 1970.

Sailor Jack and the 20 Orphans, illustrated by Robert Bartelt, Picture Puffin, 1970.
The Princess and the Clown, F. Watts, 1971.
The Railway Engine and the Hairy Brigands, Dent, 1972.
17 Kings and 42 Elephants (verse), Dent, 1972, 2nd edition edited by Phyllis J. Fogelman with illustrations by Patricia MacCarthy, Dial, 1987.
The Boy with Two Shadows, illustrated by Williams, F. Watts, 1972, Lippincott, 1989.
The Man Whose Mother Was a Pirate, illustrated by Brian Froud, Atheneum, 1972, illustrated by Margaret Chamberlain, Viking Kestrel, 1986.
Rooms for Rent, illustrated by Williams, F. Watts, 1974, published in England as *Rooms to Let,* Dent, 1975.
The Rare Spotted Birthday Party, F. Watts, 1974.
The Witch in the Cherry Tree, illustrated by Williams, Parents' Magazine Press, 1974.
Stepmother, F. Watts, 1974.
Ultra-Violet Catastrophe! Or, The Unexpected Walk with Great-Uncle Mangus Pringle, Parents' Magazine Press, 1975.
David's Witch Doctor, F. Watts, 1975.
The Wind between the Stars, Dent, 1976.
The Boy Who Was Followed Home, illustrated by Steven Kellogg, F. Watts, 1976.
Leaf Magic (also see below), Parents' Magazine Press, 1976.
Jam: A True Story, illustrated by Helen Craig, Little, Brown, 1986.

Pumpkin Man and the Crafty Creeper, illustrated by Craig, Greenwillow Books, 1991.

JUVENILE FICTION

The Great Millionaire Kidnap, illustrated by Jan Brychta, Dent, 1975.

The Nonstop Nonsense Book, illustrated by Quentin Blake, Dent, 1977.

The Great Piratical Rumbustification [and] *The Librarian and the Robbers,* illustrated by Blake, Dent, 1978.

The Birthday Burglar [and] *A Very Wicked Headmistress,* Dent, 1984, new edition with illustrations by Chamberlain, Godine, 1988.

The Dragon's Birthday, illustrated by Webb, Shortland, 1984.

Ups and Downs and Other Stories, illustrated by Webb, Shortland, 1984.

The Spider in the Shower, illustrated by McRae, Shortland, 1984.

Wibble-Wobble and Other Stories, Shortland, 1984.

The Adventures of a Kite, illustrated by David Cowe, Shortland (Auckland, New Zealand), 1985, Arnold-Wheaton (Leeds, England), 1986.

Sophie's Singing Mother, illustrated by Jo Davies, Arnold-Wheaton, 1985.

The Earthquake, illustrated by Dianne Perham, Arnold-Wheaton, 1985.

The Cake, illustrated by Cowe, Arnold-Wheaton, 1985.

The Catten, illustrated by Davies, Arnold-Wheaton, 1985.

A Very Happy Bathday, illustrated by Elizabeth Fuller, Arnold-Wheaton, 1985.

Out in the Big Wild World, illustrated by Rodney McRae, Shortland, 1985.

Rain, illustrated by Fuller, Shortland, 1985.

Clever Hamburger, illustrated by McRae, Arnold-Wheaton, 1985.

Beautiful Pig, Shortland, 1986, Arnold-Wheaton, 1987.

The Long Grass of Tumbledown Road, Shortland, 1986, Arnold-Wheaton, 1987.

The Robber Pig and the Ginger Beer, illustrated by McRae, two volumes, Shortland, 1986, Arnold-Wheaton, 1987.

Arguments, illustrated by Kelvin Hawley, Shortland, 1986,

An Elephant in the House, illustrated by Fuller, Shortland, 1986.

The Fight on the Hill, illustrated by Jan van der Voo, Shortland, 1986, Arnold-Wheaton, 1987.

Jacko, the Junk Shop Man, illustrated by Davies, Shortland, 1986.

The Mouse Wedding, illustrated by Fuller, Shortland, 1986.

Squeak in the Gate, illustrated by Davies, Shortland, 1986.

(With others) *The Three Wishes,* illustrated by McRae and others, Shortland, 1986.

Tinny Tiny Tinker, illustrated by David Cowe, Shortland, 1986.

Mr. Rooster's Dilemma, illustrated by Fuller, Shortland, 1986, published in England as *How Mr. Rooster Didn't Get Married,* Arnold-Wheaton, 1987.

My Wonderful Aunt (four volumes), illustrated by Dierdre Gardiner, Wright Group, 1986, revised edition in one volume, Children's Press, 1988.

Baby's Breakfast, illustrated by Madeline Beasley, Heinemann, 1986.

Feeling Funny, illustrated by McRae, Heinemann, 1986.

The Garden Party, illustrated by McRae, Heinemann, 1986.

The New House Villain, illustrated by Fuller, Heinemann, 1986.

A Pet to the Vet, illustrated by Philip Webb, Heinemann, 1986.

The Pop Group, illustrated by McRae, Heinemann, 1986.

Tai Taylor and His Education, illustrated by Nick Price, four volumes, Heinemann, 1986-87.

The Terrible Topsy-Turvy, Tissy-Tossy Tangle, illustrated by Vicki Smillie-McItoull, Heinemann, 1986.

Trouble on the Bus, illustrated by Wendy Hodder, Heinemann, 1986.

Mr. Rumfitt, illustrated by Price, Heinemann, 1987.

The Man Who Walked on His Hands, illustrated by Martin Bailey, Shortland, 1987.

Guinea Pig Grass, illustrated by Kelvin Hawley, Shortland, 1987.

No Dinner for Sally, illustrated by John Tarlton, Shortland, 1987.

The Girl Who Washed in Moonlight, illustrated by Robyn Belton, Heinemann, 1987.

The Haunting of Miss Cardamon, illustrated by Korky Paul, Heinemann, 1987.

Iris La Bonga and the Helpful Taxi Driver, illustrated by Smillie-McItoull, Heinemann, 1987.

The Mad Puppet, illustrated by Jon Davis, Heinemann, 1987.

As Luck Would Have It, illustrated by Gardiner, Shortland, 1988.

A Not-So-Quiet Evening, illustrated by Glenda Jones, Shortland, 1988.

Sarah, the Bear and the Kangaroo, illustrated by Fuller, Shortland, 1988.

When the King Rides By, Thornes, 1988.

Seven Chinese Brothers, illustrated by Jean and Mousien Tseng, Scholastic, 1990.

The Great White Man-Eating Shark: A Cautionary Tale, illustrated by Jonathan Allen, Dial Books for Young Readers, 1990.

Making Friends, illustrated by Wendy Smith, McElderry Books, 1990.

Keeping House, Macmillan, 1991.

The Queen's Goat, illustrated by Emma Chichester Clark, Dial Books for Young Readers, 1991.

JUVENILE FICTION WITH JOY COWLEY AND JUNE MELSER

Roly-Poly, illustrated by Gardiner, Shortland, 1982, Arnold-Wheaton, 1985.

Cooking Pot, illustrated by Gardiner, Shortland, 1982, Arnold-Wheaton, 1985.

Fast and Funny, illustrated by Lynette Vondrusha, Shortland, 1982, Arnold-Wheaton, 1985.

Sing to the Moon, illustrated by Isabel Lowe, Shortland, 1982, Arnold-Wheaton, 1985.

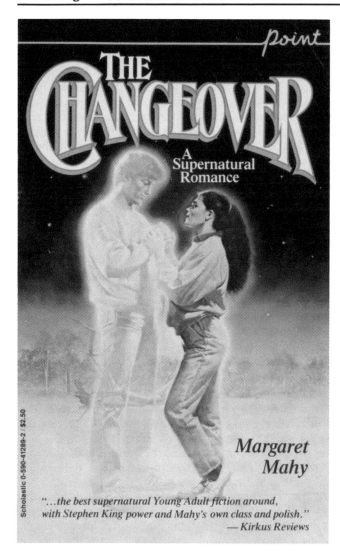

Scholastic 0-590-41289-2 /$2.50

"...the best supernatural Young Adult fiction around,
with Stephen King power and Mahy's own class and polish."
— *Kirkus Reviews*

**The Changeover: A Supernatural Romance won the
American Library Association's Children's Book of the
Year citation and a Best Books for Young Adults award
in 1986.**

Tiddalik, illustrated by Philip Webb, Shortland, 1982,
Arnold-Wheaton, 1985.

YOUNG ADULT NOVELS

Clancy's Cabin, illustrated by Trevor Stubley, Dent,
1974.
The Bus under the Leaves, illustrated by Margery Gill,
Dent, 1974.
The Pirate Uncle, illustrated by Mary Dinsdale, Dent,
1977.
Raging Robots and Unruly Uncles, illustrated by Peter
Stevenson, Dent, 1981.
*The Pirates' Mixed-Up Voyage: Dark Doings in the
Thousand Islands,* illustrated by Chamberlain,
Dent, 1983.
The Haunting (also see below), illustrated by Bruce
Hogarth, Atheneum, 1982.
The Changeover: A Supernatural Romance, Atheneum,
1984.
The Catalogue of the Universe, Atheneum, 1985.
Aliens in the Family, Scholastic, 1986.

The Tricksters, Margaret McElderry Books, 1987.
Memory, Margaret McElderry Books, 1988.
The Blood-and-Thunder Adventure on Hurricane Peak,
illustrated by Smith, Dent, 1989.
Dangerous Spaces, Viking Children's Books, 1991.

READERS

Look under "V", illustrated by Deirdre Gardiner, Wellington Department of Education, School Publications Branch (New Zealand), 1977.
The Crocodile's Christmas Sandals, illustrated by Gardiner, Wellington Department of Education, School
Publications Branch, 1982, published as *The Christmas Crocodile's Thongs,* Nelson (Melbourne), 1985.
The Bubbling Crocodile, illustrated by Gardiner, Wellington Department of Education, School Publica-
tions Branch, 1983.
Mrs. Bubble's Baby, Wellington Department of Educa-
tion, School Publications Branch, 1983.
Shopping with a Crocodile, Wellington Department of
Education, School Publications Branch, 1983.
A Crocodile in the Garden, illustrated by Gardiner, two
volumes, Wellington Department of Education,
School Publications Branch, 1983-85.
Going to the Beach, illustrated by Dick Frizzell, Welling-
ton Department of Education, School Publications
Branch, 1984.
The Great Grumbler and the Wonder Tree, illustrated by
Diane Perham, Wellington Department of Educa-
tion, School Publications Branch, 1984.
Fantail, Fantail, illustrated by Bruce Phillips, Welling-
ton Department of Education, School Publications
Branch, 1984.
Horrakopotchin, Wellington Department of Education,
School Publications Branch, 1985.

NONFICTION

New Zealand: Yesterday and Today, F. Watts, 1975.

COLLECTIONS

*The First Margaret Mahy Story Book: Stories and
Poems,* Dent, 1972.
*The Second Margaret Mahy Story Book: Stories and
Poems,* Dent, 1973.
*The Third Margaret Mahy Story Book: Stories and
Poems,* illustrated by Shirley Hughes, Dent, 1975.
A Lion in the Meadow and Five Other Favorites,
illustrated by Williams, Bartelt, Brychta, Mozley,
and Froud, 1976.
The Chewing-Gum Rescue and Other Stories, illustrated
by Jan Ormerod, Dent, 1982, Methuen, 1984.
Leaf Magic and Five other Favourites, illustrated by
Chamberlain, Dent, 1984.
The Downhill Crocodile Whizz and Other Stories, illus-
trated by Ian Newsham, Dent, 1986.
*Mahy Magic: A Collection of the Most Magical Stories
from the Margaret Mahy Story Books,* illustrated by
Hughes, Dent, 1986.
The Door in the Air and Other Stories, illustrated by
Diana Catchpole, Dent, 1988, Delacorte, 1991.
Chocolate Porridge and Other Stories, illustrations by
Hughes, 1989.

Also author of *The Horrible Story and Others,* 1987.

OTHER

The Haunting of Barney Palmer (screenplay adapted by Mahy from her novel *The Haunting*), broadcast on *Wonderworks,* Public Broadcasting Service, 1987.
The Tin Can Band and Other Poems, illustrated by Honey De Lacey, 1989.

Author of scripts "A Land Called Happy," "Wooly Valley," "Once upon a Story," and "The Margaret Mahy Story Book Theatre" for Television New Zealand, and scripts for the Gibson Group television series *Cuckooland.*

ADAPTATIONS: Cassette versions of Mahy's works include *The Haunting,* 1986, *The Chewing Gum Rescue and Other Stories,* 1988, and *The Pirate's Mixed-Up Voyage,* all read aloud by Richard Mitchley, and *Nonstop Nonsense,* read by Kenneth Stanley, all G. K. Hall.

SIDELIGHTS: Fantastical adventures that tell about how people get along in family life have made New Zealand author Margaret Mahy well-known around the world. In more than fifty titles since her first book *A Lion in the Meadow,* Mahy has written about a world full of surprising possibilities—a world familiar to children, that she insists remains real for adults. Critics place Mahy's work, which appeals to readers of all ages, with the best works of young people's literature. When writing about aliens with unusual powers, intelligent adolescents, or New Zealand, Mahy "writes with all the force and precision and richness of a poet," Elizabeth Ward observes in the *Washington Post Book World.*

Mahy's first book *A Lion in the Meadow* shows a mother in trouble because she refuses to take her son seriously. Annoyed by his warnings that there is a lion in the meadow, and thinking that he is playing a fantasy game with her, the busy mother gives the child a box of matches. Inside it, she says, is a little dragon that can grow large enough to scare the lion away. She soon vows not to lie to her children again. The fable shows that while fantasy is important to children, it is dangerous for adults not to recognize and teach the difference between fantasy and reality.

In addition to being valued for their themes, Mahy's books for children are popular and highly praised because of her skills as a poet. In the rhythmic verses in *17 Kings and 42 Elephants,* a parade of kings, elephants, tigers, and other jungle animals winds from an unnamed beginning to an unnamed finish, making a journey that is enjoyable for its own sake, say the critics. The book's language is both precise and creative, entertaining and thought-provoking, silly and serious, Arthur Yorinks comments in the *New York Times Book Review.* Patricia MacCarthy's brightly-colored batik illustrations make the second edition particularly pleasing to the eye. The *New York Times Book Review* named it one of the year's ten best illustrated books in 1987.

Mahy's books for young adults focus on family relationships and coming-of-age themes through a variety of story-telling methods that range from realism to supernaturalism. In *Memory,* an elderly woman suffering from Alzheimer's disease gets help from a teen who wants to forget his early life. In *The Haunting,* a young man finds out he is in line to inherit psychic powers that he feels are a curse more than a blessing. The novel's eight-year-old protagonist, Barney Palmer, describes a sequence of meal-time family discussions and ties them together with explanations of his own thoughts and feelings. Critics praise Mahy's ability to develop likeable characters and an ambitious theme within this framework. Barney and his family "are beautifully drawn, and perhaps because they care so much for each other, readers care for them, too," Michael Cart comments in *School Library Journal.* Hayes observes in the *Times Literary Supplement,* "*The Haunting* manages to combine a realistic approach to family life—in which how you feel about your parents and yourself is actually important—with a strong and terrifying line in fantasy."

Dangerous Spaces presents one young woman's struggle to control her habit of trying to avoid life's difficulties by escaping to a private world inhabited by her great-uncle's ghost. Anthea's own parents have died suddenly and she lives with relatives whose complicated and noisy lives are no comfort to her. Soon she is retreating to the spacious dream-world Viridian every night, and her trips become so dangerous that her life is threatened. Down-to-earth Flora, the cousin who resents the glamorous Anthea at first, charges in to Viridian to rescue her and puts an end to a haunting that has plagued the family for generations. The skillful weaving of adventure with insights into family relationships for which Mahy is known rewards readers who finish the book, a *Publishers Weekly* reviewer comments.

The importance of family relationships to young adults is just one of the author's major themes. Hayes writes in the *Times Literary Supplement,* "the double aspect of things—man and beast, [good] and evil, young and old—intrigues Margaret Mahy." In *The Catalogue of the Universe,* the main characters are high school seniors working out the problems of identity common to that age group. Angela has lived without a father for many years, and feels that the blessings of beauty, a loving mother, and intelligence have not compensated for his absence. Tycho, her friend since early childhood, who is looking to science and astronomy to provide a rational basis for his life, helps Angela in her search for her missing father. When they encounter the lost parent, disappointment forces Angela to find out who she is apart from family ties. She and Tycho also find that while forgiveness can help relationships survive, it is difficult state of mind to achieve and does not necessarily change the faults of others. Mahy's characters accept these lessons without feeling sorry for themselves and without giving up on life. "Angela shares with her friend Tycho a fascination with matters like the square root of two and the moon of Jupiter which outlast emotional pains and the novel moves lightly," Gillian Wilce maintains in the *New Statesman.* Colin Greenland notes

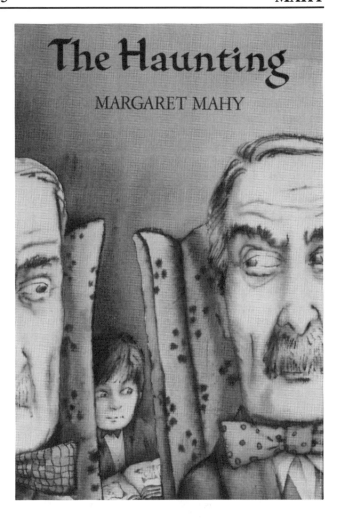

A young man suffering from painful memories befriends an elderly woman who is losing her memory to Alzheimer's disease in Mahy's young adult novel, *Memory.* (Jacket illustration by Alun Hood.)

An eight-year-old boy receives frightening supernatural messages in Mahy's *The Haunting.* (Jacket illustration by Michele Chessare.)

in the *Times Literary Supplement* that readers who "know at least a little of what it feels like to be in love" will appreciate this book.

Mahy compares the powers and limitations of magic and science in the well-received junior novel *The Blood-and-Thunder Adventure on Hurricane Peak. Times Literary Supplement* reviewer John Mole observes that in the romance between a school principal and the scientist Belladonna Doppler, "the rival claims of magic and science argue their way towards a happy marriage." The scientist sums up near the end that though sorcery had brought them into the forest, they needed science to come back out.

Mahy's ability to combine themes relevant to young adults with fantasy is matched by her consistently non-sexist perspective on roles and relationships. Jan Dalley, writing in the *Times Literary Supplement,* points out that Mahy "continually pushes at the boundaries of [fairy-tale] conventions," and "roots out the sexism that used to be integral" to fiction for young readers. For example, though the roles of rescuer, leader, and problem-solver have been traditionally assigned to males,

she gives these roles as often to females of various ages and levels of social status. In Mahy's books, the role of home economist and nurturer, traditionally assigned to women, is also assigned to men. Growth to sexual maturity is equally exciting and frightening to her male and female adolescents. Adults of both sexes are equally subject to weakness and failure to discern the needs of their children. All her characters face the same challenges to strike a balance between freedom and commitment, reason and emotion. And they all benefit from recognizing the power of the imagination, which they learn to celebrate as well as to contain.

In her work as a librarian, Mahy is called upon to segregate works of fact from works of fiction, as if imagined stories somehow do not contain elements of truth about life. Unlike the many fault lines that score the geography of her homeland, she believes the dividing line between fact and fiction is an imaginary rift. Pointing to changes in scientific theories about how the world began, she comments in a lecture published in *Journal of Youth Services in Libraries* that what we think of as scientific fact sometimes proves to be wrong in the light of new discoveries, "and the truest thing in science is wonder just as it is in story. And I never forget that story is as important to human beings as science."

In her lecture, she says that one does not have to impose the truth onto children, because "they demand to be told. When a child writes and asks me 'Do you believe in supernatural things?' they may be asking me to confirm that a story like *The Haunting* is literally true. But mostly they are asking 'Just where am I to fit this story in my view of the world?' ... Part of giving them the truest answer we can give also involves telling stories of desire: once there was a man who rode on a winged horse, once there was a boy who spoke to the animals, and the animals talked back to him, once there was a girl who grew so powerful that she was able not only to overcome her enemy but to overcome the base part of herself. Beware or the wolf will eat you and then you will become part of the wolf until something eats the wolf and so on." Story-telling is always risky because writers don't know what sense readers will make of their stories after they have read them. Commenting on her own work, she sums up, "I have told the children all the truth I know from personal experience."

WORKS CITED:

Cart, Michael, review of *The Haunting, School Library Journal,* August, 1982, p. 119.
Dalley, Jan, "Fantastical Flights," *Times Literary Supplement,* November 25, 1988, p. 1323.
Eccleshare, Julia, "Comforting Corners," *Times Literary Supplement,* December 13, 1985, p. 1435.
Greenland, Colin, "Ritual Dismembering," *Times Literary Supplement,* November 8, 1985, p. 1274.
Hayes, Sarah, "Adding another Dimension," *Times Literary Supplement,* July 13, 1984, p. 794.
Hayes, "Unearthing the Family Ghosts," *Times Literary Supplement,* September 17, 1982, p. 1001.
Mahy, "May Hill Arbuthnot Lecture, A Dissolving Ghost: Possible Operations of Truth in Children's Books and the Lives of Children," *Journal of Youth Services in Libraries,* summer, 1989, p. 313-329.
Mole, John, "Abandoning Reality," *Times Literary Supplement,* April 7, 1989, p. 378.
Review of *Dangerous Spaces, Publishers Weekly,* February 1, 1991, p. 80.
Ward, Elizabeth, "Space to Dream," *Washington Post Book World,* October 12, 1986, p. 11.
Wilce, Gillian, "Waking Up to the Kid Next Door," *New Statesman,* November, 1985, pp. 27-28.
Yorinks, Arthur, "Lots of Pachyderms," *New York Times Book Review,* November 8, 1987, p. 40.

FOR MORE INFORMATION SEE:

BOOKS

Children's Literature Review, Volume 7, Gale, 1984, pp. 176-188.

PERIODICALS

Christian Science Monitor, June 6, 1986, p. B6; November 4, 1988, p. B3; January 25, 1989, p. 13.
Fantasy Review, March, 1985, p. 27.
Growing Point, November 21, 1982, p. 3985.

Horn Book, November/December, 1984, p. 764; November/December, 1989, pp. 772-773; March, 1991, p. 201.
Journal of Youth Services in Libraries, summer, 1989, p. 313-329.
Junior Bookshelf, February, 1983, p. 45.
Listener, November 8, 1984, p. 27.
New Statesman, November, 1985, pp. 27-28.
New York Times Book Review, July 13, 1986, p. 22; May 17, 1987, pp. 31, 44; November 8, 1987, p. 40.
Publishers Weekly, February 1, 1991, p. 80.
School Librarian, September, 1984, p. 260; April, 1991, p. 121.
School Library Journal, August, 1982, p. 119; April, 1991, p. 98.
Times Literary Supplement, September 17, 1982, p. 1001; July 13, 1984, p. 794; November 8, 1985, p. 1274; December 13, 1985, p. 1435; August 1, 1986, p. 850; October 9, 1987, p. 1120; November 25, 1988, p. 1323; April 7, 1989, p. 378.
Voice of Youth Advocates, June, 1987, p. 80.
Washington Post Book World, October 12, 1986, p. 11; January 14, 1990, p. 10.

* * *

MARK, Jan 1943-

PERSONAL: Full name is Janet Marjorie Mark; born June 22, 1943, in Welwyn, Hertfordshire, England; daughter of Colin Denis and Marjorie Brisland; married Neil Mark (a computer operator), March 1, 1969 (divorced, 1989); children: Isobel, Alexander. *Education:* Canterbury College of Art, N.D.D., 1965. *Politics:* Labour. *Religion:* None.

ADDRESSES: Home—98 Howard St., Oxford OX4 3BG, England. *Agent*—Murray Pollinger, 4 Garrick St., London WC2E 9BH, England.

JAN MARK

CAREER: Southfields School, Gravesend, Kent, England, teacher of art and English, 1965-71; full-time writer, 1975—. Oxford Polytechnic, Arts Council Writer Fellow, 1982-84.

AWARDS, HONORS: Penguin/*Guardian* Award, 1975, and Library Association Carnegie Medal, 1976, both for *Thunder and Lightnings; The Ennead* was named a Notable Children's Trade Book in the field of social studies by the National Council for Social Studies and the Children's Book Council, 1978; runner-up for Library Association Carnegie Medal, 1981, for *Nothing to Be Afraid Of;* co-winner of Young *Observer*/Rank Teenage Fiction Prize, 1982, for *Aquarius;* Library Association Carnegie Medal, 1983, for *Handles;* Angel Literary Award for fiction, 1983, for *Feet,* and 1987, for *Zeno Was Here;* British nominee for International Hans Christian Andersen Medal, 1984; runner-up for *Guardian* Award for Children's Fiction, 1986, for *Trouble Halfway.*

WRITINGS:

NOVELS; FOR CHILDREN AND YOUNG ADULTS, EXCEPT WHERE INDICATED

Thunder and Lightnings (ALA notable book), illustrated by Jim Russell, Kestrel, 1976, Crowell, 1979.
Under the Autumn Garden, illustrated by Colin Twinn, Kestrel, 1977, U.S. edition illustrated by Judith Gwyn Brown, Crowell, 1979.
The Ennead, Crowell, 1978.
Divide and Rule, Kestrel, 1979, Crowell, 1980.
The Short Voyage of the Albert Ross, illustrated by Gavin Rowe, Granada, 1980.
The Dead Letter Box, illustrated by Mary Rayner, Antheneum Books, 1982.
Aquarius, Kestrel, 1982, Antheneum, 1984.
At the Sign of the Dog and Rocket, Longman, 1985.
Handles, illustrated by David Parkins, Kestrel, 1983, Antheneum, 1985.
Trouble Halfway, illustrated by David Parkins, Viking Kestrel, 1985, Antheneum, 1986.
Dream House, illustrated by Jon Riley, Viking Kestrel, 1987.
The Twig Thing, illustrated by Sally Holmes, Viking Children's, 1988.
Zeno Was Here (for adults), Cape, 1987, Farrar, Straus, 1988.
Man in Motion, illustrated by Jeff Cummins, Viking Kestrel, 1989.
Finders, Losers, Orchard, 1990.
The Hillingdon Fox, Turton & Chambers, 1991.

STORY COLLECTIONS; FOR CHILDREN AND YOUNG ADULTS

Nothing to Be Afraid Of (includes "William's Version"), illustrated by David Parkins, Kestrel, 1980, Harper, 1981.
Hairs in the Palm of the Hand (contains "Time and the Hour" [also see below] and "Chutzpah"), illustrated by Jan Ormerod, Kestrel, 1981, published as *Bold as Brass,* Hutchinson, 1984.

Feet and Other Stories (includes "Posts and Telecommunications," "Enough Is Too Much Already" [also see below] and "A Little Misunderstanding"), illustrated by Bert Kitchen, Kestrel, 1983.
Two Stories (contains "Childermas" and "Mr. and Mrs. Johnson"), illustrated by Clive King, Inky Parrot Press (Oxford), 1984.
Frankie's Hat (includes "It Wasn't Me"), illustrated by Quentin Blake, Viking Kestrel, 1986.
Enough Is Too Much Already and Other Stories, Bodley Head, 1988.
(Editor) *School Stories,* Kingfisher, 1989.
A Can of Worms, Bodley Head, 1990.
In Black and White (ghost stories), Viking, 1991.

Contributor of stories to anthologies and periodicals.

OTHER; FOR CHILDREN AND YOUNG ADULTS, EXCEPT WHERE INDICATED

The Long Distance Poet (picture book), illustrated by Steve Smallman, Dinosaur, 1982.
Izzy (three-act play), Longman, 1985.
Fur (picture book), illustrated by Charlotte Voake, Harper, 1986.
Out of the Oven (picture book), illustrated by Antony Maitland, Viking Kestrel, 1986.
Interference (three-act play), Longman, 1987.
(With Stephen Cockett) *Captain Courage and the Rose Street Gang* (two-act play), Collins, 1987.
Fun (picture book), illustrated by Michael Foreman, Gollancz, 1987, Viking Kestrel, 1988.
Strat and Chatto (picture book), illustrated by David Hughes, Walker, 1989.
Time and the Hour (two plays), Longman, 1990.
Great Frog and Mighty Moose, (travel), Walker, 1992.

Author of television plays and radio dramas; contributor of articles for adults to magazines.

ADAPTATIONS: The Dead Letter Box was adapted as an audiocassette, Puffin/Cover to Cover, 1987; *Frankie's Hat, Hairs on the Palm of the Hand,* and *Nothing to Be Afraid Of* were adapted as audiocassettes, Chivers Press, 1987, 1988, and 1989, respectively; works have been adapted for television, including *Izzy,* 1983, *Interference,* 1986, and *Handles,* 1989.

SIDELIGHTS: One of Great Britain's most notable children's authors, Jan Mark has written a variety of works, including picture books, plays, stories, and novels. Her writings appeal to a wide audience, from young children to adults. Although most of her work attracts young readers, Mark once told *SATA* that "I do not write specifically for children, any more than I write for adults. I tend rather to write about children." With this approach, Mark has created some unusually sophisticated books for young readers. Critics praise Mark's unique characters, sharp wit, and clear prose, noting that she comments insightfully on the behavior, problems, and joys of young people. Unlike the majority of children's authors, she often provides a bleak and uncompromising view of the world. "Mark stretches the range of children's books," *New York Times Book*

Review contributor Jane Langton declared. "She provides for young people the combination of fine prose and strong realism generally reserved for adults."

Born in Welwyn, England, Mark spent a great deal of time reading as a child. She once told *SATA:* "My educational career comprised fourteen glorious years of state-subsidized reading time. I cannot recall doing very much else, certainly not learning, since I reckoned, along with one of my fictional characters, that anything I wanted to know would stick." Mark learned to read at the age of three and was able to write by age four. The author was soon attracted to writing fiction, and she wrote stories, poems, and plays, hoping to become a published author before she even finished high school. Although this goal was never realized, Mark continued to write; in college she composed fragments of a novel. After graduating from college, however, Mark found that her job teaching art and English kept her busy, leaving her little of the spare time or energy that writing required.

Mark was married with two children when a newspaper advertisement inspired her to finally pursue a career in writing. The London *Guardian* was sponsoring a writing contest in which an award would be given for the best children's novel by an unpublished author. Mark wrote *Thunder and Lightnings* for the competition—and won. Reflecting upon her somewhat late start in writing, Mark commented: "I did not begin writing seriously until I was in my thirties and am in retrospect glad of it, since I had by then developed a voice of my own." The author continued, "I started well by winning a competition for new fiction but this has imposed on me the challenge to produce always something at least as good as the first book. I dare not fall below that standard."

In addition to winning the *Guardian* contest, *Thunder and Lightnings* received a Carnegie Medal. The novel examines an unlikely friendship between two young boys—Andrew, a bright though naive middle-class youngster, and Victor, a working-class boy who is uninterested in school but who knows much about the ways of the world. Winifred Whitehead observed in *The Use of English* that "behind the apparent simplicity, [and] the everydayness of the story's events ... lies a penetrating analysis of the two boys and their lives." Graham Hammond, writing in *Children's Literature in Education,* described *Thunder and Lightnings* as "a series of contrasts: between appearance and reality, official estimation and real worth, formal schooling and out-of-school learning, artificial projects and genuine interests, fear and love."

Thunder and Lightnings also addresses life's injustices; when Andrew tells his mother about an incident in which Victor was punished unfairly, his mother responds that "nothing's fair," Robbie March-Penney quoted from the book in *Children's Literature in Education.* "There's no such thing as fairness. It's a word made up to keep children quiet. When you discover it's a fraud then you're starting to grow up." Though Mark's message may seem disheartening, it is softened, review-

ers noted, by humor and gentle irony. Hammond observed that "for all her serious intent, [Mark] has a light touch, a flair for word play, and a warm sense of fun."

With *Thunder and Lightnings,* as with later novels such as *Under the Autumn Garden, The Dead Letter Box,* and *Trouble Halfway,* Mark was noted for her attention to detail, well-rounded characters, and realistic dialogue. These novels for younger readers frequently lack plot development, focusing instead on characters and relationships in school or home settings. Mark often gives a bittersweet look at childhood and adolescence. *Times Educational Supplement* contributor Neil Philip remarked: "What is so refreshing about her writing both about and for children ... is the accuracy with which she reflects the real concerns of childhood; an accuracy born of careful observation."

Mark's power of observation is also evident in her short fiction. Her story collections, which include *Nothing to Be Afraid Of, Hairs in the Palm of the Hand,* and *Feet,* are considered to be among the best examples of her work. In a *Horn Book* article Mark described the differences between writing stories and novels: "I much prefer writing short stories. I have to explain this to schoolchildren. They think I like writing short stories because short stories are quickly done and therefore easy.... In fact, writing short stories is harder than writing novels. You can't get away with anything in a short story.... It is said that in a novel every chapter must count; in a short story every sentence must count." Also writing in *Horn Book,* Aidan Chambers noted that *Nothing to Be Afraid Of* "indicated just how appropriate the [short story] form is for [Mark's] talents. The collection is funny, uncomfortably accurate in its dialogue and in the persuasiveness of its narrative situations, and written throughout with the combination of an unflinchingly sharp eye for human foible and a detached sympathy for the underdog ... that makes fiction ... more potent than real life for the observing reader."

Though her portrayal of life as difficult and unjust surfaces in many of her books, it is especially evident in *The Ennead, Divide and Rule,* and *Aquarius,* three novels written specifically for an older, young adult audience. These books stand apart from Mark's works for younger readers; requiring a more sophisticated audience, the novels have a bleaker tone, exploring such issues as manipulative relationships, the power of religion, and the fate of those who are unwilling to conform to the rules of society. Instead of being set in contemporary England like most of Mark's writings, these works are set in fictitious societies and have sometimes been labeled science fiction. The main characters in these books are, as Mark described in *SATA,* "likely to be ... amoral or downright corrupt." Her protagonists are not victims; Mark explained that they are, rather, "authors of their own downfalls.... The forces of evil currently fashionable are not supernatural, but human ignorance and complacency."

Winner of the Carnegie Medal

Jan Mark

HANDLES

'Cannot fail to entertain'
—Sunday Times

Mark explores an adolescent girl's need for acceptance in her 1983 Carnegie Medal winner, *Handles*. (Cover illustration by Garry Walton.)

Mark discussed these works for older children with Philip, commenting that "the idea of manipulation is what I'm working on in all three books. Not only why we do it, but why do we allow it? How much capital do you think you can make out of allowing yourselves to be used?" Mark also noted in *Books for Keeps* that in the three books "I'm setting up situations and inviting the reader to explore the situation along with the writer. They're for a sophisticated reader and they're deliberately written to discourage an unsophisticated reader.... I like to make the reader work hard."

Although some critics faulted Mark for the despairing message she presents in *The Ennead, Divide and Rule,* and *Aquarius,* M. Crouch asserted in the *Junior Bookshelf* that "it is some indication of the power of her writing that ... Mark leaves us exhilarated rather than depressed." In *Painted Desert, Green Shade,* David Rees

observed that "scarcely anyone writing today presents youth with a more somber picture of life than does Jan Mark. Sometimes the reader may feel that her novels go to an extreme beyond which it is not possible to venture in books for children and teenagers. This doesn't matter: the harsh truths of her vision of the world are infinitely preferable to the cozy pap that is sometimes served up for the young."

WORKS CITED:

"Authorgraph No. 25: Jan Mark," *Books for Keeps,* March 1984, pp. 12-13.
Chambers, Aidan, "Letters from England: A Mark of Distinction," *Horn Book,* September/October, 1984, pp. 665-70.
Crouch, M., review of *The Ennead, Junior Bookshelf,* February, 1979, pp. 56-57.
Hammond, Graham, review of *Thunder and Lightnings, Children's Literature in Education,* summer, 1982, pp. 58-59.
Langton, Jane, review of *Handles, New York Times Book Review,* July 28, 1985, p. 25.
March-Penney, Robbie, "I Don't Want to Learn Things, I'd Rather Just Find Out: Jan Mark's *Thunder and Lightnings,*" *Children's Literature in Education,* spring, 1979, pp. 18-24.
Mark, Jan, "The Short Story," *Horn Book,* January/February, 1988, pp. 42-45.
Mark, Jan, *Thunder and Lightnings,* Crowell, 1979.
Philip, Neil, "Read Mark, Learn," *Times Educational Supplement,* June 3, 1983, p. 37.
Rees, David, "No Such Thing as Fairness: Jan Mark," *Painted Desert, Green Shade: Essays on Contemporary Writers of Fiction for Children and Young Adults,* Horn Book, 1984, pp. 62-74.
Something about the Author, Volume 22, Gale, 1981, p. 182.
Whitehead, Winifred, "Jan Mark," *The Use of English,* spring, 1982, pp. 32-39.

FOR MORE INFORMATION SEE:

BOOKS

Children's Literature Review, Volume 11, Gale, 1986.

PERIODICALS

Bulletin of the Center for Children's Books, December, 1978; June, 1980; April, 1982; July/August, 1984; May, 1985; April, 1986.
Children's Literature in Education, winter, 1983.
Growing Point, July, 1982.
Horn Book, October, 1978; July/August, 1986; March/April, 1987.
New York Times Book Review, July 17, 1988.
Publishers Weekly, April 15, 1988.
Times Literary Supplement, July 23, 1982; November 24, 1989.

—Sketch by Michelle M. Motowski

O

OBERLE, Joseph 1958-

PERSONAL: Surname is pronounced "oh-ber-lee"; born January 4, 1958, in Mankato, MN; son of Anthony George (a business agent) and Mary Ann (a line worker; maiden name, Sieberg) Oberle; married Lora Lee Polack (a publishing project manager), April 21, 1990; children: Seth Joseph. *Education:* St. John's University, B.A., 1981. *Politics:* Democrat. *Religion:* Catholic. *Hobbies and other interests:* Football, softball, hockey, music, literature, cross-country skiing, camping, travel.

ADDRESSES: Home—2721 Georgia Ave. S., St. Louis Park, MN 55426. *Office*—Skyway News Publications, 33 South Fifth St., Minneapolis, MN 55402.

CAREER: Loyola High School, Mankato, MN, publicity writer, c. 1981-83; *TV Guide* (magazine), Radnor, PA, editor, 1984-88; *Training* (magazine), Minneapolis, MN, editor, 1989; free-lance writer, 1990-91; Skyway News Publications, Minneapolis, editor of *Minnesota Sports* magazine and an editor for *Skyway News* (Minneapolis newspaper), 1991—.

AWARDS, HONORS: Honorable Mention for best feature, Neighborhood Press Association, 1987, for "Saga of a Renovation."

WRITINGS:

(Editor and contributor) *Papal Bull* (humorous dictionary), Meadowbrook Press, 1989.
Anchorage, Dillon Press, 1990.

Contributor to newspapers, including *Whittier Globe.*

WORK IN PROGRESS: Minneapolis, "another juvenile education book like the Anchorage title"; *A Humorous Guide to Softball for Softball Widows and Widowers.*

SIDELIGHTS: Joseph Oberle told *SATA:* "I can still remember the first poem that I ever wrote. It was actually more of a rhyme I made up as I was walking home from school in the second grade, and it was called 'As I Walk to School Each Day.' The first and only poem

JOSEPH OBERLE

that I ever published was a seventh grade poetry class assignment. We had a choice between an essay and a poem and I thought a poem would be easier. It was called 'Freedom Isn't Free,' and it placed first in a Mankato Catholic Daughters poetry contest and third place in the state. I got a real kick out of being paid five dollars at each contest for doing homework. Although I don't feel that the two poems were a major influence on my career to date (or epics of major importance in the literary community), they do illustrate a couple of things about myself to me. One, the sound of the written word had impressed me somewhere along the line and had become a part of me, and two, if I was going to have to write, I would write about something from my own experience."

As an adult, Oberle learned about Dillon Press's books on American cities. "It had always been a goal, sometimes seeming more like a dream, to witness the beauty of Alaska. I applied to write one of Dillon Press's books by writing sample chapters of the book, bought my plane ticket, and hoped for the best. I received the contract and flew into Anchorage one day before the *Exxon Valdez* oil tanker ran aground in Prince William Sound" on March 24, 1989, causing the worst oil spill in U.S. history. Oberle remarked: "The abundant beauty of the state made it easy to put aside the disaster for a time, especially for a first-time visitor. One trip to Kodiak Island and another to Mount McKinley and Fairbanks gave me only a small glimpse of our country's largest state. But the variety of natural beauty and the immense grandeur of Alaska have been calling me back ever since.

"Since *Anchorage* was finished, I have contacted some publishers about future projects and am cultivating ideas, although free-lance time is a premium. My wife and I recently had our first child, so I hope to have more works for him to read by the time he comes of the age. As I will be spending plenty of time taking care of the baby, I'm sure the baby will be the source of inspiration in the future.

"I enjoy my work as a writer, especially the freedom of free-lance work. Even though it is a struggle to maintain a stable income, writing is the one job I've always wanted to do. More than anything, I enjoy the creative process, the transferring of my imagination to the paper, to something tangible. I believe my best writing comes from the sometimes odd relationship I see between separate things, and I achieve a great sense of satisfaction out of giving form to those thoughts and ideas. If in some way they make an impression on the readers, especially to the point of sparking another idea or thought in them, I feel my work has been a success."

P

PARKER, Nancy Winslow 1930-

PERSONAL: Born October 18, 1930, in Maplewood, NJ; daughter of Winslow Aurelius (a textile executive) and Beatrice McCelland (Gaunt) Parker. *Education:* Mills College, B.A., 1952; attended Art Students League, 1956-57, and School of Visual Arts, 1966-67. *Hobbies and other interests:* "Travel, all things French, carpentry, tennis, gardening."

ADDRESSES: Home—51 East 74th St., No. 3R, New York, NY 10021.

CAREER: National Broadcasting Company (NBC), New York City, sales promoter, 1956-60; New York Soccer Club, New York City, sports promoter, 1961-63; Radio Corporation of America (RCA), New York City, sales promoter, 1964-67; Appleton-Century-Crofts (publishers), New York City, art director, 1968-70; Holt, Rinehart & Winston (publishers), New York City, graphic designer, 1970-72; free-lance writer and illustrator, 1972—.

MEMBER: Authors Guild, Mills College Club of New York, Mantoloking Yacht Club.

AWARDS, HONORS: Jane Tinkham Broughton fellowship in writing for children, Bread Loaf Writers Conference, 1975; notable children's book in the field of social studies, 1975, for *Warm as Wool, Cool as Cotton: The Story of Natural Fibers,* and 1976, for *The Goat in the Rug; The Goat in the Rug* was cited as best of the season in children's books, *Saturday Review,* 1976; *Willy Bear* received a year's best children's book citation from the *Philadelphia Inquirer* and a Christopher Award, both 1976; *Poofy Loves Company* was an American Library Association (ALA) Notable book, a *School Library Journal* best books of spring, and was named to New York Public Library list of children's books, all 1981; *My Mom Travels a Lot* received a Christopher Award and was named one of the ten best illustrated books by *New York Times,* both 1981; New York Academy of Science honorable mention, 1981, Sequoyah Children's Book Award, Oklahoma Library Association, 1983-84,

Alabama Library Association Children's Choice, 1985, all for *The President's Car; The Christmas Camel* and *The United Nationals from A to Z* were named to New York Public Library list of children's books, 1983, and 1985 respectively; Association of Booksellers for Children Choice, 1988, for *Bugs.* Several of Parker's books have been Junior Literary Guild selections.

WRITINGS:

SELF-ILLUSTRATED CHILDREN'S BOOKS

The Man with the Take-Apart Head, Dodd, 1974.
The Party at the Old Farm, Atheneum, 1975.
Mrs. Wilson Wanders Off, Dodd, 1976.
Love from Uncle Clyde, Dodd, 1977.
The Crocodile under Louis Finneberg's Bed, Dodd, 1978.
The President's Cabinet (nonfiction), Parents Magazine Press, 1978, revised as *The President's Cabinet and How It Grew,* introduction by Dean Rusk, Harper-Collins, 1991.
The Ordeal of Byron B. Blackbear, Dodd, 1979.
Puddums, the Cathcarts' Orange Cat, Atheneum, 1980.
Poofy Loves Company, Dodd, 1980.
The Spotted Dog, Dodd, 1980.
The President's Car (nonfiction), introduction by Betty Ford, Crowell, 1981.
Cooper, the McNallys' Big Black Dog, Dodd, 1981.
Love from Aunt Betty, Dodd, 1983.
The Christmas Camel, Dodd, 1983.
The United Nations from A to Z, Dodd, 1985.
(With Joan R. Wright) *Bugs,* Greenwillow, 1987.
(With Wright) *Frogs, Toads, Lizards and Salamanders,* Greenwillow, 1990.

ILLUSTRATOR

John Langstaff, *Oh, A-Hunting We Will Go!* (songbook), Atheneum, 1974.
Carter Hauck, *Warm as Wool, Cool as Cotton: The Story of Natural Fibers,* Seabury, 1975.
Charles L. Blood and Martin Link, *The Goat in the Rug,* Parents Magazine Press, 1976.
Mildred Kantrowitz, *Willy Bear,* Parents Magazine Press, 1976.

A young boy's efforts in caring for a camel are rewarded on a magical Christmas Eve in Nancy Winslow Parker's self-illustrated *The Christmas Camel*.

Langstaff, *Sweetly Sings the Donkey* (songbook), Atheneum, 1976.

Ann Lawler, *The Substitute,* Parents Magazine Press, 1977.

Langstaff, *Hot Cross Buns and Other Old Street Cries* (songbook), Atheneum, 1978.

Jane Yolen, *No Bath Tonight,* Crowell, 1978.

Caroline Feller Bauer, *My Mom Travels a Lot,* Warne, 1981.

Henry Wadsworth Longfellow, *Paul Revere's Ride,* Greenwillow, 1985.

Eve Rice, *Aren't You Coming Too?,* Greenwillow, 1988.

Rachel Field, *General Store,* Greenwillow, 1988.

Rice, *Peter's Pockets,* Greenwillow, 1989.

Nietzel, *The Jacket I Wear in the Snow,* Greenwillow, 1989.

Rice, *At Grammy's House,* Greenwillow, 1990.

Ginger Foglesong Guy, *Black Crow, Black Crow,* Greenwillow, 1990.

Patricia Lillie, *When the Rooster Crowed,* Greenwillow, 1991.

John Greenleaf Whittier, *Barbara Frietchie,* Greenwillow, 1991.

ADAPTATIONS: My Mom Travels a Lot was adapted into a filmstrip by Live Oak; *The Ordeal of Byron B. Blackbear* was made into a film.

SIDELIGHTS: Nancy Winslow Parker is an award-winning children's book author and illustrator. Parker insists that her illustrations and stories have one characteristic in common; they are all done in the spirit of fun. Critiquing a representative group of Parker's works, Dulcy Brainard, writing in *Publishers Weekly,* remarked, "The books are marked by a fresh simplicity and an observant, ironic sense of humor that is particularly apparent in the unexpected ways her pictures expand on the text."

Parker was born in Maplewood, New Jersey, in 1930. Her favorite reading material was *National Geographic,* a magazine that her family collected. Although Parker had dreamed of being an artist since childhood, her family did not think it was a legitimate or profitable career and instead urged her to get a mainstream job. So, after college, Parker moved to New York City and began working for a magazine and as a secretary, although she continued her artwork on the side. Eventually, however, she went to the School of Visual Arts and soon found work as an art director and book designer. Parker tried to market herself as a free-lance illustrator, but realized that she would have to illustrate *and* write stories before being noticed by publishers. After she took this approach, she realized immediate success. In an interview with Brainard in *Publishers Weekly,* Parker commented, "My first story was *The Man with the Take-Apart Head.* It's one of my favorites, and as good as any I've written."

Parker often finds inspiration for her books in real-life situations. Her 1980 work *Poofy Loves Company,* was based on an actual incident in which her overly friendly dog ambushed a visiting youngster, messing up her clothes and stealing her cookie. In a *Junior Literary Guild* review of *Poofy Loves Company,* the author recalled that the story "took about fifteen minutes to write, the whole thing coming at once in a delicious outburst of creativity." Praising Parker's re-creation of this event, the critic remarked that the book contained "hilarious four-color pictures."

As shown by *Poofy Loves Company,* animals, especially dogs, are Parker's favorite subjects. Sometimes she includes more exotic animals in her books and is forced to conduct extensive research to ensure the accuracy of her drawings and facts. *Love from Uncle Clyde* is the story of a boy named Charlie who receives an unusual Christmas present—a three thousand pound hippopotamus from Africa. These same characters reappear in *The Christmas Camel.* In this book Charlie receives a camel from eccentric Uncle Clyde and labors over the wooly animal's care. However this beast is magical and whisks Charlie to Bethlehem on Christmas Eve for an extraordinary experience.

Parker also illustrates works written by other authors. Two of the books she has illustrated—*Willy Bear,* by Mildred Kantrowitz, and *My Mom Travels a Lot,* by Caroline Feller Bauer—earned the prestigious Christopher Award. Both of these works focus on children handling new, and somewhat scary, situations. In *Willy Bear* a youngster uses his teddy bear to act out his fear of going to school, and in *My Mom Travels a Lot,* a young girl examines the positive and negative aspects of her mother's hectic business career. In each instance, Parker's drawings were credited by reviewers as complimenting the text, thus helping to produce superior picture books.

Although Parker has achieved success with fiction for children, she has also delved into the field of nonfiction in her writing and illustrating career. For instance, her 1987 work, *Bugs,* written with Joan R. Wright, examines the physical structure and habitats of several types of insects. Patti Hagan, writing in the *New York Times Book Review,* about *Bugs* remarked that "the color illustrations, with precise anatomical tags, are a fine tool for introducing children" to the creatures portrayed in the book.

WORKS CITED:

Brainard, Dulcy, interview with Nancy Winslow Parker in *Publishers Weekly,* February 22, 1985, pp. 161-162.
Hagan, Patti, review of *Bugs, New York Times Book Review,* February 7, 1988, p. 29.
Review of *Poofy Loves Company, Junior Literary Guild,* March, 1980, p. 8.

*   *   *

PARNALL, Peter 1936-

PERSONAL: Born May 23, 1936, in Syracuse, NY; married; children: one son, one daughter. *Education:* Attended Cornell University and Pratt Institute School of Art.

ADDRESSES: Home—Rural Route 3, Waldoboro, ME 04572.

CAREER: Illustrator and author. Worked as an art director and free-lance designer, 1958-67.

AWARDS, HONORS: New York Times Best Illustrated Book list, 1967, for *A Dog's Book of Bugs* and *Knee-Deep in Thunder,* and 1968, for *Malachi Mudge;* Dutton Junior Animal Award, 1968, Dorothy Canfield Fisher Award, 1970, and William Allen White Award, 1971, all for *Kavik the Wolf Dog;* Commonwealth Club of California Award, 1971, Woodward Park School Award, 1972, Newbery Honor Award, 1972, Christopher Medal, 1972, and Art Books for Children Award, 1973, all for *Annie and the Old One;* Art Books for Children

PETER PARNALL

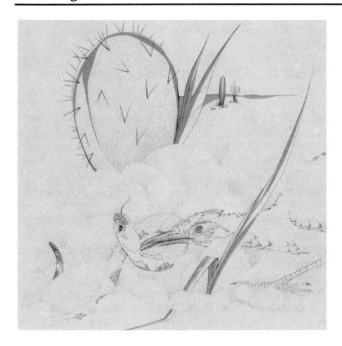

Parnall shows his deep love of wildlife by drawing animals in their natural habitats in illustrations like this one from Naomi Lewis's *Roadrunner.*

Award, 1976, for *Everybody Needs a Rock; Boston Globe-Horn Book* Award, 1976, Caldecott Honor Medal, 1976, New York Academy of Sciences Award, 1976, Steck-Vaughn Award, 1976, Art Books for Children Award, 1977, 1978, and 1979, all for *The Desert Is Theirs;* Caldecott Honor Medal, 1977, for *Hawk, I'm Your Brother;* Caldecott Honor Medal, 1979, for *The Way to Start a Day;* Parents' Choice Award, 1980, for *Roadrunner;* New York Academy of Sciences Award, 1985, for *The Daywatchers.*

WRITINGS:

SELF-ILLUSTRATED

The Mountain, Doubleday, 1971.
The Great Fish, Doubleday, 1973.
Alfalfa Hill, Doubleday, 1975.
A Dog's Book of Birds, Scribner, 1977.
The Daywatchers, Macmillan, 1984.
Winter Barn, Macmillan, 1986.
Apple Tree, Macmillan, 1987.
Feet, Macmillan, 1988.
Quiet, Morrow, 1989.
Cats from Away, Macmillan, 1989.
The Woodpile, Macmillan, 1990.
The Rock, Macmillan, 1991.
Marsh Cat, Macmillan, 1991.
Stuffer, Macmillan, 1992.

ILLUSTRATOR

Hal Borland, *Beyond Your Doorstep,* Knopf, 1962.
Wayne Short, *The Cheechakoes,* Random House, 1964.
Eunice de Chazneau, *Of Houses and Cats,* Random House, 1965.
Mary Francis Shura, *A Tale of Middle Length,* Atheneum, 1966.

Elizabeth Griffen, *A Dog's Book of Bugs,* Atheneum, 1967.
Sheila Moon, *Knee-Deep in Thunder,* Atheneum, 1967.
William O. Douglas, *A Farewell to Texas,* McGraw, 1967.
Harold E. Burtt, *The Psychology of Birds,* Macmillan, 1967.
Edward Cecil (pseudonym of Cecil Maiden), *Malachi Mudge,* McGraw, 1967.
Frank Lee DuMond, *Tall Tales of the Catskills,* Atheneum, 1968.
Jean Craighead George, *The Moon of the Wild Pigs,* Crowell, 1968.
Murray Goodwin, *Underground Hideaway,* Harper, 1968.
Walt Morey, *Kavik the Wolf Dog,* Dutton, 1968.
Patricia Coffin, *The Gruesome Green Witch,* Walker, 1969.
Miska Miles, *Apricot ABC,* Little, Brown, 1969.
Peggy Parish, *A Beastly Circus,* Simon & Schuster, 1969.
Aileen Lucia Fisher, *But Ostriches,* Crowell, 1970.
George Mendoza, *The Inspector,* Doubleday, 1970.
Jan Wahl, *Doctor Rabbit,* Delacorte, 1970.
Cora Annett, *When the Porcupine Moved In,* F. Watts, 1971.
Angus Cameron, *The Nightwatchers,* Four Winds Press, 1971.
Mendoza, *Big Frog, Little Pond,* McCall, 1971.
Mendoza, *Moonfish and Owl Scratchings,* Grosset, 1971.
Miles, *Annie and the Old One,* Little, Brown, 1971.

Parnall evokes the relationships between human beings and the land they inhabit in his illustrations of Byrd Baylor's *The Desert Is Theirs.*

Wahl, *The Six Voyages of Pleasant Fieldmouse,* Delacorte, 1971.

Margaret Hodges, *The Fire Bringer,* Little, Brown, 1972.

Jane Yolen and Barbara Green, *The Fireside Song Book of Birds and Beasts,* Simon & Schuster, 1972.

Mary Anderson, *Emma's Search for Something,* Atheneum, 1973.

Kent Durden, *Gifts of an Eagle,* Simon & Schuster, 1972.

Mary Ann Hoberman, *A Little Book of Little Beasts,* Simon & Schuster, 1973.

Laurence P. Pringel, *Twist, Wiggle, and Squirm: A Book about Earthworms,* Crowell, 1973.

Miriam Schlein, *The Rabbit's World,* Four Winds Press, 1973.

Josephine Johnson, *Seven Houses,* Simon & Schuster, 1973.

Byrd Baylor, *Everybody Needs a Rock,* Scribner, 1974.

Berniece Freschet, *Year on Muskrat Marsh,* Scribner, 1974.

Keith Robertson, *Tales of Myrtle the Turtle,* Viking, 1974.

Baylor, *The Desert Is Theirs,* Scribner, 1975.

Sally Carrighar, *The Twilight Seas,* Weybright & Talley, 1975.

Millard Lampell, *The Pig with One Nostril,* Doubleday, 1975.

Alice Schick, *The Peregrine Falcons,* Dial Press, 1975.

Baylor, *Hawk, I'm Your Brother,* Scribner, 1976.

Victor B. Scheffer, *A Natural History of Marine Mammals,* Scribner, 1976.

Baylor, *The Way To Start a Day,* Scribner, 1977.

(With Virginia Parnall) Anna Michel, *Little Wild Chimpanzee,* Pantheon, 1978.

William Humphrey, *The Spawning Run,* Delacorte, 1979.

(With V. Parnall) Michel, *Little Wild Elephant,* Pantheon, 1979.

Baylor, *Your Own Best Secret Place,* Scribner, 1979.

Baylor, *The Other Way to Listen,* Scribner, 1980.

Baylor, *If You Are a Hunter of Fossils,* Scribner, 1980.

(With V. Parnall) Naomi John, *Roadrunner,* Dutton, 1980.

Baylor, *Desert Voices,* Scribner, 1981.

(With V. Parnall) Terry Williams, *Between Cattails,* Scribner, 1985.

Baylor, *I'm in Charge of Celebrations,* Scribner, 1986.

Jean Chapman, compiler, *Cat Will Rhyme with Hat: A Book of Poems,* Scribner, 1986.

SIDELIGHTS: Author and illustrator Peter Parnall brings a deep love of wildlife to his work. Although he originally planned on becoming a veterinarian, Parnall changed his mind when he discovered that he preferred drawing animals in their natural habitats to studying them in an office or lab. Parnall always keeps his young audience in mind, working slowly to insure that his depictions are accurately rendered. Musing on his success in the *Third Book of Junior Authors and Illustrators,* Parnall noted that publishing has "been very kind to me and I have been very kind to it by working like a slave trying to improve the fare we publish for our children. Seeing my little neighbors

smile at a drawing makes me feel I could make the rain fall up."

Parnall began illustrating books for children in the 1960s. He found inspiration for many of his works by taking long walks in parks and wooded areas. Critics praised the results of these intense periods of observation. "Superbly detailed, elegant in line, bold in composition, Parnall's drawings ... are a striking accompaniment to his series of pieces on the various birds of prey he has observed," wrote a reviewer in the *Bulletin of the Center for Children's Books* about *The Daywatchers.* Another reviewer for the *Bulletin,* commenting on Parnall's *Winter Barn,* remarked that the illustrations "have a still-life quality; their precise drafting and spacious composition underscore the brittle quiet of intense cold. A wintry mood piece."

In recent years, Parnall has worked at home on his farm. He produces about three books a year and admits to enjoying the writing aspect of his work as much as illustrating. "I found I wanted to share some of my love of nature and ecology with children and chose to do it by writing about 'stuff,'" Parnall wrote in an essay for *Something about the Author Autobiography Series.* "Just stuff that is hanging around here and there, like a woodpile, or maybe a stone wall. Things children often ignore. Like a tree."

WORKS CITED:

de Montreville, Doris, and Donna Hill, editors, *Third Book of Junior Authors and Illustrators,* H. W. Wilson, 1972, pp. 220-21.

Review of *The Daywatchers, Bulletin of the Center for Children's Books,* March, 1985.

Something about the Author Autobiography Series, Volume 11, Gale, 1991, pp. 259-73.

Review of *Winter Barn, Bulletin of the Center for Children's Books,* February, 1987.

FOR MORE INFORMATION SEE:

BOOKS

Kingman, Lee, compiler, *Illustrators of Children's Books, 1957-66,* Horn Book, 1968.

PERIODICALS

Booklist, November 15, 1975.

Horn Book, October, 1975.

New York Times Book Review, January 2, 1972.

Saturday Review, September 18, 1971.*

*   *   *

PATENT, Dorothy Hinshaw 1940-

PERSONAL: Born April 30, 1940, in Rochester, MN; daughter of Horton Corwin (a physician) and Dorothy Kate (Youmans) Hinshaw; married Gregory Joseph Patent (a professor of zoology), March 21, 1964; children: David Gregory, Jason Daniel. *Education:* Stanford University, B.A., 1962; University of California, Berkeley, M.A., 1965, Ph.D., 1968; also studied at Friday

DOROTHY HINSHAW PATENT

Harbor Laboratories, University of Washington, 1965-67. *Hobbies and other interests:* Gardening, cooking, and racquetball.

ADDRESSES: Home—5445 Skyway Dr., Missoula, MT 59801.

CAREER: Writer. Sinai Hospital, Detroit, MI, post-doctoral fellow, 1968-69; Stazione Zoologica, Naples, Italy, post-doctoral researcher, 1970-71; University of Montana, Missoula, faculty affiliate in department of zoology, 1975—, acting assistant professor, 1977.

MEMBER: International Woman's Writing Guild, American Institute of Biological Sciences, Authors Guild, Society of Children's Book Writers.

AWARDS, HONORS: The National Science Teachers Association has cited more than forty of Patent's books as outstanding science trade books; Golden Kite Award in nonfiction, Society of Children's Book Writers, 1977, for *Evolution Goes On Every Day,* and 1980, for *The Lives of Spiders;* "Notable Book" citation, American Library Association, 1982, for *Spider Magic;* "Best Book for Young Adults" citation, American Library Association, 1986, for *The Quest for Artificial Intelligence;* Eva L. Gordon Award, American Nature Study Society, 1987, for the body of her work.

WRITINGS:

FOR CHILDREN

Weasels, Otters, Skunks and Their Family, illustrations by Matthew Kalmenoff, Holiday House, 1973.
Microscopic Animals and Plants, Holiday House, 1974.
Frogs, Toads, Salamanders and How They Reproduce, illustrations by M. Kalmenoff, Holiday House, 1975.
How Insects Communicate, Holiday House, 1975.
Fish and How They Reproduce, illustrations by M. Kalmenoff, Holiday House, 1976.
Plants and Insects Together, illustrations by M. Kalmenoff, Holiday House, 1976.
Evolution Goes On Every Day, illustrations by M. Kalmenoff, Holiday House, 1977.
Reptiles and How They Reproduce, illustrations by M. Kalmenoff, Holiday House, 1977.
The World of Worms, Holiday House, 1978.
Animal and Plant Mimicry, Holiday House, 1978.
(With Paul C. Schroeder) *Beetles and How They Live,* Holiday House, 1978.
Butterflies and Moths: How They Function, Holiday House, 1979.
Sizes and Shapes in Nature: What They Mean, Holiday House, 1979.
Raccoons, Coatimundis and Their Family, Holiday House, 1979.

In *The Quest for Artificial Intelligence,* Patent explains how the brain extracts the essential elements of simple images—like those pictured here—and identifies them.

Bacteria: How They Affect Other Living Things, Holiday House, 1980.

The Lives of Spiders, Holiday House, 1980.

Bears of the World, Holiday House, 1980.

Horses and Their Wild Relatives, Holiday House, 1981.

Horses of America, Holiday House, 1981.

Hunters and the Hunted: Surviving in the Animal World, Holiday House, 1981.

Spider Magic, Holiday House, 1982.

A Picture Book of Cows, photographs by William Munoz, Holiday House, 1982.

Arabian Horses, Holiday House, 1982.

Germs!, Holiday House, 1983.

A Picture Book of Ponies, photographs by W. Munoz, Holiday House, 1983.

Whales: Giants of the Deep, Holiday House, 1984.

Farm Animals, photographs by W. Munoz, Holiday House, 1984.

Where the Bald Eagles Gather, photographs by W. Munoz, Clarion, 1984.

Baby Horses, photographs by W. Munoz, Dodd, 1985.

Quarter Horses, photographs by W. Munoz, Holiday House, 1985.

The Sheep Book, photographs by W. Munoz, Dodd, 1985.

Thoroughbred Horses, Holiday House, 1985.

Draft Horses, photographs by W. Munoz, Holiday House, 1986.

Buffalo: The American Bison Today, photographs by W. Munoz, Clarion, 1986.

Mosquitoes, Holiday House, 1986.

Maggie: A Sheep Dog (Junior Literary Guild selection), photographs by W. Munoz, Dodd, 1986.

The Quest for Artificial Intelligence, Harcourt, 1986.

Christmas Trees (Junior Literary Guild selection), Dodd, 1987.

All about Whales, Holiday House, 1987.

Dolphins and Porpoises, Holiday House, 1987.

The Way of the Grizzly, photographs by W. Munoz, Clarion, 1987.

Wheat: The Golden Harvest, photographs by W. Munoz, Dodd, 1987.

A computer plays chess against a human opponent in this photo from Patent's *The Quest for Artificial Intelligence*. Patent has won praise for presenting complex scientific information in a clear, lively manner.

Appaloosa Horses, photographs by W. Munoz, Holiday House, 1988.

Babies!, Holiday House, 1988.

A Horse of a Different Color, photographs by W. Munoz, Dodd, 1988.

The Whooping Crane: A Comeback Story, photographs by W. Munoz, Clarion, 1988.

Humpback Whales, photographs by Mark J. Ferrari and Deborah A. Glockner-Ferrari, Holiday House, 1989.

Grandfather's Nose: Why We Look Alike or Different, illustrations by Diane Palmisciano, F. Watts, 1989.

Singing Birds and Flashing Fireflies: How Animals Talk to Each Other, illustrations by Mary Morgan, F. Watts, 1989.

Where the Wild Horses Roam, photographs by W. Munoz, Clarion, 1989.

Wild Turkey, Tame Turkey, photographs by W. Munoz, Clarion, 1989.

Looking at Dolphins and Porpoises, Holiday House, 1989.

Looking at Ants, Holiday House, 1989.

Seals, Sea Lions and Walruses, Holiday House, 1990.

Yellowstone Fires: Flames and Rebirth, photographs by W. Munoz, Holiday House, 1990.

An Apple a Day: From Orchard to You, photographs by W. Munoz, Cobblehill, 1990.

Flowers for Everyone, photographs by W. Munoz, Cobblehill, 1990.

Gray Wolf, Red Wolf, photographs by W. Munoz, Clarion, 1990.

How Smart Are Animals? (Junior Literary Guild selection), Harcourt, 1990.

A Family Goes Hunting, photographs by W. Munoz, Clarion, 1991.

Miniature Horses, photographs by W. Munoz, Cobblehill, 1991.

The Challenge of Extinction, Enslow, 1991.

Where Food Comes From, photographs by W. Munoz, Holiday House, 1991.

African Elephants: Giants of the Land, photographs by Oria Douglas-Hamilton, Holiday House, 1991.

Feathers, photographs by W. Munoz, Cobblehill, 1992.

Places of Refuge: Our National Wildlife Refuge System, photographs by W. Munoz, Clarion, 1992.

Nutrition: What's in the Food We Eat, photographs by W. Munoz, Holiday, 1992.

FOR ADULTS

(With Diane E. Bilderback) *Garden Secrets,* Rodale Press, 1982, revised and expanded edition published as *The Harrowsmith Country Life Book of Garden Secrets: A Down-to-Earth Guide to the Art and Science of Growing Better Vegetables,* Camden House, 1991.

(With D. E. Bilderback) *Backyard Fruits and Berries,* Rodale Press, 1984.

Contributor to gardening and farming magazines.

WORK IN PROGRESS: Patent is preparing a book on pelicans for Clarion, one on habitat preservation for Enslow, and a three book series comparing the behavior of domesticated animals with their wild relatives for Carolrhoda. Projects scheduled for 1993 publication include books on ospreys and prairie dogs for Clarion, a book on killer whales for Holiday, books on animal tails and a Newfoundland search-and-rescue dog named Hugger for Cobblehill, and one on the loss of diversity in our food sources for Harcourt. Future projects include books on deer, elk, and alligators for Clarion. Patent told *SATA* that she has been "trying her hand at fiction for children with the help of a local critique group."

SIDELIGHTS: "The story of my life is a story of love of the earth and of the world of living things," remarks Dorothy Hinshaw Patent in the *Something about the Author Autobiography Series* (*SAAS*). Her childhood curiosity about animals and the natural world evolved into educational interests and finally into a lifelong career as a writer. Whether writing about salamanders, eagles, or grizzly bears, Patent transforms hours of research both in the library and in the wild into easily understood books that respect their audience as much as their subject. Her nonfiction books for young people have won over twenty awards from the National Science Teachers Association, and she has been commended by critics for presenting complex scientific information in a clear, spirited style.

"Many writers have known for as long as they can remember that they wanted to write. Not me," says Patent in *SAAS.* "I knew that I loved animals, the woods, and exploring, and I always wanted to learn everything possible about something that interested me. But I never yearned to be a writer." Patent says that she grew up a tomboy, exploring the terrain around her family's homes in Minnesota and later California with her older brother. She was always more interested in catching tadpoles, playing with toads, and collecting insects than in the more conventional interests shared by girls her age. In fact, Patent remembers having trouble making girl friends in school: "To this day I'm not sure why, but maybe it was because I'd never spent much time with girls and didn't know how to act around them."

When she was in elementary school, Patent received a gift from her mother that turned her general interest in nature into a firm resolve to know all that she could of a specific subject. As a reward for practicing the piano, her mother bought her a pair of golden guppies and she recalls in *SAAS:* "The morning after we bought the fish, I peered into the bowl to check on my new pets. To my surprise, the adult fish weren't alone—three new pairs of eyes stared out at me from among the plants. I couldn't believe this miracle—the female fish had given birth during the night, and now I had five fish instead of two!" Patent's enthusiasm led her to read every book she could about tropical fish and to frequent a special Japanese fish store to learn even more, which came in handy later on, she says, when she wrote *Fish and How They Reproduce.* Another book, *The Challenge of Extinction,* was written partly because of Patent's experience with animals that were abundant in her childhood but are now almost extinct.

Patent's curiosity helped her to excel in school, as did the encouragement of her family. "Learning was highly valued in my family," she says in *SAAS.* Despite her success academically, she felt like a misfit socially. "I wanted to be like the 'in' crowd ...," she recalls. "I admired the girls who became prom queens and cheerleaders. At the time, there was no way I could understand that some of them were living the best part of their lives during high school while the best parts of my life were yet to come and would last much longer." After high school Patent went to nearby Stanford University, one of the few highly rated schools in the nation that was coeducational at the time and had a strong science program. Patent blossomed in college, where her intelligence and intellectual curiosity were valued. Despite a terrible tragedy during her freshman year—the suicide of her roommate—which put her "into a dark emotional frame of mind that lasted the entire four years," she says in her autobiographical sketch that she became involved with international folk dancing, made good friends, and had interesting, challenging classes. Many of her classes

emphasized writing, and "by the end of my freshman year," she recollects, "I could set an internal switch for a paper of a certain length and write it. I'm sure this discipline and training helped me in my writing career." After a trip to Europe with a friend, Patent enrolled in graduate school at the University of California at Berkeley, where she met the man she would marry, Greg Patent, a teaching assistant in her endocrinology class.

Patent and her new husband continued their graduate work and research in Friday Harbor, Washington; Detroit, Michigan; and Naples, Italy; settling for a while in North Carolina before moving to Montana. Searching for a job that would allow her to spend time with her two young boys, Patent recalls in *SAAS:* "When people asked me questions about biology, they often complimented my answers by saying that I explained things well. Maybe I could write about biology. And since I had children, perhaps writing for kids would be a good idea. There was so much exciting information about living things that I could share. I could write for children who were like me, who wanted to learn everything they could about nature."

Though her first two books were not published, one of them piqued the interest of an editor at Holiday House who eventually approached Patent with an idea for a book about the weasel family. Although she knew next to nothing about weasels, Patent agreed to write the book. She spent hours doing research at the University of Montana library in Missoula, and received help from a professor at the university who happened to be one of the world's experts on weasels. She soon developed a pattern of careful research and organization that allowed her to write first one, then two, then three books a year. "Each book was a review," she explains in *SAAS,* "in simple language, of everything known up to that time about the subject. I chose most of the subjects myself, and they were the things that had interested me as a child—frogs, tropical fish, reptiles, butterflies."

In the early 1980s Patent began to work with photographer William Munoz, whose name she found in a Missoula newspaper. The two would travel together to photograph the animals for a book, and became a successful team. The first few books that Patent wrote with the help of Munoz allowed her to stay in Montana, but her desire to write books on grizzly bears, whooping cranes, and wolves soon took them to Alaska, New Mexico, Texas, and other states. Becoming increasingly concerned with the plight of wildlife, Patent says in her autobiographical sketch that "wild things always seem to lose out in today's world.... We need to realize that we are part of nature, that without nature, we are not whole."

Patent's books, the majority of which explain the history, breeding, growth and habits of various groups of animals, have been widely praised for their clarity, thoroughness, and readability. Whether she is describing worms or whales, Patent's works appeal to students of all ages, from the bright eight-year-old to the curious high school student. She may use difficult vocabulary, but she explains the words used and often supplies a helpful glossary. Also, humorous examples of strange animal behavior and vivid pictures frequently combine to make her books more interesting than the ordinary textbook. In *Children and Books*, Zena Sutherland and May Hill Arbuthnot comment that Patent "communicates a sense of wonder at the complexity and beauty of animal life by her zest for her subject," and Sarah Gagne, who has reviewed many of Patent's works, says that she "could probably make interesting the life and ancestors of even a garden mole."

Patent wrote in *SAAS:* "I hope that my writing can help children get in touch with the world of living things and realize how dependent we are on them, not just on the wild world but on domesticated plants and animals as well. We owe our existence to the earth, and it is the balance of nature that sustains all life; we upset that balance at our peril. I believe that well-informed children can grow up into responsible citizens capable of making the wise but difficult decisions necessary for the survival of a liveable world. I plan to continue to write for those children, helping to provide them with the information they will need in the difficult but exciting times ahead."

WORKS CITED:

Gagne, Sarah, review of *Horses and Their Wild Relatives, Horn Book,* October, 1981, pp. 558-559.

Patent, Dorothy Hinshaw, article in *Something about the Author Autobiography Series,* Volume 13, Gale, 1991, pp. 137-154.

Sutherland, Zena, and May Hill Arbuthnot, "Informational Books," in *Children and Books,* 7th edition, Scott, Foresman, 1986, pp. 484-548.

FOR MORE INFORMATION SEE:

BOOKS

Children's Literature Review, Volume 19, Gale, 1990, pp. 147-166.

PERIODICALS

Appraisal: Children's Science Books, fall, 1974, p. 33; winter, 1976, p. 33; spring, 1979, pp. 47-48; winter, 1980, pp. 45-46; winter, 1982, p. 52; fall, 1983, p. 52; spring, 1985, p. 32; winter, 1987, pp. 55-56; spring, 1988, p. 28; fall, 1989.

Booklist, June 15, 1987; May 15, 1989; March 15, 1990; June 1, 1991.

Bulletin of the Center for Children's Books, November, 1991.

Horn Book, October, 1973; April, 1978; October, 1979; February, 1980.

Los Angeles Times Book Review, November 14, 1982, p. 8; April 26, 1987, p. 4.

Missoulian, December 19, 1981; May 4, 1984.

New York Times Book Review, May 4, 1975, p. 45.

San Rafael Independent-Journal, January 26, 1974.

School Library Journal, February, 1977, p. 67; March, 1979, p. 150; February, 1980, p. 71; February, 1981, p. 77; November, 1984, p. 127; October, 1985, p.

BONNIE PRYOR

186; August, 1987, p. 87; August, 1988, p. 91; January, 1989; March, 1990.

—Sketch by Tom Pendergast

*   *   *

PRYOR, Bonnie 1942-

PERSONAL: Born December 22, 1942, in Los Angeles, CA; daughter of George A. (an electrical engineer) and Helen B. (Bowden) Gehr; married Robert E. Pryor (a tool and die maker), 1960; children: Rick, Suzanne Stevens, Tonya Baughman, Dirk, Christina, and Jennifer. *Education:* Attended Central Ohio Tech.

ADDRESSES: Home and office—19600 Baker Rd., Gambier, OH 43022.

CAREER: Writer of books for children. Kid's Shelf (children's book store), Mt. Vernon, OH, proprietor, 1989—.

MEMBER: Society of Children's Book Writers, Association of Children's Booksellers.

AWARDS, HONORS: Child Study award, Children's Book Committee at Bank Street College, 1986, for *Mr. Z. and the Time Clock;* Notable Children's Trade Book in the Field of Social Studies award, National Association for the Social Studies/Children's Book Council,

1987, for *The House on Maple Street*, and 1988, for *Seth of the Lion People;* Outstanding Science Trade Book for Children award, National Science Teachers Association/Children's Book Council, 1987, for *The House on Maple Street;* Irma Simonton Black award, Bank Street College, 1990, for *Porcupine Mouse.*

WRITINGS:

Grandpa Bear, illustrated by Bruce Degen, Morrow Junior Books, 1985.
Grandpa Bear's Christmas, illustrated by Degen, Morrow Junior Books, 1986.
Amanda and April, illustrated by Diane DeGroat, Morrow Junior Books, 1986.
Rats, Spiders, and Love, Morrow Junior Books, 1986.
Mr. Z. and the Time Clock, Dillon Press, 1986.
The House on Maple Street, illustrated by Beth Peck, Morrow Junior Books, 1987.
Vinegar Pancakes and Vanishing Cream, illustrated by Gail Owens, Morrow Junior Books, 1987.
Jenny's Baby Sister, illustrated by Carolyn Bracken, Simon & Schuster, 1987.
Happy Birthday Mama, illustrated by Bracken, Simon & Schuster, 1987.
Mr. Munday and the Rustlers, illustrated by Wallup Munyon, Simon & Schuster, 1987.
Perfect Percy, illustrated by Jerry Smath, Simon & Schuster, 1988.
Seth of the Lion People, Morrow Junior Books, 1988.
Mr. Munday and the Space Creatures, illustrated by Leo Lorentz, Simon & Schuster, 1989.
Porcupine Mouse, illustrated by Maryjane Begin, Morrow Junior Books, 1989.
Plum Tree War, illustrated by Dora Leder, Morrow Junior Books, 1989.
Twenty Four Hour Lipstick Mystery, Morrow Junior Books, 1990.
Merry Christmas Amanda and April, illustrated by DeGroat, Morrow Junior Books, 1990.
Greenbrook Farm, illustrated by Mark Graham, Simon & Schuster, 1991.

Contributor of articles to periodicals, including *Ladies' Circle, Women's World,* and *Bobcat.*

WORK IN PROGRESS: Six books scheduled for release through 1993: *Beaver Boys, Lottie's Dream, Horse in the Garage, Poison Ivy and Eyebrowwigs, Birthday Blizzard,* and *Louie and Dan Are Friends;* finishing an untitled mystery; researching pre-historic Native Americans.

SIDELIGHTS: The experiences of childhood and motherhood provide Bonnie Pryor with much of the material for her books. Rather than relying entirely on imagina-

tion to create her stories, Pryor scrutinizes her own life for moments of humor and insight. Her approach to creative writing developed gradually. Pryor first began to write in 1983. But after some initial success publishing articles in magazines, she found herself struggling to come up with original book ideas. She solved this problem by recasting childhood memories as the adventures of the characters in her books.

Pryor has been interested in books and reading since she was a young girl. Commenting on her school days, she told *SATA:* "Most of my childhood was spent hiding under the dining room table or locked in the bathroom with a book. I was very shy, and if my teachers remember me at all, it is probably because of the number of times I had to be scolded for hiding a novel inside of my math book." Delighted by the possibilities that literature held for escape, Pryor indulged in fantasy and day-dreams. "I lived in a world of my own creating," she recalled, "It was a secret world in which I, the heroine, pursued dastardly villains and survived the end of the world."

These flights of fancy did not immediately translate themselves into writing. Years passed before Pryor finally decided to write for publication. After a year of study and practice, she sold her first magazine articles. Despite these sales, Pryor still felt as if something were missing. She had always enjoyed reading to her children; armed with a new typewriter, and her husband's encouragement, she set out to write a children's book: "I stared at a blank paper for weeks trying to think what I had to say that was any different from all those other books. While I sat there, funny family incidents would pop into my head. I thought about how it felt to be a middle child. I remembered the time my mother admonished me to keep my new shoes out of the fresh tar on the road. So, I took them off, walked through with my new white socks, and then put the shoes back on. I thought about how excited my daughter was to find an arrowhead in our backyard." Memories like these resulted in three published works: *Grandpa Bear, Amanda and April,* and *The House on Maple Street.* "To keep myself from growing stale I try all kinds of stories," Pryor told *SATA.* Fresh memories and other books have followed.

To stay abreast of developments in children's literature, and to make available a wide variety of writing for children, Pryor has opened a bookshop in Mt. Vernon, Ohio. She commented: "I still get a thrill reading all the new books as they come in, so I can recommend them to my customers. Luckily for me I am a night person, and in spite of a rather whirlwind life, I find time to write everyday—usually between 11 p.m. and 3 a.m."

R

READE, Deborah 1949-

PERSONAL: Born April 7, 1949, in Berkeley, CA; daughter of Rawlinson Whitney (an industrial contractor) and Rubye (a homemaker; maiden name, Campodonico) Reade; children: Francisco Aschwanden, Sophie Aschwanden. *Education:* Attended University of Washington, Seattle, 1966-1968; University of California, Berkeley, B.A., 1970; attended Laney Junior College, 1976-77. *Politics:* "Work in antiwar and anti-nuclear activities."

ADDRESSES: Home and office—100 El Rancho Rd. S., Santa Fe, NM 87501.

CAREER: Legal researcher, 1970-72; did pasteup and typesetting for various companies, 1976-78; Flights of Fancy (design firm), owner and operator, 1978-80; John Muir Publications, Santa Fe, NM, typesetter and illustrator, 1980-84; self-employed craft designer, illustrator, and map designer, 1978—. Lecturer on nuclear waste and nuclear waste repositories, 1990-92. *Exhibitions:* Work has been shown at Laney College, Oakland, CA, and in several museums and galleries in Albuquerque, Espanola, and Santa Fe, NM.

MEMBER: Phi Beta Kappa.

ILLUSTRATOR:

Gordon Morrell, *Computer-Ease: Selecting Your Personal Computer,* John Muir, 1982.
(With Jennifer Owings Dewey) Stephen Trimble, *The Village of Blue Stone,* Macmillan, 1990.

Also contributor of illustrations to books, including *The Traveling Angler,* by Ernest Schwiebert; *The Traveling Golfer,* by Glen Waggoner; and *The Traveling Skier: Twenty Five-Star Vacations,* all published by Doubleday, 1991. Contributor of maps to numerous books, including *Japan in 22 Days,* by David Olds, John Muir, 1987; *The Sagebrush Ocean: The Natural History of the Great Basin,* by Trimble, University of Nevada Press, 1989; and *An Introduction to the Geology of Death*

DEBORAH READE

Valley, by Michael Collier, Death Valley Natural History Association, 1990.

WORK IN PROGRESS: An illustrated, three-part history of New Mexico; research on the prehistory of the American Southwest and on various aspects of nuclear waste.

SIDELIGHTS: Deborah Reade told *SATA:* "When I was in the fifth grade, I read every book in our local library on ancient Egypt and for many years was determined to be an Egyptologist. Other interests and circumstances intervened and, though never gone, my interest in ancient civilizations slipped to the background. The opportunity to illustrate *The Village of Blue Stone* rekindled all my former interest.

"The research involved in drawing the cultural artifacts of the ancient Anasazi was fascinating. Now I am

163

studying *all* the Indians of the ancient Southwest. My particular favorites are the Anasazi of Chaco Canyons and Paleo-Indians—those who lived more than ten thousand years ago and hunted animals now extinct.

"Being a book illustrator seems to satisfy the two sides of my personality—the technical/intellectual and the artistic. My drawings are quite realistic, and I usually learn much about a new subject when I research to illustrate a new book. Lately, I have been specializing in maps. The opportunity to map many different areas and in the styles of different periods is like a trip through time and space. The technical aspects of producing illustrations for book publication also satisfy some—perfectionist(!)—aspect of my personality. At the same time, trying to create a drawing as beautiful as the natural object, or putting form and texture together to make something jewel-like, continually challenges my creative/artistic side."

*　　*　　*

REAVER, Chap 1935-

PERSONAL: Given name is Herbert R. Reaver; born June 10, 1935, in Cincinnati, OH; son of Herbert R., Sr. (a chiropractor) and Mildred (Vordenburg) Reaver; married Dixie (a realtor; maiden name, Reece), September 3, 1959; children: Chappie, Scott. *Education:* Palmer College of Chiropractic, D.C., 1957. *Politics:* Republican. *Religion:* "No preference." *Hobbies and other interests:* Racquet sports, fishing, gardening.

CHAP REAVER

ADDRESSES: Home—1570 West Sandtown Rd., Marietta, GA 30064. *Office*—627 Cherokee N.E., Marietta, GA 30060.

CAREER: Private practice in chiropractic, Cincinnati, OH, 1957-80, Marietta, GA, 1980—; writer. Part-time writing instructor at Marietta Junior High School, in association with the Marietta Community School Program. *Military service:* Served in the Air Force Reserve.

AWARDS, HONORS: Delacorte Press Prize for an Outstanding First Young Adult Novel, 1990, and Edgar Allan Poe Award for best young adult mystery, Mystery Writers of America, 1991, both for *Mote;* Hugo Award nomination for short story, World Science Fiction Society, 1992, for "Feel Good Stuff."

WRITINGS:

Mote (young adult mystery), Delacorte, 1990.
A Little Bit Dead (young adult western), Delacorte, 1992.

Contributor of articles and short stories to periodicals, including *Amazing Stories* and several humor publications.

WORK IN PROGRESS: A young adult novel.

SIDELIGHTS: Chap Reaver never planned to become a writer. He was perfectly contented with his private practice as a chiropractor and active family life. But then in 1980 he moved with his wife and two children to Marietta, Georgia, where they did not have many friends or relations. Reaver decided to use some of his free time for writing. After publishing only a few short stories and articles, his first novel, *Mote,* won the most prestigious prize for mystery fiction in the United States—the Edgar Allan Poe Award. "What is nice is that it does happen," Reaver stated in an interview for *Something about the Author* (*SATA*). "I'm a real ordinary guy who wrote a book, and the long shot came and got it published, which is a thousand to one or whatever. Not only got published, but got nominated for an Edgar; not only got nominated, but won the damn thing. It can happen; so keep your courage up."

Reaver—who's given name is Herbert—got his nickname the day he was born in his family's home in Cincinnati, Ohio. "Dad said, 'What a cute little chap,'" the author recalled. "And I take his word for it; I've been Chap as long as I know." Like his father, Reaver received his degree in chiropractic and established a private practice. He would have remained in his home town, except that his wife, whom Reaver first met when he was stationed at an Air Force base in Georgia, missed living in the South. After moving to Georgia, Reaver drew on his wife's career as a source of inspiration: "I did a few pieces about my wife's real estate activities from the standpoint of the long-suffering husband. Then I did a lot of humor pieces in professional magazines like problems of ethics and morals. It is always with a light approach, hopefully to entertain, because if I don't keep that in mind I tend to start preaching."

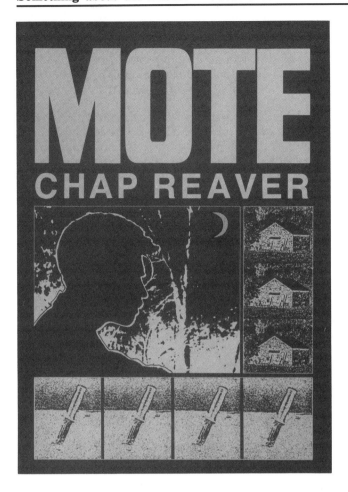

Reaver's first novel, *Mote,* was awarded the prestigious Edgar Allan Poe Award for best young adult mystery of 1991. (Cover design by Marietta Anastassatos.)

Unlike many beginning writers, Reaver had little trouble getting his articles published. "It really helped that I was ignorant," he commented to *SATA.* "I didn't know that it was hard to do, and that you had to get three hundred rejections. So I just wrote a story and sold it, and then they wanted some more and I sold the first five or six before I got a rejection slip. So I guess I've got some kind of natural storytelling ability." Before his novel, *Mote,* was accepted by a publisher, Reaver received a scant eight rejections, an unusually low amount. Nevertheless, he told *SATA:* "What I've learned is that the publishing business doesn't seem like a very nice business to me. The people in children's and young adults' publishing seem like the cream of the crop. They really seem well motivated; they're not just—I don't think—in it for the money. They're really trying to write good books for kids."

Reaver had originally planned *Mote* to be for an adult audience, but after it was written he and his editor decided it was more suited to young adults. "My vocabulary is about that level," the author confided to *SATA.* "That's kind of my natural voice." Reaver also commented, "I find that to be a very interesting time of life anyway and set it there. I did not set out to write a young adult novel. My first submission was to Peachtree

Publishers, they're local here, and the editor was wonderfully generous to write at length about my book: first of all, how much she liked the book, and then some very practical advice on some problems I'm going to have with an adult book with a teenager as narrator. The problem is the booksellers don't know where to put it on the shelf. She said, 'I know that doesn't seem like a problem to you as a writer, but it is a big marketing problem.' And she suggested that I consider going one way or the other, more toward adult or more toward young adult. I went slightly more toward young adult in the rewriting process. This is, I think, a first for publishers. They debated long and hard on how to come out with it. So anyway, they're coming out with the paperback as just an adult book. The same words, the same content, but a new cover, an adult cover, and it won't say 'fourteen and up' on the inside. The publishers call it a crossover book, and I think it probably is."

Mote concerns a teenager named Chris and his investigation of the murder of one of his teachers. The police believe that Chris's friend, a vagabond Vietnam veteran nicknamed "Mote," is responsible because one of his knives was found at the scene. Chris, however, is certain that Mote could never commit murder. With the help of a black police detective named Steinert, Chris conducts a search for the killer that leads him into the hands of a white supremacist group called Equal Rights for White Americans and its African-American counterpart, the Black Brigade. Racism, then, becomes one of the important themes in the story.

Reaver's concern about this topic dates back to an experience he had as a child. One day his father, who had a dark complexion and had gotten very tan after a trip to Florida, was refused a ticket to the theater. "He looked dark enough that the ticket seller was in doubt and refused seating," Reaver told *SATA.* "It really had an effect on my father who up to that time had never given a thought to racial matters. He became very active in the NAACP, and rose to national vice president, and we had meetings in our house. I think I grew up in as racially liberal an atmosphere as possible." Reaver's background made him impatient with prejudiced people. "When I see racism it seems like such a waste of time. We should have been through that a long time ago."

Because the author considers the viewpoints of racist people to be ridiculous, their ideas can seem laughable until he becomes aware of "their potential for harm and unhappiness." Then he gets angry. Still, Reaver acknowledged, "I tend to deal with them in a humorous way. I think it's more effective." "I think that my best thing is to write with a humorous approach to serious problems," Reaver revealed at one point. In addition to the issue of racism, *Mote* deals with other serious matters like divorce and the tragic memories of Vietnam.

Despite the presence of themes like divorce and racism, the main theme of *Mote,* Reaver revealed, concerns "coming of age. I think it's more a book about friendship, bonding and friendship between the kid and Steinert, and the kid and Mote, cross-cultural and cross-racial friendships, and the commonality of that." Reaver also admitted that there are a lot of autobiographical elements in *Mote.* For one thing, Chris and the author both enjoy fly fishing and are avid tennis players. But more than this, Reaver said that all the main characters in the story express some side of himself. "This was a wonderful vehicle for me because I think, like most males, part of me is still very immature and stuck in this childish mode of being sixteen. So it's not a problem for me to speak in that voice. I think Chris's narrative sounds like a sixteen-year old. It was not hard for me to duplicate that because part of me is still there. Part of my emotional reactions are still very little-boyish. But then part of me is Mote's stuff too. I know what's important now. When I had something to say that needed a wiser, more experienced voice, I had Mote, or when I needed kind of a street-wise thing to say, I had Steinert, and when I had a juvenile thing to say, or a little uncertain thing to say, I had Chris or Billy. And so I had all the various parts of myself, the parent and the child. I think there's some kind of psychological system that talks about that, that we each have a parent side and a child side. I had mouths through which to speak all the sides of myself."

Because the characters and their relationships in the book are what was important to Reaver, he was surprised *Mote* was considered for the Edgar Allan Poe Award. "I never figured the who-done-it aspect was its strongest point." But winning an Edgar has not changed Reaver's attitude towards writing in any way. "People pay a little bit more attention to you now that you've got an award that says you wrote a good book. I get invited to more things; I'm doing an interview tonight. I'm glad I won, but I wish the system would allow a little bit of something for second and third. Just being nominated is a marvelous honor with all the mysteries that are written every year."

As a writer for young adults, Reaver feels a certain obligation towards his audience. "It's important that I remind myself to entertain because if I don't I'm going to go to preaching, and the kids are going to turn me off and I don't blame them. I don't want to be preached to either. I'm old enough! And I didn't like it back then and that's what everybody's doing. I think the kids need to learn that they're okay." He then added, "I think it's a greater responsibility writing for teens or young adults than it is writing for adults because their values have not all been shaped yet and you'll have a greater influence. You have to be more careful and you have to feel that responsibility more and really think about what you're doing. Those are young precious lives, and it's an honor if you can just have their attention for a while, much less have any influence. You don't want to squander that."

Reaver has also had an influence on teenagers as a creative writing teacher for high school students. "I really get a kick out of it. I would like to do more, but there are some educators here that are a little bit afraid of *Mote.* It's a little bit too provocative for them, and it's

got the F-word in there, and it's got racial epithets." Reaver later observed, "I think a lot of people write down to kids. I think it's a terrible mistake. They pick that up so quick, and I think that a lot of people try to moralize to them. They don't need that."

As for his future writing, Reaver has no definite plans about sticking to one type of book. His next project is a "New Age mystic Western where the protagonist has a near-death experience. It's really a weird sequence of events. It's altogether different from *Mote,* and I'm really pleased that it worked." Other possibilities for the future include a novel about sex abuse, a sequel to *Mote,* and a cable television screenplay based on *Mote.* When asked whether he had any other career plans, Reaver replied: "I'm really lucky. I've got a lifestyle I enjoy. I like practicing chiropractic a lot; I'm good at it, and I like exercising and fishing and writing. It seems like everything I do is fun, and some of it I get paid for. A lot of people ask if I was going to retire, or retire to write full-time. I don't think I could. I don't think my attention span is such that I could write full-time anyway." "I've got things just about the way I like them," he said later, "and isn't that a lucky guy? Really, I enjoy my whole day. I might hire a boy to cut the grass, but everything else would be about the same."

WORKS CITED:

Reaver, Herbert, interview conducted by Kevin S. Hile for *Something about the Author,* June 12, 1991.

FOR MORE INFORMATION SEE:

PERIODICALS
Publishers Weekly, July 13, 1990.

—*Sketch by Kevin S. Hile*

* * *

REES, David 1936-

PERSONAL: Full name is David Bartlett Rees; born May 18, 1936, in London, England; son of Gerald (a civil servant) and Margaret (Healy) Rees; married Jenny Lee Watkins (a teacher), July 23, 1966 (divorced, 1974); children: Stephen, Adam. *Education:* Queens' College, Cambridge, B.A., 1958. *Hobbies and other interests:* Travel, classical music, attending concerts.

ADDRESSES: Home—69 Regent Street, Exeter, Devon EX2 9EG, England.

CAREER: Wilson's Grammar School, London, England, schoolmaster, 1960-65; Vyners School, Ickenham, England, schoolmaster, 1965-68; St. Luke's College, Exeter, England, lecturer, 1968-73, senior lecturer in English, 1973-78; University of Exeter, lecturer in English, 1978-84; free-lance writer, 1984—. California State University, San Jose, visiting professor, 1982-83, 1985, and 1987.

AWARDS, HONORS: Guardian Award commendation, 1976, for *Storm Surge;* Carnegie Medal from British

DAVID REES

Library Association, 1978, for _The Exeter Blitz;_ Other Award from Children's Rights Workshop, 1980, for _The Green Bough of Liberty._

WRITINGS:

FOR YOUNG CHILDREN

The House That Moved, illustrated by Lazlo Acs, Hamish Hamilton, 1978.
The Night before Christmas Eve, illustrated by Peter Kesteven, Wheaton, 1980, Pergamon, 1982.
A Beacon for the Romans, illustrated by Kesteven, Wheaton, 1981.
The Mysterious Rattle, illustrated by Maureen Bradley, Hamish Hamilton, 1982.
The Burglar, illustrated by Ursula Sieger, Arnold/Wheaton, 1986.
Friends and Neighbours, illustrated by Clare Herroneau, Arnold/Wheaton, 1986.

FOR CHILDREN

Landslip, illustrated by Gavin Rowe, Hamish Hamilton, 1977.
The Exeter Blitz, Hamish Hamilton, 1978, Elsevier/Nelson, 1980.
Holly, Mud and Whisky, illustrated by David Grosvenor, Dobson, 1981.
The Flying Island, Third House, 1988.

FOR YOUNG ADULTS

Storm Surge, illustrated by Trevor Stubley, Lutterworth, 1975.
Quintin's Man, Dobson, 1976, Elsevier/Nelson, 1979.
The Missing German, Dobson, 1976.
The Spectrum, Dobson, 1977.
The Ferryman, illustrated with old maps and prints, Dobson, 1977.
Risks, Heinemann, 1977.
In the Tent, Dobson, 1979, Alyson, 1985.

Silence, Dobson, 1979, Elsevier/Nelson, 1981.
The Green Bough of Liberty, illustrated with old maps and prints, Dobson, 1979.
The Lighthouse, Dobson, 1980.
Miss Duffy Is Still with Us, Dobson, 1980.
The Milkman's on His Way, GMP, 1982.
Waves, Longman, 1983.

FOR ADULTS

The Marble in the Water: Essays on Contemporary Writers of Fiction for Children and Young People, Horn Book, 1980.
The Estuary, GMP, 1983.
Out of the Winter Gardens, Olive Press, 1984.
Painted Desert, Green Shade: Essays on Contemporary Writers for Children and Young Adults, Horn Book, 1984.
A Better Class of Blond: A California Diary, Olive Press, 1985.
Islands (short stories), Knights Press, 1985.
Watershed, Knights Press, 1986.
The Hunger, GMP, 1986.
(Editor and contributor, with Peter Robins) _Oranges and Lemons: Stories by Gay Men,_ Third House, 1987.
Twos and Threes, Third House, 1987.
Flux (short stories), Third House, 1988.
Quince, Third House, 1988.

Quintin's Man **is one of three young adult novels Rees completed in a creative burst in 1974.** (Jacket illustration by Robert Chronister.)

The Wrong Apple, Knights Press, 1988.

The Colour of His Hair, Third House, 1989.

Letters to Dorothy (essays and stories), Third House, 1990.

What Do Draculas Do?: Essays on Contemporary Writers for Children and Young Adults, Third House, 1990.

(With Robins) *Fabulous Tricks,* Inbook, 1991.

Dog Days, White Nights (essays), Third House, 1992.

Not for Your Hands (autobiography), Third House, 1992.

Packing It In (travel guide), Millivres Books, 1992.

OTHER

Rees's work is represented in anthologies, including *Remember Last Summer?,* edited by John Foster, Heinemann, 1980; *Cracks in the Image,* GMP, 1981; *School's O.K.,* edited by Josie Karavasil, Evans, 1982; *Messer Rondo and Other Stories,* GMP, 1983; *Knockout Short Stories,* Longman, 1988; *The Freezer Counter,* Third House, 1989. Author of column in *Gay Times;* regular contributor of book reviews to *Children's Literature in Education, Horn Book, Journal of the Royal Society of the Arts, School Librarian,* and *Times Literary Supplement;* contributor to various literature and library journals. Author's manuscripts are included in collection at University of Exeter, England.

WORK IN PROGRESS: Critical essays on contemporary novelists and composers.

SIDELIGHTS: David Rees uses his writing to reevaluate his past by letting fictional characters resolve the conflicts he experienced in his early life. In the many books he has written for young adults, the author's characters experience situations similar to those from his own adolescence, regardless of their sex or whether the story has a historical or modern setting. "My teenagers do things I never did, but which I perhaps would have enjoyed doing," Rees commented in an autobiographical essay for *Something about the Author Autobiography Series* (*SAAS*). "I give them more chances and opportunities than I had, and I like to put them in situations where they grow up a bit, where they take a step towards maturity." Unlike many books of the genre, the author's young adult novels deal openly with controversial subjects such as homosexuality. As difficult as the subject matter may be for some to confront, Rees's books are critically respected for their honest, sensitive portrayal of the adolescent passage from youth to adulthood.

Rees was a boy of three when World War II began, and he lived with his family in a suburb of London during the blitz of 1940-41 when Germany was bombing the city almost daily. Even as an adult, he continued to have vivid memories of being awakened by the whine of air-raid sirens, or crouching in the dark listening for the "thump" of anti-aircraft guns repelling an enemy attack. "I don't think I have ever forgiven the Nazis for what they did to my childhood," Rees recalled. "When I was twenty I visited Germany for the first time; I drove across the frontier from Denmark, thinking—it's ridicu-

lous, of course—that I'd put my head in a noose: S.S. storm-troopers would jump out of the bushes and kill me. It was a very unpleasant, creepy feeling. And that was eleven years after it was all over!" The intense childhood memories of this period of his life eventually caused Rees to write *The Exeter Blitz,* his best-known book, for which he received the Carnegie Medal in 1978.

Rees and his family left London for the safety of a less-populated area, but found that air raids over the seaside resorts along England's southern coast occurred just as frequently. "Bournemouth had proved no safer than London," he recounted, "so we set off again, this time to a farm by the sea in an utterly remote area of Devon, in southwest England. The village—so tiny and scattered it scarcely deserves the name of 'village'—was called Welcombe. And welcome it was for sure. Here, you didn't know the war existed. I learned to swim and surf at Welcombe." It was at this point in his life, at the age of eight, that Rees began to write. "I realized one day that I was turning, in my head, everything I was doing into the third person, as if I wasn't me but someone else, and that I had been doing this, without knowing it, for weeks. It was a short step from thinking in the third person to writing in it."

At the end of World War II, Rees and his family returned to their home in Surbiton, but the memories of those few years in Welcombe provided the fabric for several of his later novels, such as *The Missing German, The Milkman's on His Way,* and *Waves.* Meanwhile, he was enrolled at King's College School, Wimbledon, where he continued his education until the age of eighteen. This period of his life was not as happy as those months in Welcombe and would never find a place in his books. The school headmaster criticized the young Rees as being "too much of an individual" because of his opposition to the school emphasis upon sports and the compulsory participation in activities such as the Cadet Corps, both of which the boy felt encouraged conformity. The young Rees felt himself marked as an outsider for other things as well, such as his Roman Catholicism, the Irish heritage with which he strongly identified, his physical immaturity, and the fact that he came from a less affluent background than many of the other students. Although his years at school were socially unhappy ones, Rees excelled in his academics and was able to win a scholarship to Cambridge where he graduated with a degree in English in 1958. At the age of twenty-two, after spending two years in travel throughout parts of Europe, Rees started on the teaching career which he pursued until 1984.

Rees's profession as a fiction writer began in earnest when he began to research his family history. He had always had a fascination with his ancestors, stemming in part from the close relationship he had with his grandparents as a young child. As he delved further and further back in time, some fascinating stories began to emerge which demanded a retelling. *The Green Bough of Liberty* was the result of his curiosity, as well as a culmination of both an increasing involvement in the teaching of children's literature and his enthusiasm for

Noted for his character-driven novels, Rees has occasionally relied on disaster—such as the murder in *Risks*—to propel his stories. (Jacket illustration by Robert McMahon.)

the works of several writers for young adults. The novel recounts the Irish uprising of 1798—in which Rees's ancestors had participated—as seen through the eyes of the young protagonist, Ned Byrne. Although the plot revolves around a political rebellion which resulted in war and death, the story, on a deeper level, is an examination of one young man's ability to come to terms with the emotional aspects of the situation: the false heroics, unmet romantic expectations, the death of a brother, and the true cost of the rebellion to both his family and himself. In other books Rees employs a more contemporary setting. For example, *The Exeter Blitz* takes place during its author's own lifetime, giving readers a vivid account of everyday life amidst the German bombing of Exeter, England, during World War II.

With books such as *In the Tent, The Lighthouse,* and *The Milkman's on His Way,* Rees began to confront directly the central concerns of his own adolescence: the emotional experiences he underwent while coming to terms with his homosexuality. In *The Milkman's on His Way,* within a setting that recalls summers spent at Welcombe during the war, Rees tells the story of Ewan, who is beginning to suspect that he is gay. The young man experiences a great deal of emotional turmoil, guilt, and uncertainty due to the growing awareness that he

feels a sexual attraction for his best friend, Leslie, who is heterosexual. Through the course of the novel, Ewan gradually learns to deal with his feelings, finally being put into a situation where he must openly confront his parents with his homosexuality. By the novel's end, Ewan has come to terms with his own identity and makes the decision to leave home and live in a gay community in London as a symbolic transition to independent adulthood. Although the book was rejected by Rees's usual publisher, Dobson, due to its sometimes graphic portrayals of sexual activity, David Keyes wrote in *Voice of Youth Advocates* that "the frankness seems essential and does not linger." The critic added, "This novel is an important addition to others focusing on this theme." It also proved to be a bestseller.

Rees has been an instructor of English for most of his adult life and enjoys teaching his craft to enthusiastic young writers. "I believe anyone can write, provided he or she can spell, punctuate, and string a sentence together," he said in *SAAS*. "It isn't some extraordinary, special gift of the gods. The chief thing is to want to do it enough. It helps, too, to be able to enjoy reading a lot, to be happy in one's own company, to like being house-bound for much of the time, and to refuse to give up because of rejections, or the naggings that come from within. I've taught children who are potentially much better writers than I will ever be, but who, as adults, have written nothing; the only difference between us is this—they have no real urge to do it. Nobody can teach you how; you learn [writing] by doing it. Believe in yourself, and just get on with it!"

WORK CITED:

Something about the Author Autobiography Series, Volume 5, Gale, 1988, pp. 251-265.
Voice of Youth Advocates, February, 1984, p. 340.

FOR MORE INFORMATION SEE:

BOOKS

Burton, Peter, *Talking To...*, Third House, 1991.
Holmes Holze, Sally, editor, *Fifth Book of Junior Authors and Illustrators,* H. W. Wilson, 1983.
Kingman, Lee, and others, compilers, *Illustrators of Children's Books: 1967-1976,* Horn Book, 1978.
Twentieth Century Children's Writers, St. Martin's Press, 1989.

PERIODICALS

Booklist, December 15, 1978, p. 680; September 1, 1980, p. 40; April 15, 1984, p. 1145.
School Librarian, September, 1984, pp. 210-211; August, 1989, pp. 88-90.
Times Literary Supplement, December 10, 1976, p. 1548; March 28, 1980, p. 362; November 21, 1980, p. 1322.

REY, H. A. 1898-1977
(Uncle Gus)

PERSONAL: Original surname, Reyersbach; legally changed to Hans Augusto Rey; born September 16, 1898, in Hamburg, Germany; immigrated to United States, 1940, naturalized U.S. citizen, 1946; died August 26, 1977, in Boston, MA; son of Alexander and Martha (Windmuller) Reyersbach; married Margret Elizabeth Waldstein (an author and illustrator), 1935. *Education:* Attended University of Munich, 1919-20, and University of Hamburg, 1920-23. *Hobbies and other interests:* Watching nature, reading, making gadgets, swimming and snorkeling, and stargazing.

ADDRESSES: Home—14 Hilliard St., Cambridge, MA 02138; (summer) Waterville Valley, Campton P.O., NH.

CAREER: Executive in import/export business, Rio de Janeiro, Brazil, 1924-36; writer and illustrator of children's books, Paris, France, 1937-40; writer and illustrator of books, mainly juvenile, New York City, 1940-63, Cambridge, MA, 1963-77. Taught astronomy at Cambridge Center for Adult Education. *Military service:* German Army, 1916-19; served with Infantry and Medical Corps in France and Russia.

MEMBER: American Association for the Advancement of Science, Federation of American Scientists, Amateur Astronomers Association, Astronomical League, Waterville Valley (NH) Athletic and Improvement Association.

AWARDS, HONORS: Lewis Carroll Shelf Award, 1960, for *Curious George Takes a Job;* Children's book award, Child Study Association of America, 1966, for *Curious George Goes to the Hospital; Curious George* was named best picture book in the 1987 Children's Choice Awards held by *School Library Journal* and a notable book by the American Library Association.

WRITINGS:

JUVENILE BOOKS, EXCEPT WHERE INDICATED; ALL SELF-ILLUSTRATED

Zebrology (drawings), Chatto & Windus, 1937.
Aerodome for Scissors and Paint, Chatto & Windus, 1939.
Raffy and the Nine Monkeys, Chatto & Windus, 1939, published in U.S. as *Cecily G. and the Nine Monkeys,* Houghton, 1942.
Au Clair de la lune and Other French Nursery Songs, Greystone, 1941.
(Under pseudonym Uncle Gus) *Christmas Manger* (with text from the Bible), Houghton, 1942.
(Under pseudonym Uncle Gus) *Uncle Gus's Circus,* Houghton, 1942.
(Under pseudonym Uncle Gus) *Uncle Gus's Farm,* Houghton, 1942.
Elizabite: The Adventures of a Carnivorous Plant, Harper, 1942.
(Compiler) *Humpty Dumpty and Other Mother Goose Songs,* Harper, 1943.

H. A. REY

(Compiler) *We Three Kings and Other Christmas Carols* (music arranged by Henry F. Waldstein), Harper, 1944.
Look for the Letters: A Hide-and-Seek Alphabet, Harper, 1945.
The Stars: A New Way to See Them (for adults), Houghton, 1952, published in England as *A New Way to See the Stars,* Hamlyn, 1966, enlarged edition, Houghton, 1967.
Find the Constellations, Houghton, 1954, revised edition, 1976.

WITH WIFE, MARGRET REY; ALL SELF-ILLUSTRATED

How the Flying Fishes Came into Being, Chatto & Windus, 1938.
Anybody at Home? (verse; puzzle book), Chatto & Windus, 1939, Houghton, 1942.
How Do You Get There? (puzzle book), Houghton, 1941.
Tit for Tat (verse), Harper, 1942.
Tommy Helps, Too, Houghton, 1943.
Where's My Baby (verse; puzzle book), Houghton, 1943.
Feed the Animals (verse; puzzle book), Houghton, 1944.
Billy's Picture, Harper, 1948.
See the Circus (verse; puzzle book), Houghton, 1956.

"CURIOUS GEORGE" SERIES (PUBLISHED IN ENGLAND AS "ZOZO" SERIES BY CHATTO & WINDUS, 1942-67)

Curious George, Houghton, 1941.

(With M. Rey) *Curious George Takes a Job,* Houghton, 1947.

(With M. Rey) *Curious George Rides a Bike,* Houghton, 1952, new edition, 1973.

Curious George Gets a Medal, Houghton, 1957.

(With M. Rey) *Curious George Flies a Kite,* Houghton, 1958.

Curious George Learns the Alphabet, Houghton, 1963.

(With M. Rey) *Curious George Goes to the Hospital,* Houghton, 1966.

ILLUSTRATOR

Margaret Wise Brown, *The Polite Penguin,* Harper, 1941.

Brown, *Don't Frighten the Lion!,* Harper, 1942.

Emmy Payne, *Katy No-Pocket,* Houghton, 1944.

Charlotte Zolotow, *The Park Book,* Harper, 1944.

M. Rey, *Pretzel,* Harper, 1944.

M. Rey, *Spotty,* Harper, 1945.

M. Rey, *Pretzel and the Puppies,* Harper, 1946.

Mary Had a Little Lamb, Penguin, 1951, published in England as *Mary Had a Little Lamb and Other Nursery Songs,* Puffin, 1951.

Christian Morgenstern, *The Daynight Lamp and Other Poems,* translation from German by Max Knight, Houghton, 1973.

Contributor, with wife, Margret Rey, to the "Zozo Page for Children," *Good Housekeeping,* 1951.

ADAPTATIONS:

MOVIES AND FILMSTRIPS

Curious George Rides a Bike (animated film; with teaching guide), Weston Woods Studios, 1958, released as filmstrip, 1960.

Curious George (filmstrip; with record and teaching guide), Teaching Resources Films, 1971, released as animated film, Churchill Films, 1986.

Curious George Flies a Kite (filmstrip; with record and teaching guide), Teaching Resources Films, 1971.

Curious George Gets a Medal (filmstrip; with record and teaching guide), Teaching Resources Films, 1971.

Curious George Goes to the Hospital (filmstrip; with record and teaching guide), Teaching Resources Films, 1971.

Curious George Takes a Job (filmstrip; with record and teaching guide), Teaching Resources Films, 1971, released as slides with recorded narration and music, Knowledge Systems, 1982.

Curious George Learns the Alphabet (filmstrip; with cassette), Teaching Resources Films, 1977.

Pretzel and Other Stories (filmstrip; with cassette), Educational Enrichment Materials, 1978.

"Curious George" was also the subject of eighteen animated shorts, produced in 1972, and compiled on videotape in three volumes by Sony.

RECORDINGS

Curious George and Other Stories about Curious George (includes *Curious George Takes a Job, Curious George Rides a Bike,* and *Curious George Gets a* *Medal*), read by Julie Harris, Caedmon Records, 1972.

Curious George Learns the Alphabet and Other Stories about Curious George, read by Harris, Caedmon Records, 1973.

BOOKS; ALL TITLES ALSO KNOWN AS MARGRET AND H. A. REY'S ...

(Edited by Margret Rey and Alan J. Shalleck) *Curious George Goes Fishing,* adapted from Curious George animated film series, Houghton, 1987.

(Edited by M. Rey and Shalleck) *Curious George Visits a Police Station,* adapted from animated film series, Houghton, 1987.

(Edited by M. Rey and Shalleck) *Curious George Goes to an Ice Cream Shop,* adapted from the animated film series, Houghton, 1987.

Rey's character was also adapted to the books *Curious George Bakes a Cake, Curious George Goes Camping, Curious George Goes to a Toy Store,* and *Curious George Goes to an Air Show.*

SIDELIGHTS: H. A. Rey was the creator of the widely popular Curious George stories, for which he won awards from both the Child Study Association of America and *School Library Journal.* In addition to writing and illustrating seven Curious George books, Rey lent his talents to numerous other books. He was also an accomplished astronomer who created two books on stargazing, illustrated stories by other authors, and created puzzle and "pop-up" books. His books have been translated into nine languages and have combined sales of more than twenty million copies.

Rey was born in Hamburg, Germany. By the age of two he was displaying a talent for drawing. He developed his artistic skill during his school years, often drawing in his sketchbook during other lessons. When World War I broke out he was drafted into the army, but as he stated in *Junior Book of Authors:* "I did better with my pencil than with my rifle." When he got out of the army, Rey wanted to go to an art school, but he could not afford the tuition. Instead he attended two German universities and did free-lance art work in his spare time. Before Rey formally finished school, family members offered him a job at their import/export firm in Rio de Janeiro, Brazil—Rey accepted. While in Brazil, he met Margret Waldstein, a young woman who had also grown up in Hamburg. The two shared an interest in art and a distaste for the Nazi government of Germany; they were soon married. They moved to Paris where Rey began to write and draw children's books. In 1940 they were forced to flee Paris on bicycles when Nazi Germany invaded France. They took with them only a small amount of food and some of Rey's manuscripts. Escaping France, they travelled to America.

Rey completed several books before moving to the States, often collaborating on them with Margret. Most of the books involve animals as the main characters. When he was growing up, Rey lived near a zoo. Visiting the zoo often, he developed a fondness for a variety of

When Curious George made his first appearance in *Cecily G. and the Nine Monkeys* in 1942, Rey never dreamed that his creation was to become a series that would earn him lasting fame.

exotic animals. "I ... was more familiar with elephants and kangaroos than with cows or sheep," he stated in *Junior Book of Authors*. The first book that Rey wrote and illustrated, *Cecily G. and the Nine Monkeys,* displayed his love of animals. In the story, Cecily G. is a lonely giraffe (the 'G' in her name stands for giraffe) who has been separated from her family. The nine monkeys are a family who have been driven out of their home by woodcutters and are travelling in search of a new place to live. Cecily and the monkeys meet and instantly become friends. The monkeys stay in Cecily's home with her, sleep in her long giraffe's bed, and play inventive games with her. In addition to using her long body as a bridge, they ski down her neck, use her as a see-saw, parachute off her head with their umbrellas, and even use her as a makeshift harp during a concert. *Cecily G. and the Nine Monkeys* introduced readers to an important character. In listing each of the monkeys, Rey used two words to describe the monkey named George, clever and *curious*. Rey found George so entertaining that he devoted an entire book to the little monkey's adventures. He titled it simply *Curious George.*

Curious George begins with George playing in his African jungle home. Rey introduces his character with this description: "He was a good little monkey and always very curious." While playing, George notices a man, dressed in yellow and wearing a large yellow hat, watching him. Naturally, George is very curious about this man. When the man places his hat on the ground, George cannot resist the urge to investigate. Before George knows what has happened, the man with the yellow hat—the only name he is given in the books—has snatched the little monkey up and taken him back to his ship. The man explains to George that he is taking him to the city to live in a zoo. He tells George that he may look around the boat, but to be careful and stay out of trouble. George does just the opposite and ends up falling into the ocean while trying to fly like a sea gull. Once in the city George finds himself in more trouble. He plays with a phone and accidently dials the fire department. The fire department arrives, finds there is no fire, and puts George in jail for playing pranks. He escapes from the jail, grabs a bunch of balloons, and sails off over the city. In the end George is found by the man with the yellow hat and is taken to his happy new home in the zoo.

The universal appeal of *Curious George* is illustrated by an incident that occurred shortly after Rey finished the book. Just prior to fleeing France, the Reys—suspected of spying—were arrested by the French police. During the Reys' interrogation, an officer came across the *Curious George* manuscript. Attempting to find evidence in the book that would confirm the Reys as spies, the man instead found himself amused and enchanted by the story of the little monkey. Reasoning that the person who wrote such an innocent and funny book could not possibly be a spy, the officer released the Reys, and they were able to escape the Nazi invasion.

Over the course of six more books Rey continued George's adventures, often collaborating on them with Margret. "The share of my wife's work varies," Rey once told *SATA*. "Basically I illustrate and Margret writes." During the course of the series, George gets a job, rides a bike, and flies a kite—managing to cause something of a ruckus in each case. Along the way he also receives a medal, gets to fly in outer space, and even appears in a motion picture. Rey makes it clear that George's intentions are good, but his curiosity just seems to get the best of him. Regardless of the amount of trouble George manages to get into, the man with the yellow hat always arrives in time to rescue George from disaster.

Before his death, Rey worked on two Curious George stories—*Curious George Learns the Alphabet* and *Curious George Goes to the Hospital*—that differed from his previous books in their attempt to be both educational and entertaining. In *Curious George Learns the Alphabet,* the man with the yellow hat teaches George his ABCs. In *Curious George Goes to the Hospital,* George comes down with mysterious stomach pains and must be taken to the hospital. He is taken to the children's ward where he meets young boys and girls who also need medical attention. George does not feel well at first, but after the doctors help him, he bounces back to his old, curious self. He decides to explore the hospital and, as

Rey found George so entertaining that he devoted an entire book to the little monkey's adventures and titled it simply *Curious George.*

In *Curious George Goes to the Hospital,* George comes down with mysterious stomach pains and must be taken to the hospital. Written by Rey and his wife Margret, the story is designed to be both entertaining and educational.

usual, causes a commotion due to his curiosity. The Reys collaborated with the Children's Hospital Medical Center in Boston, Massachusetts, to familiarize children with hospitals, their procedures, and the people who work in them. By presenting the hospital in a story with a comforting and familiar character like George, the Reys hoped to ease some of the anxiety a child entering a hospital might have.

Readers of all ages are fascinated by George. Children love George because his appearance and behavior are very similar to that of a child: He has wild adventures and is never punished for his antics. While his escapades always cause trouble, they usually result in some good and George is rewarded or praised. "Good intentions, even motivated by curiosity, lead to poetic justice," opined Louisa Smith in *Dictionary of Literary Biography.* Discussing the reasons for George's popularity, Margot Dukler commented in *Elementary English:* "The most important is the ease with which the children can identify with him. He is an animal who is doing the

things that they would like to do but don't dare." Adults also like George. Their children can identify with him yet, because he is a monkey, can distinguish between George's world and reality. George is drawn in a cartoon style, one that illustrates his good nature and innocence. "You see a very likable monkey, with a very sweet, simple face," described Dukler in *Elementary English.* "He can look happy or sad, or maybe surprised, but he never loses the sweetness in his expression."

In addition to the Curious George series, Rey worked on several other books. He wrote and illustrated *Elizabite: The Adventures of a Carnivorous Plant,* the story of a plant with a large appetite for just about anything it can get its leaves on. *Pretzel* tells the story of a dachshund, named Pretzel, who is extraordinarily long. Pretzel is unhappy because his appearance does not please Greta, the female dog that he loves. When Greta gets into trouble, Pretzel's length enables him to rescue her, and she sees his true, unique beauty. Rey also combined his interests in stargazing and drawing in two books about

Rey's *Find the Constellations* features bright, colorful illustrations and a unique system—invented by Rey himself—that easily identifies the constellations.

astronomy: *Find the Constellations,* which he wrote for children, and *The Stars: A New Way to See Them,* written for adults. Each of the books features Rey's bright, colorful illustrations and a unique system—invented by Rey himself—that easily identifies the constellations.

"Making picture books for children is the most wonderful profession I can think of," stated Rey in *Junior Book of Authors.* "Not only do you have fun doing it but your fellow men even pay you for it." Rey's career as an author and illustrator spanned more than thirty years. In that time he created some of the most beloved books in children's literature. The humor in his books, borrowed from the slapstick comedy of Charlie Chaplin and the simple logic of comic strips, make them all the more appealing to children. Rey brought a basic sensibility to all of his books. He summarized his work ethic in *SATA:* "I believe I know what children like. I know what *I* liked as a child, and I don't do any book that I, as a child, *wouldn't* have liked."

WORKS CITED:

Dukler, Margot, *Elementary English,* January, 1958, pp. 3-11.
Junior Book of Authors, H. W. Wilson Company, second edition, revised, 1951, pp. 255-56.
Rey, H. A., *Curious George,* Houghton, 1941.
Smith, Louisa, "H. A. Rey," *Dictionary of Literary Biography,* Volume 22: *American Writers for Children, 1900-1960,* Gale, 1983, pp. 286-89.
Something about the Author, Volume 26, Gale, 1982, p. 165.

FOR MORE INFORMATION SEE:

BOOKS

Children's Literature Review, Volume 5, Gale, 1983
Twentieth-Century Children's Writers, 2nd edition, St. Martin's, 1983.

PERIODICALS

Cricket, Volume 1, number 2, 1973.
People, June 1, 1987, p. 98.

OBITUARIES:

PERIODICALS

AB Bookman's Weekly, October 17, 1977.
New York Times, August 28, 1977.
Publishers Weekly, October 3, 1977.*

—*Sketch by David Galens*

*   *   *

RHINE, RICHARD
    See SILVERSTEIN, Alvin
and SILVERSTEIN, Virginia B.

*   *   *

RIVERSIDE, John
    See HEINLEIN, Robert A.

*   *   *

ROBERTSON, Keith (Carlton) 1914-1991
    (Carlton Keith)

OBITUARY NOTICE—See index for *SATA* sketch: Born May 9, 1914, in Dows, IA; died of cancer, September 23, 1991, in Hopewell, NJ. Business executive and author. Robertson is remembered for his five-book "Henry Reed" series for children and his adult murder mysteries written under the pseudonym Carlton Keith. He began writing children's books in 1948, continuing to do so while employed as president of a ceramics manufacturing company from 1958 to 1969. Two of Robertson's books, *Henry Reed, Inc.* and *Henry Reed's Baby-Sitting Service,* earned the William Allen White Children's Award. His other publications for children include *Ticktock and Jim, The Mystery of Burnt Hill, The Money Machine,* and *Henry Reed's Think Tank.* Among Robertson's adult works are *The Diamond-Studded Typewriter, The Hiding Place,* and *The Missing Book-Keeper.*

OBITUARIES AND OTHER SOURCES:

BOOKS

The Writers Directory, 1990-1992, St. James Press, 1990.

PERIODICALS

Chicago Tribune, October 2, 1991, section 3, p. 12.
Los Angeles Times, October 4, 1991, p. A26.
New York Times, September 30, 1991, p. B9.
Washington Post, October 1, 1991, p. B7.

RODDENBERRY, Gene 1921-1991

OBITUARY NOTICE—See index for *SATA* sketch: Full name is Eugene Wesley Roddenberry; born August 19, 1921, in El Paso, TX; died of a heart attack, October 24, 1991, in Santa Monica, CA. Pilot, film and television executive, screenwriter, and author. Roddenberry is remembered as the creator of the 1960s space-age science fiction television series *Star Trek*, which inspired motion pictures, a sequel series, and devoted fans known as Trekkies. Roddenberry's career in television began after he served as a pilot in World War II—earning a Distinguished Flying Cross—and worked for a commercial airline. From 1953 to 1962 he wrote scripts for such programs as *Goodyear Theater, Dragnet,* and *Naked City,* winning an Emmy Award for the 1950s western series *Have Gun, Will Travel.* It was with *Star Trek,* however, that Roddenberry received substantial critical acclaim, including a Hugo Award. He stressed characterization in the series and predicted that the future held the promise of harmonious relationships throughout the universe. The premiere episode aired in 1966, and although new shows were produced for only three seasons, reruns have been broadcast on more than two hundred television stations throughout America and in nearly fifty countries. This continuing popularity led to spin-offs, and when the first *Star Trek* motion picture was filmed in 1979, Roddenberry served as producer and became the executive consultant for the next three films. He was also the executive producer of the television sequel series, *Star Trek: The Next Generation,* which began in 1987. Roddenberry's books include *The Making of "Star Trek," Star Trek: The Motion Picture,* and *The Making of "Star Trek: The Motion Picture."*

OBITUARIES AND OTHER SOURCES:

BOOKS

Who's Who in America, 46th edition, Marquis, 1990.

PERIODICALS

Chicago Tribune, October 25, 1991, section 1, p. 10; October 27, 1991, section 2, p. 10.
Los Angeles Times, October 25, 1991, p. A3; October 26, 1991, p. F1.
New York Times, October 25, 1991, p. B5; October 26, 1991, p. 26.
Washington Post, October 25, 1991, p. C4.

*　　*　　*

RODGERS, Frank 1944-

PERSONAL: Born August 12, 1944, in Bellshill, Scotland; son of Frank and Mary (Budis) Rodgers; married Elizabeth Morton (an artist), August, 1969; children: Zoe, Adam. *Education:* Attended Glasgow School of Art, 1961-65, and Jordanhill College of Education, 1965-66. *Hobbies and other interests:* Singing old rock 'n' roll tunes at his piano.

FRANK RODGERS

ADDRESSES: Home—32 Banavie Rd., Patrickhill, Glasgow G11 5AN, Scotland. *Agent*—Caroline Sheldon, 71 Hillgate Pl., London W8 7SS, England.

CAREER: Educator, artist, illustrator, and author. Art teacher in secondary schools in Glasgow, Scotland, 1966-87; driver, 1974-75; musician, 1975-76; full-time artist and illustrator, 1987—.

AWARDS, HONORS: Book of the Year citations from Children's Book Federation, 1990, for *A Is for Aaargh!,* and 1991, for *The Jolly Witch; The Bunk-Bed Bus* was chosen by the Education Department to be part of the national curriculum for seven-year-olds in England and Wales.

WRITINGS:

Think of Magic (musical), S. French, 1986.
A Second Chance (young adult novel), Deutsch, 1992.

Also author of comedy scripts for television programs.

SELF-ILLUSTRATED

Who's Afraid of the Ghost Train?, Viking/Puffin, 1988, Harcourt, 1989.
A Is for Aaargh!, Viking/Puffin, 1989.
The Bunk-Bed Bus, Viking/Puffin, 1989.
The Summertime Christmas Present, Viking/Young Puffin, 1989, published as *Ricky's Summertime Christmas Present,* 1991.

In Rodgers's self-illustrated story, *Who's Afraid of the Ghost Train?*, young Robert learns to overcome his fears by imagining them in an unthreatening way.

Cartoon Fun, Scholastic, 1990.
Doodle Dog, Dutton Children's Books, 1990.
The Intergalactic Kitchen, Viking/Young Puffin, 1990.
Animal Art, Scholastic, 1991.
Can Piggles Do It?, Viking, 1991.
I Can't Get to Sleep!, Simon & Schuster Books for Young Readers, 1991.
The Intergalactic Kitchen Goes Prehistoric, Viking, 1991.
Looking After Your First Monster, Scholastic, 1991.
B Is for Book!, Viking, 1992.
Comic Fun, Scholastic, 1992.
Ricky, Zedex, and the Spooks, Viking, 1992.
Millie's Letter, Simon & Schuster, in press.
Teacher's or Creatures?, Viking, in press.

ILLUSTRATOR

Brenda Sivers, *The Case of the Baffling Burglary,* Beaver, 1980.
Paul Biegel, *The Curse of the Werewolf,* Blackie, 1981.
Constance Milburn, *Sasha: Looking After Your First Puppy,* Blackie, 1981.
Sivers, *Count Doberman of Pinscher,* Abelard, 1981.
Sivers, *Hound and the Perilous Pekes,* Abelard-Schuman, 1981.
Sivers, *Hound and the Curse of Kali,* Abelard, 1982.
Jane Waller, *Below the Green Pond,* Abelard, 1982.
Humphrey Carpenter, *Mr. Majeika,* Kestrel, 1984.
Carpenter, *Mr. Majeika and the Music Teacher,* Viking Kestrel, 1986.

Carpenter, *Mr. Majeika and the Haunted Hotel,* Viking Kestrel, 1987.
Carpenter, *Mr. Majeika and the Dinner Lady,* Viking Kestrel, 1989.
Linda Dearsley, *Mrs. Smith's Crocodile,* Macdonald, 1989.
Dick King-Smith, *The Jolly Witch,* Simon & Schuster, 1990.
Terence Blacker, *Nasty Neighbours/Nice Neighbours,* Pan/Macmillan, in press.
Penelope Lively, *Judy and the Martian,* Simon & Schuster, in press.

SIDELIGHTS: Some of Frank Rodgers's most widely reviewed children's books hinge on the power of imagination. *Doodle Dog* opens as Sam, who can't have a dog because his family lives in an apartment, follows his mother's advice and makes a drawing of a dog instead. He goes to sleep with the drawing beside him and wakes up to find what seems to be a real live dog licking his face. As Denise Anton Wright noted in *School Library Journal,* Rodgers "leaves readers wondering whether [this dog] is part of Sam's imagination or a magical dog who appears at will." Robert, the young hero of *Who's Afraid of the Ghost Train?,* learns to fight his fears of everyday objects around the house, such as vacuum cleaners and fur coats. Taking advice from his lion-tamer grandfather, he learns that anything can become less intimidating if you can imagine it in an unthreatening way. Robert proves himself when he joins his friends for a ride on the scary "Ghost Train" at a local carnival.

When monsters appear, Robert's friends run away in terror, but he triumphs by imagining how harmless the creatures would look in their underwear.

Rodgers told *SATA:* "I remember my first primary school readers. They had stories, fables, and poems illustrated with sinewy black-and-white pen drawings and enchanting watercolors. They made a big impression on me. The combination of pictures and text seemed so right. The *idea* of it seemed so right.

"Those books are with me still. As an adult I searched them out and collected them and other examples of children's literature. Looking at them now I still get a small thump of excitement in my chest. Not so much from nostalgia but more, I think, from the delight of recognizing, as if for the first time, the emotive power of simple stories well illustrated.

"This is the feeling I try to bring to each book that I work on. I feel very strongly that children deserve well-written and well-illustrated books and should never be shortchanged.

"I liked to create things as a child: drawings, models, stories. As a teenager this creative urge took me to Glasgow School of Art, where I graduated in silversmithing and jewelry. A strange beginning to my eventual career as an author/illustrator but at that time in my life I had no idea in which direction I was going, knowing only that it was going to be connected with art in some way.

"I duly became an art teacher in secondary schools in Glasgow. That there was an author/illustrator in me waiting its chance to emerge there is no doubt, however, as in my first year of teaching I wrote and illustrated a poem for children and sent it to a publisher in London. It was promptly rejected. When I look at it now I can see why, but at the time I felt there was no future in that line of creativity and embarked on another—writing rock music.

"This caused an attempt at a career change in 1974, when my wife and I moved to London with a band I was writing for and playing in. The music business proved fickle, however, and soon I had to look for alternative employment as our 'deal' fell through. A stint as a hire-car driver and then one as a guitar player in a cabaret-type band filled in the next two years, during which time my daughter was born.

"This was the catalyst. Not only did I become aware of the ocean of contemporary children's literature, but my wife got to know some couples at the baby clinic. We became friends with one of these couples and it transpired that they had written a children's story. I illustrated it. I was on my way! Well, not quite. It was scheduled to be published as a coloring book but again the 'deal' fell through. However, on our return to Glasgow in 1976 I began to think seriously about children's illustration. I went to London with some drawings and was fortunate enough to see an editor at

Blackie who liked my work. Shortly afterwards I was given my first book illustration commission. Over the next few years I illustrated a number of books for Blackie and then for Viking/Puffin.

"My son was born in 1978, and I became more and more intrigued by and drawn to the idea of creating my own stories, as both myself and my wife made up bedtime stories for him and our daughter.

"At this point my musical creativity was still going strong. I was involved with a youth theater group for whom I wrote two rock musicals, one of which was published.

"Writing and illustrating for children, however, was taking a stronger hold on my imagination. This led to me working out a picture-book story called *Who's Afraid of the Ghost Train?* in the mid-1980s, based on my own memories of childhood fears and the wild imaginings of my own children. I sent it to London and two publishers each took a year to tell me they liked it—but not enough to publish it, as it seemed to have a flaw. As I was working as a teacher at that time, plus doing illustration work, a year for a publisher to make a decision was, if not exactly acceptable, at least tolerable. Now, of course, I expect a reply within a couple of weeks! I persevered with the story, however, and discovered what was wrong with it. The center section, where the little boy learns to use his imagination to conquer his fears, was too obviously educative and solemn. I made it funny and the story worked!

"At the same time, I had been working on two other picture book ideas: *A Is for Aaargh!*—an anarchic alphabet story inspired by our children's brushes with bullies at school and by my own experiences as a teacher (the book, in fact, could have been called *The Teacher's Revenge!*)—and *The Bunk-Bed Bus,* again growing from our children's bunk-bed antics. In the summer of 1987 I took all three projects in complete book 'dummy' form round about a dozen London publishers and struck gold. Most wanted to publish one or two, but Viking/Puffin wanted all three. *This* time I was on my way!

"I left teaching and began my career as an author/illustrator in the autumn of that year. I love it. Because of my early experience of illustrating other people's work, I have developed a critical, editorial view of my own work (helped by my wife as deputy-editor!) so that rejected ideas are few and far between.

"I am now swimming in that ocean of contemporary children's literature I first discovered in the mid-1970s, and think I am now getting the hang of the rhythm. I feel there is always room for improvement, however, as I am constantly seeing others gliding through the same waves with the silkiest of strokes.

"Like those first three books, my subsequent stories all have their beginning and reason for being in some part, large or small, of a child's experience. Something that a child reading the story can identify with, be entertained by, find humor in and perhaps learn from. This year, for instance, will see the publication of a novel for teenagers—a new area for me. It is at present entitled *A Second Chance* and contains elements from my own adolescence.

"Most experience is common, shared. What seems unique at the time has been felt or is being felt by countless others. This is where the writer comes in—to give voice to those open secrets of shared experience."

WORKS CITED:

Wright, Denise Anton, review of *Doodle Dog* in *School Library Journal,* July, 1990, p. 64.

FOR MORE INFORMATION SEE:

PERIODICALS

Junior Bookshelf, August, 1989; June, 1991.
School Library Journal, October, 1989.

S

SANFORD, Doris 1937-

PERSONAL: Born August 3, 1937, in Kansu province, China; daughter of Malcolm (a missionary) and Lillian (a missionary; maiden name, Hurst) Phillips; married Albert Sanford (a professor), March 21, 1964 (deceased); children: Christine Sanford Burch, Timothy Sanford. *Education:* Attended Good Samaritan Hospital School of Nursing, 1956-59; Azusa Pacific University, B.A., 1971, M.A., 1977. *Politics:* Democrat. *Religion:* Presbyterian.

ADDRESSES: Home—16332 Southeast Heart Place, Milwaukie, OR 97267. *Office*—Heart to Heart, 2115 Southeast Adams St., Milwaukie, OR 97222.

CAREER: Became registered nurse, 1959. Citrus College, Glendora, CA, professor of nursing, 1970-77; Mount Hood Community College, Gresham, OR, professor of social science, 1977-86; Heart to Heart, Inc., Milwaukie, OR, president and co-owner, 1986—. Play therapist for preschool children, 1988—; State of Oregon, Children's Services Division, consultant, 1990—; speaker.

MEMBER: Oregon Education Association, Bereavement Network, Young Life Committee.

AWARDS, HONORS: C. S. Lewis Award for children's literature, 1985; selected outstanding small business for Oregon by Small Business Administration, 1985.

WRITINGS:

"HURTS OF CHILDHOOD" SERIES; ILLUSTRATED BY GRACI EVANS

Don't Look at Me: A Child's Book about Feeling Different, Multnomah, 1986.
I Can't Talk about It: A Child's Book about Sexual Abuse, Multnomah, 1986, stage play adaptation, produced in Los Angeles, CA, 1989.
It Must Hurt a Lot: A Child's Book about Death, Multnomah, 1986.

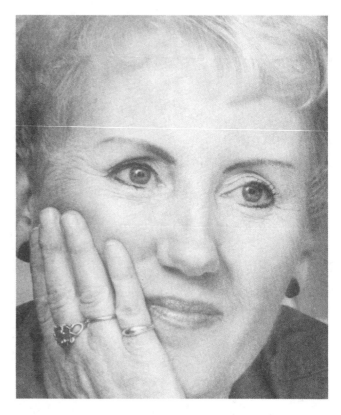

DORIS SANFORD

Please Come Home: A Child's Book about Divorce, Multnomah, 1986.
I Can Say No: A Child's Book about Drug Abuse, Multnomah, 1987.
I Know the World's Worst Secret: A Child's Book about Living with an Alcoholic Parent, Multnomah, 1987.
Don't Make Me Go Back, Mommy, Multnomah, 1990.

"ADVANCED THEOLOGY FOR VERY TINY PERSONS" SERIES, VOLUME ONE; ILLUSTRATED BY EVANS

The Child of God, Multnomah, 1988.
The Friends of God, Multnomah, 1988.
The Names of God, Multnomah, 1988.
The World of God, Multnomah, 1988.

"IN OUR NEIGHBORHOOD" SERIES; ILLUSTRATED BY EVANS

Brian Was Adopted, Multnomah, 1989.
David Has Aids, Multnomah, 1989.
Lisa's Parents Fight, Multnomah, 1989.
Maria's Grandmother Gets Mixed Up, Multnomah, 1989.

"YOU'LL NEVER GUESS WHAT" SERIES; ILLUSTRATED BY EVANS

Once I Told a Lie, Multnomah, 1990.
Once I Was a Bully, Multnomah, 1990.
Once I Was a Thief, Multnomah, 1990.
Once I Was Obnoxious, Multnomah, 1990.

"CHILDREN OF COURAGE" SERIES; ILLUSTRATED BY EVANS

Don't Be Afraid of the Darkness, Multnomah, 1992.
Fire Escape, Multnomah, 1992.
My Friend, The Enemy, Multnomah, 1992.
Yes I Can, Multnomah, 1992.

OTHER

The Comforter, Multnomah, illustrated by Evans, 1989.
Love Letters (correspondence between author and readers), Multnomah, 1992.

Contributor to numerous periodicals.

ADAPTATIONS: The "Hurts of Childhood" series has been adapted for video by Franciscan Communications; *I Can't Talk about It* has been adapted for audio cassette by Steve & Steve Productions.

SIDELIGHTS: Doris Sanford told *SATA:* "I grew up in China during a time of Japanese invasion and experienced much trauma as a young child. My parents were missionaries. Later, when I was married, my husband died while my children were both under three years old. I know that children heal from trauma if they are supported by caring adults. The focus of our work is for young children who have experienced a painful life trauma. Our aim has been to teach them and comfort them. I believe that wounds of childhood linger into adult years apart from healing. I also believe that children are supported by knowing that God loves them and helps them through gentle adults."

*   *   *

SAUNDERS, Caleb
See HEINLEIN, Robert A.

*   *   *

SAY, Allen 1937-

PERSONAL: Born August 28, 1937, in Yokohama, Japan; came to the United States c. 1953; son of Masako Moriwaki; children: Yuriko (daughter). *Education:* Studied at Aoyama Gakuin, Tokyo, Japan, three years, Chouinard Art Institute, one year, Los Angeles Art Center School, one year, University of California,

ALLEN SAY

Berkeley, two years, and San Francisco Art Institute, one year. *Hobbies and other interests:* Fly fishing.

ADDRESSES: Home—San Francisco, CA.

CAREER: EIZO Press, Berkeley, CA, publisher, 1968; commercial photographer and illustrator, 1969—; writer and illustrator.

AWARDS, HONORS: American Library Association Notable Book and Best Book for Young Adults, both 1979, both for *The Inn-Keeper's Apprentice; New York Times* Best Illustrated award, 1980, for *The Lucky Yak; Horn Book* honor list, 1984, and Christopher Award, 1985, both for *How My Parents Learned to Eat; New York Times* Ten Best Illustrated Children's Books, 1988, for *A River Dream; Boston Globe/Horn Book* Award, 1988, American Library Association Notable Children's Book, 1988, and Caldecott Honor Book, 1989, all for *The Boy of the Three Year Nap.*

WRITINGS:

SELF-ILLUSTRATED

Dr. Smith's Safari, Harper, 1972.
Once under the Cherry Blossom Tree: An Old Japanese Tale, Harper, 1974.
The Feast of Lanterns, Harper, 1976.
The Innkeeper's Apprentice (young adult), Harper, 1979.
The Bicycle Man, Houghton, 1982.
A River Dream, Houghton, 1988.
The Lost Lake, Houghton, 1989.
El Chino, Houghton, 1990.
Tree of Cranes, Houghton, 1991.

Say's illustrations for Ina Friedman's *How My Parents Learned to Eat* explore her theme of the crossing of two cultures.

ILLUSTRATOR

Brother Antoninus, *A Canticle to the Waterbirds,* EIZO Press, 1968.

Wilson Pinney, editor, *Two Ways of Seeing,* Little, Brown, 1971.

Eve Bunting, *Magic and Night River,* Harper, 1978.

Annetta Lawson, *The Lucky Yak,* Parnassus Press, 1980.

Thea Brow, *The Secret Cross of Lorraine,* Houghton, 1981.

Ina R. Friedman, *How My Parents Learned to Eat,* Houghton, 1984.

Dianne Snyder, *The Boy of the Three Year Nap,* Houghton, 1988.

WORK IN PROGRESS: Grandfather's Journey.

SIDELIGHTS: Allen Say is a gifted author and illustrator whose books describe the richness of his native culture but also explore the complexities of being both Japanese and American. His tales often narrate the tenuous ways that young boys find guidance and strength from older men. In *A River Dream* and *The Lost Lake,* outdoor experiences provide the setting for youths to understand the natural world and to bond with an important male. Critics praise Say's messages of nonviolence and coexistence with nature but, more than anything, they applaud his consistently vivid, imaginative illustrations. Liz Rosenberg, writing in the *New York Times Book Review,* calls Say "an extraordinarily thoughtful illustrator whose work invariably connects to and comments on the text."

Say was born in Yokohama, Japan in 1937, and told Leonard S. Marcus, in a *Horn Book* interview, that he began drawing before he could walk, and drew on everything, even the walls. As he grew older, however, his parents discouraged his talent: "At home, drawing really wasn't acceptable. My father, particularly, wanted a successful businessman for a son. To have an artist in the family was a disaster. So I drew, not in a closet, but always with a sense of guilt."

Say received encouragement in his artistic endeavors, however, from two teachers. The first, Mrs. Morita, was an elementary school teacher who treated her students as family, for her husband had been killed in World War II. She taught Say that it was acceptable to draw, and helped him surmount some of his childhood fears. The second teacher was Noro Shinpei, a well-known Japanese cartoonist. Say told Marcus: "Cartoonists were cultural heroes. But it was very unusual in post-war Japan to actually apprentice yourself to a master cartoonist, as I did when I was twelve." Shinpei taught Say all that he knew of Western and Japanese drawing styles, and from him Say inherited the habit of mixing ancient and modern themes in his work. He also found in Shinpei a "spiritual father," telling Marcus that "I didn't know it at the time I first went to see him, but I was trying to replace my father. I was looking for a mentor, and this is what I found." In the award-winning *The Inn-Keeper's Apprentice,* Say recreates the relationship that he developed with Shinpei.

Say moved to the United States when he was sixteen, but recalled that he had virtually stopped drawing and painting by the time he was twenty-five. Hoping to avoid the draft, Say enrolled in architecture school in Berkeley, California, but was drafted anyway. "I was sent to Germany," he told Marcus, "and became the firing-panel operator of a missile system which carried a nuclear warhead—the same A-bomb they dropped on Hiroshima. I was very near to that one as an eight-year-old child. I had a camera, and in order to keep my sanity I started taking pictures." His photos soon appeared in military magazines, and he began a career as a commercial photographer.

Though he had published a few books, Say's first critical success as an author/illustrator came with the 1982 publication of *The Bicycle Man.* The book depicted an encounter between a group of Japanese schoolchildren and two American soldiers in post-World War II Japan. The pen-and-ink and watercolor illustrations capture the tentative understanding that develops between the two groups as the black soldier performs tricks on the principal's bicycle. The Christopher Medal-winning *How My Parents Learned to Eat,* written by Ina Friedman and illustrated by Say, also explores the crossing of cultures as a young Oriental boy's parents learn a new way of approaching food.

By the mid-1980s, Say had decided to give up working on children's books and devote himself entirely to photography. However, an editor cajoled him into doing the illustrations for one last book: *The Boy of the Three-Year Nap.* Say resisted at first, but told Marcus that as he worked on the book, he "started having a very intense experience, and suddenly I decided, at age fifty,

Say's watercolor illustrations in *El Chino* explode with color as its hero Bong Way Wong, the first Chinese matador, discovers his calling.

that this, more than anything else, was what I wanted to do. I reverted to my childhood, to my happiest days when I used to go to my master's studio, warm my hands in front of one of the charcoal braziers, loosen my fingers, and start working on his beautiful drawings." Say has continued to work as an author/illustrator since then, producing in *El Chino* some of his most intense and dramatic illustrations. The first part of the book describes the life of Bong Way Wong in sepia half-tones, but when Wong becomes "El Chino," the first Chinese bullfighter, the illustrations explode in brilliant watercolors. The message, that people truly flower when they discover their calling, is among Say's most moving and most autobiographical.

When Marcus asked Say whether his early apprenticeship had proven useful to him as a picture-book artist, Say responded: "I learned that action is of the essence. Everything has to be moving. Everything has to be dramatized.... Years ago, I read in the *New Yorker* a remark that had a profound effect on me. Enzo Ferrari [an Italian car designer] wrote that it excited him to take nuts and bolts and breathe life into them. That is what an artist tries to do. Or at least what I try to do."

WORKS CITED:

Marcus, Leonard S., "Rearrangement of Memory: An Interview with Allen Say," *Horn Book,* May/June, 1991, pp. 295-303.
Rozenberg, Liz, "Ole, Billy Wong!," *New York Times Book Review,* November 11, 1990, p. 51.

FOR MORE INFORMATION SEE:

BOOKS

Children's Literature Review, Volume 22, Gale, 1991, pp. 208-212.

PERIODICALS

Horn Book, March/April, 1989, pp. 174-175.
Library Journal, September 15, 1972, p. 2941; May 15, 1974, p. 1469.
New York Times Book Review, May 5, 1974, p. 47; October 24, 1982, p. 41; November 6, 1988, p. 37.
School Library Journal, January, 1977, p. 85; March, 1979, p. 150; January, 1983, p. 66; December, 1988, pp. 101-102; December, 1989, p. 88.
Washington Post Book World, May 19, 1974; May 4, 1975.

*   *   *

SCHWEITZER, Byrd Baylor
See BAYLOR, Byrd

*   *   *

SEWALL, Marcia 1935-

PERSONAL: Born November 5, 1935, in Providence, RI; daughter of Edgar Knight and Hilda (Osgood) Sewall. *Education:* Pembroke College, B.A., 1957; Tufts University, M.Ed., 1958; studied art at Rhode Island School of Design and Boston Museum School. *Religion:* Unitarian Universalist.

ADDRESSES: Home—Boston, Massachusetts.

MARCIA SEWALL

CAREER: Writer and illustrator of children's books. Children's Museum, Boston, MA, staff artist, 1961-63; teacher of art in Winchester, MA, 1967-75. Participant in Boston Adult literacy program and School Volunteers of Boston.

AWARDS, HONORS: Come Again in the Spring was named one of the outstanding books of the year, *New York Times,* 1976, and was selected for exhibition by American Institute of Graphic Arts, 1985; notable book citation, American Library Association, 1978, for *Little Things,* and 1981, for *The Song of the Horse;* best picture book of the year designation, *New York Times,* 1978, for *The Nutcrackers and the Sugar-Tongs; The Leprechaun's Story* was selected for exhibition by the American Institute of Graphic Arts, 1979; Parent's Choice Award for illustration, 1980, for *Crazy in Love;* outstanding book of the year designation, *New York Times,* 1980, for *Stone Fox; The Story of Old Mrs. Brubeck and How She Looked for Trouble and Where She Found Him* was named one of best picture books of the year and *The Marzipan Moon* named one of outstanding books of the year, *New York Times,* both 1981; selection for exhibition at Bratislava International Biennale, 1983, for *The Song of the Horse,* and 1985, for *Finzel the Far-sighted; Boston Globe/Horn Book* Award for nonfiction, 1987, for *The Pilgrims of Plimoth.*

WRITINGS:

SELF-ILLUSTRATED

(Reteller) *The Little Wee Tyke,* Atheneum, 1979.
(Reteller) *The Wee, Wee Mannie and the Big, Big Coo* (Scottish folk-tale), Little, Brown, 1979.
(Reteller) *The Cobbler's Song,* Dutton, 1982.
Ridin' That Strawberry Roan, Viking, 1985.
(Reteller) *The World Turned Upside Down: An Old Penny Rhyme,* Atlantic Monthly, 1986.
The Pilgrims of Plimoth, Atheneum, 1986.
Animal Song, Joy Street Books, 1988.
People of the Breaking Day, Atheneum, 1990.

ILLUSTRATOR; TEXT BY RICHARD KENNEDY

The Parrot and the Thief, Little, Brown, 1974.
Come Again in the Spring (also see below), Harper, 1976.
The Porcelain Man (also see below), Little, Brown, 1976.
The Rise and Fall of Ben Gizzard, Little, Brown, 1978.
The Leprechaun's Story, Dutton, 1979.
Crazy in Love, Dutton, 1980.
The Song of the Horse, Dutton, 1981.
Richard Kennedy: Collected Stories (includes *Inside My Feet, The Porcelain Man,* and *Come Again in the Spring*), Harper, 1987.

ILLUSTRATOR

Joseph Jacobs, adapter, *Master of All Masters: An English Folktale,* Little, Brown, 1972.
P. C. Asbjoornsen and J. E. Moe, *The Squire's Bride: A Norwegian Folk Tale,* Atheneum, 1975.
Jacobs, *Coo-My-Dove, My Dear,* Atheneum, 1976.
Drew Stevenson, *The Ballad of Penelope Lou and Me,* Crossing Press, 1978.

Anne Eliot Crompton, *The Lifting Stone,* Holiday House, 1978.
Anne Laurin, *Little Things,* Atheneum, 1978.
Edward Lear, *The Nutcrackers and the Sugar-Tongs,* Little, Brown, 1978.
Paul Fleischman, *The Birthday Tree,* Harper, 1979.
Phyllis Krasilovsky, *The Man Who Tried to Save Time,* Doubleday, 1979.
John Reynolds Gardiner, *Stone Fox,* Crowell, 1980.
Nancy Willard, *The Marzipan Moon,* Harcourt, 1981.
Lore Segal, *The Story of Old Mrs. Brubeck and How She Looked for Trouble and Where She Found Him,* Pantheon, 1981.
Clyde Robert Bulla, *Poor Boy, Rich Boy,* Harper, 1982.
Lynn Hoopes, *When I Was Little,* Dutton, 1983.
Fleischman, *Finzel the Far-sighted,* Dutton, 1984.
Walter Wangerin, *Thistle,* Harper, 1984.
Jane Resh Thomas, *Say Goodbye to Grandma,* Clarion, 1988.
Roni Schotter, *Captain Snap and the Children of Vinegar Lane,* Orchard, 1989.
Patricia Foley, *John and the Fiddler,* Harper, 1990.
Ruth Young, *Daisy's Taxi,* Orchard, 1991.

OTHER

Contributor to periodicals, including *Horn Book.*

ADAPTATIONS: The Pilgrims of Plimoth was adapted for inclusion in a Read-Along Cassette series, Weston Woods, 1988.

SIDELIGHTS: Author and illustrator Marcia Sewall was raised in the coastal town of Providence, Rhode Island, entering Pembroke College at Brown University in 1953. Now living and working in Boston, Massachusetts, a city steeped in colonial American history, she is much more influenced by traditions from the past than by the modern city visible from her studio window. Sewall's love for the history and landscape of her New England heritage is embodied within her work, adding a unique vitality to the books she writes and illustrates for children.

Although never formally trained as an illustrator of children's books, Sewall demonstrated an early interest in both drawing and painting. She majored in art while in college and at one point after graduation spent a summer at the prestigious Rhode Island School of Design in an accelerated art program. As she once told *SATA,* "I never worked so hard in my life, and I learned a tremendous sense of discipline there. It was the first extremely structured art training I'd had. I needed it, and loved it." Before becoming a illustrator, Sewall taught art to high school students and was employed as a staff artist at the Children's Museum in Boston. Her desire to become a working illustrator motivated her to show her portfolio to several publishers. There was enthusiasm for her artistic style, and she launched a successful career in book illustration.

The first volume published with Sewall's illustrations was *Master of All Masters: An English Folktale.* As with all the books she has chosen to illustrate, she was

The humor and eccentricity of the characters within its pages attracted Sewall to the first book she illustrated—*Master of All Masters: An English Folk Tale.*

immediately drawn to the humor and eccentricity of the characters within its pages. She once told *SATA,* "I don't think you can force a book. If a manuscript seems natural and comfortable and appealing, I accept it readily. You work so hard for three or four months on the material that you must be comfortable with it. I love the wisdom, the character, and the tradition in folk people, so I often choose books with that sort of quality.

"When I first receive a manuscript," explained Sewall, "I walk through the story and divide it into pictures. If it's to be a thirty-two page book then I am limited to about thirteen double-page spreads. I begin to immediately struggle with the sense of character, the movement of character, and then on to the transformation of that flat surface into a believable space. An author gives me clues as to person and place and then it's a matter of sorting them out. The illustrator often makes decisions about the period and costuming. I next try to capture the rhythm and movement of the story in the dummy."

Sewall has illustrated seven books for author Richard Kennedy, including his anthology, *Richard Kennedy: Collected Stories.* "Sometimes I know immediately how a book must look," she commented. "As I read the manuscript for [Kennedy's] *The Song of the Horse,* I visualized the story in scratchboard. Scratchboard is a black ink surface over a white gessoed board. Instead of putting a black line down on white paper you scratch a white line away from a black surface. It is sort of electrical, magnetic. It has a vibrancy that seemed appropriate for that particular story.

"Although I may not immediately 'see' a character, I have to believe that it's within me to see him or her. On reading and rereading a manuscript, a sense of person begins to emerge and it is that which I try to capture in my initial sketches. It took a stack of paper and lots of drawing of *Old Mrs. Brubeck* before she would materialize for me. At first I had difficulty with her as a personality. She worried too much. Then I thought, 'My gosh, she's me and she's everybody I know!' I began to

Sewall's decorative paintings in *The World Turned Upside Down* encourage young readers to look at the "ordinary" with a fresh and inquisitive eye.

feel that there was humor about her, and then she just took shape. I thought if I gave her wooden shoes we would not only see but could hear her move about the house in her search for 'Trouble' and, as a final statement, I distilled her anxious movements in silhouettes against the endpapers."

The Cobbler's Song, published in 1982, was Sewall's first full-color book. "What an absolute joy it was to sit down and paint, and use colors that seemed to express the changing moods of the story. I used gouache which is an opaque watercolor paint not unlike poster paint. The story is a variation of the old 'rich man, poor man' theme. It deals with feelings, so it made sense to use full-color and to put paint on expressively."

Periodically, Sewall has taken a break from illustrating books by other authors to illustrate some of her own texts. Sometimes she has adapted ethnic folk-tales to a picture-book format and in other instances has written original stories, all characteristically embroidered with Sewall's love of traditional folklore and history. *Ridin' That Strawberry Roan* is based on a traditional ballad from the American West and tells the story of the taming of an outlaw horse. Written in jaunty rhyming couplets, the book is illustrated throughout with bright

watercolor paintings reflecting the story's humorous theme. *The Pilgrims of Plimoth* (1987), although based on actual diary entries made by William Bradford and other passengers of the *Mayflower,* was retold by Sewall as an original prose-poem and has been commended—along with its companion volume, *People of the Breaking Day*—for its "scholarship and sensitivity," by a critic in *School Library Journal.*

Taken together, these two books give a sensitive account of the day-to-day experiences of the early settlers of Plimoth Plantation and the Wampanoag Indians, a tribe then making their home in southeastern Massachusetts. Throughout both books, Sewall focuses on the strong fibers of family ritual and community support that unite these two very different groups of people in their struggle to survive the harshness of their common surroundings. Whether it be a young English lad standing on the deck of the *Mayflower* as the ship makes its way along the coast of Cape Cod towards a land full of mystery, or a young Indian girl collecting firewood within a dark, wintery forest, each contributes to the family, thereby playing an integral role in the survival of the entire community. Although somewhat critical of Sewall's attempt at recreating Native American speech patterns as being "overly mystical," a reviewer for *Horn*

Book praised *People of the Breaking Day* as "a fine resource that is resonant with integrity, intelligence, and eloquence." The vibrant and impressionistic illustrations accompanying both books draw the reader deeply into that harshly beautiful New England wilderness, which faced the first settlers upon their landing at Plymouth rock.

Sewall's success as an author has not diminished her desire to continue working as an illustrator. With an artist's eye for culling details from everyday life, she is continuously inspired by her surroundings. As she explained, "I have always enjoyed the sensation of movement ... and that has really helped me with moving figures about a page. My characters are not based on real people, though I notice when I illustrate a book that sometimes people I know will appear. Months later, it will occur to me that I have illustrated the boy in the corner market, or I discover that one of my figures sits like someone I know. I think an artist is constantly taking in visual impressions, but not always consciously. And you don't deliberately pull them out. They come."

WORKS CITED:

Bulletin of the Center for Children's Books, December, 1985.
Horn Book, January, 1991, p. 88.
New York Times Book Review, September 17, 1989.
School Library Journal, January, 1991, p. 106-107.
Something about the Author, Volume 37, Gale, 1985, pp. 170-174.

FOR MORE INFORMATION SEE:

BOOKS

Holmes Holtze, Sally, editor, *Fifth Book of Junior Authors and Illustrators,* H. W. Wilson, 1983, pp. 280-81.
Kingman, Lee, and others, compilers, *Illustrators of Children's Books: 1967-1976,* Horn Book, 1978.

PERIODICALS

Booklist, October 1, 1985, p. 269; September 15, 1986, p. 134; October 1, 1990, p. 329.
Graphis, Number 200, 1979.
Horn Book, December, 1979, p. 657; February, 1983, p. 40; January, 1988, pp. 32-34; July 1990, p. 153; January, 1991, p. 88.
New York Times Book Review, November 23, 1986, p. 32.
Publishers Weekly, January 24, 1977, p. 333; November 5, 1982, p. 71; November 2, 1990, p. 73-74.
School Library Journal, April, 1977, p. 57; December, 1979, p. 77; May, 1986, p. 85.

*   *   *

SILVERSTEIN, Alvin 1933-
(Ralph Buxton, Richard Rhine, Dr. A, joint pseudonyms)

PERSONAL: Born December 30, 1933, in New York, NY; son of Edward (a carpenter) and Fannie (Wittlin)

ALVIN and VIRGINIA B. SILVERSTEIN

Silverstein; married Virginia B. Opshelor (a writer and translator), August 29, 1958; children: Robert Alan, Glenn Evan, Carrie Lee, Sharon Leslie, Laura Donna, Kevin Andrew. *Education:* Brooklyn College (now Brooklyn College of the City University of New York), B.A., 1955; University of Pennsylvania, M.S., 1959; New York University, Ph.D., 1962. *Hobbies and other interests:* Vegetable gardening, sports, drawing and painting.

ADDRESSES: Home—3 Burlinghoff Lane, P.O. Box 537, Lebanon, NJ 08833. *Office*—Department of Biology, College of Staten Island of the City University of New York, 715 Ocean Ter., Staten Island, NY 10301.

CAREER: Junior High School No. 60, New York City, science teacher, 1959; College of Staten Island of the City University of New York, instructor, 1959-63, assistant professor, 1963-66, associate professor, 1966-70, professor of biology, 1970—; chair of biology department, 1978-79; writer.

MEMBER: Authors Guild, American Association for the Advancement of Science, American Chemical Society, American Institute of Biological Sciences, National Collegiate Association for the Conquest of Cancer (national chairperson, 1968-70).

AWARDS, HONORS: All with wife, Virginia B. Silverstein: Children's Book of the Year citations, Child Study

Association of America, 1969, for _A World in a Drop of Water_, and 1972, for _The Code of Life, Nature's Defenses,_ and _Nature's Pincushion; A World in a Drop of Water_ was named an Outstanding Children's Book of 1969, _World Book Yearbook,_ 1970; _Circulatory Systems_ was named a Science Educators' Book Society Selection; awards from New Jersey Institute of Technology, 1972, for _Guinea Pigs: All about Them,_ 1980, for _Aging,_ and 1983, for _The Robots Are Here_ and _The Story of Your Mouth;_ Outstanding Science Books for Children citations, National Science Teachers Association and Children's Book Council, 1972, for _The Long Voyage, The Muscular System, The Skeletal System, Cancer, Nature's Pincushion,_ and _Life in a Bucket of Soil,_ 1973, for _Rabbits: All about Them,_ 1974, for _Animal Invaders_ and _Hamsters: All about Them,_ 1976, for _Potatoes: All about Them_ and _Gerbils: All about Them,_ 1983, for _Heartbeats,_ 1987, for _The Story of Your Foot,_ 1988, for _Wonders of Speech_ and _Nature's Living Lights,_ and 1990, for _Overcoming Acne._

Alcoholism was selected among the Notable Trade Books in the Field of Social Studies, National Council for the Social Studies and Children's Book Council, 1975; Older Honor citation, New York Academy of Sciences, 1977, for _Potatoes: All about Them;_ Junior Literary Guild selection, and Children's Book of the Year citation, Bank Street College, 1977, both for _The Left-Hander's World;_ Books for the Teen Age selections, New York Public Library, 1978, for _Heart Disease,_ and 1987, for _AIDS: Deadly Threat;_ special certificate of commendation, John Burroughs List of Nature Books for Young Readers, 1988, for _Nature's Living Lights._

WRITINGS:

The Biological Sciences (college textbook), Holt, 1974.
Conquest of Death, Macmillan, 1979.
Human Anatomy and Physiology (college textbook), Wiley, 1980, 2nd edition, 1983.

NONFICTION CHILDREN'S BOOKS; WITH WIFE, VIRGINIA B. SILVERSTEIN

Life in the Universe, illustrated by L. Ames, Van Nostrand, 1967.
Unusual Partners, illustrated by Mel Hunter, McGraw, 1968.
Rats and Mice: Friends and Foes of Mankind, illustrated by Joseph Cellini, Lothrop, 1968.
The Origin of Life, illustrated by L. Ames, Van Nostrand, 1968.
The Respiratory System: How Living Creatures Breathe, illustrated by George Bakacs, Prentice-Hall, 1969.
A Star in the Sea, illustrated by Simeon Shimin, Warne, 1969.
A World in a Drop of Water, Atheneum, 1969.
Carl Linnaeus, illustrated by L. Ames, John Day, 1969.
Frederick Sanger, illustrated by L. Ames, John Day, 1969.
Cells: Building Blocks of Life, illustrated by G. Bakacs, Prentice-Hall, 1969.
Germfree Life: A New Field in Biological Research, Lothrop, 1970.

Living Lights: The Mystery of Bioluminescence, Golden Gate, 1970.
Circulatory Systems: The Rivers Within, illustrated by G. Bakacs, Prentice-Hall, 1970.
The Digestive System: How Living Creatures Use Food, illustrated by G. Bakacs, Prentice-Hall, 1970.
Bionics: Man Copies Nature's Machines, McCall Publishing, 1970.
Harold Urey: The Man Who Explored from Earth to Moon, illustrated by L. Ames, John Day, 1971.
The Nervous System: The Inner Networks, illustrated by Mel Erikson, Prentice-Hall, 1971.
Mammals of the Sea, illustrated by Bernard Garbutt, Golden Gate, 1971.
Metamorphosis: The Magic Change, Atheneum, 1971.
The Sense Organs: Our Link with the World, illustrated by M. Erikson, Prentice-Hall, 1971.
The Endocrine System, illustrated by L. Ames, Prentice-Hall, 1971.
The Reproductive System: How Living Creatures Multiply, illustrated by L. Ames, Prentice-Hall, 1971.
The Code of Life, Atheneum, 1971.
Guinea Pigs: All about Them, photographs by Roger Kerkham, Lothrop, 1972.
The Long Voyage: The Life Cycle of a Green Turtle, illustrated by Allan Eitzen, Warne, 1972.
(Under joint pseudonym Ralph Buxton) _Nature's Defenses,_ illustrated by Angus M. Babcock, Golden Gate, 1972.
The Muscular System: How Living Creatures Move, illustrated by L. Ames, Prentice-Hall, 1972.
The Skeletal System, illustrated by L. Ames, Prentice-Hall, 1972.
Cancer, John Day, 1972, first revised edition, illustrated by Andrew Antal, 1977, second revised edition published as _Cancer: Can It Be Stopped?,_ Lippincott, 1987.
The Skin, illustrated by L. Ames, Prentice-Hall, 1972.
(Under joint pseudonym Ralph Buxton) _Nature's Pincushion,_ illustrated by A. M. Babcock, Golden Gate, 1972.
The Excretory System, illustrated by L. Ames, Prentice-Hall, 1972.
(Under joint pseudonym Richard Rhine) _Life in a Bucket of Soil,_ illustrated by Elsie Wrigley, Lothrop, 1972.
Exploring the Brain, illustrated by Patricia De Veau, Prentice-Hall, 1973.
The Chemicals We Eat and Drink, Follett, 1973.
Rabbits: All about Them, photographs by R. Kerkham, Lothrop, 1973.
Sleep and Dreams, Lippincott, 1974.
(Under joint pseudonym Ralph Buxton) _Nature's Water Clown,_ illustrated by A. M. Babcock, Golden Gate, 1974.
Animal Invaders: The Story of Imported Animal Life, Atheneum, 1974.
Hamsters: All about Them, photographs by Frederick Breda, Lothrop, 1974.
Epilepsy, Lippincott, 1975.
Oranges: All about Them, illustrated by Shirley Chan, Prentice-Hall, 1975.

THE ROBOTS ARE HERE

Husband-and-wife team Alvin and Virginia B. Silverstein bring an extensive knowledge of science to collaborations such as the award-winning 1983 title, *The Robots Are Here.*

Beans: All about Them, illustrated by S. Chan, Prentice-Hall, 1975.

Alcoholism, introduction by Gail Gleason Milgrom, Lippincott, 1975.

(Under joint pseudonym Ralph Buxton) *Nature's Glider,* illustrated by A. M. Babcock, Golden Gate, 1975.

Apples: All about Them, illustrated by S. Chan, Prentice-Hall, 1976.

Potatoes: All about Them, illustrated by S. Chan, Prentice-Hall, 1976.

Gerbils: All about Them, photographs by F. Breda, Lippincott, 1976.

Heart Disease, Follett, 1976.

The Left-Hander's World, Follett, 1977.

Allergies, introduction by Sheldon Cohen, Lippincott, 1977.

Itch, Sniffle and Sneeze: All about Asthma, Hay Fever and Other Allergies, illustrated by Roy Doty, Four Winds, 1978.

Cats: All about Them, photographs by F. Breda, Lothrop, 1978.

So You're Getting Braces: A Guide to Orthodontics, illustrated by Barbara Remington, with photo-graphs by Virginia B. and Alvin Silverstein, Lippincott, 1978.

(With son Glenn Silverstein) *Aging,* F. Watts, 1979.

World of Bionics, Methuen, 1979.

The Sugar Disease: Diabetes, introduction by consulting editor Charles Nechemias, Lippincott, 1980.

The Genetics Explosion, Four Winds, 1980.

Mice: All about Them, photographs by son Robert A. Silverstein, Lippincott, 1980.

Nature's Champions: The Biggest, the Fastest, the Best, illustrated by Jean Zallinger, Random House, 1980.

The Story of Your Ear, illustrated by Susan Gaber, Coward, McCann & Geoghegan, 1981.

Runaway Sugar: All about Diabetes, illustrated by Harriett Barton, Lippincott, 1981.

Futurelife: The Biotechnology Revolution, illustrated by Marjorie Thier, Prentice-Hall, 1982.

Heartbeats: Your Body, Your Heart, illustrated by Stella Ormai, Lippincott, 1983.

The Story of Your Mouth, illustrated by Greg Wenzel, Coward-McCann, 1984.

The Robots Are Here, Prentice-Hall, 1984.

Headaches: All about Them, Lippincott, 1984.

Heart Disease: America's Number One Killer, Lippincott, 1985.

The Story of Your Hand, illustrated by G. Wenzel, Putnam, 1985.

Dogs: All about Them, introduction by John C. McLoughlin, Lothrop, 1986.

World of the Brain, illustrated by Warren Budd, Morrow, 1986.

AIDS: Deadly Threat, foreword by Paul Volberding, Enslow Publishers, 1986, revised and enlarged edition, 1991.

The Story of Your Foot, illustrated by G. Wenzel, Putnam, 1987.

Mystery of Sleep, illustrated by Nelle Davis, Little, Brown, 1987.

Wonders of Speech, illustrated by Gordon Tomei, Morrow, 1988.

Nature's Living Lights: Fireflies and Other Bioluminescent Creatures, illustrated by Pamela and Walter Carroll, Little, Brown, 1988.

Learning about AIDS, foreword by James Oleske, Enslow Publishers, 1989.

Glasses and Contact Lenses: Your Guide to Eyes, Eyewear, and Eye Care, Harper, 1989.

Genes, Medicine, and You: Genetic Counseling and Gene Therapy, Enslow Publishers, 1989.

(With R. A. Silverstein) *Overcoming Acne: The How and Why of Healthy Skin Care,* preface by Christopher M. Papa, illustrated by Frank Schwarz, Morrow, 1990.

Life in a Tidal Pool, illustrated by P. and W. Carroll, Little, Brown, 1990.

(With R. A. Silverstein) *Lyme Disease, the Great Imitator: How to Prevent and Cure It,* preface by Leonard H. Sigal, AVSTAR, 1990.

(With R. A. Silverstein) *So You Think You're Fat: Obesity, Anorexia Nervosa, Bulimia, and Other Eating Disorders,* Harper, 1991.

(With R. A. Silverstein) *Addictions Handbook,* Enslow Publishers, 1991.

(With R. A. Silverstein) *Steroids: Big Muscles, Big Problems,* Enslow Publishers, in press.

(With R. A. Silverstein) *Smell, the Subtle Sense,* Morrow, in press.

(With R. A. Silverstein) *Recycling: Meeting the Challenge of the Trash Crisis,* Putnam, in press.

(With R. A. Silverstein) *Food Power! Proteins,* Millbrook, in press.

(With R. A. Silverstein) *Food Power! Fats,* Millbrook, in press.

(With R. A. Silverstein) *Food Power! Carbohydrates,* Millbrook, in press.

(With R. A. Silverstein) *Food Power! Vitamins and Minerals,* Millbrook, in press.

Also author with wife, Virginia B. Silverstein, under joint pseudonym Dr. A, of syndicated juvenile fiction column, "Tales from Dr. A," which appeared in about 250 American and Canadian newspapers, 1972-74.

"FAMOUS NAME" SERIES; WITH VIRGINIA B. SILVERSTEIN

(With family members Robert A., Linda, Laura, and Kevin Silverstein) *John, Your Name Is Famous: Highlights, Anecdotes, and Trivia about the Name John and the People Who Made It Great,* AVSTAR, 1989.

(With R. A. Silverstein) *John: Fun and Facts about a Popular Name and the People Who Made It Great,* AVSTAR, 1990.

(With R. A. Silverstein) *Michael: Fun and Facts about a Popular Name and the People Who Made It Great,* AVSTAR, 1990.

SIDELIGHTS: Husband-and-wife team Alvin and Virginia B. Silverstein have formed a successful writing partnership, producing almost one hundred scientific information books for young people. Their works cover a wide spectrum, from contemporary issues like bionics, recycling, robotics, and genetics to detailed studies of various animals, foods, body systems, and diseases. Both authors bring an extensive knowledge of science to their collaborations—Virginia is a former chemist and Alvin is a biology professor—and they deal with complex issues in a comprehensible manner. Their books are accessible to young audiences and are often praised as straightforward, detailed, and authoritative. Their "work is carefully organized and written in a clear, direct style, and is dependably accurate," according to Zena Sutherland and May Hill Arbuthnot in *Children and Books.* "The more complicated subjects are not always covered in depth, but they are given balanced treatment, and the Silversteins' writing usually shows their attention to current research and always maintains a scientific attitude."

Both Alvin and Virginia enjoyed similar interests throughout their childhoods. Alvin grew up an avid reader, sometimes even reading the encyclopedia for fun, and found he was particularly fond of scientific literature. "I began a lifelong hobby of 'science watching' practically as soon as I learned to read," he revealed in *Fifth Book of Junior Authors and Illustrators.* "My

first love was astronomy, but I also was crazy about animals." Virginia, too, remembers herself as an enthusiastic reader, who especially loved books about animals. "When I was seven or eight," she recalled in *Fifth Book of Junior Authors and Illustrators,* "I used to total up my money saved in terms of how many Thornton Burgess [a prolific animal writer] ... books it would buy." In time she discovered an aptitude for chemistry and languages and was attracted to both fields. Ultimately, though, she decided to study chemistry, as did Alvin. The couple met at the University of Pennsylvania during the late 1950s—in a chemistry lab.

Nearly ten years after their marriage in 1958, Alvin and Virginia collaborated on their first children's book, *Life in the Universe.* "That book was quickly signed up," Virginia related in *Fifth Book of Junior Authors and Illustrators,* "and we plunged happily into children's science writing. Then followed twenty-three straight rejections. We would probably have given up if we hadn't already had a manuscript accepted." The duo persisted, however, and went on to complete more than ninety books, many of which have been named outstanding science books for children, awarded children's book of the year citations, and recognized by the New Jersey Institute of Technology and the New York Academy of Sciences. Among these are works like *Gerbils,* which includes a history of the animals as well as information about their intelligence and behavior, and *Aging,* which encompasses such areas as senility, retirement, and the role of the elderly in families. Other Silverstein books examine topics of high interest to many adolescents, such as eating disorders, braces, acne, or glasses, while still others delve into subjects like dreams, chemicals, allergies, or cancer.

Both Silversteins are content with their working relationship. Virginia once told *SATA* that she and Alvin "have an almost perfect meshing of minds." Alvin agrees that he and his wife work well together. "I was fortunate to find a marriage that has been both emotionally satisfying and a successful professional partnership," he told *SATA* in 1976. That partnership was expanded in 1988, when the Silversteins' eldest son, Robert, joined the writing team full time.

"Since Bob joined us, it seems as though our ideas have grown exponentially," Alvin recently told *SATA.* "We even tried a brief venture into the publishing end and loved the experience of having complete control of a book project from its conception to the finished product. We're proud of the results, and the books were very well reviewed, but we discovered that the profits weren't good enough to compensate for the time and headaches involved in production, promotion, and marketing. Now we're back to just writing, but Bob and I are seriously exploring the possibilities of doing some of the illustrations for new Silverstein books." Virginia adds, "We'd also like to expand the scope of our books, doing more for younger children, books with a lighter touch, and perhaps some imaginative fiction. We get the feeling sometimes that our editors have us a bit too stereotyped."

WORKS CITED:

Silverstein, Alvin, and Virginia B. Silverstein, *Fifth Book of Junior Authors and Illustrators,* edited by Sally Holmes Holtze, H. W. Wilson, 1983, pp. 289-291.

Something about the Author, Volume 8, Gale, 1976, pp. 188-190.

Sutherland, Zena, and May Hill Arbuthnot, "Informational Books," *Children and Books,* fifth edition, Scott, Foresman, 1977, pp. 444-505.

FOR MORE INFORMATION SEE:

BOOKS

Contemporary Literary Criticism, Volume 17, Gale, 1981.

PERIODICALS

Appraisal, fall, 1974; spring, 1975; fall, 1975; spring, 1976; fall, 1976; spring, 1977; spring, 1978; fall, 1978; winter, 1981; spring/summer, 1982; fall, 1983; spring, 1985; winter, 1987.

Booklist, October 1, 1989; May 15, 1990.

Bulletin of the Center for Children's Books, December, 1973; February, 1977; February, 1980; May, 1981; December, 1986; January, 1988.

Horn Book, June, 1981; June, 1983; January/February, 1987; March/April, 1988.

Junior Bookshelf, June, 1972.

Junior Literary Guild, September, 1977.

Kirkus Reviews, March 15, 1972.

School Library Journal, March, 1981; February, 1982; March, 1983; November, 1984; March, 1985; September, 1986; December, 1986; October, 1987; December, 1987; June/July, 1988; September, 1988; May, 1989; September, 1989; June, 1990.

Science Books, May, 1970.

Science Books and Films, January/February, 1985; November/December, 1988; May/June, 1989; September/October, 1989; November/December, 1990.

Wilson Library Bulletin, October, 1986.

* * *

SILVERSTEIN, Virginia B. 1937-
(Ralph Buxton, Richard Rhine, Dr. A, joint pseudonyms)

PERSONAL: Full name is Virginia Barbara Opshelor Silverstein; born April 3, 1937, in Philadelphia, PA; daughter of Samuel W. (an insurance agent) and Gertrude (Bresch) Opshelor; married Alvin Silverstein (a professor of biology and writer), August 29, 1958; children: Robert Alan, Glenn Evan, Carrie Lee, Sharon Leslie, Laura Donna, Kevin Andrew. *Education:* Attended McGill University, summer, 1955; University of Pennsylvania, A.B., 1958. *Hobbies and other interests:* Reading, listening to classical music, working on various handcrafts, grandchildren (Emily, Shara, and Bobby Lee).

ADDRESSES: Home—3 Burlinghoff Lane, P.O. Box 537, Lebanon, NJ 08833.

In *The Mystery of Sleep,* Alvin and Virginia B. Silverstein investigate what happens to people during sleep—and sleep deprivation. (Jacket illustration by Nelle Davis.)

CAREER: American Sugar Company, Brooklyn, NY, analytical chemist, 1958-59; free-lance translator of Russian scientific literature, 1960—; writer.

MEMBER: Authors Guild, American Translators Association.

AWARDS, HONORS: All with husband, Alvin Silverstein: Children's Book of the Year citations, Child Study Association of America, 1969, for *A World in a Drop of Water,* and 1972, for *The Code of Life, Nature's Defenses,* and *Nature's Pincushion; A World in a Drop of Water* was named an Outstanding Children's Book of 1969, *World Book Yearbook,* 1970; *Circulatory Systems* was named a Science Educators' Book Society Selection; awards from New Jersey Institute of Technology, 1972, for *Guinea Pigs: All about Them,* 1980, for *Aging,* and 1983, for *The Robots Are Here* and *The Story of Your Mouth;* Outstanding Science Books for Children citations, National Science Teachers Association and Children's Book Council, 1972, for *The Long Voyage, The Muscular System, The Skeletal System, Cancer, Nature's Pincushion,* and *Life in a Bucket of Soil,* 1973, for *Rabbits: All about Them,* 1974, for *Animal Invaders* and *Hamsters: All about Them,* 1976, for *Potatoes: All about Them* and *Gerbils: All about Them,* 1983, for *Heartbeats,* 1987, for *The Story of Your Foot,* 1988, for

Wonders of Speech and *Nature's Living Lights,* and 1990, for *Overcoming Acne.*

Alcoholism was selected among the Notable Trade Books in the Field of Social Studies, National Council for the Social Studies and Children's Book Council, 1975; Older Honor citation, New York Academy of Sciences, 1977, for *Potatoes: All about Them;* Junior Literary Guild selection, and Children's Book of the Year citation, Bank Street College, 1977, both for *The Left-Hander's World;* Books for the Teen Age selections, New York Public Library, 1978, for *Heart Disease,* and 1987, for *AIDS: Deadly Threat;* special certificate of commendation, John Burroughs List of Nature Books for Young Readers, 1988, for *Nature's Living Lights.*

WRITINGS:

NONFICTION CHILDREN'S BOOKS; WITH HUSBAND, ALVIN SILVERSTEIN

Life in the Universe, illustrated by L. Ames, Van Nostrand, 1967.
Unusual Partners, illustrated by Mel Hunter, McGraw, 1968.
Rats and Mice: Friends and Foes of Mankind, illustrated by Joseph Cellini, Lothrop, 1968.
The Origin of Life, illustrated by L. Ames, Van Nostrand, 1968.
The Respiratory System: How Living Creatures Breathe, illustrated by George Bakacs, Prentice-Hall, 1969.
A Star in the Sea, illustrated by Simeon Shimin, Warne, 1969.
A World in a Drop of Water, Atheneum, 1969.
Carl Linnaeus, illustrated by L. Ames, John Day, 1969.
Frederick Sanger, illustrated by L. Ames, John Day, 1969.
Cells: Building Blocks of Life, illustrated by G. Bakacs, Prentice-Hall, 1969.
Germfree Life: A New Field in Biological Research, Lothrop, 1970.
Living Lights: The Mystery of Bioluminescence, Golden Gate, 1970.
Circulatory Systems: The Rivers Within, illustrated by G. Bakacs, Prentice-Hall, 1970.
The Digestive System: How Living Creatures Use Food, illustrated by G. Bakacs, Prentice-Hall, 1970.
Bionics: Man Copies Nature's Machines, McCall Publishing, 1970.
Harold Urey: The Man Who Explored from Earth to Moon, illustrated by L. Ames, John Day, 1971.
The Nervous System: The Inner Networks, illustrated by Mel Erikson, Prentice-Hall, 1971.
Mammals of the Sea, illustrated by Bernard Garbutt, Golden Gate, 1971.
Metamorphosis: The Magic Change, Atheneum, 1971.
The Sense Organs: Our Link with the World, illustrated by M. Erikson, Prentice-Hall, 1971.
The Endocrine System, illustrated by L. Ames, Prentice-Hall, 1971.
The Reproductive System: How Living Creatures Multiply, illustrated by L. Ames, Prentice-Hall, 1971.
The Code of Life, Atheneum, 1971.

Guinea Pigs: All about Them, photographs by Roger Kerkham, Lothrop, 1972.
The Long Voyage: The Life Cycle of a Green Turtle, illustrated by Allan Eitzen, Warne, 1972.
(Under joint pseudonym Ralph Buxton) *Nature's Defenses,* illustrated by Angus M. Babcock, Golden Gate, 1972.
The Muscular System: How Living Creatures Move, illustrated by L. Ames, Prentice-Hall, 1972.
The Skeletal System, illustrated by L. Ames, Prentice-Hall, 1972.
Cancer, John Day, 1972, first revised edition, illustrated by Andrew Antal, 1977, second revised edition published as *Cancer: Can It Be Stopped?,* Lippincott, 1987.
The Skin, illustrated by L. Ames, Prentice-Hall, 1972.
(Under joint pseudonym Ralph Buxton) *Nature's Pincushion,* illustrated by A. M. Babcock, Golden Gate, 1972.
The Excretory System, illustrated by L. Ames, Prentice-Hall, 1972.
(Under joint pseudonym Richard Rhine) *Life in a Bucket of Soil,* illustrated by Elsie Wrigley, Lothrop, 1972.
Exploring the Brain, illustrated by Patricia De Veau, Prentice-Hall, 1973.
The Chemicals We Eat and Drink, Follett, 1973.
Rabbits: All about Them, photographs by R. Kerkham, Lothrop, 1973.
Sleep and Dreams, Lippincott, 1974.
(Under joint pseudonym Ralph Buxton) *Nature's Water Clown,* illustrated by A. M. Babcock, Golden Gate, 1974.
Animal Invaders: The Story of Imported Animal Life, Atheneum, 1974.
Hamsters: All about Them, photographs by Frederick Breda, Lothrop, 1974.
Epilepsy, Lippincott, 1975.
Oranges: All about Them, illustrated by Shirley Chan, Prentice-Hall, 1975.
Beans: All about Them, illustrated by S. Chan, Prentice-Hall, 1975.
Alcoholism, introduction by Gail Gleason Milgrom, Lippincott, 1975.
(Under joint pseudonym Ralph Buxton) *Nature's Glider,* illustrated by A. M. Babcock, Golden Gate, 1975.
Apples: All about Them, illustrated by S. Chan, Prentice-Hall, 1976.
Potatoes: All about Them, illustrated by S. Chan, Prentice-Hall, 1976.
Gerbils: All about Them, photographs by F. Breda, Lippincott, 1976.
Heart Disease, Follett, 1976.
The Left-Hander's World, Follett, 1977.
Allergies, introduction by Sheldon Cohen, Lippincott, 1977.
Itch, Sniffle and Sneeze: All about Asthma, Hay Fever and Other Allergies, illustrated by Roy Doty, Four Winds, 1978.
Cats: All about Them, photographs by F. Breda, Lothrop, 1978.
So You're Getting Braces: A Guide to Orthodontics, illustrated by Barbara Remington, with photo-

graphs by Virginia B. and Alvin Silverstein, Lippincott, 1978.

(With son Glenn Silverstein) *Aging,* F. Watts, 1979.

World of Bionics, Methuen, 1979.

The Sugar Disease: Diabetes, introduction by consulting editor Charles Nechemias, Lippincott, 1980.

The Genetics Explosion, Four Winds, 1980.

Mice: All about Them, photographs by son Robert A. Silverstein, Lippincott, 1980.

Nature's Champions: The Biggest, the Fastest, the Best, illustrated by Jean Zallinger, Random House, 1980.

The Story of Your Ear, illustrated by Susan Gaber, Coward, McCann & Geoghegan, 1981.

Runaway Sugar: All about Diabetes, illustrated by Harriett Barton, Lippincott, 1981.

Futurelife: The Biotechnology Revolution, illustrated by Marjorie Thier, Prentice-Hall, 1982.

Heartbeats: Your Body, Your Heart, illustrated by Stella Ormai, Lippincott, 1983.

The Story of Your Mouth, illustrated by Greg Wenzel, Coward-McCann, 1984.

The Robots Are Here, Prentice-Hall, 1984.

Headaches: All about Them, Lippincott, 1984.

Heart Disease: America's Number One Killer, Lippincott, 1985.

The Story of Your Hand, illustrated by G. Wenzel, Putnam, 1985.

Dogs: All about Them, introduction by John C. McLoughlin, Lothrop, 1986.

World of the Brain, illustrated by Warren Budd, Morrow, 1986.

AIDS: Deadly Threat, foreword by Paul Volberding, Enslow Publishers, 1986, revised and enlarged edition, 1991.

The Story of Your Foot, illustrated by G. Wenzel, Putnam, 1987.

Mystery of Sleep, illustrated by Nelle Davis, Little, Brown, 1987.

Wonders of Speech, illustrated by Gordon Tomei, Morrow, 1988.

Nature's Living Lights: Fireflies and Other Bioluminescent Creatures, illustrated by Pamela and Walter Carroll, Little, Brown, 1988.

Learning about AIDS, foreword by James Oleske, Enslow Publishers, 1989.

Glasses and Contact Lenses: Your Guide to Eyes, Eyewear, and Eye Care, Harper, 1989.

Genes, Medicine, and You: Genetic Counseling and Gene Therapy, Enslow Publishers, 1989.

(With R. A. Silverstein) *Overcoming Acne: The How and Why of Healthy Skin Care,* preface by Christopher M. Papa, illustrated by Frank Schwarz, Morrow, 1990.

Life in a Tidal Pool, illustrated by P. and W. Carroll, Little, Brown, 1990.

(With R. A. Silverstein) *Lyme Disease, the Great Imitator: How to Prevent and Cure It,* preface by Leonard H. Sigal, AVSTAR, 1990.

(With R. A. Silverstein) *So You Think You're Fat: Obesity, Anorexia Nervosa, Bulimia, and Other Eating Disorders,* Harper, 1991.

(With R. A. Silverstein) *Addictions Handbook,* Enslow Publishers, 1991.

(With R. A. Silverstein) *Steroids: Big Muscles, Big Problems,* Enslow Publishers, in press.

(With R. A. Silverstein) *Smell, the Subtle Sense,* Morrow, in press.

(With R. A. Silverstein) *Recycling: Meeting the Challenge of the Trash Crisis,* Putnam, in press.

(With R. A. Silverstein) *Food Power! Proteins,* Millbrook, in press.

(With R. A. Silverstein) *Food Power! Fats,* Millbrook, in press.

(With R. A. Silverstein) *Food Power! Carbohydrates,* Millbrook, in press.

(With R. A. Silverstein) *Food Power! Vitamins and Minerals,* Millbrook, in press.

Also author with husband, Alvin Silverstein, under joint pseudonym Dr. A, of syndicated juvenile fiction column, "Tales from Dr. A," which appeared in about 250 American and Canadian newspapers, 1972-74.

"FAMOUS NAME" SERIES; WITH ALVIN SILVERSTEIN

(With family members Robert A., Linda, Laura, and Kevin Silverstein) *John, Your Name Is Famous: Highlights, Anecdotes, and Trivia about the Name John and the People Who Made It Great,* AVSTAR, 1989.

(With R. A. Silverstein) *John: Fun and Facts about a Popular Name and the People Who Made It Great,* AVSTAR, 1990.

(With R. A. Silverstein) *Michael: Fun and Facts about a Popular Name and the People Who Made It Great,* AVSTAR, 1990.

TRANSLATOR FROM RUSSIAN

V. N. Kondratev, *Kinetics of Chemical Gas Reactions,* Atomic Energy Commission, 1960.

M. A. Elyashevich, *Spectra of the Rare Earths,* Atomic Energy Commission, 1960.

L. K. Blinov, *Hydrochemistry of the Aral Sea,* Office of Technical Services, 1961.

R. A. Belyaev, *Beryllium Oxide,* Atomic Energy Commission, 1963.

G. V. Samsonov, *High-Temperature Compounds of Rare Earth Metals with Nonmetals,* Plenum, 1965.

M. B. Neiman, *Aging and Stabilization of Polymers,* Plenum, 1965.

Contributor of translations to about twenty scientific journals; translator of monthly journals *Biokhimiya* and *Molekulyarnaya Genetika, Mikrobiologiya, i Virusologiya.*

SIDELIGHTS: Virginia B. Silverstein and her husband, Alvin Silverstein, have combined their writing talents and mutual love of science to become successful authors of more than ninety scientific books for young readers. Please refer to Alvin Silverstein's sketch in this volume for their Sidelights essay.

SOWTER, Nita

ADDRESSES: Office—c/o HarperCollins Publishers Ltd., 77-85 Fulham Palace Rd., London W6 8JB, England.

WRITINGS:

People at Work, Jackdaw for Thames Television, 1976.
Up and Down, Jackdaw for Thames Television, 1977.
Maisie Middleton, A. & C. Black, 1977.
On the Farm, Blackie & Son, 1978.
Little Boy Blue, Harper, 1982.
Hey Diddle Diddle, Blackie & Son, 1984.
Maisie Middleton at the Wedding, Collins, 1988.

ILLUSTRATOR

Baa Baa Black Sheep, Dinosaur Publications, 1971.
Little Miss Muffet [and] *Humpty Dumpty,* Dinosaur Publications, 1971.
Little Bo Beep [and] *Hickory Dickory Dock,* Dinosaur Publications, 1971.
The Old Woman Who Lived in a Shoe, Dinosaur Publications, 1971.
Althea, *Whirling Windmills,* Colourmaster International, 1972.
Althea, *Going to the Doctor,* Dinosaur Publications, 1973.
Althea, *The New Baby,* Souvenir Press, 1973.
M. F. Howard and A. Podersoo, editors, *Education and Training: Industry, Commerce, Hospitals, Public Service: Your Guide to Over 6,000 Training Opportunities,* Hobsons Press, 1974.
Rosamund Cross, *The Runaway Balloon,* Dinosaur Publications, 1974.
Althea, *I Go to Playschool,* Souvenir Press, 1976.
Rosemary Creek, *Guinea Pigs,* Dinosaur Publications, 1977.
Creek, *Rabbits,* Dinosaur Publications, 1977.
Catherine Storr, *Hugo and His Grandma,* Dinosaur Publications, 1977.
Storr, *Hugo and His Grandma's Washing Day,* Dinosaur Publications, 1978.

Sheila Lavelle, *Oliver Ostrich,* A. & C. Black, 1978.
Anne Wellington, *Apple Pie,* Prentice-Hall, 1978, published in England as *Mr. Bingle's Apple Pie,* Abelard, 1978.
Lavelle, *Everybody Said No!,* A. & C. Black, 1978.
Diana S. Stoker, *Rainbow Party Pack,* Jackdaw for Thames Television, 1978.
Marjorie Darke, *Carnival Day,* Kestrel Books, 1979.
Wellington, *Grandfather Gregory,* Abelard, 1980.
Una Leavy, *Shoes for Tom,* Abelard, 1981.
Leavy, *Tom's Garden,* Abelard, 1981.
Joan Cass, *The Persistent Mouse,* Abelard, 1983.
Cass, *Six Too Many Mice,* Blackie & Son, 1985.

SIDELIGHTS: Nita Sowter's illustrations for children's books often focus on teaching young children basic concepts, such as up and down, and explaining what adults do to make a living. Her book *People at Work* gives examples of such everyday occupations as policeman, newspaper seller, and nurse, so that children can learn more about what the people they normally encounter actually do. Sowter's illustrations for the book include cut-out costumes for several occupations and a set of finger puppets as well.

In her books *Maisie Middleton* and *Maisie Middleton at the Wedding,* Sowter tells of a young tomboy. In *Maisie Middleton,* Maisie cooks her own breakfast, while in *Maisie Middleton at the Wedding,* she reluctantly serves as a bridesmaid at her aunt's wedding. The *Books for Keeps* reviewer finds *Maisie Middleton at the Wedding* to be "a book to go 'Ah!' over—we all did!"

WORKS CITED:

Review of *Maisie Middleton at the Wedding, Books for Keeps,* July, 1989, p. 7.

FOR MORE INFORMATION SEE:

PERIODICALS

Growing Point, December, 1976, pp. 3026-3027; October, 1977, pp. 3186-3187.
Publishers Weekly, February 24, 1984, p. 140.*

T

TOMES, Margot (Ladd) 1917-1991

OBITUARY NOTICE—See index for *SATA* sketch: Born August 10, 1917, in Yonkers, NY; died June 25, 1991, in New York, NY. Designer and illustrator. Tomes began her career as a children's book illustrator in 1963 and thereafter supplied artwork for more than fifty fairy tales, historical stories, cookbooks, and songbooks. Educated at the Pratt Institute in Brooklyn, Tomes worked as a fabric and wallpaper designer before turning to children's books. Her artwork has earned substantial acclaim; for example Beatrice S. De Regniers's *Little Sister and the Month Brothers* was included in the Children's Book Showcase in 1977, and *Jack and the Wonder Beans*, written by James Still, was named a *New York Times* best illustrated children's book of 1977. Tomes's illustrations also appear in *The Lap-Time Song and Play Book* and Wanda Gag's *The Earth Gnome* and *The Sorcerer's Apprentice.*

OBITUARIES AND OTHER SOURCES:

BOOKS

Who's Who in American Art, 1991-1992, 19th edition, Bowker, 1990.

PERIODICALS

School Library Journal, August, 1991, p. 21.

*   *   *

TUDOR, Tasha 1915-

PERSONAL: Name originally Starling Burgess; legally changed; born August 28, 1915, in Boston, MA; daughter of William Starling Burgess (a naval architect) and Rosamond Tudor (a portrait painter); married Thomas Leighton McCready, Jr. (an author), 1938 (divorced); children: Bethany Wheelock, Seth Tudor, Thomas Strong, Efner Strong Tudor Holmes. *Education:* Studied at the Boston Museum Fine Arts School. *Politics:* "Not at all interested." *Religion:* "Stillwater."

ADDRESSES: Office—c/o The Jenny Wren Press, P.O. Box 505, Mooresville, IN 46158.

TASHA TUDOR

CAREER: Author and illustrator of children's books, 1938—; Jenny Wren Press (small press publisher), Mooresville, IN, partner, 1989—. *Exhibitions:* Period clothing collection, books, and artwork featured in exhibit "A Time to Keep," at Conner Prairie Settlement in Noblesville, IN, 1991.

MEMBER: Pembroke Walsh Coral Club, American Primrose Society, American Goat Association, American Lilac Society.

AWARDS, HONORS: Children's Spring Book Festival Younger Honor, *New York Herald Tribune,* 1941, for *A Tale for Easter;* Caldecott Honor Books, American

Tudor's love of the past is reflected in the Victorian motifs of her illustrations for *Mother Goose*.

Library Association (ALA), 1945, for *Mother Goose,* and 1957, for *1 Is One;* Chandler Book Talk Reward of Merit, 1963; Regina Medal, Catholic Library Association, 1971; *The Night Before Christmas* was named a Children's Book of the Year in 1975 by the Child Study Association; Chicago Book Clinic Award, 1982, for *A Child's Garden of Verses.* Junior Literary Guild citation for *Increase Rabbit;* ALA Notable Book citation for *The Dolls' House.*

WRITINGS:

SELF-ILLUSTRATED

Pumpkin Moonshine, Oxford University Press, 1938, enlarged edition, Walck, 1962.
Alexander the Gander, Oxford University Press, 1939, enlarged edition, Walck, 1961.
The County Fair, Oxford University Press, 1940, enlarged edition, Walck, 1964.
Snow Before Christmas, Oxford University Press, 1941.
A Tale for Easter, Oxford University Press, 1941.
Dorcas Porkus, Oxford University Press, 1942, enlarged edition, Walck, 1963.
The White Goose, Farrar, 1943.
Linsey Woolsey, Oxford University Press, 1946.
Thistly B, Oxford University Press, 1949.
The Dolls' Christmas, Walck, 1950.
Amanda and the Bear, Oxford Unversity Press, 1951.
Edgar Allan Crow, Oxford Unversity Press, 1953.
A Is for Annabelle (verse), Oxford University Press, 1954.
1 Is One (verse), Oxford University Press, 1956.
Around the Year (verse), Walck, 1957.
Becky's Birthday, Viking, 1960.
(With others) *My Brimful Book,* edited by Dana Bruce, Platt, 1961.
Becky's Christmas, Viking, 1961.

First Delights: A Book about the Five Senses, Platt, 1966.
Corgiville Fair, Crowell, 1971.
A Time to Keep: The Tasha Tudor Book of Holidays, Rand McNally, 1977.
Tasha Tudor's Sampler: A Tale for Easter, Pumpkin Moonshine, [and] *The Dolls' Christmas,* McKay, 1977.
An Advent Calendar, Rand McNally, 1978.
(With Linda Allen) *Tasha Tudor's Favorite Christmas Carols,* McKay, 1978.
A Book of Christmas, Collins, 1979.
(With L. Allen) *Tasha Tudor's Old-Fashioned Christmas Gifts,* McKay, 1979.
The Springs of Joy, Rand McNally, 1979.
Rosemary for Remembrance, Philomel Books, 1981.
Tasha Tudor's Seasons of Delight: A Year on an Old-Fashioned Farm, Philomel Books, 1986.
Give Us This Day: The Lord's Prayer, Philomel Books, 1987.

ILLUSTRATOR OF BOOKS BY HUSBAND, THOMAS LEIGHTON McCREADY, JR.

Biggity Bantam, Ariel Books, 1954.
Pekin White, Ariel Books, 1955.
Mr. Stubbs, Ariel Books, 1956.
Increase Rabbit, Ariel Books, 1958.
Adventures of a Beagle, Ariel Books, 1959.

ILLUSTRATOR OF BOOKS BY DAUGHTER, EFNER TUDOR HOLMES

The Christmas Cat, Crowell, 1976.
Amy's Goose, Crowell, 1977.
Carrie's Gift, Collins, 1978.
Deer in the Hollow, Philomel Books, 1990.

ILLUSTRATOR OF BOOKS BY OTHER AUTHORS

Mother Goose: Seventy-Seven Verses, Walck, 1944.
Hans Christian Andersen, *Fairy Tales from Hans Christian Andersen,* Oxford University Press, 1945.
Robert Louis Stevenson, *A Child's Garden of Verses,* Oxford University Press, 1947, revised edition, Rand McNally, 1981.
Rumer Godden, *The Dolls' House,* Georgian Webb, 1947.
Juliana Horatia Ewing, *Jackanapes,* Oxford University Press, 1948.
First Prayers, Oxford University Press, 1952.
First Graces, Oxford University Press, 1955.
And It Was So: Words from the Scripture, selected and edited by Sara Klein Clarke, Westminster Press, 1958.
The Lord Will Love Thee, scriptures selected and edited by S. K. Clarke, Westminster Press, 1959.
Clement C. Moore, *The Night Before Christmas,* St. Onge, 1962, revised edition, Rand McNally, 1975.
Frances Hodgson Burnett, *The Secret Garden,* Lippincott, 1962.
F. H. Burnett, *A Little Princess,* Lippincott, 1963.
Louisa May Alcott, *A Round Dozen: Stories,* selected with a foreword by Anne Thaxter Eaton, Viking, 1963.

The Twenty-Third Psalm, St. Onge, 1965, reissued as *The Lord Is My Shepherd: The Twenty-Third Psalm,* Philomel Books, 1980.

Kenneth Grahame, *The Wind in the Willows,* World Publishing, 1966.

First Poems of Childhood, Platt, 1967.

More Prayers, Walck, 1967.

Henry Augustus Shute, *The Real Diary of a Real Boy,* R. R. Smith, 1967.

H. A. Shute, *Brite and Fair,* R. R. Smith, 1968.

Mary Mason Campbell, *New England Butt'ry Shelf Cookbook: Receipts for Very Special Occasions,* World Publishing, 1968.

L. M. Alcott, *Little Women,* World Publishing, 1968.

M. M. Campbell, *New England Butt'ry Shelf Almanac,* World Publishing, 1970.

M. M. Campbell, *Betty Crocker's Kitchen Gardens,* Golden Press, 1971.

Tasha Tudor's Bedtime Book, edited by Kate Klimo, Platt, 1977.

A Basket of Herbs: A Book of American Sentiments, edited by M. M. Campbell, New England Unit, Inc., of Herb Society of America, Inc., 1983.

Emily Dickinson, *A Brighter Garden* (verse), collected by Karen Ackerman, Philomel Books, 1989.

EDITOR AND ILLUSTRATOR

The Tasha Tudor Book of Fairy Tales, Platt, 1961.

Wings from the Wind: An Anthology of Poems, Lippincott, 1964.

Tasha Tudor's Favorite Stories, Lippincott, 1965.

Take Joy! The Tasha Tudor Christmas Book, World Publishing, 1966.

All for Love, Philomel Books, 1984.

SIDELIGHTS: During her youth Tasha Tudor yearned to become a farmer—to experience the fulfillment that accompanies simple rural living and hard work. She was also fascinated with the lifestyle of nineteenth-century New Englanders, who lived without benefit of modern conveniences, and envisioned a similiar existence. Never abandoning these aspirations, Tudor followed in the footsteps of her mother, a portrait painter, by pursuing an interest in art, a penchant that eventually led to a long and successful career as an author and illustrator of children's books. Her love of the past became evident in her work as she frequently included Victorian motifs and painted her characters in old-fashioned clothing and settings. She first published a book in her early twenties and has since written the text and drawn the pictures for more than thirty books for children, illustrated some thirty others, and edited five more. She has retold and reillustrated popular fairy tales and nursery rhymes, as well as invented the characters and situations for original stories based on actual people and occurrences. Many reviewers praise her soft watercolors, pen and ink drawings, and flowery prose for evoking the ideals, beauty, and sentimentality of a bygone era, and some compare her artistry to that of nineteenth-century British illustrator Kate Greenaway. Tudor's work is "always steeped ... in old-fashioned romantic ambience," a *Booklist* reviewer observed.

"Tasha Tudor has given children a very special ray of sunshine—that of pictures which ... carr[y] the imagination of children into history, into the human heart, into the joys of family life, into love of friendship itself," assessed Ilse L. Hontz in *Catholic Library World.* The critic asserted that "Tudor radiates a deep appreciation of family life, animals, nature," and "brings another world of peacefulness into our consciousness." Her work reflects "charm, excellence, and tranquility," echoed Sister Julanne Good in a speech made during the Regina Medal Award presentations in 1971, reprinted in *Catholic Library World.* Adding that Tudor's mix of "nineteenth-century style with the realism of the story reflects a talent which is difficult to duplicate," she called the artist's style "natural and expressive, revealing a creative and imaginative personality."

Tudor was born in Boston, Massachusetts, in 1915, to Rosamond Tudor and yacht designer William Starling Burgess. Originally named Starling Burgess, she was nicknamed "Natasha" by her father, who admired nineteenth-century Russian writer Leo Tolstoy's heroine in *War and Peace.* She eventually changed her name to Tasha Tudor, legally adopting her mother's maiden name as a surname. Unenthusiastic about school in her youth, Tudor nevertheless loved to draw and read works illustrated by Edmund Dulac, Randolph Caldecott, Walter Crane, and Beatrix Potter, among others. At the age of nine, when her mother and father divorced, she was sent to live with friends of her parents in Redding, Connecticut. Her mother opted to relocate to Greenwich Village to pursue her art career and felt the free-spirited lifestyle of 1920s New York City was inappropriate for her young daughter.

Tudor's new surroundings, however, were a far departure from the formal and reserved milieu she had experienced in Boston before her parents separated. "I was dumped into the most unconventional atmosphere you can imagine," noted Tudor in *Drawn from New England,* her 1979 biography written by daughter Bethany Tudor. Describing her mother's change in environment as "exhilarating," Bethany writes that "in Connecticut [Tudor] could run wild in a state of utter relaxation from discipline. Nothing was ever on schedule at Aunt Gwen's house, except on weekends when [Uncle Michael] came home from his job in the city." Tudor, herself, credits her "aunt" with helping tap her creativity.

While living in Redding, Tudor became interested in theater, often dressing up in antique clothing and costumes. Together with a few friends, she presented plays written by Aunt Gwen. She also grew fond of dance, nature, and country living. She dreamed of owning a farm one day. Later, in her teenage years, Tudor rejoined her mother. Subsequently, they spent a number of winters in Bermuda and their summers on a farm that Rosamond purchased in Redding. While in Bermuda, Tudor established a nursery school in order to raise money—her goal was to obtain enough funds to purchase a cow after she returned to Connecticut. Her summers were spent developing her art as well as

Tudor's Vermont home was the model for the house in her illustrations for Clement C. Moore's *The Night Before Christmas*.

tending to her newly acquired cow and a flock of chickens.

During her late teens Tudor decided on a career as an illustrator after reading *The Vicar of Wakefield,* illustrated by Hugh Thompson. "I just loved ... Thompson's work, and right then and there decided, I would be an illustrator!," declared Tudor in *Drawn from New England.* Daughter Bethany adds: "My mother was not particularly fond of writing, but in order to have something to illustrate, she began to write little stories for children, often based on real incidents she had observed." She created her first book—an unpublished story of a farm girl—at age nineteen.

In 1938 Tudor married fellow Redding resident Thomas Leighton McCready, Jr., who had been raised in the New York City area. Described by Bethany as "a suburbanite at heart," McCready agreed to help his new bride realize her dream of farming. He also encouraged Tudor to find a publisher for a book, *Pumpkin Moonshine,* that she had originally written and illustrated as a gift for his English niece Sylvie Ann, who serves as the story's main character. The volume, which charts the young girl's adventures as she seeks and later carts home the largest pumpkin on her grandmother's property, was rejected by numerous New York publishers. Tudor finally struck a deal with Oxford University Press, however, beginning a long association with the firm. *Pumpkin Moonshine* is still in print more than fifty years later.

Tudor managed to find time to write and illustrate in addition to her farm duties. By the mid-1940s Tudor had borne two children and longed to resettle in a more rustic environment. The family found such a locale in Webster, New Hampshire. Tudor, meanwhile, began work as an illustrator of books by other authors. The royalties from her work on a 1944 version of *Mother Goose* helped her purchase the rural home, which was in need of renovation. The family eventually increased by two more children. In time all of the Tudor offspring were trained to run various aspects of the old farm. Devoid of many modern conveniences, including running water and electricity, the homestead was restored and filled with antique furnishings. Various facets of nineteenth-century living were observed in the Tudor-McCready home. For example, Tudor washed clothes by hand, became proficient in spinning and weaving flax, made bread from scratch, sewed much of her children's clothing, and planted a vast garden of flowers and vegetables.

"My mother often said she wanted to live a life similar to that of New Englanders in the past century," explained Bethany in *Drawn from New England.* "So that is what our family did, in a way, for many a year. It was not easy, but the rewards were most satisfying. One could say my mother's whole career has been inspired by her lifestyle, plus the farm pets and animals." The family kept a number of cows, geese, ducks, chickens, corgi dogs, horses, cats, and other animals. Many of these "pets" accompanied the family on picnics; some appeared as subjects of Tudor's books, including *Alexander the Gander, Thistly B.,* and *Edgar Allan Crow.*

Tudor often drew pictures of her children in their youth, dressing them in period clothing. "Sometimes, after being sketched, we were allowed to keep on the dresses and enjoy an afternoon tea party in the best parlor [of the farmhouse]," recalled Bethany. "We felt as if we were actually living some of the wonderful old fairy tales and stories my mother read to us so constantly." Tudor frequently included illustrations of her children in her books, most often in real-life situations and occurrences. For example, one of Bethany's birthday parties is recreated in *Becky's Birthday,* while the family custom of Easter egg tree decoration is depicted in *A Time to Keep.* The author and illustrator also acquainted her children with her world of fantasy. She passed on her love of acting out plays and playing with dolls—two pastimes that had broken the monotony of boarding school in her youth. Together, Tudor and her children devised a number of activities for their dolls, holding fairs and parties, making miniature Christmas presents for them, sending letters and parcels through their own special mail service called the "Sparrow Post," and even staging a doll marriage. The dolls themselves have been featured in Tudor's books, including *The Dolls' Christmas* and *A Is for Annabelle.*

Tudor's unusual lifestyle and special brand of fantasy are evident in her other books as well. Many critics have delighted over her simple stories as well as her sentimental, "Victorian" pastel illustrations. Among her more notable volumes are the award-winning *A Tale for Easter* and *1 Is One,* which she wrote and illustrated herself. The former work describes through text and pictures the days preceding Easter. A *New York Herald Tribune Books* reviewer described the tale as "a jewel of prettiness," while Ellen Lewis Buell in *New York Times Book Review* praised the volume for exuding an "unforgettable air of joy." *1 Is One,* named a Caldecott Honor book, helps youngsters learn to count. Critics called the book charming, beautiful, and pleasing.

Tudor's illustrations for other authors' texts have also received much critical praise. Her drawings for *Mother Goose,* another Caldecott Honor book, were lauded by many reviewers. A writer for the *New York Herald Tribune,* for example, observed that the reader feels that Tudor "has seen deeper into the character than many of her predecessors." Tudor's drawings for Clement C. Moore's *Night Before Christmas* were also well received by both the public and reviewers, as were her illustrations for fairy tales, Christmas narratives, biblical verses, and bedtime stories. In addition to reillustrating popular works like Robert Louis Stevenson's *Child's Garden of Verses,* Tudor has also lent her artistic vision to texts written by family members, including first husband McCready and daughter Efner.

Amid the success of Tudor's books she was able to realize another life-long dream—that of living in Ver-

mont. In the early 1970s Tudor purchased property adjoining that of her son Seth, who built his mother a new home, modeled after a nineteenth-century farmhouse. According to a 1977 article by Angela Taylor in the *New York Times,* the Tudor home "is set in a pine clearing reached by a narrow, rutted road no ordinary car can navigate. The house itself has had electricity for only two years and there is no running water in the kitchen; it is carried in buckets from the barn." Tudor continues to heed old-fashioned mores and belongs to a group dedicated to nineteenth-century living called "Stillwater." She told Taylor, "We are great venerators of nature, believe in peaceful living, in live and let live, and discipline for children." In addition to her farming and children's book activities, Tudor became a partner with Mrs. David Mathers in the Mooresville, Indiana-based Jenny Wren Press, a small press publisher, in 1989.

WORKS CITED:

Booklist, February 1, 1985, p. 784.
Buell, Ellen Lewis, "A Picture Book," *New York Times Book Review,* March 30, 1941, p. 10.
Good, Sister Julanne, "Regina Medal Presentation," *Catholic Library World,* July-August, 1971, pp. 614-15.
Hontz, Ilse L., "Tasha Tudor," *Catholic Library World,* February, 1971, pp. 351-54.
Review of *Mother Goose, New York Herald Tribune,* November 12, 1944, p. 12.
"Other Books Chosen for Honor," a review of *A Tale for Easter, New York Herald Tribune Books,* May 11, 1941, p. 10.
Taylor, Angela, "An Illustrator Who Works at the Art of 19th-Century Living," *New York Times,* July 5, 1977.
Tudor, Bethany, *Drawn from New England: Tasha Tudor,* Collins, 1979, pp. 15-16, 26-27, 36, and 49.

FOR MORE INFORMATION SEE:

PERIODICALS

Booklist, December 15, 1977; January 15, 1980; February 1, 1980.
Bulletin of the Center for Children's Books, July-August, 1962; May, 1978.
Canadian Forum, December, 1960.
Horn Book, December, 1960.
Kirkus Reviews, October 15, 1971; May 15, 1977.
New York Herald Tribune, November 12, 1950; November 14, 1954; November 18, 1956; September 11, 1960.
New York Times Book Review, November 3, 1940; October 25, 1942; October 10, 1943; November 28, 1971; April 15, 1973; February 5, 1978.
Publishers Weekly, October 26, 1984; November 28, 1991.
Saturday Review, November 11, 1961.
School Library Journal, March, 1980; March, 1985.

—Sketch by Kathleen J. Edgar

U–V

UNCLE GUS
See REY, H. A.

* * *

VOS, Ida 1931-

PERSONAL: Born December 13, 1931, in Groningen, Netherlands; daughter of Joseph (a commercial agent) and Bertha (Blok) Gudema; married Henk Vos (an insurance broker), April 3, 1956; children: Josephine, Karel, Bert. *Education:* Kweekschool Voorbereidend Ondervijs Training College, teaching certificates, 1950 and 1952.

ADDRESSES: Home—Dr. Wibautlaan 6G, Rijswijk, Holland 2285XY, Netherlands. *Translator*—Therese Edelstein, 1342 Devonshire, Grosse Pointe Park, MI 48230.

CAREER: Writer. Teacher in Den Haag, Rijswijk, Holland, Netherlands.

MEMBER: Dutch Writers Association, Women's Club.

AWARDS, HONORS: Has received numerous Dutch awards for writings.

WRITINGS:

IN ENGLISH TRANSLATION

Hide and Seek, translated by Therese Edelstein and Inez Smidt, Houghton, 1991 (originally published as *Wie niet weg is wordt Gezien,* Leopold, 1981).

UNTRANSLATED WORKS

Vijfendertig tranen (poetry; title means "35 Tears"), [Holland], 1975.
Schiereiland (poetry; title means "Peninsula"), Nijgh and van Ditmar, 1979.
Miniaturen (title means "Miniature"), Nijgh and van Ditmar, 1980.
Anna is er nog (title means "Anna Is Still There"), Leopold, 1986.

IDA VOS

Dansen op de brug van Avignon (title means "Dancing on the Bridge of Avignon), Leopold, 1989.

Author of *Witte zwanen zwarte zwanen,* 1992.

Also author of radio play, *De bevrijding van Rosa Davidson* (title means "The Liberation of Rosa Davidson"), broadcasted, 1984. Contributor of articles and short stories to various periodicals.

SIDELIGHTS: In her homeland of the Netherlands, Ida Vos is well-known as the author of seven books, numerous short stories, and many articles. While only one of Vos's works—*Hide and Seek*—has been translated into English, readers and critics in America have come to view Vos as a sensitive and talented writer.

Reviewers praised *Hide and Seek* for its compelling portrayal of the experiences of a young Jewish girl during the Nazi invasion of Holland. Eight-year-old Rachel Hartog's life is suddenly turned upside during World War II. The invading Nazis force Rachel to wear a yellow star to indicate her Jewish heritage, to attend a school for Jewish children only, and forbid Rachel to enter the local parks or use the neighborhood swimming pool. Rachel cannot understand these injustices and wrestles with the many intense emotions she feels as she and her family struggle to survive.

A reviewer for *Publishers Weekly* remarked: "Drawing on her own experiences during World War II, Vos fills the narrative with understated but painfully realistic moments.... Vos's novel deserves special attention for its sensitive and deeply affecting consideration of life after liberation." And Hazel Rochman suggested in *Booklist* that "any number of the vignettes—wearing the star for the first time, hiding with the Dutch underground, Rachel's parting from her parents, and later from her foster parents—would make a gripping booktalk/read-aloud that will move children to imagine 'What if it happened to me?'"

Vos told *SATA* how she came to be a writer: "I was born in Groningen, Netherlands. Here I lived until 1936, when my family moved to Rotterdam. Both my parents are Jewish and I grew up in a traditional Jewish family. In 1940, Germany started the war with Holland and my life changed totally. The big bombardment on Rotterdam on May 14, 1940, made a deep impression on me. Seeing the Germans enter our city shocked me terribly. All my books are connected with World War II.

"I started reading when I was a kid of four. At this age, I managed to read books and newspapers. My parents felt unhappy about my reading habits. I could read for hours. They thought that a child of my age should play outside instead of reading all the time. My books brought me to places I never visited. By reading I could fly from reality and forget the terrible world around me.

"At the age of eight, I had already started writing poems and stories. Unfortunately nothing has been kept—the Nazis stole everything from our home.

"I wrote many letters to my grandparents in Groningen. Most of the time the letters started as follows: 'Dear Grandpa, Dear Grandma. Mom is knitting, Daddy is reading and I am writing.' Thereafter followed a report of my experiences at school. I suppose that writing letters has been a good exercise for writing books.

"After the bombardment of Rotterdam in 1940, my parents, my younger sister, Esther, and me, moved to Rijswijk (a small city near the Hague). Here I entered the fourth grade of the elementary school. Unfortunately I was forced to change schools rather quickly because of measures against the Jews. We were forbidden a lot of things: Entering a park, visiting a cinema, library, or swimming pool. We were not allowed to travel by train, enter restaurants, etc. So many things were forbidden that it would be too much to mention them all. We had to wear big yellow stars of David on our clothing with

Hide and Seek is based on Vos's family's life during the years of World War II. (Jacket illustration by Donna Diamond.)

the inscription 'Jew' so that everybody could see that we were Jewish. I had to change schools because Jewish children were not allowed to sit together with Christian kids. My new school was only for Jewish children; all our teachers had to be Jewish as well.

"People, including many of our relatives, friends, and acquaintances, were brought to concentration camps. All the time more and more people. Then my grandparents! When it became too dangerous in 1943, my parents decided to go into hiding. With the help of the resistance movement, we found people that would hide us. Regularly we had to change addresses because of the danger of betrayal. We had to move so many times that I really don't remember all the people that helped us. I owe a lot to all of them. They risked their lives and that of their families in order to save us. The first year of hiding I was together with my parents and my sister. Then we had to split up: my parents at one address, my sister and me at another. I had to take care of my younger sister, telling her stories when she was afraid, playing with her, etc. Of course, I was also afraid but couldn't afford to show it. As a child of eleven, I had to play the role of the older and wiser sister. During the hiding, I had sometimes the opportunity to continue my writing. I still possess a very long poem I wrote during this period about a gnome. Like myself, this small guy hadn't an easy life."

"After nearly three years of hiding, the liberation of Europe occurred in 1943. It was good the Germans were gone from our country, but I couldn't feel happiness. The counting had started—counting all our relatives and friends who didn't come back from the concentration camps, being murdered—gassed—by the invading Nazis.

"I went back to school at thirteen years old. The school officials put me in the fifth grade, since I had forgotten many of the things I learned before the war. I felt stupid sitting between younger children. Fortunately, I was soon allowed to enter a high school. After high school I went to a training college. I was very anxious to work with children. I studied many subjects: Psychology, pedagogics, art history, painting, drawing, modeling, speech training, French, English, and German, and the literature of these languages."

In 1956, I married Henk Vos, who is still my husband. We had three children—one girl and two boys. We were a happy family until 1973 when I broke down mentally. All the grief of the war came back to me. I wanted to stay in bed all the time. I wept the whole day and didn't see any future. Finally I had to be nursed in a psychiatric clinic. It was a clinic only for war victims and people from the resistance movement. I stayed there for about three months and it did me a lot of good. I was never fully cured but I could endure life again.

"However, an unbelievable thing happened during my stay at the clinic. I started writing about the war. Poems flew out of my pen and I couldn't stop. The poems were printed and I got enthusiastic reviews. Now the author Ida Vos was born. I wrote another two volumes of poems. Many volumes of my poems have been sold which is very surprising as the publishing market is rather thin in Holland.

"I also wrote several short stories. The subject was World War II. Some of them were printed in newspapers, periodicals, and a volume of short stories. An editor, reading some of them, asked me to write a book about my life during World War II. First I refused, thinking that I was not able to stand it, being also afraid that I would again break down mentally.

"One day, however, I read in a newspaper about certain articles printed in the German press, such as opinions that the Holocaust was an invention of the Jewish people. The reports were exaggerated the article said—the number of six million Jews murdered was a big lie.

"I was terribly shocked and it made me change my mind. Now I wanted to tell the truth. People should know what really happened. Then I wrote my book, *Wie niet weg is wordt Gezien,* which was translated and published in the United States as *Hide and Seek.*

"After this book, I wrote another three books. In all my books, I describe my experiences during World War II.

"I divide my time between my family, writing, and visiting schools. I am regularly invited by libraries and schools to talk about my writing, books, the Holocaust, and the war. Children are very interested. I have received many letters and paintings from them. I am very happy about my contacts with youth. Through my lectures I am able to warn them against war, discrimination, and fascism."

WORKS CITED:

Review of *Hide and Seek, Publishers Weekly,* February 15, 1991, p. 90.
Rochman, Hazel, review of *Hide and Seek, Booklist,* March 15, 1991, p. 1504.

W

WALTER, Mildred Pitts 1922-

PERSONAL: Born September 9, 1922, in Sweetville, LA; daughter of Paul (a log cutter) and Mary (a midwife and beautician; maiden name, Ward) Pitts; married Earl Lloyd Walter (a social worker and civil rights activist), 1947 (died June 11, 1965); children: Earl Lloyd Jr., Craig Allen. *Education:* Southern University, B.A., 1944; attended California State College, 1950-52; Antioch College, M.Ed., 1977.

CAREER: Shipwright helper in Vancouver, WA, 1943-44; City Dye Works, Los Angeles, CA, salesperson, 1944-48; Los Angeles Public Schools, personnel clerk, 1949-52, elementary school teacher, 1952-70; consultant and lecturer on cultural diversity for educational institutions, 1971-73. Civil rights activist for Congress of Racial Equality (CORE), during 1950s and 1960s. Northeast Women's Center, Denver, CO, cofounder and administrator, 1982-86. Delegate to Second World Black and African Festival of the Arts and Culture, Lagos, Nigeria, 1977.

MEMBER: Society of Children's Book Writers.

AWARDS, HONORS: Runner-up for Irma Simonton Black Award, 1981, for *Ty's One-Man Band; Parents' Choice* awards, 1984, for *Because We Are,* and 1985, for *Brother to the Wind;* Coretta Scott King awards from Social Responsibility Round Table of American Library Association, honorable mention, 1984, for *Because We Are,* honorable mention, 1986, for *Trouble's Child,* winner, 1987, for *Justin and the Best Biscuits in the World.*

WRITINGS:

FICTION FOR YOUNG PEOPLE

Lillie of Watts: A Birthday Surprise (novel), illustrations by Leonora E. Prince, Ritchie, 1969.
Lillie of Watts Takes a Giant Step (novel), illustrations by Bonnie H. Johnson, Doubleday, 1971.
The Liquid Trap, illustrations by John Thompson, Scholastic, 1975.

MILDRED PITTS WALTER

Ty's One-Man Band, illustrations by Margot Tomes, Four Winds, 1980.
The Girl on the Outside (novel), Lothrop, 1982.
Because We Are (novel), Lothrop, 1983.
My Mama Needs Me, illustrations by Pat Cummings, Lothrop, 1983.
Brother to the Wind, illustrations by Diane and Leo Dillon, Lothrop, 1985.
Trouble's Child (novel), Lothrop, 1985.

Justin and the Best Biscuits in the World (novel), illustrations by Catherine Stock, Lothrop, 1986.
Mariah Loves Rock (novel), illustrations by Cummings, Bradbury, 1988.
Have a Happy (novel), illustrations by Carole Byard, Lothrop, 1989.
Two and Too Much, illustrations by Cummings, Bradbury, 1990.
Mariah Keeps Cool (novel), illustrations by Cummings, Bradbury, 1990.

OTHER

The Mississippi Challenge (nonfiction), Bradbury, 1992.

Contributor of articles to periodicals, including *Publishers Weekly. Los Angeles Times,* book reviewer and guest book editor, 1965-68, drama reviewer, 1969-71.

SIDELIGHTS: "I think family is everything within the lives of human beings," said Mildred Pitts Walter in an interview with *Something about the Author* (*SATA*). "Not just the nuclear family, but the extended family—grandmothers, uncles, cousins, friends, community, city, country." As an African American born in rural Louisiana in 1922, Walter grew up facing the twin obstacles of poverty and racial prejudice. But she drew strength from her home and community and went on to a meaningful career as a teacher, civil rights activist, and award-winning children's author. Her books often show how a sense of family and community can enrich anyone's life. "That's how we learn to extend ourselves to people," she observed—"when we have a wonderful foundation in our own family."

In Walter's childhood home, self-respect and work were the basic virtues. "My parents gave me a sense of pride in myself," she told *SATA,* "a sense that I am beautiful—not in terms of physical appearance but in the way I look at life. That is the gift they gave me: the understanding that I am a person who is whole and who is loved, and who is capable of loving." Her parents' faith was particularly remarkable because their lives were very difficult. Walter was the seventh child born into her family. Her mother worked as a beautician and a midwife. Walter's father cut logs for timber companies during the 1920s and then found, as the Great Depression took hold in the 1930s, that such jobs were no longer available. The family was forced to split up for a time, with the father and an older brother and sister going to Houston, Texas, in search of work. Despite all the hardship, Walter grew up with the sense that work was always worth doing and doing well. "I always knew that I could do any kind of work," she recalled to *SATA.* "And if I set my mind to it, I could do anything I wanted. That was the way I had been brought up."

In the Deep South of Walter's youth, African Americans were still subject to much of the racism that had been visited on their grandparents as slaves. They worked long hours for little money and were regularly threatened or abused by whites. Walter's parents tried to shield their children from the pain of racism, but it often intruded anyway. Sometimes racism was mean and

petty: for instance, Walter had to buy shoes without knowing whether they would fit because white store-owners wouldn't allow a black child to be seen trying on their goods. Sometimes racism was more openly threatening. "I was often frightened by strange people, especially white men, coming into our neighborhood," Walter told *SATA.* "A lot of times they had been drinking alcohol. They would knock on our doors late at night and my mother was frightened, therefore I was frightened. A lot of times the police would pass and shine their lights in our window. Young white boys would throw firecrackers out of cars at us when we were walking from church on Sunday evening."

Even as a young child Walter sensed that these things were happening because she was black. "My parents never said anything about color to me—they just said I was beautiful," Walter observed. As for those who harassed black people, "I guess we understood that they were probably more afraid of us than we were of them. And I don't know why they would be afraid unless it was because we knew what we were about. We had our own school, our own church, our own way of doing things." Shunned by whites, African Americans in the rural South developed close-knit communities of their own that were sources of support, affection, and joy. "Because we were together, and isolated in that way, it made us strong," Walter told *SATA.* "We depended upon each other to overcome our fears and to live a full, healthy life. We were able to laugh and play games and tell our stories and sing our songs." Within her community, Walter recalled, "everybody was concerned about me—not just my mother and father but all the neighbors—and I knew they were concerned and I could not do things that were detrimental to myself. I couldn't smoke and do things like that. They just wouldn't allow it!" Later in life, when Walter traveled throughout the world, she realized where those strong community values had come from. They were part of her heritage from the traditional village life of Africa.

For Walter, two pillars of community life were her church and her school. "Ministers, teachers, and church members expected great things from us," she recalled in an article for the *Something about the Author Autobiography Series,* "and we felt an obligation to live up to those expectations." Walter, who loved school from the start, was especially impressed when the school hired a group of sophisticated young women who had trained at Southern University—a black college just outside the state capitol of Baton Rouge. By the time she graduated from high school in 1940, she had resolved to go on to Southern, making her the first person in her family to attend college. To pay for her education Walter had to work very hard, holding two or even three jobs at once during the summer. Since her schooling coincided with World War II, when jobs with good pay were available in defense industries, she even took a year's leave of absence and worked in a shipyard on the far-off Pacific Coast.

Was college worth the struggle? "Yes, it was, yes!" Walter wrote in her autobiography. "I learned to

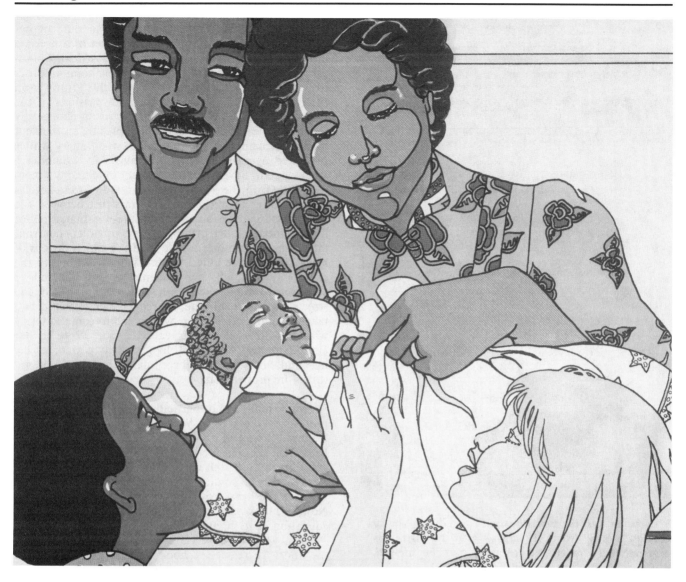

One of Walter's major themes is the importance of family life. (Illustration by Pat Cummings from *My Mama Needs Me,* by Walter.)

question, to seek an understanding of what was happening around and beyond me." Leading African American thinkers, including W. E. B. Du Bois and Howard Thurman, came to speak at Southern; Frank Yerby, who went on to become a major black novelist, was one of her teachers. Soon after Walter graduated, though, she realized that she would have to leave Louisiana. "I needed to go away to get work that was satisfying," she told *SATA.* "Where I grew up in the South the only thing that we could do, if we did anything beyond housework or work in service, was to teach, and teaching at that time paid very little compared to work that I could get outside the state." Walter decided to move to Los Angeles, a city that intrigued her because it was on the Pacific Coast. When she reached the town, she knew hardly anyone there and she had only ten dollars with her.

Los Angeles was not as openly racist as Louisiana, but beneath the surface it was still very intolerant. For example, Walter hoped to stay at the Young Women's

Christian Association (YWCA) when she arrived, but found that it wouldn't rent rooms to black people. She finally got settled with help from fellow African Americans, and soon she was attending a black church just as she had back home. Helping to run the Sunday school was a remarkable man, Earl Walter, whom she married in 1947. "My husband was very quiet, but deep," Walter told *SATA.* "He believed in nonviolence, not just as a theory but as a practical way of life." Nonviolence was about to become a central issue in African American life, as a generation of civil rights leaders—ranging from Martin Luther King, Jr., to James Farmer—advocated nonviolent protest as the best way for black people to achieve equal rights. Walter's husband put his beliefs into practice by joining Farmer's Congress of Racial Equality (CORE), for which he served as a local leader and eventually a national vice chairman. Walter joined her husband in his work. The couple earnestly discussed all variety of social issues—including equality of the sexes, which both strongly advocated. Through CORE

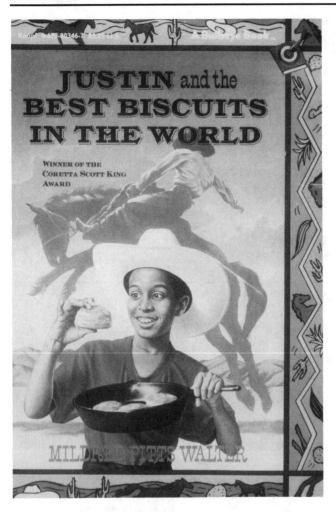

In *Justin and the Best Biscuits in the World,* Justin gains a new sense of purpose after he visits his grandfather's ranch and learns to cook for himself. (Cover illustration by Paul Tankersley.)

they met many civil rights activists, famous and unknown, black and white.

Soon Walter found herself in the midst of the great movement for civil rights that crested in the late 1950s and the 1960s. When California made it illegal for hotels and motels to deny rooms to people because of their race, the Walters became part of a CORE team that compelled owners to accept the law. Walter and her husband would drive to a motel on a Sunday afternoon, bringing their luggage and one of their young sons with them, and ask for a room. Often the desk clerk would claim the motel was filled, and the Walters would drive away. At once a second CORE couple would appear—this time, white—and if the motel suddenly had a vacancy, CORE would confront the owners with evidence of their discrimination. Owners who refused to change their policies could be sued under the new law. This campaign, Walter believes, helped to end such discrimination throughout Los Angeles.

But the struggles of the civil rights era were often more difficult. Many activists, including Walter, were arrested because of demonstrations they made against racist practices in housing or business. At the time of her arrest Walter was protesting construction of a housing development in Los Angeles that barred African Americans. Twice the Walters mortgaged their home in order to provide financial support to civil rights efforts. And there was always the chance that the passions of the times would spill over into violence. As an elementary school teacher, Walter was deeply upset by an incident in Birmingham, Alabama, in 1963, when angry whites retaliated against civil rights activists by bombing a black church. Several children attending Sunday school were killed. In the Watts neighborhood of Los Angeles where Walter taught, simmering mistrust between the poor, black population and the white-dominated police force helped to touch off several days of violent confrontations in the summer of 1965, during which dozens of black people were killed. When Walter returned to the classroom that fall, her students were frightened or embittered and police with shotguns patrolled the streets. In the meantime, moreover, her husband had taken ill and died, and she was forced to come to terms with the crisis alone. "I realized," she wrote in her autobiography, "that I had lost not only a kind, loving husband, but a friend and confidant who helped me put things in proper perspective."

As with many who participated in the civil rights protests of the sixties, Walter came away with mixed feelings. "I walked on a picket line with Martin Luther King, Jr., ... in Los Angeles," she recalled in her autobiography. "I felt we were making great strides. We were so busy on so many fronts, we had no time, nor did we have the heart, to compare our losses to our gains. Now, as I look back, I see that our gains in employment, education, and housing were minimal." Even as the 1990s began, she observed, "Los Angeles is still one of the most segregated school districts in the nation. Unemployment remains high and police harassment continues."

Asked what she might have done differently in the sixties, Walter didn't know: in such a time of crisis, people simply did the best they could. "My husband always said that as long as you are doing something about these things, you can find consolation in the fact that you are not succumbing to the evil," she told *SATA.* "You grieve, but you move on to ending this kind of grief. I think people who remain helpless for a long time become hopeless. The main thing was not to feel helpless." Most of all, she observed, "I'm proud that we stayed in there, and that we gave to a generation to come an example of how struggle can be waged without losing your conscience, without losing your self-respect, and without feeling that you have destroyed humanity. That gives me the greatest satisfaction about that struggle. We came out of it stronger spiritually because we did not leave behind dead bodies and wounded spirits, as in most struggles."

Meanwhile Walter continued her work in the Los Angeles schools, where she had been a teacher since the 1950s. "The children who came to me," she told *SATA,* "were open and anxious to learn. They were honest—

they said exactly what they meant and they meant what they said—and that is the kind of personality I like best. They gave me a lot in terms of keeping my spirit free." Though Walter believed in work and discipline, she realized that young children need work of a special kind. "If you watch young kittens and cubs, they learn by playing," she told *SATA*. Children, she realized, learn in much the same way. "Play is really the work of children," she explained. "It is that way that they learn and grow and develop. Too many of our children are not playing now—they are sitting watching TV; they start them early in reading and sitting at desks. I saw children who were different from that," she declared. "I saw them wanting to learn by playing. And providing that kind of play-work activity for them was the thing that inspired me."

Walter was so inspired that she started writing children's books. "I didn't want to do it," she told *SATA*. "I didn't think I could become a writer. I was interested in teaching—I was interested in books about and by black people for my students, who were all black." As late as the 1960s, however, hardly any such books existed. One day she found herself talking to Dick Lewis, a book salesman who owned part of the local publishing house of Ward Ritchie Press. "I asked him to meet that need," she recalled in her autobiography. "He suggested that I write those books. I felt he was passing the buck and told him so. He insisted." Soon Walter was at work on *Lillie of Watts: A Birthday Discovery.* The title character, a girl who has just turned eleven, finds out that the love within her family is a source of strength that can help her to cope with money troubles and the other struggles of life in her neighborhood. Reviewers praised Walter for her ability to understand and accurately portray the concerns of her characters. She soon followed the book with a sequel, *Lillie of Watts Takes a Giant Step,* in which Lillie stands up for her heritage by joining a campaign to celebrate the birthday of black leader Malcolm X at her school.

As someone who became an author in spite of herself, Walter had some special advice for aspiring writers. "The first book is very difficult," she cautioned in her *SATA* interview. "You're not just writing for yourself. Although you might understand what you are writing very well, somebody else picks it up and they don't! They ask you so many questions that you realize that you haven't really said what you wanted people to understand." In the long run, Walter observed, "you have to have more than a story to tell—you have to have a love for telling a story, a love for words to make that story come alive." Writing, she explained, is like carpentry—there are a lot of basic skills to master before you can do your work with confidence and add the special touches that are distinctively your own. "You have to keep doing pieces of work before you become the *artist*—and that's what every writer strives for."

A writer, Walter learned, also has to be resilient, because getting published is a continual struggle. After *Lillie of Watts Takes a Giant Step* appeared in 1971, Walter saw the market for her work disappear. "In the late sixties it had been less difficult for writers of color to get published because of the great demand for books by and about them," she explained in her autobiography. "President [Lyndon] Johnson, in his push for equality in education, had pressured Congress to allot a great sum of money for books and other materials for schools serving people of color. In the seventies these programs were drastically cut. Opportunities for black writers lessened."

Walter found that the friendship and support of other writers and editors could help her through the impasse. After moving to Colorado in 1970 she encountered Mary Elting and Franklin Folsom, a pair of well-established children's authors who gave her a scholarship to attend writing workshops and polish her skills. At one such workshop she met Frances Keene, a former editor from New York who introduced her to several colleagues back East. Eventually Walter piqued the interest of a number of New York editors—including several African Americans—who remained willing, in spite of the times, to encourage writers of color. One editor was Ray Shepard, who worked on reading textbooks for the publishers of *Scholastic* magazine. He asked Walter to write a lively easy reader that became *The Liquid Trap,* the story of a girl in Louisiana's bayou country who has a suspenseful escape from a quicksand hole. Shepard also showed Walter's work to editors at *Scholastic*'s Four Winds Press, which published general-interest books for children. Four Winds editor Barbara Lalicki encouraged Walter to turn some of her own childhood memories into a storybook for the young. The work was published in 1980 as *Ty's One-Man Band*—Walter's first mass-market children's book in almost ten years.

Ty's One-Man Band begins on a hot, slow summer day, when young Ty has "nothing fun to do." He heads for a local pond to cool off in the shade, and there he spots Andro, a one-legged man who apparently travels from place to place with all his belongings in a bag slung over his back. Andro calls himself a one-man band, and he offers to perform if Ty will meet him in town that evening with a few simple items: a washboard, a wooden spoon, a tin pail, and a comb. Ty's family can scarcely accept the story when he rushes home—"How can he make music with just those old things?" his father asks—but they lend him what he needs anyway. That night all Ty's friends are laughing at him in disbelief, but then Andro appears and soon has the whole town dancing. At the end of the story, only Ty sees Andro "slip away back into the night," leaving as mysteriously as he came. Reviewers were charmed with *Ty's One-Man Band.* "[It] has a magical quality," said a writer for *Booklist,* hailing the book as "a fine work, with music of its own."

Walter so enjoyed working with Lalicki on *Ty's One-Man Band* that she sought out the editor with further book projects for years thereafter, even when Lalicki moved on to new jobs at the Lothrop and Bradbury publishing houses. What's it like for a writer to work with a good editor? "It's very much like having a good relationship with members of your family," Walter told

SATA. "It's like handing over your child to an aunt or a cousin or a grandmother—you say: 'Here he is, I have done the best I can to make him a healthy, well-behaved child, so I hope you will enjoy taking care of him.' When you give a book to your editor, it's like saying: 'This is my creation, I have done the best that I could to make it beautiful, artistic, and honest. Going out into the world it will do well because many will love it.' If the editor doesn't love that creation"—or if she loves it so much that she tries to make it her personal property—"that breaks your heart because that is all you have of yourself." Fortunately, Walter continued, "I have not had that kind of relationship with editors. They have helped me to make my work better the way that I want it to go. And that's the way it is within a family: they help you to bring your child up the way *you* feel is the best way—giving advice, shaping here and there, but always with you in control of your creation."

As the 1980s began Walter focused on writing novels for young people. Her years of struggle and training paid off as she developed a distinctive voice as an author. "If there is any one theme that runs through my work it is the dynamics of choice, courage, and change," she wrote in her autobiography. "My characters must make choices," she explained to *SATA,* "and once they have made those choices they have to work them through. That's what life is—making a series of choices—and people who cannot choose for themselves don't grow."

The Girl on the Outside (1982) shows two teenage girls who gain new maturity by making important moral choices. The novel was inspired by the early years of the civil rights struggle in the 1950s, when the segregated public schools of Little Rock, Arkansas—well-funded for whites and poorly funded for blacks—were integrated by court order to provide an equal education for all children. Set in the fictional town of Mossville, the book has two main characters whose lives gradually intertwine. Eva Collins, with encouragement from her parents and her minister, agrees to become one of the first African American students at Mossville's Chatman High School. As the school year approaches, she dreads the growing anger among the white community but feels duty-bound to fulfill the hopes that her own community has for her: with calm courage, she must prove by her actions that the cause of equality is just. "Most of the students [at Chatman] really have not decided whether they want you there, or not," says a civil rights activist who advises Eva and her friends. "So you must act in a way that, if they have to take sides, they'll choose *our* side." Meanwhile Sophia Stuart, daughter of a wealthy white family, cannot accept the coming of outsiders to the closed, predictable world of her high school. But when Eva arrives at the school steps and prays to God for help as she is attacked by an angry white mob, Sophia is so moved that—much to her own surprise—she helps Eva to safety. Elizabeth Muther of the *Christian Science Monitor* wrote that *The Girl on the Outside* was "well crafted and focused" and "sizzling with details" that young adult readers would enjoy.

In several of Walter's novels, the characters grow as people while they learn about their African American heritage. As the grandfather says in *Justin and the Best Biscuits in the World,* "you must know where you've come from in order to find the way to where you want to go." The title character of *Justin* is a ten-year-old boy whose father has died and left him without a man to look up to. Picked on by his sisters because he is clumsy at household chores, he rebels by acting as irresponsible as he dares and declaring that all housework is "women's work." Finally Justin finds a role model in his own grandfather, a black cowboy who takes him to his Missouri ranch and convinces him that cowboys are strong, self-sufficient men partly because they know how to cook their own food and otherwise care for themselves. Justin also learns about the origins of black cowboys: they were freed slaves who braved racist opposition in order to move west, buy land, and run their own farms. The high point of the book comes when Justin and his grandfather attend a black rodeo, where Justin wins several prizes for playing classic farm games like horseshoe pitching and his grandfather wins a cooking prize for "the best biscuits in the world." (The recipe was inspired by Walter's own father—"I guess the idea is really rooted in me," she told *SATA,* "that fathers make good biscuits.") Justin masters biscuit-making, goes back home, and proves to his sisters that he can take care of himself—even in a kitchen. *Justin* earned Walter national acclaim when it won the 1987 Coretta Scott King Award.

But Walter couldn't attend the meeting where she was granted the prize. An experienced traveler, she had accepted an invitation to visit what was then the Soviet Union and join a march in favor of world peace. "I had to choose between going on the walk or going to the awards ceremony," she recalled in her autobiography. "This was the kind of choice my characters have had to make." So she wrote a speech, which was later read at the ceremony by the editor in chief of the Lothrop publishing house. "What ... is most in keeping with the spirit of the Coretta Scott King Award," the speech asked—"accepting the award in person, or putting myself wholly on the line to make a statement that the nuclear arms race must end if we are to survive? My answer came. I chose to walk."

Walter had been traveling since the days of her marriage, part of an ongoing effort to broaden her understanding of people—and of herself. She and her husband "started out by seeing every state in the Union," she told *SATA.* "We would go to all the national parks and everywhere. Then we went to Mexico, Canada, and the Caribbean Islands. We were preparing to go to Africa the year he died. We wanted to know our country very well so that when we went overseas we would have a sense of who we were in terms of being American." Why travel? "Places and people give me a sense of who I am very much," Walter said. "They help me in their differences to see who I really am."

Walter's most important journey probably occurred in 1977, when she first visited Africa as an American delegate to the Second World Black and African Festival of the Arts and Culture (FESTAC). She found that her encounter with Africa, like her work with the civil rights movement, inspired mixed emotions. Her first feeling was elation, because reaching Africa allowed her to vanquish some unpleasant memories of her childhood. As a young girl, she explained in her autobiography, "myths about the inferiority of blackness weighed heavily upon me.... Pictures then showed Africans as uncivilized, half-naked with elongated lips, and with bones in their noses. Scenes from the so-called dark continent provoked nervous, boisterous laughter.... I knew but repressed knowing that I was treated inferiorly because, somehow, I was connected to that place that was so terribly ridiculed." Landing in Africa with the FESTAC delegation refuted all those childhood memories at once. "We were met and surrounded by smiling faces that looked very much like people I already knew, people who were near and dear to me," she recalled. "An overwhelming feeling brought tears of joy as I joined others in our delegation in a chant: 'We're home! We're home!'"

But Walter soon realized that for an American descendant of African slaves, going "home" to Africa wasn't so simple. African writers, she found, sometimes didn't want black Americans to join their groups—how could an American be an African? The African tourguide who showed Walter through a slave-traders' fortress seemed to feel little identification with the Africans who had been kidnapped and forced into slavery in the New World. "The brutal events of slavery," Walter decided in her autobiography, "had created a situation of grief and pain that made it impossible for our African relatives to keep us in mind, to carry memories and hopes of our return. Imagine knowing that thousands were disappearing with no knowledge or word of one return!" Walter concluded that she wasn't simply "African" or "American," but a unique mixture of the two. "Caught between two cultures," she wrote, "I had an opportunity to choose the best from each."

What did she choose? From Africa, Walter chose the spirit of community, a spirit of closeness and unity much like what she knew when she was growing up. In African philosophies, she told *SATA,* there is a feeling "that we are one with all living things"—the kind of feeling that caused all the people in her neighborhood to look out for her. "Religion is not a Sunday thing, but an everyday thing, interwoven with your life," just as religious values pervaded her childhood. "Art is interwoven with your life"—just as the people she grew up with could entertain one another with stories, dance, and song. "In America," she continued, "I like the *idea* of freedom, the idea of freedom is a great idea, the idea of democracy is a powerful idea. African Americans," she declared, "have the kind of heritage that could make a powerful community, a powerful statement about what life could be. If we could combine what we bring from the Mother Land with what exists in this new land, we could have it all."

Inspired by Walter's interest in African folk tales, *Brother to the Wind* tells how the wind accepts young Emeke as a brother and enables him to fly. (Cover illustration by Diane and Leo Dillon.)

Fulfilling that dream, Walter knows, will be a great struggle—especially for younger African Americans. The obstacles that confronted her in her youth, Walter told *SATA,* "were *nothing* like what they see today. We had poverty of course, but we were *together.*" Years ago, she said, African Americans "were in small communities. We were an agrarian people, close to the land. We had a warmth, a feeling...." With her whole community urging her to succeed, "I *had* to do it in spite of the Depression." But since then, she continued, "we have come into an urban world where we are alienated—where there is no time to care about other people's children. There seems to be a fear of caring, a fear of knowing what's going on, and our children are suffering from that. They are not given direct care—I mean discipline that comes from the community." As a result, Walter declared, "Our children are suffering. They don't know boundaries in terms of behavior, and they are *longing* for those boundaries. They need maps and there is nobody to give them that, and when you do not have maps on the road you are lost."

"My greatest concern for African Americans," Walter continued, "is that we lose this uniqueness that we have—the spontaneity, the laughter, the loving, and the caring that we as a people always had. That we will lose the idea of the extended family, which goes from the immediate family into the community. My greatest hope, of course, is that those of us who have the knowledge of who we were and are—in terms of caring

Holidays bring all kinds of happiness... Sometimes when you least expect it

Have A Happy...

by Coretta Scott King Award-winning author
Mildred Pitts Walter
Illustrated by Carole Byard

AVON
CAMELOT
$2.95 U.S.

In Walter's *Have a Happy,* Chris finds a special joy in Kwanzaa—a celebration of his African heritage that stresses such traditional virtues as faith, self-determination, and cooperation with others. (Cover illustration by Carole Byard.)

and supporting and giving our children values—will share what we know with our children and with the world, and make for a peaceful place for all children. I hope that we as African Americans, who came unwillingly to this country but stayed and carved out a way of life that is unique and has wonderful values, will cling to that, and spread it, and share it."

So Walter shares the strength of her heritage through her books. In *Have A Happy ...,* eleven-year-old Chris and his family find the strength to weather tough economic times as they celebrate Kwanzaa, an African American holiday that commemorates traditional African virtues such as *imani* (faith), *umoja* (unity), and *ujima* (collective work and responsibility). Chris wants a bicycle so he can earn money as a paperboy, but his unemployed father can't afford it; in accord with the principles of Kwanzaa, relatives chip in to give Chris the bike, and Chris, in turn, helps his father to get a job supervising him and the other news carriers. "I was thinking about children whose parents are out of work," Walter told *SATA.* "I wanted them to feel that they were not alone, that this *is* happening, and that they can find strength in wanting to help and support the family."

"There are some wonderful things happening in the realm of children's books," Walter told *SATA*—"books that are dealing with real issues, dealing with history, talking directly to children, telling them about things they can really relate to." However, she noted, "all the different cultures are not well represented. Less than one percent of American authors are people of color. In terms of diversity I don't think we have reached the golden age yet." What should be done? "First of all," Walter observed, "we should get some of these diverse people into the publishing business as readers, as receptionists, as editors, as vice presidents. Then the material that is coming from people of color would have a better chance of being read with a different perspective. If you have a friend in the business, or a person who is like you, and they see that you have potential, they can help you—they will take the time." And that's important, for Walter, because children's books are so important. "Children's literature is the only true literature now," she said, because it is willing—unlike many movies, television shows, or books for adults—to teach positive values. "Children's books," Walter declared, "are really the mainstay of our literature."

WORKS CITED:

Muther, Elizabeth, "Novel of Courage, Determination," *Christian Science Monitor,* October 8, 1982, p. B11.
Review of *Ty's One-Man Band, Booklist,* September 15, 1980, p. 122-23.
Walter, Mildred Pitts, *The Girl on the Outside,* Lothrop, 1982.
Walter, interview by telephone with Thomas Kozikowski for *Something about the Author,* August 6, 1991.
Walter, *Justin and the Best Biscuits in the World,* Lothrop, 1986.
Walter, *Something about the Author Autobiography Series,* Volume 12, Gale, 1991, pp. 283-301.
Walter, *Ty's One-Man Band,* Four Winds Press, 1980.

FOR MORE INFORMATION SEE:

BOOKS

Children's Literature Review, Volume 15, Gale, 1988.

PERIODICALS

Booklist, November 1, 1983, p. 404; September 1, 1989, p. 82; April 15, 1990, p. 1636.
Bulletin of the Center for Children's Books, November, 1982, p. 58.
English Journal, March, 1972, p. 435.
Horn Book, July, 1985, p. 446; March, 1989, p. 212.
Kirkus Reviews, July 1, 1988, p. 979; August 1, 1989, p. 1170.
Library Journal, February 15, 1970, p. 782.
New York Times Book Review, October 12, 1980, p. 39.
Publishers Weekly, April 14, 1969, p. 97; July 29, 1988, p. 234.
School Library Journal, March, 1983, p. 167; October, 1985, p. 188; April, 1990, p. 100.
Wilson Library Bulletin, June, 1990, p. 117.

—Sketch by Thomas Kozikowski

ANN E. WEISS

WEISS, Ann E. 1943-

PERSONAL: Full name is Ann Edwards Weiss; born March 21, 1943, in Newton, MA; daughter of Donald Loring (a teacher) and Dorothy (a teacher; maiden name, Poole) Charlton; married Malcolm E. Weiss (a writer), January 31, 1966; children: Margot Elizabeth, Rebecca Bates. *Education:* Pembroke College (now Brown University), A.B., 1965.

CAREER: Scholastic Magazines, Inc., New York City, writer and assistant editor, 1965-69, associate editor, 1969-72; free-lance writer, 1972—.

AWARDS, HONORS: Christopher Award, 1974, for *Save the Mustangs,* 1984, for *The Nuclear Arms Race,* and 1989, for *Lies, Deception, and Truth; Save the Mustangs, The School on Madison Avenue, God and Government, The Supreme Court,* and *Prisons* were named notable children's trade books in the field of social studies by the National Council on the Social Studies and Children's Book Council for 1974, 1978, 1982, 1987, and 1988, respectively; Outstanding Science Trade Book for Children Award, National Science Teachers Association Children's Book Council, 1976, for *The Vitamin Puzzle* and 1981, for *The Nuclear Question.*

WRITINGS:

NONFICTION; FOR CHILDREN AND YOUNG ADULTS

Five Roads to the White House, Messner, 1970.
We Will Be Heard: Dissent in the United States, Messner, 1972.
Save the Mustangs! How a Federal Law Is Passed, Messner, 1974.
(With husband, Malcolm E. Weiss) *The Vitamin Puzzle,* Messner, 1976.
The American Presidency, Messner, 1976.

The American Congress, Messner, 1977.
News or Not? Facts and Feelings in the News Media, Dutton, 1977.
Polls and Surveys: A Look at Public Opinion Research, F. Watts, 1979.
The School on Madison Avenue: Advertising and What It Teaches, Dutton, 1979.
What's That You Said? How Words Change, illustrated by Jim Arnosky, Harcourt, 1980.
Party Politics, Party Problems, Harper, 1980.
The Nuclear Question, Harcourt, 1981.
Tune In, Tune Out: Broadcasting Regulation in the United States, Houghton, 1981.
God and Government: The Separation of Church and State, Houghton, 1982.
The Nuclear Arms Race: Can We Survive It?, Houghton, 1983.
Over-the-Counter Drugs, F. Watts, 1984.
Biofeedback: Fact or Fad?, F. Watts, 1984.
Bioethics: Dilemmas in Modern Medicine, Enslow Publishers, 1985.
Good Neighbors? The U.S. and Latin America, Houghton, 1985.
Seers and Scientists: Can the Future Be Predicted?, illustrated by Paul Plumer, Harcourt, 1986.
The Supreme Court, Enslow Publishers, 1988.
Prisons: A System in Trouble, Enslow Publishers, 1988.
Lies, Deception, and Truth, Houghton, 1988.
Who's to Know? Information, the Media, and Public Awareness, Houghton, 1990.
Welfare: Helping Hand or Trap?, Enslow Publishers, 1990.
Lotteries: Who Wins, Who Loses?, Enslow Publishers, 1991.

WORK IN PROGRESS: A book about "the business of sports."

SIDELIGHTS: Ann E. Weiss is known for her thought-provoking yet accessible books for children and young adults. In her numerous nonfiction works, Weiss explores contemporary topics such as nuclear weapons, medical ethics, advertising, politics, U.S. prisons, and the public welfare system. The author highlights the complexities of these often controversial issues, encouraging readers to discuss them and form their own opinions. Weiss's work has earned several honors, including three Christopher awards.

Born in Newton, Massachusetts, Weiss grew up in the town of Rockland, in the house where her mother was born. She lived with her parents, grandfather, and younger brother, and recalls that reading and storytelling were important aspects of her youth. Weiss noted in *Something about the Author Autobiography Series* (*SAAS*) that "I grew up surrounded by books in a family of readers, and find it impossible to remember a time when I wasn't snuggled up next to someone being read aloud to."

Her grandfather, Gang, amused her with stories of her ancestors and eventually taught her to read. "I'm not sure whether he really set out to," explained Weiss in

Weiss probes the concept of scientific and mystic prediction in *Seers and Scientists,* encouraging her readers to form their own opinions with the possibilities set before them.

SAAS. "Mostly I just watched the pages as he read, and, gradually, sounds and printed words began to make sense together." Gang was well read and provided Weiss with background information on a variety of subjects, from history to science to mythology. In *SAAS* the author credited her grandfather with "spark[ing] my interest in looking beneath surfaces and in examining and asking questions instead of simply accepting other people's assumptions and assertions."

As a child, Weiss enjoyed creating stories to entertain her brother at bedtime. Later she found she relished writing factual pieces and joined the staff of her high school newspaper. In addition, Weiss remarked in *SAAS* that in school she "honestly enjoyed writing essays and research papers. It was fun looking up information, discovering how I felt about it, organizing it, then putting it back down on paper in a way that made it my own."

The daughter of two college graduates, Weiss planned to continue her education after high school. Her mother had attended Pembroke College (now Brown University) and Weiss decided to do so as well. She intended to major in English literature and find a job in publishing upon graduation, because "working with words was

something I liked doing," she commented in *SAAS*. "I was never particularly athletic, or social, or musical, or artistic, but writing came naturally to me and I could always put words together in a way that brought me great delight."

When she graduated from college in 1965, Weiss headed for New York City, intending to start her career by becoming a secretary at a publishing company. She told *SAAS* that at the time she had no "delusions of grandeur about becoming an author.... Being 'in publishing,' handling books, and perhaps meeting the occasional writer, that seemed ambition enough." The author's hopes of being a secretary for a publishing company were not realized, however, since "each publisher's interview had turned out to include a spelling quiz, and I cannot spell." Weiss then applied for a position as a writer at Scholastic Magazines, a company that published current events newsletters for children. She submitted two sample articles to the company (after having a friend check her spelling) and was hired.

Weiss found that Scholastic was an ideal place to polish her writing skills. Writing for children was a challenge; she was often required to write short, simple articles about complex world events. Weiss maintains that children are a difficult audience to write for because they do not have the background knowledge of adults. In *SAAS* she declared that "anyone who can write for children will have little difficulty writing for adults. Most people think it's the other way around.... If only they knew how wrong they are."

Scholastic writers and editors often free-lanced and wrote books in their spare time. One such person was Malcolm E. Weiss, a science writer whom Weiss met at Scholastic and married in 1966. After the birth of their first child, Malcolm urged Weiss to speak to a publisher about writing a book. He proposed that such a project would keep her from being bored during her three-month maternity leave. Weiss agreed and submitted a sample chapter to editor Lee Hoffman. Typically editors wish to see a sample chapter and an outline of a projected book before recommending that the author proceed. "In my case, Lee was unsure," admitted Weiss in *SAAS*. "Still, after several false starts, we agreed to go ahead."

The result was *Five Roads to the White House,* written "partly in longhand, and partly on an old sticky-keyed manual typewriter perched on a flimsy TV table in front of Malcolm's and my living room couch," commented Weiss in *SAAS*. "By the time I began work on the actual book, Margot was six months old and I was back at Scholastic, so I did most of my writing at night." Weiss later found that she was able to write on the bus to and from work as well as in the playground where she often spent time with her daughter.

Five Roads to the White House, which contains short biographies of presidents Franklin D. Roosevelt, Harry S Truman, Dwight D. Eisenhower, John F. Kennedy, and Lyndon B. Johnson, was published in 1970. Since then, Weiss has written more than twenty books, generating ideas from a variety of sources. Some books were written at the suggestions of editors—*Five Roads to the White House, Bioethics: Dilemmas in Modern Medicine,* and *Lies, Deception, and Truth* came about in this manner. Other books were derived from what Weiss calls the "indignation factor." She declared in *SAAS* that "sometimes as I read the newspaper, I get so annoyed at something—or so downright angry—that I dash off an outline and send it to an editor I suspect feels the way I do about the topic." This approach has resulted in books such as *The Nuclear Arms Race: Can We Survive It?* and *Prisons: A System in Trouble.* Sometimes Weiss obtains book ideas from her earlier works. She explained in *SAAS* that "after finishing *Prisons,* I found myself pondering the social conditions—poverty, joblessness, and lack of opportunity—that are one reason so many Americans land behind bars." Her interest in the subject led her to write *Welfare: Helping Hand or Trap?*

Weiss was even inspired to write a book by a class of Oregon fourth-graders. When she worked at Scholastic, she received letters from the class describing their efforts to persuade the U.S. Congress to enact a law protecting the nation's wild horses, animals that were often hunted for sport or for use in pet food. The

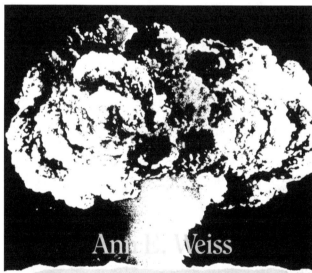

This chronicle of the nuclear arms race originated in the author's indignation at current events.

children's campaign was successful, and they hoped their story would appear in Scholastic's *Explorer* magazine. The story did appear in the magazine as well as in Weiss's book, *Save the Mustangs! How a Federal Law Is Passed.* In it the author describes the children's undertaking, using their story to illustrate how laws are formed in the United States.

Reviewers have praised Weiss for her clear writing style and her ability to inform and interest readers. She is also lauded for addressing issues objectively, though she observed in *SAAS* that "it is impossible to write on any subject without expressing an opinion about it." The author continued, "My opinions are there, but I don't 'put' them in [my books]. I do, however, make every effort to present other people's points of view about whatever subject I'm working on."

Weiss clearly enjoys writing and has commented to *SATA* that "my favorite 'hobby' is what I do for a living—reading and writing books." She described her *School on Madison Avenue: Advertising and What It Teaches* as the book she had the most fun writing. "I found myself simultaneously appalled and amused by advertising, and I wrote the book in a series of gasps and giggles," the author once remarked to *SATA.* Weiss continues to write prolifically, noting in *SAAS* that "I enjoy more than ever transforming words into sentences, paragraphs, chapters, [and] books." When asked what she would be doing if she were not a writer, she responded in *SAAS:* "I can't imagine."

WORKS CITED:

Something about the Author, Volume 30, Gale, 1983, pp. 205-06.
Weiss, Ann E., essay in *Something about the Author Autobiography Series,* Volume 13, Gale, 1991, pp. 247-62.

FOR MORE INFORMATION SEE:

PERIODICALS

Booklist, March 15, 1974; February 1, 1980; May 15, 1984; February 15, 1987; October 1, 1990.
Bulletin of the Center for Children's Books, November, 1982; April, 1987; October, 1988.
Horn Book, August, 1982; January, 1987; July, 1990.
Kirkus Reviews, October 1, 1970; June 15, 1977; November 15, 1977.
School Library Journal, February, 1980; February, 1981; September, 1981; November, 1981; March, 1982; September, 1984; December, 1985; February, 1987; March, 1987; November, 1988; May, 1989; May, 1990; June, 1990.
Voice of Youth Advocates, December, 1985; February, 1989.

—Sketch by Michelle M. Motowski

WELLS, Rosemary 1943-

PERSONAL: Born January 29, 1943, in New York City; married Thomas Moore Wells (an architect), 1963; children: Victoria, Marguerite. *Education:* Studied at the Museum School in Boston, MA.

ADDRESSES: Home—732 Sleepy Hollow Rd., Briarcliff Manor, NY 10510.

CAREER: Allyn and Bacon, Inc., Boston, MA, art editor; Macmillan Publishing Co., Inc., New York City, art designer; free-lance author and illustrator, 1968—. *Exhibitions:* The American Institute of Graphic Arts displayed *Morris's Disappearing Bag* in the Bias-Free Illustration Show and included *Impossible Possum, Noisy Nora, Max's Toys,* and *Two Sisters and Some Hornets* in the Children's Book Shows.

AWARDS, HONORS: Children's Book Showcase award, Children's Book Council, 1974, for *Noisy Nora;* Art Book for Children citation, Brooklyn Museum and Brooklyn Public Library, 1975, 1976, 1977, for *Benjamin and Tulip;* Irma Simonton Black Award, for *Benjamin and Tulip,* and 1975, for *Morris's Disappearing Bag: A Christmas Story;* runner-up for Edgar Allan Poe award, Mystery Writers of America, for *Through the Hidden Door,* and 1981, for *When No One Was Looking; Hazel's Amazing Mother* was named one of the *New York Times* Best Illustrated Books, 1985; Washington Irving Children's Book Choice Award, Westchester Library Association, 1986, for *Peabody,* and 1988, for *Max's Christmas;* Boston Globe-Horn Book Award, 1989, for *Shy Charles.*

Noisy Nora, Morris's Disappearing Bag, Leave Well Enough Alone, Stanley and Rhoda, Max's Toys, Max's Breakfast, Max's Bedtime, Max's Bath, When No One Was Looking, Max's Christmas, Shy Charles, and *Max's*

ROSEMARY WELLS

Chocolate Chicken were named among the best books of the year by *School Library Journal;* American Library Association (ALA) Notable Book citations for *Noisy Nora, Benjamin and Tulip, Morris's Disappearing Bag, Max's Breakfast, Max's Christmas, Max's Chocolate Chicken,* and *Max's Dragon Shirt;* ALA Best Books for Young Adults citation for *Through the Hidden Door; Bulletin of the Center for Children's Books* Blue Ribbon for *The Little Lame Prince;* American Bookseller Pick of the Lists citations for *Abdul, Stanley and Rhoda, Goodnight Fred, Timothy Goes to School, A Lion for Lewis, Forest of Dreams,* and *Max's Chocolate Chicken; Booklist* Children's Editor's Choice citations for *Max's Toys, Timothy Goes to School,* and *Through the Hidden Door;* Child Study Association Children's Books of the Year citations for *Morris's Disappearing Bag* and *Don't Spill It Again, James; Horn Book* Fanfare citation and West Australian Young Readers' Book Award, both for *When No One Was Looking;* Virginia Young Readers Award and New York Public Library Books for Teenagers citation, both for *The Man in the Woods;* Parents' Choice Award, Parents' Choice Foundation, for *Shy Charles;* Golden Kite Award, Society of Children's Book Writers, and International Reading Association Teacher's Choices List, both for *Forest of Dreams;* International Reading Association Children's Choices citation for *Max's Chocolate Chicken;* International Reading Association/Children's Book Council Children's Choice citations for *Timothy Goes to School, A Lion for Lewis,* and *Peabody;* Cooperative Children's Book Center citation for *Max's Bedtime.*

WRITINGS:

The Fog Comes on Little Pig Feet, Dial, 1972.
None of the Above, Dial, 1974.
Leave Well Enough Alone, Dial, 1977.
When No One Was Looking, Dial, 1980.
The Man in the Woods, Dial, 1984.
Through the Hidden Door, Dial, 1987.
Forest of Dreams, illustrated by Susan Jeffers, Dial, 1988.
(With Joanna Hurley) *Cooking for Nitwits,* Dutton, 1989.

SELF-ILLUSTRATED

Martha's Birthday, Bradbury, 1970.
Miranda's Pilgrims, Bradbury, 1970.
Unfortunately Harriet, Dial, 1972.
Benjamin and Tulip, Dial, 1973.
Noisy Nora, Dial, 1973.
Abdul, Dial, 1975.
Morris's Disappearing Bag: A Christmas Story, Dial, 1975.
Don't Spill It Again, James, Dial, 1977.
Stanley and Rhoda, Dial, 1978.
Good Night, Fred, Dial, 1981.
Timothy Goes to School, Dial, 1981.
A Lion for Lewis, Dial, 1982.
Peabody, Dial, 1983.
Hazel's Amazing Mother, Dial, 1985.
Shy Charles, Dial, 1988.
The Little Lame Prince, Dial, 1990.

In Wells's self-illustrated *Good Night Fred,* a young boy's imagination helps him to conquer his fears in the night.

Fritz and the Mess Fairy, Dial, 1991.
Voyage to the Bunny Planet, Dial, 1992.

Also authored several self-illustrated books in the late 1960s.

"MAX" SERIES; SELF-ILLUSTRATED

Max's First Word, Dial, 1979.
Max's New Suit, Dial, 1979.
Max's Ride, Dial, 1979.
Max's Toys: A Counting Book, Dial, 1979.
Max's Bath, Dial, 1985.
Max's Bedtime, Dial, 1985.
Max's Breakfast, Dial, 1985.
Max's Birthday, Dial, 1985.
Hooray for Max, Dial, 1986.
Max's Christmas, Dial, 1986.
Max's Chocolate Chicken, Dial, 1989.
Max's Dragon Shirt, Dial, 1991.

ILLUSTRATOR

Williams Schwenck Gilbert and Arthur Sullivan, *A Song to Sing, O!* (from *Yeoman of the Guard*), Macmillan, 1968.
Gilbert and Sullivan, *W.S. Gilbert's "The Duke of Plaza Toro"* (from *The Gondoliers*), Macmillan, 1969.
Paula Fox, *Hungry Fred,* Bradbury, 1969.
Ellen Conford, *Impossible Possum,* Little, Brown, 1971.
Virginia A. Tashjian, editor, *With a Deep-Sea Smile: Story Hour Stretches for Large or Small Groups,* Little, Brown, 1974.
Lore G. Segal, *Tell Me a Trudy,* Farrar, Straus, 1977.

Also illustrator of books written by Robert William Service, Charlotte Pomerantz, Rudyard Kipling, Winifred Rosen Casey, Marjorie Weinman Sharmat, Beryl Williams, and Dorrit Davis.

ADAPTATIONS: Max's Christmas and *Morris's Disappearing Bag* have been adapted as short films by Weston Woods.

SIDELIGHTS: "I am firmly convinced that the story comes first," author/illustrator Rosemary Wells declared of the relationship between text and pictures in children's books in an article for *Publishers Weekly.* "The child may be charmed, intrigued or even inspired by good illustration, but it is the sound of the words and the story that first holds the child's attention." However, while storyline might be responsible for first attracting children to a particular book, Wells asserted in an essay for *Something about the Author Autobiography Series* (*SAAS*) that in order of development, "writing is always the last of the arts to show up as a talent in children." She also stated that "very few young people who grow up to be writers know this lies in store for them, even if they write reams and reams. Young writers do odd things that they almost never acknowledge. They listen compulsively to other people's conversations (eavesdropping) and become so proficient at this (and at concealing it) that they are virtually human video tape recorders." The author further commented that in contrast to the secrecy and late development of writing, "drawing is quite different. Children who draw well early, like children who play music or hit a baseball three hundred feet, are noticed, complimented, and ascribed a future. They are called 'talented.'" Evaluating her present abilities, Wells, who is the creator of the popular "Max" series of board books for very young children as well as the author of several young adult novels, stated: "I can say the writing is the better part of my skills. I try mightily to improve my illustrations but writing is much easier."

Wells studied at the museum school in Boston in the early sixties. Never a good student in any institution, she was not at home with the abstract expressionism that was then in vogue. Wells told *SATA* that as an illustrator she could not find instruction in technique that disregarded representational drawing. When one of her professors dismissed her as "nothing but an illustrator," Wells lost patience. She left the school in 1963. That same year she married Tom Wells, who was then a student at Dartmouth College, and began a career as a book designer at Allyn and Bacon. She referred to her hiring at Allyn and Bacon as "my first lucky break and the only one I ever needed." When her husband became an architecture student in New York, Wells joined the staff of Macmillan, a New York publishing company. The author said of her time at Macmillan: "I began to learn the art of book design. One day when I was on staff as a designer at Macmillan I presented a small illustrated dummy of a Gilbert and Sullivan song to the editor-in-chief. It was published and I was on my way." Also at Macmillan, Wells met Susan Jeffers, who has collaborated with her on several picture books.

Wells developed her understanding of story structure from the theater: "I learned almost everything I know about poetry from memorizing lyrics of Broadway musicals," she told *SATA.* "I learned much about

From Wells's award-winning *Max's Christmas*, an illustration of Max, the inspiration of two films and a doll.

comedy from Sid Caesar and Imogene Coco." Writing in *SAAS*, Wells continued, "I learned much more from Sid Caesar than from Shakespeare. Those playlets ... contained the three most important ingredients for short stories (or picture-book plots): humor, recognizable characters and settings, and emotional content. They were theatre—and picture books are theatre, too." Because young children like to hear stories repeated many times, the author "began to figure out how to invent some extremely simple stories that wouldn't drive parents up the wall when they had to repeat them over and over," she revealed in an interview with *Publishers Weekly*. "I wanted to give children adventures they could understand and include jokes parents would recognize." *Bulletin of the Center for Children's Books* reviewer Zena Sutherland asserted that Wells's *Stanley & Rhoda*, in addition to entertaining young children, "is one of those unusual books that can also beguile adult readers-aloud."

Wells often uses elements of her home life in producing her picture books. "Our West Highland white terrier, Angus, had the shape and expressions to become Benjamin and Tulip, Timothy, and all the other animals I have made up for my stories," she revealed in *SAAS*. Writing in *Horn Book*, Wells commented on the origin of her popular "Max" series of books: "Many of the stories in my books come from our two children, Victoria and Beezoo [Marguerite]. Ruby and Max are Victoria and Beezoo. They appeared on my drawing board in the summer of 1977. Victoria was then five and Beezoo nine months. Victoria had taken it upon herself to teach her baby sister about the world and dragged her, like a sack of flour, because she was too heavy to really carry, from object to object shouting, 'Table, Beezoo!

say table. TA-BLE!' Beezoo did not cooperate at all and was always off in a world of her own."

Later in her *Horn Book* article, the author said of the stories about Max and Ruby: "I submitted them to my editor, Phyllis Fogelman, hesitantly because there had never been any books like them. Phyllis did not take them hesitantly." The "Max and Ruby" books were the first funny stories for very young children. In addition to being a hallmark of her own work, originality is something that Wells urges for children's literature in general. In her *Publishers Weekly* article, she asserted that "Children do not need someone else to illustrate *Alice in Wonderland, Peter Rabbit, The Wind in the Willows* or anything else that was perfectly done the first time.... There is a crying need out there for funny, original and inspired writing. Publishers are looking for it, children need it and the time is right."

In addition to writing and illustrating picture books, Wells has also written novels for teenagers. *Washington Post Book World* contributor Katherine Paterson said of the mystery *Leave Well Enough Alone:* "I began this book laughing with delight at Rosemary Wells's marvelous re-creation of fourteenness.... I ended it in goose-bumps. In between I had gobbled up red herrings like gum drops." Though Wells was brought up in a Protestant religious background, the heroine of *Leave Well Enough Alone* is an Irish-Catholic girl modeled after the author's best friend in grade school. *Leave Well Enough Alone* captured the quirks of Catholic school so well that a review of the novel "stated that the author had indisputably drawn on her Irish-Catholic background, her intimacy with nuns as teachers especially, in creating the heroine," Wells recalled in the *Publishers Weekly* interview.

"The job I have now—writing and illustrating children's books, writing novels for teenagers—is pure delight," Wells stated in an her *SAAS* essay, adding, "There are hard parts but no bad or boring parts, and that is more than can be said for any other line of work I know."

WORKS CITED:

Paterson, Katherine, "The Case of the Curious Babysitter," *Washington Post Book World,* May 1, 1977, p. E4.

Sutherland, Zena, review of *Stanley & Rhoda, Bulletin of the Center for Children's Books,* February, 1979, p. 108.

Wells, Rosemary, "The Artist at Work: The Writer at Work," *Horn Book,* March/April 1987, pp. 163-170.

Wells, Rosemary, interview with Jean F. Mercier, *Publishers Weekly,* February 29, 1980, pp. 72-73.

Wells, Rosemary, "Words & Pictures: The Right Order," *Publishers Weekly,* February 27, 1987, p. 146.

Wells, Rosemary, essay in *Something about the Author Autobiography Series,* Volume 1, Gale, 1986, pp. 279-291.

FOR MORE INFORMATION SEE:

BOOKS

Children's Literature Review, Volume 16, Gale, 1989.
Contemporary Literary Criticism, Volume 12, Gale, 1980.

PERIODICALS

Horn Book, January/February 1990.
Junior Literary Guild, September, 1977; March, 1981.
Wilson Library Bulletin, January, 1992, pp. 105-107.

*   *   *

WESTALL, Robert 1929-

PERSONAL: Full name is Robert Atkinson Westall; born October 7, 1929, in Tynemouth, England; son of Robert (a foreman and fitter at the local gas works) and Maggie Alexandra (Leggett) Westall; married Jean Underhill (an administrator), July 26, 1958 (divorced, 1990); children: Christopher (deceased). *Education:* University of Durham, B .A. (with first class honors), 1953; University of London, D.F.A., 1957. *Politics:* "Left-wing conservative." *Religion:* Church of England. *Hobbies and other interests:* Designing, building and sailing model yachts; "cats (you have to earn their friendship), old clocks, Buddhist statues, bird-watching and people-watching, other people's gardens, ruins and the sea."

ADDRESSES: Home—1, Woodland Ave., Lymm, Cheshire WA13 0BT, England.

ROBERT WESTALL

CAREER: Sir John Deane's College, Northwich, England, art teacher and head of department, 1960-85, head of careers guidance, 1970-85; antiques dealer, 1985-87; full-time writer, 1987—. Director of Telephone Samaritans of Mid-Cheshire, 1965-75. *Military service:* British Army, Royal Signals, 1953-55.

AWARDS, HONORS: Carnegie Medal from Library Association of Great Britain, 1976, for *The Machine-Gunners,* and 1982, for *The Scarecrows;* Boston *Globe/Horn Book* Honor Books citations, 1978, for *The Machine-Gunners,* 1982, for *The Scarecrows,* and 1983, for *Break of Dark; The Devil on the Road* was selected by the American Library Association as a best book for young adults, 1979; Carnegie Medal nomination, 1979, for *The Devil on the Road;* Leseratten Prize (Germany), 1988, for *The Machine-Gunners,* 1990, for *Futuretrack Five,* and 1991, for *The Promise;* Children's Book prize nomination, 1988, for *Urn Burial;* Senior Smarties Prize, 1989, and Children's Book Award commendation, both for *Blitzcat;* Carnegie Award commendation, and Sheffield Children's Book Prize, both 1991, both for *The Promise; Guardian* Award and Carnegie Award runner-up, both for *The Kingdom by the Sea.*

WRITINGS:

FICTION FOR YOUNG ADULTS

The Machine-Gunners, London, Macmillan, 1975; New York, Greenwillow, 1976.
The Wind Eye, London, Macmillan, 1976; New York, Greenwillow, 1977.
The Watch House, London, Macmillan, 1977; New York, Greenwillow, 1978.
The Devil on the Road, London, Macmillan, 1978; New York, Greenwillow, 1979.
Fathom Five, London, Macmillan, 1979; New York, Greenwillow, 1980.
The Scarecrows, London, Chatto & Windus, and New York, Greenwillow, 1980.
Break of Dark, London, Chatto & Windus, and New York, Greenwillow, 1981.
The Haunting of Chas McGill and Other Stories, London, Macmillan, and New York, Greenwillow, 1983.
Futuretrack Five, London, Kestrel, 1983; New York, Greenwillow, 1984.
The Cats of Seroster, London, Macmillan, and New York, Greenwillow, 1984.
The Other: A Christmas Story, London, Macmillan, 1985.
The Witness, London, Macmillan, 1985.
Rachel and the Angel and Other Stories, London, Macmillan, 1986; New York, Greenwillow, 1987.
Rosalie, London, Macmillan, 1987.
Urn Burial, London, Viking Kestral, 1987; New York, Greenwillow, 1988.
The Creature in the Dark, illustrated by Liz Roberts, London, Blackie, 1988.
Ghosts and Journeys, London, Macmillan, 1988.
Ghost Abbey, London, Macmillan, 1988; New York, Scholastic, 1989.

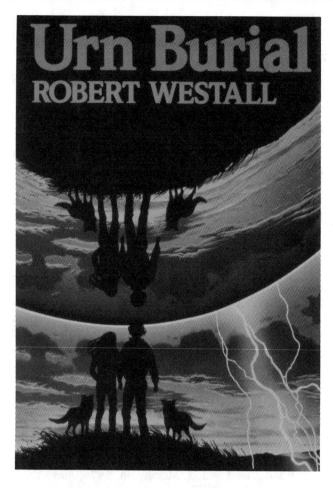

Westall's fiction ranges from historical realism to the supernatural suspense of *Urn Burial*, in which a young man opens a coffin and awakens a dangerous alien force. (Jacket illustration by Alun Hood.)

Antique Dust: Ghost Stories, London, Viking Kestral, and New York, Viking, 1989.
Blitzcat, London, Macmillan, 1989; New York, Scholastic, 1990.
Old Man on a Horse, London, Blackie, 1989.
A Walk on the Wild Side, London, Methuen, 1989.
The Call, London, Viking Kestral, 1989.
Echoes of War, London, Viking Kestral, 1989.
Cat!, London, Methuen, 1989.
The Kingdom by the Sea, London, Methuen, 1990; New York, Farrar, Straus, 1991.
Stormsearch, London, Blackie, 1990.
If Cats Could Fly...?, London, Methuen, 1990.
The Promise, New York, Scholastic, 1991.
The Christmas Cat, London, Methuen, 1991.
The Stones of Muncaster Cathedral, London, Kestral, 1991.
Yaxley's Cat, London, Macmillan, 1991; New York, Scholastic, 1992.
The Fearful Lovers, London, Macmillan, 1992.
Size Twelve, London, Heinemann, 1992.
The Ghost in the Tower, London, Methuen, 1992.
A Place for Me, London, Macmillan, 1993.

OTHER

(Editor) *Children of the Blitz: Memories of Wartime Childhood,* London, Viking, 1985.
The Machine-Gunners (play; adapted from his own story), London, Macmillan, 1986.

Staff writer for *Cheshire Life,* 1968-71. Art and architecture critic for *Chester Chronicle,* 1962-73; art critic for *Guardian,* 1970, 1980.

WORK IN PROGRESS: A book about horror in a shipbreaker's yard.

SIDELIGHTS: Robert Westall is one of the most original and controversial novelists for young adults writing today. His books range from the realistic fiction of the Carnegie Award-winning *The Machine-Gunners* and *The Scarecrows* to the historical fantasy *The Devil on the Road* and the terrifying future society of *Futuretrack Five.* Although some critics protest Westall's use of violence and swearing, many others celebrate his versatility and uncompromising depictions of youth caught in struggle.

Robert Westall commented, "Since I write for young people, I have always used the experiences of my own childhood a lot—a childhood growing more distant all the time. A childhood where everybody over the age of fourteen expected to have a job. A childhood where our fathers understood nearly all the factors in their lives that could affect them, and could largely control them. My father needed to understand four things to feel secure: the machinery of the works where he was foreman, the plants in his large garden, the world of buying and selling, and the temperament of my mother. All these he managed pretty well."

Westall goes into more detail about his relationship with his father in his *Something about the Author Autobiography Series (SAAS)* entry. "A growing boy gets his image of masculinity from his father." Westall writes that his father believed "a man was one who could make things, and put things right." Westall's father excelled in both these areas. "At home ... it was make, make, make. Radios; elaborately decorated cabinets for radios; model galleons." "Best of all, though," Westall continues, "were the stupendous toys he made for me in his spare time at work, in the summer when things were slack in the gas business. A full-sized model of a Vickers heavy machine gun; a three-foot model of a battle cruiser. He would simply walk in some evening, his face full of glee, say 'Shut your eyes' and when I opened them, there was something wonderful." Westall's father also helped his son learn to read and to draw.

"My father's effect on my writing was huge," Westall writes in his *SAAS* entry. "He is the father of *The Machine-Gunners* and *Fathom Five.* But more than that, he is the source of wizardry in my books; he showed me a world in which things could be transformed beyond belief; he made the miraculous possible in my writing." The self-reliance that Westall's father installed in his son stood the boy in good stead when he started school. "I realize now," he writes in *SAAS*, "that the children round me, labouring painfully over their work with their tongues out, were already starting to be crushed by the system. They were becoming panicky about being too slow; with every mistake they made, their confidence went down. Work became depressing for them, something to be endured, something imposed by a cruel ultimate authority.... I honestly don't think I started off brighter than other people; I was simply not crushed and maimed in my confidence in myself."

Westall began writing while still in school. "I think I was a bad writer, the worst kind of writer, from the time I could first hold a pencil," he declares in his *SAAS* entry. "I wrote my first novel in the summer holidays when I was twelve," largely because he had just started high school and was too shy to make new friends. "It was execrable." Four more novels followed, each longer than the one before it and equally as bad. As Westall made new friends, however, he abandoned writing, except for required school papers. "With a couple of exceptions," he states in *SAAS*, "I stayed dead as a writer for another fourteen years." Instead, Westall enrolled in the local university to study fine arts, married, graduated, and had a son of his own.

"Perhaps all the best books," Westall writes in *Signal*, "start by being written for only one child, and that child very close to you. They start when the child-within-the-author turns to the real child and says, 'Come away with me and I will show you a place you otherwise will never see, because it is buried under thirty, or three hundred or three thousand years of time.'... That is why I wrote *The Machine-Gunners*. No thought of publication: it lay over a year in manuscript before I even bothered to have it typed up. I wrote it only for my son, then twelve. To tell him how it felt to be me, when I was twelve. As I read it out to him, chapter by chapter, we were, for the first and last time, twelve-year-olds standing side by side. He had 'come away' with me. Twelve spoke to twelve, without interruption."

The Machine-Gunners takes place in northern England (Tyneside) in 1940. A German bomber, flying over the area on a night raid, is shot down by English fire. The first to discover the wreckage is a young local boy, Chas McGill, who notices the undamaged machine gun at the rear of the downed plane and decides to scavenge it. He puts together a gang of boys and sets up the gun to use against other enemy bombers. Unfortunately, the team does not really know what it is doing and, states Westall in *Library Association Record*, "as a result of using violence [Chas] loses his best friend, his gang, his most precious possession (the machine gun) and his good name." Chas's adventures and his relations with the community in which he lives "add up to a vivid, three-dimensional picture of that time and place," writes Aidan Chambers in the *Times Literary Supplement*: "the battered streets, the refugee families, the weary nights and days, the shortages, the acts of courage, love, and decent neighbourliness, and the moments of desperation, cowardice and stupidity too."

The Machine-Gunners won Great Britain's prestigious Carnegie Medal in 1976, an honor that was questioned by some librarians who objected to the book's blunt portrayal of violence and swearing. "The book has much bad language, which is accepted as everyday speech by the children in the story, and the descriptions of the violence are altogether too vivid," write some of the objecting librarians in *Library Association Record*. "Surely these traits should be discouraged in children." Many others, however, celebrated Westall's uncompromising authenticity. "I can think of few writers," declares Margery Fisher in *Growing Point*, "who have put on paper as successfully ... the sheer muddle of [the Second World War] and the day-to-day difficulty, for civilians at least, of deciding what was important."

Westall's books since *The Machine-Gunners* have dealt with a variety of topics, ranging from witch-hunting in the seventeenth century to ghosts that haunt other ghosts to a race of intelligent cats. John Webster, the cat-fancying, time-traveling hero of Westall's 1978 novel *The Devil on the Road*, was based on Westall's son Christopher—killed in a motorcycle accident in his eighteenth year. Westall's second Carnegie Medal book, *The Scarecrows*, tells the story of Simon Brown, a young boy who, outraged by his mother's remarriage to a man he feels is unsuitable, becomes entangled in what might be a supernatural intrusion from the past into the present day, but which equally might be a projection from Simon's fevered imagination. *The Cats of Seroster* uses elements of traditional fantasy to tell how telepathic cats restore the heir of a dukedom to his rightful place.

"I cannot say I like the way the world is going," Westall remarked. "There have been advances; more prosperity in the West; a growth of conscience among the Western middle classes; the liberation, still incomplete, of women. But there has been a decay in the way people belonged together, looked after each other, and were proudly determined to stand on their own two feet. So when I found I could go back into history, I didn't see any reason why I shouldn't keep going. You can never turn the clock back; but you can be like a miner, burrowing back into the past to try to rescue some of the good things that we have forgotten in the rush for 'progress.' Each of my books is a separate prospecting-expedition."

"There is really very little more to tell," writes Westall in his *SAAS* entry; "since then, it has simply been doing more of the same—it is the story of everyday, and writers' everydays are not thrilling at all—much less than those of pilots or deep-sea divers."

WORKS CITED:

Chambers, Aidan, "War Efforts" (review of *The Machine-Gunners*), *Times Literary Supplement*, September 19, 1975, p. 1056.

Fisher, Margery, review of *The Machine-Gunners*, *Growing Point*, October, 1975, pp. 2707-08.

Jones, Mrs. P. S., and others, "Bad Language Honoured," *Library Association Record,* October, 1976, p. 497.

Westall, Robert, "Defense of—and by—Author Robert Westall," *Library Association Record,* January, 1977, pp. 38-39.

Westall, Robert, "How Real Do You Want Your Realism?," *Signal,* January, 1979, pp. 34-46.

Westall, Robert, *Something about the Author Autobiography Series,* Volume 2, Gale, 1986, pp. 305-23.

FOR MORE INFORMATION SEE:

BOOKS

Children's Literature Review, Volume 13, Gale, 1987.
Contemporary Literary Criticism, Volume 17, Gale, 1981.
Holtze, Sally Holmes, editor, *Fifth Book of Junior Authors and Illustrators,* H. W. Wilson, 1983.

PERIODICALS

Horn Book, August, 1976.
Junior Bookshelf, April, 1979.
New York Times Book Review, May 16, 1982.
School Librarian, June, 1979.
Times Literary Supplement, December 10, 1975; December 14, 1979; March 27, 1981; July 23, 1982; November 30, 1984; October 11, 1985.
Washington Post Book World, November 7, 1976; November 11, 1979.

* * *

WIGNELL, Edel 1936-

PERSONAL: Born October 19, 1936, in Echuca, Victoria, Australia; daughter of Burton Robert (a farmer) and Elizabeth Jane (a homemaker; maiden name, Benson) Paynter; married Geoffrey Wignell (a bank manager), February 7, 1966. *Education:* Toorak Teachers' College, teachers certificate, 1956, diploma, 1972. *Hobbies and other interests:* "In my spare time I like to read, attend plays and the cinema, and visit art galleries with my husband. On holidays, we like lazing on the beach and travelling in the country to see places of historical and architectural interest."

ADDRESSES: Home—Glen Iris, Victoria, Australia 3146. *Office*—P.O. Box 135, Glen Iris, Victoria, Australia 3146.

CAREER: Education Department of Victoria, Victoria, Australia, infant teacher, 1957-61 and 1963-64, teachers' college lecturer in infant teaching, 1965, teachers' college lecturer in English, 1967-72; London Education Authority, South Lambeth, London, England, infant teacher, 1962; free-lance writer, compiler, and journalist, 1979—.

MEMBER: Australian Society of Authors, Fellowship of Australian Writers, Australian Writers Guild, Children's Book Council of Australia, Society of Children's Book Writers (USA).

Edel Wignell holding her novel *Escape by Deluge* and the photograph of the 1972 Melbourne flood that inspired the story.

AWARDS, HONORS: Children's short story commendation, McGregor Literary Competition, 1982, for "Lottie and the Swaggie Joes"; Mary Grant Bruce Short Story Award, 1983, for "Richard Goes West" (highly commended citation), 1985, for "Catastrophe's Ninth Life," and 1986, for "Clever Juice" (second place) and "Arachne Returns" (commended citation); commended ballad in open poetry section, Ballarat Begonia Literary and Arts Festival, 1985, for "The Cycling Shearers' Race"; highly commended reading citation in short story competition, St. George-Sutherland Branch of Fellowship of Australian Writers, 1987, for "It's Your Money, Do What You Like with It"; open poetry prize, Mackay Arts Festival, 1987, for "Devlin's Ghost"; honor award, Most Beautiful Books from around the World competition, Leipzig Book Fair, 1989, for *Raining Cats and Dogs*; Viewpoint short story competition award, 1989, for "Deep-Frozen Fire"; *Escape by Deluge* was also named a notable book by the Children's Book Council of Australia, 1990.

WRITINGS:

(Editor with Don Drummond) *Reading: A Source Book,* Primary Education, 1975.
(With Heather Chatfield) *Reading Responses: A Literature Program for Primary Schools,* Thomas Nelson, 1976.
(Compiler) *A Boggle of Bunyips,* Hodder & Stoughton, 1981.
Crutches Are Nothing: A Collection of Twelve Stories about Disabled Children, Greenhouse, 1982.

A mix of fantasy and reality, Wignell's *Escape by Deluge* features the mythical Australian water creature known as the bunyip.

Rick's Magic (part of the Australian Magpie series), Rigby Education, 1982.

The Ghostly Jigsaw, Hodder & Stoughton, 1985.

A Bluey of Swaggies, Edward Arnold, 1985.

Omar's Opal Magic (part of the "Wheels" series), Harcourt, 1985.

She'll Fall in, for Sure! (part of the "Water" series), Harcourt, 1986.

A Gift of Squares, Hamish Hamilton, 1986.

The Car Wash Monster, illustrated by Kim Lynch, Ashton, 1986.

Born to Lead, Rigby Education, 1986.

(Compiler) *Inviting Authors and Illustrators,* Primary English Teaching Association, 1986, revised edition, 1987.

Fiorella's Cameo, Macmillan, 1987.

Missing, Macmillan, 1987.

The Tie Olympics, Macmillan, 1987.

What's Your Hobby?, Macmillan, 1987.

Marmalade, Jet and the Finnies, Hamish Hamilton, 1987.

Raining Cats and Dogs, illustrated by Rodney McRae, Hodder & Stoughton, 1987.

You'll Turn into a Rabbit!, Hodder & Stoughton, 1988.

What's in the Red Bag? (novel; adaptation of Wignell's five-part television script for Channel 10 in Australia), Hamish Hamilton, 1988, published as *No Pets Allowed,* Transworld, 1990.

Spider in the Toilet, illustrated by Margaret Power, Lothian, 1988.

I Know That Place!, Primary English Teaching Association, 1989.

Amanda's Warts, Harcourt, 1989.

Big April Fools, Harcourt, 1989.

Mischief Makers, Harcourt, 1989.

Escape by Deluge, Walter McVitty Books, 1989, Holiday House, 1990.

A Bogy Will Get You!, Harcourt, 1990.

Battlers of the Great Depression, Harcourt, 1990.

The Portland Fairy Penguins, Harcourt, 1990.

Saving Wildlife, Harcourt, 1990.

The Little Girl and Her Beetle, Mimosa, 1990.

The Nursery Rhyme Picnic, Mimosa, 1990.

Ghost Dog, Era Publications, 1990.

Voices, Era Publications, 1990.

Also author of numerous booklets. Author, with husband Geoffrey Wignell, of "Manpower Series" adult literacy unit. Contributor to anthologies, including *Stories to Share,* compiled by Jean Chapman, Hodder & Stoughton, 1983; *Win Some, Lose Some,* compiled by Jo Goodman, Fontana, 1985; *Do Frogs Wear Jeans?,* compiled by Pam Chessell and Hazel Edwards, Longman Cheshire, 1985; *Bushfire and Other Stories,* Macmillan, 1987; *Frightfully Fearful Tales,* Macmillan, 1987; *Bubbles,* Gazelle, 1987; *English Magic,* Brooks Waterloo, 1988; *Reaping a Harvest,* edited by Michael Kavanagh, Noel Kilby, and Wilfred Savage, Longman Cheshire, 1988; and *Stay Loose, Mother Goose,* compiled by Sue Machin, Omnibus Books, 1990. Contributor to reference books, including *The Dictionary of Australian Quotations,* edited by Stephen Murray-Smith, Heinemann, 1984, and *The Macmillan Australian Children's Encyclopedia,* 1986.

Former columnist for *Australian Grade Teacher* and *Primary Education Magazine.* Contributor of articles, poems, and short stories to numerous newspapers and periodicals, including *The Age, The Australian Author, Comet, Explore, Family Circle, Good Health, New Woman,* and *Short Story International—Seedling Series.*

Some of Wignell's works have been recorded on audiocassette.

WORK IN PROGRESS: "A historical novel for young adults. It has two threads—one set at the turn of the century and the other in 1950."

SIDELIGHTS: Edel Wignell told *SATA:* "I am the second in a family of six girls. We lived on a wheat farm approximately eleven kilometers west of the township of Echuca in Victoria, southeastern Australia. When irrigation came, my father changed to sheep farming. We had an orchard with many different fruits, a huge vegetable garden, and several cows.

"There were many jobs to do, and we took turns at them. I hated milking and housework, but I liked shepherding sheep and driving the tractor. I loved swimming in the dam in summer—except for the yabbies (freshwater prawns), which tweaked my toes. We swam in the irrigation channel, too, but I was terrified of the leeches.

"My love of stories came from the family. My grandparents' house was nearby and grandma was a storyteller. My mother loved reading and my father talked entertainingly about country life. At night when I went to the backyard lavatory, I was scared that the hobyahs (bogies) would carry me away. My mother bought new torch batteries for me every Friday, but I used them up immediately, reading under the blankets that night!

"I attended Wharparilla West Rural School which usually had about twelve pupils. I liked writing, reading, and being a monitor—helping the little kids. Our library books came in a box by train each month, and I read every one. I traveled to Echuca High School by bus. The teachers there encouraged my reading and writing. I quickly moved from schoolgirl stories to historical novels and adult fiction. In the first year I became editor of *The Murray Log* school magazine. I liked athletics, swimming, and playing on the hockey team. At the age of seventeen, I went to Melbourne, the capital city, to attend Toorak Teachers' College.

"After three years I graduated as an infant teacher and taught for eight years in both city and country primary schools. Then I taught for seven years at a teachers' college. Meanwhile, I took two trips abroad. The first was to London in 1962 where I taught for six months and traveled through the United Kingdom and Europe with two young women. After I married Geoffrey Wignell in 1966, we spent a year honeymooning by campervan in the United Kingdom and Europe.

"While I was teaching, I was a columnist for two educational magazines, in turn: *Australian Grade Teacher* and *Primary Education Magazine.* I continued this work for several years after I left teaching, and I wrote a teachers' textbook while I took the opportunity to try several arts and crafts, including drawing, painting, printmaking, and gold and silversmithing.

"In 1979 I increased my writing, becoming a full-time writer, compiler, and journalist. I write for both adults and children. My work includes short stories, picture books, novels, verse, nonfiction, anthologies, feature articles for newspapers and magazines, and a children's television serial.

"My ideas for writing come from my own childhood experiences and those of children I know, including nine nieces and nephews. For example, the delight and terror of two of my nieces (aged four and six) when my husband and I took them through a car wash for the first time inspired a picture-story book, *The Car Wash Monster.* The story parodies the folktale 'The Three Billy Goats Gruff.' It includes three 'good' characters and one 'bad,' three happenings, and repetitive language such as 'I'm coming to eat you up.'

"I like to play with the English language, taking mad sayings and idioms literally by asking 'What if?' In my picture book *Raining Cats and Dogs,* illustrated by Rodney McRae, it literally rains cats and dogs! Another experience I used occurred at school. I often ate salad while the other teachers ate sandwiches and pies. They used to say, 'You'll turn into a rabbit!' Years later I remembered this and wrote a juvenile novel, *You'll Turn into a Rabbit!* In it, a girl named Rowena discovers a magic eating formula that enables her to turn into a rabbit any time she likes. She has some scary and funny adventures as a result.

"My first children's book was an anthology called *A Boggle of Bunyips.* The bunyip is a terrifying water monster—a creature in the folktales of Australia's aborigines. In the last century, scientists expected to find it. My collection includes stories, verse, extracts, legends, descriptions, reports, and letters to the newspapers that were written from the 1820s to the present day.

"I included the bunyip in my first full-length novel, *Escape by Deluge.* The story is a blend of fantasy and reality with two interwoven threads. Shelley, who lives on the ninth floor of a building in the heart of Melbourne, hears strange sounds at midnight. 'Boom, boom, boom! Yalloooooo!' No one else hears this booming and wailing, so she investigates and discovers that something—a creature of the water—is trapped in a drain below the building. She wonders how she can set it free and thus release herself from its haunting presence. The second thread of the novel describes the bunyip and the aboriginal people living in the Yarra Valley from the mythic era called Dreamtime until the present. *Escape by Deluge* was inspired by a wonderful photograph of the 1972 Melbourne flood, and my husband's assertion, 'The bunyip caused the flood!'

"Currently, I am researching a full-length historical novel for young adults set in 1901 and 1950. The main characters are two girls who are mysteriously linked across time. It's too soon to tell any more than that, but I hope it will be published in a year or two."

FOR MORE INFORMATION SEE:

PERIODICALS

Booklist, July, 1990, p. 2096.

*   *   *

WILDSMITH, Brian 1930-

PERSONAL: Born January 22, 1930, in Penistone, Yorkshire, England; son of Paul (a coal miner) and Annie Elizabeth (Oxley) Wildsmith; married Aurelie Janet Craigie Ithurbide, 1955; children: Clare, Rebecca, Anna, Simon. *Education:* Attended Barnsley School of Art, c. 1946-49; Slade School of Fine Art, University College, London, D.F.A., 1952. *Religion:* Roman Catho-

BRIAN WILDSMITH

lic. *Hobbies and other interests:* Abstract painting, playing the piano, cricket, squash.

ADDRESSES: Home—11 Castellaras le Vieux, 06370 Mouans-Sartoux, France.

CAREER: Selhurst Grammar School for Boys, London, England, art teacher, 1954-57; free-lance artist and creator of books for children, 1957—. Maidstone College of Art, lecturer, c. 1957. Set and costume designer for USA-USSR Leningrad film production of *The Blue Bird. Military service:* National Service, 1952-54; became sergeant.

AWARDS, HONORS: Kate Greenaway Medal, 1962, for *ABC;* Kate Greenaway commendations, 1963, for *The Lion and the Rat* and *Oxford Book of Poetry for Children,* 1967, for *Birds,* and 1971, for *The Owl and the Woodpecker;* Art Books for Children citation, 1965, for *Brian Wildsmith's 1, 2, 3s;* runner-up for Hans Christian Andersen Award, 1966 and 1968; *Birds* was listed among the *New York Times* Choice of Best Illustrated Children's Books of the Year in 1967; Brooklyn Art Books for Children citation, c. 1979, for *Hunter and His Dog;* runner-up for the Maschler award, 1982, and Parent's Choice citation for illustration, 1983, both for *Pelican;* Soka Eakkai Japan Education Medal, 1988; USHIO Publication Culture Award, 1991.

WRITINGS:

SELF-ILLUSTRATED; FOR CHILDREN

A Brian Wildsmith Portfolio, F. Watts, 1962-66.
ABC (sometimes cited as *Brian Wildsmith's ABC*), Oxford University Press, 1962, F. Watts, 1963.
(Reteller) *The Lion and the Rat: A Fable* (based on the story by Jean de La Fontaine), F. Watts, 1963.
(Reteller) *The North Wind and the Sun* (based on the story by J. de La Fontaine), F. Watts, 1964.
Brian Wildsmith's Mother Goose: A Collection of Nursery Rhymes, F. Watts, 1964.
Brian Wildsmith's 1, 2, 3s, F. Watts, 1965, published in England as *1, 2, 3,* Oxford University Press, 1965.
(Reteller) *The Rich Man and the Shoemaker* (based on the story by J. de La Fontaine), F. Watts, 1965.
(Reteller) *The Hare and the Tortoise* (based on the story by J. de La Fontaine), F. Watts, 1967.
Wild Animals (sometimes cited as *Brian Wildsmith's Wild Animals*), F. Watts, 1967.
Birds (sometimes cited as *Brian Wildsmith's Birds*), F. Watts, 1967.
Fishes (sometimes cited as *Brian Wildsmith's Fishes*), F. Watts, 1968.
(Reteller) *The Miller, the Boy, and the Donkey* (based on the story by J. de La Fontaine), F. Watts, 1969.
Brian Wildsmith's Circus, F. Watts, 1970 (published in England as *The Circus,* Oxford University Press, 1970).
Puzzles (sometimes cited as *Brian Wildsmith's Puzzles*), Oxford University Press, 1970, F. Watts, 1971.
The Owl and the Woodpecker, Oxford University Press, 1971, F. Watts, 1972.
The Twelve Days of Christmas, F. Watts, 1972.
The Little Wood Duck, Oxford University Press, 1972, F. Watts, 1973.
The Lazy Bear, Oxford University Press, 1973, F. Watts, 1974.
Squirrels, Oxford University Press, 1974, F. Watts, 1975.
Python's Party, Oxford University Press, 1974, F. Watts, 1975.
(Adapter) *Maurice Maeterlinck's "Blue Bird,"* F. Watts, 1976.
The True Cross, Oxford University Press, 1977.
What the Moon Saw, Oxford University Press, 1978.
Hunter and His Dog, Oxford University Press, 1979.
Animal Games, Oxford University Press, 1980.
Animal Homes, Oxford University Press, 1980.
Animal Shapes, Oxford University Press, 1980.
Animal Tricks, Oxford University Press, 1980.
Professor Noah's Spaceship, Oxford University Press, 1980.
Seasons, Oxford University Press, 1980.
Bear's Adventure, Pantheon, 1981.
Cat on the Mat, Oxford University Press, 1982.
Pelican, Pantheon, 1982.
The Trunk, Oxford University Press, 1982.
All Fall Down, Oxford University Press, 1983.
The Apple Bird, Oxford University Press, 1983.
The Island, Oxford University Press, 1983.
The Nest, Oxford University Press, 1983.
Daisy, Pantheon, 1984.

(Illustration by Wildsmith from his retelling of Maurice Maeterlinck's *The Blue Bird*.)

Wildsmith decided to publish his costume designs for *The Blue Bird* when he was disappointed with the movie adaptation he created them for.

Toot, Toot, Oxford University Press, 1984.
Whose Shoes?, Oxford University Press, 1984.
Give a Dog a Bone, Pantheon, 1985.
Goat's Trail, Knopf, 1986.
My Dream, Oxford University Press, 1986.
What a Tale, Oxford University Press, 1986.
Giddy Up, Oxford University Press, 1987.
If I Were You, Oxford University Press, 1987.
Carousel, Knopf, 1988.
A Christmas Story, Knopf, 1989.

ILLUSTRATOR; FOR CHILDREN

Eileen O'Faolain, *High Sang the Sword,* Oxford University Press, 1959.

Rene Guillot, *Prince of the Jungle,* S. G. Phillips, 1959.

Frederick Grice, *The Bonny Pit Laddy,* Oxford University Press, 1960, published as *Out of the Mines,* F. Watts, 1961.

Nan Chauncy, *The Secret Friends,* Oxford University Press, 1960, F. Watts, 1962.

Eleanor Graham, *The Story of Jesus,* Hodder & Stoughton, 1960.

N. Chauncy, *Tangara: "Let Us Set Off Again,"* Oxford University Press, 1960.

Madeleine Polland, *The Town across the Water,* Constable, 1961.

Veronique Day, *Landslide!,* Bodley Head, 1961.

Tales from the Arabian Nights, Oxford University Press, 1961, F. Watts, 1962.

Roger L. Green, *Myths of the Norsemen,* Bodley Head, 1962.

Geoffrey Trease, *Follow My Black Plume,* Macmillan, 1963.

Edward Blishen, editor, *Oxford Book of Poetry for Children,* F. Watts, 1963.

Charlotte Morrow, *The Watchers,* Hutchinson, 1963.

Geoffrey Trease, *A Thousand for Sicily,* Macmillan, 1964.

Mother Goose, *Nursery Rhymes,* Oxford University Press, 1964.

Kevin Crossley-Holland, *Havelok the Dane,* Macmillan, 1964, Dutton, 1965.

Charles Dickens, *Barnaby Rudge,* Ginn, 1966.

Robert L. Stevenson, *A Child's Garden of Verses,* F. Watts, 1966.

Philip Turner, *Brian Wildsmith's Illustrated Bible Stories,* F. Watts, 1968.

Alan Wildsmith, *Ahmed, Prince of Ashira,* Deutsch, 1969.

Frances Hodgson Burnett, *Sara Crewe,* Scholastic Inc., 1986.

Daisaku Ikeda, *The Snow Country Prince,* translated by Geraldine McCaughrean, Oxford University Press, 1990, Knopf, 1991.

D. Ikeda, *The Cherry Tree,* retold by Geraldine McCaughrean, Oxford University Press, 1991.

D. Ikeda, *The Princess and the Moon,* Oxford University Press, 1991.

Also illustrator of D. Ikeda's *Over the Deep Blue Sea,* 1992.

WORK IN PROGRESS: Passion of Christ.

SIDELIGHTS: Brian Wildsmith is one of England's most renowned contemporary authors and illustrators of children's books. Bringing brilliant colors and an exuberant style to his drawings, he burst onto the children's literary scene with his *ABC,* which won the Kate Greenaway Medal in 1962. Since then, he has produced a variety of acclaimed books, including *Birds, Hunter and His Dog,* and *Goat's Trail.* All of his works feature drawings born out of a painterly style that many consider to border on fine art. Wildsmith, in fact, believes in introducing art and culture to very young children and feels compelled to produce children's books of high quality. "I believe in the Jesuit saying 'Give me a child under seven years and he is mine forever,'" Wildsmith said in *Library Journal.* "How often have we left all that is good and free in our culture to be brought before the child too late, when his taste has already been formed, maltreated, warped and destroyed by the everlasting rubbish that is still thought by many to be good enough for children. I hope my picture books will help alleviate this, and perhaps guide them to finer and greater paths."

Born in Penistone, a small mining town in Yorkshire, England, Wildsmith was the oldest of four children. His father worked as a miner and often found time to spend with his son. "My father was always very kind towards me. . . . He was not a strict man, my mother being the disciplinarian of the two," Wildsmith said in *Something about the Author Autobiography Series (SAAS).* "[My mother] was the one who made us go to church on Sundays, do our homework, tidy our rooms, keep our lives in an orderly manner." Despite his mother's meticulous ways, Wildsmith adored her sense of humor as well as her warmth and understanding. "She encouraged us in our every interest," he said in *SAAS,* "leading us to believe that if we were to embark on any activity, whether physical or mental, it would only be of value unless we put ourselves entirely to it."

Having moved when Wildsmith was two years old to a town called Hoyland Common, the Wildsmith family moved to a second house in that town shortly before the onset of World War II. It was there that Wildsmith developed his fondness for the game of cricket. "I played the game with a passion I believe many Yorkshiremen share, wrecking [by means of a cricket ball and bat] the most fragile parts of the neighbourhood," Wildsmith said in *SAAS.* At the age of ten, he earned a scholarship to the Delasalle College for boys, where he excelled at playing not only cricket but football and other sports. Also at Delasalle, Wildsmith developed a love for science and decided that he would be a chemist.

"One day, however, at the age of sixteen, I realized I was on the wrong tracks," Wildsmith said in *SAAS.* "I was on my way to a chemistry class when I turned on my heels, went to see the headmaster and told him I was leaving to go to art school." Wildsmith was accepted at the Barnsley Art School, where he told *SAAS,* "there was only one teacher, along with the headmaster, and both disliked me. I admired artists of the likes of [twentieth-century abstract painters Pablo] Picasso and

[Paul] Klee; they regarded me as some way-out weirdo leftie who did not appreciate the boring, conventional work of artists like Russell Flint (a Royal Academician)."

Wildsmith later was accepted at the Slade School of Fine Art in London. "The course I followed at the Slade gave me a sound foundation within the artistic world.... I drew quite well there," Wildsmith told *SAAS*. He added, though, that "in retrospect I believe I would have benefitted far more from [my education] had I applied some five to eight years later." Only nineteen years old at the time, Wildsmith was befuddled by what he considered contradictory teaching methods combined with a practice of being left with virtually no guidance in order to discover his own creative direction. "The Slade, at the time," Wildsmith said in *SAAS*, "was a place to go where one could extend oneself after having acquired a certain amount of artistic experience and [at the age of nineteen], I had very little."

Despite receiving a somewhat unsettling education from Slade, the artist earned a diploma in fine art from there in the early 1950s, at which time he was called upon to serve in England's military service. He disliked the rigid rules of army life and, in order to make his stay tolerable, asked to serve in a teaching capacity. Granted his wish, he taught math for the remainder of his eighteen-month stay in the army. Finishing his military duty in 1954, he began teaching art at a boy's grammar school. While there, Wildsmith engaged in a free-lance art career, at night designing book covers for publishers. He enjoyed the work but, having yet to establish financial security as an artist, felt obligated to keep his teaching post. "My last year as an art teacher became affected by a general sense of frustration," noted Wildsmith in *SAAS*. "Everything I did outside school was done in haste and I found myself desperately reaching out for more time—there was none unless I were to spend my life sleepless."

Wildsmith, who had married in 1955, was soon persuaded by his wife to quit teaching and pursue that which would make him happy—a full-time career in art. To his delight, "after a year of working free-lance," Wildsmith said in *SAAS*, "I had earned twice as much as I had when in full employment." His initial success was encouraged by Mabel George, an editor at Oxford University Press, "who was later to play a major part in my development as a children's illustrator," Wildsmith said in *SAAS*. After three years of commissioning the artist for book covers and black-and-white book illustrations, George asked Wildsmith to produce color plates for the book *Tales from the Arabian Nights*. The finished product drew mixed reviews, with one critic according the work particularly harsh judgment: "The descent is steep to Brian Wildsmith's attack on the Arabian Nights," Wildsmith quoted the review in *Library Journal*. "The seemingly aimless scribbles are splashed lavishly and untidily with bright smudges of paint."

"'Well,' I thought, 'that's the end of you, Wildsmith,'" the illustrator related his musings in *British Children's*

Wildsmith's drawings are born out of a painterly style that borders on fine art. (From *Give a Dog a Bone,* written and illustrated by Wildsmith.)

Authors as he doubted he would have a future with Oxford University Press. The publisher, though, had faith in Wildsmith and asked him to do a book of ABCs. The result was a resounding success and, as the artist said in *SAAS*, "from thereon it seems that my career as a children's illustrator took off."

Wildsmith proceeded to produce a variety of popular books during the 1960s. He illustrated several works based on fables by J. de La Fontaine, including *The Lion and the Rat* and *The North Wind and the Sun*. After illustrating some Mother Goose rhymes in 1964, Wildsmith endeavored to produce more educational works for children. His picture books *Birds, Wild Animals,* and *Fishes* are intended to broaden readers' vocabularies; accompanying his radiantly colored illustrations are such phrases as "a wedge of swans," "a battery of barracuda," and "a skulk of foxes." He followed with *Brian Wildsmith's Circus* and *Puzzles,* books that challenge children to put words to what they see on the page.

"By 1970 ...," Wildsmith said in *SAAS*, "I had made a conscious decision to span, if possible, with the use of form, colour, and words, the whole educational range of a young child from its initial introduction to our alphabet and numerical system to the foundation of sound humanitarian-based principles, necessary for the development of its responsibility towards the society in which it lives. I wanted to feed the eyes and minds of children with lusciously colourful images, representative of the potential beauty of our planet and its inhabitants." With this resolution, Wildsmith ventured to write story lines for his own books; his initial efforts resulted in the acclaimed *Owl and the Woodpecker*.

Now that he was both writing and illustrating, the artist required more inspiration, and the Wildsmiths, who by then had four children, moved from England to the south of France. Fond of the region's beautiful countryside and multitude of cultural centers, the family settled in a small village named Castellaras. "From my work room," Wildsmith said in *SAAS*, "I can look out onto hills covered in pine, olive, and mimosa trees that roll towards the sea; stare at the magnificent sunsets that light up the sky at nightfall; relish the spectacular view that on a clear day allows one to see Corsica, sixty miles away. I have found the ideal home: a place where I can work."

The move indeed proved fruitful for Wildsmith, who succeeded in producing several more books over the next three years, among them *The Little Wood Duck* and *Squirrels*. His quick pace was interrupted, though, when in 1974 he was asked to design the sets and costumes for a film adaptation of Maurice Maeterlinck's classic children's fable, *The Blue Bird*. Enthusiastically accepting the offer, Wildsmith made several trips to Russia, where the film was being produced. Eager to design imaginative pieces for the fantastical film, Wildsmith was eventually frustrated when a series of disasters and general disorganization adversely affected the quality of the movie. "I was so disappointed with the outcome of my designs of the film," Wildsmith said in *SAAS*, "that I decided to publish them." The result, *Maurice Maeterlinck's "Blue Bird,"* appeared in 1976. "Naturally I had to alter the drawings in order to combine them with a narrative, but I believe the book gives a good idea of how I envisaged the film should have looked."

Following his stint with moviemaking, Wildsmith resumed creating children's books on a regular basis. Producing *The True Cross* and *What the Moon Saw* in the late 1970s, Wildsmith is perhaps better known for his books about animals, which include *Hunter and His Dog* and *Bear's Adventure*. "Animals, I believe, can teach humans many things," the illustrator said in *SAAS*. In addition to creating books with a variety of subjects, Wildsmith has produced works with differing techniques, making in the 1980s a set of small, simple books for very young children as well as a series of split-page books. Despite brandishing differing subjects and formats, all of Wildsmith's works are characterized by vibrant, kaleidoscopic color and vigorous design. According to Patience M. Daltry in the *Christian Science Monitor,* "Brian Wildsmith's picture-books are among the brightest happenings in children's illustrating."

Having succeeded in the field of children's book illustration, Wildsmith has pursued his lifelong dream of being a painter. "It has taken me a long time to feel ready and mature enough to approach a blank canvas," Wildsmith said in *SAAS,* "and one of the reasons for this delay is the simple fact that I fell in love with making children's books, finding the process exciting, ever-changing, and fully enjoyable." Whether illustrating or painting, Wildsmith, based on his advice to children in *British Children's Authors,* will surely succeed: "No matter what you do ... I've always thought that the best thing ... is

to do something that you love doing. I think if you love doing it, you'll do it well. Do it to the best of your ability, and perhaps someday you'll become the best in the world at doing what it is you like best to do."

WORKS CITED:

Daltry, Patience M., review of *Birds, Christian Science Monitor,* August 31, 1967, p. 5.
Jones, Cornelia, and Olivia R. Way, "Brian Wildsmith," *British Children's Authors,* American Library Association, 1976, pp. 155-66.
Wildsmith, Brian, "Antic Disposition: A Young British Illustrator Interviews Himself," *Library Journal,* November 15, 1965, pp. 5035-38.
Wildsmith, Brian, *Something about the Author Autobiography Series,* Volume 5, Gale, 1988, pp. 303-26.

FOR MORE INFORMATION SEE:

BOOKS

Children's Literature Review, Volume 2, Gale, 1976.

PERIODICALS

Book World, November 3, 1968.
Children's Book Review, October, 1971; December, 1972.
Christian Science Monitor, July 5, 1985.
Horn Book, February, 1981; August, 1984; June, 1986; May, 1987.
Junior Bookshelf, February, 1967; August, 1967; February, 1968.
Kirkus Reviews, February 1, 1979; October 15, 1986.
New York Times Book Review, August 18, 1968; December 3, 1972.
Publishers Weekly, April 2, 1979; February 29, 1980; September 26, 1980; December 26, 1980; March 25, 1983; June 24, 1983; September 14, 1984; September 20, 1985; August 22, 1986; November 11, 1988.
School Library Journal, September, 1975; April, 1981; August, 1982; September, 1983; August, 1984; October, 1985; January, 1986; February, 1989.
Times Educational Supplement, October 22, 1982.
Times Literary Supplement, March 27, 1981.

—*Sketch by Janice Jorgensen*

*   *   *

WOLLHEIM, Donald A(llen) 1914-1990 (David Grinnell)

OBITUARY NOTICE—Born October 1, 1914, in New York, NY; died of a heart attack, November 2, 1990, in New York, NY. Publishing executive, editor, and author. Wollheim is remembered as the founder and president of DAW Books, a paperback science fiction and fantasy publishing house. He held editorial posts at several publishing companies, including Ace Magazines, Avon Books, and Ace Books, before founding DAW Books in 1971. In addition, Wollheim edited a number of science fiction anthologies and wrote the "Mike Mars" series and several other science fiction novels, some under the pseudonym David Grinnell. In 1963 he won the Hugo Award for his contributions to book publishing, and in 1975 he received the Ann Radcliffe Award. Wollheim's novels include *The Secret of Saturn's Rings, One against the Moon, Mike Mars: Astronaut,* and *Mike Mars and the Mystery Satellite.* Among the anthologies he edited are *The Pocket Book of Science Fiction, Adventures in the Far Future,* and *DAW Science Fiction Reader.* Wollheim also edited *The 1988 Annual World's Best Science Fiction,* and *The World's Best Science Fiction, 1989.*

OBITUARIES AND OTHER SOURCES:

BOOKS

Who's Who in America, 45th edition, Marquis, 1988.

PERIODICALS

Publishers Weekly, November 16, 1990, p. 13.

Y

YEP, Laurence Michael 1948-

PERSONAL: Born June 14, 1948, in San Francisco, CA; son of Thomas Gim (a postal clerk) and Franche (a homemaker; maiden name, Lee) Yep. *Education:* Attended Marquette University, 1966-68; University of California, Santa Cruz, B.A., 1970; State University of New York at Buffalo, Ph.D., 1975.

ADDRESSES: Home—921 Populus Place, Sunnyvale, CA 94086. *Agent*—Maureen Walters, Curtis Brown Agency, 10 Astor Place, New York, NY 10003.

CAREER: Writer. Part-time instructor of English, Foothill College, Mountain View, CA, 1975, and San Jose City College, San Jose, CA, 1975-76; University of California, Berkeley, visiting lecturer in Asian American studies, 1987-1989, writer-in-residence, 1990.

MEMBER: Science Fiction Writers of America, Society of Children's Book Writers.

AWARDS, HONORS: Book-of-the-Month-Club Writing Fellowship, 1970; *Dragonwings* was named one of the *New York Times* Outstanding Books of the Year, 1975; Newbery Medal Honor Book, American Library Association (ALA), Children's Book Award, International Reading Association, Jane Addams Children's Book Award Honor Book, Jane Addams Peace Association, and Carter G. Woodson Book Award, National Council for Social Studies, all 1976, *Boston Globe-Horn Book* Award Honor Book, 1977, Lewis Carroll Shelf Award, University of Wisconsin, 1979, selected as one of New York Public Library's Books for the Teen Age, 1980, 1981, and 1982, and Friends of Children and Literature Award, 1984, all for *Dragonwings; Child of the Owl* was named one of *School Library Journal*'s Best Books for Spring, and one of the *New York Times* Outstanding Books of the Year, both 1977; *Boston Globe-Horn Book* Award for fiction, 1977, and Jane Addams Children's Book Award, 1978, both for *Child of the Owl;* Commonwealth Club of California Silver Medal, 1979, for *Sea Glass; Dragon Steel* was selected one of Child Study Association of America's Children's Books of the Year,

LAWRENCE MICHAEL YEP

1986; *Boston Globe-Horn Book* Honor Award, 1989, for *The Rainbow People.*

WRITINGS:

FOR CHILDREN

Sweetwater, illustrated by Julia Noonan, Harper, 1973.
Dragonwings, Harper, 1975.
Child of the Owl, Harper, 1977.
Sea Glass, Harper, 1979.
Kind Hearts and Gentle Monsters, Harper, 1982.
The Mark Twain Murders, Four Winds Press, 1982.
Dragon of the Lost Sea, Harper, 1982.
Liar, Liar, Morrow, 1983.

DRAGONWINGS
by Laurence Yep

Yep's *Dragonwings* is a fictionalized account of Fung Joe Guey, who built and flew his own flying machine in 1909. (Jacket illustration by Ronald Himler.)

The Serpent's Children, Harper, 1984.
The Tom Sawyer Fires, Morrow, 1984.
Dragon Steel, Harper, 1985.
Mountain Light (sequel to *The Serpent's Children*), Harper, 1985.
Shadow Lord, Harper, 1985.
The Curse of the Squirrel, illustrated by Dirk Zimmer, Random House, 1987.
Age of Wonders (play), produced by Asian American Theater Company, 1987.
Pay the Chinaman, and Fairy Bones (play), produced in San Francisco, 1987.
(Reteller) *The Rainbow People* (collection of Chinese-American folk tales), illustrated by David Weisner, Harper, 1989.
Dragon Cauldron, HarperCollins, 1991.
Lost Garden, Messner, 1991.
The Star Fisher, Morrow, 1991.
Tongues of Jade, HarperCollins, 1991.

FOR ADULTS

Seademons, Harper, 1977.
Monster Makers, Inc., Arbor House, 1986.

Work represented in anthologies, including *World's Best Science Fiction of 1969,* edited by Donald A. Wollheim and Terry Carr, Ace Books, 1969; *Quark #2,* edited by

Samuel Delaney and Marilyn Hacker, Paperback Library, 1971; *Protostars,* edited by David Gerrold, Ballantine, 1971; *The Demon Children,* Avon, 1973; *Strange Bedfellows: Sex and Science Fiction,* edited by Thomas N. Scortia, Random House, 1973; *Last Dangerous Visions,* edited by Harlan Ellison, Harper, 1975; and *Between Worlds,* Theater Communication Group, 1990. Contributor of short stories to periodicals, including *Worlds of If* and *Galaxy.*

ADAPTATIONS: Dragonwings, a filmstrip with record or cassette, Miller-Brody, 1979; *The Curse of the Squirrel,* a cassette, Random House, 1989. *Sweetwater* is available in braille and as a "talking book."

SIDELIGHTS: As a Chinese-American boy growing up in a black neighborhood in San Francisco, Laurence Michael Yep found the issue of identity a difficult one. To friends in the neighborhood, Yep stated in *Literature for Today's Young Adults,* "I was the all-purpose Asian. When we played war, I was the Japanese who got killed; then, when the Korean war came along, I was a North Korean Communist." Yep attended school in San Francisco's Chinatown, but he felt an outsider there since he did not speak Chinese like many of his peers. His sense of social identity became even more complicated when he began attending a predominantly white high school. Now an award-winning children's novelist best known for his books about children from multicultural backgrounds, Yep claims that writing has aided him in his search for cultural identity. He once explained in *Something about the Author,* "In a sense I have no one culture to call my own since I exist peripherally in several. However, in my writing I can create my own." His quest to find or create an identity in his fiction has a wide appeal to young adult readers of many backgrounds. "Probably the reason that much of my writing has found its way to a teenage audience is that I'm always pursuing the theme of being an outsider—an alien—and many teenagers feel they're aliens," Yep wrote in *Literature for Today's Young Adults.*

While he was in high school, Yep discovered—and began writing—science fiction, publishing his first story when he was eighteen years old. Five years, and many stories later, Yep published *Sweetwater,* a science fiction novel about Tyree, a young man belonging to a minority group of transplanted aliens on the planet Harmony. The group's struggle for survival in a frequently hostile environment evokes themes of family bonds, individual freedom, cultural traditions, and racism. *Sweetwater* elicited favorable reactions from critics, many of whom concurred with *Vector 78* contributor Brian Stableford's observation that "*Sweetwater* has one powerful thing going for it, and that is the fact that its writing is, in every sense of the word, beautiful."

Yep's second and one of his most acclaimed novels, *Dragonwings,* was the product of six years' research into Chinese-American history. While Yep was able to uncover factual information, he could find little about the human experience of the Chinese immigrants to the United States. He found that from the 1850s to the

In *Child of the Owl,* a Chinese-American girl learns about her dual heritage from her grandmother's tale of a transformed owl. (Jacket illustration by Allen Say.)

1930s males from economically distressed areas of southern China came to work in the United States, earning money to send back to their impoverished families. Although these men generally went back to China when circumstances allowed, while they worked in America they formed a bachelor society. In later years, Chinese women began to join their husbands and raise families in the United States. The new Chinese-American family society, although often set apart from white society, strove to adapt to American customs. Many, such as Yep's own family, lost touch with the rich cultural traditions of their homeland and the history of the founding Chinese bachelor society. For a third generation Chinese-American like Yep, an understanding of the experiences of his ancestors required a powerful imagination as well as extensive research.

In his research Yep came across the story of Fung Joe Guey, a Chinese-American man who built and flew his own flying machine in 1909, around the same time the Wright brothers received international attention for their early flights. Desiring to use Fung Joe Guey as a basis for a novel, but finding only two short newspaper articles about the man and his flight, Yep found it necessary to round out the factual information with his own sense of the human story. In order to mentally recreate Chinatown and its bachelor society of the early 1900s, he went through a unique process of imaginative

discovery, which he compares to growing up. "I would have to project myself back into the past and see how I myself would react to others in that same situation," Yep related in *Reading Teacher.* "I had grown up as a child in the 1950s so that my sense of reality was an American one. Now I had to grow up again, but this time in the 1900s, developing a Chinese sense of reality.... I would also have to discover what relationships would be like within that bachelor society—that lonely group of men who spent most of their adult years apart from family and home." He knew he had succeeded when, one day, the design of a familiar American checkered tablecloth looked strangely foreign to his new Chinese sensibility.

Dragonwings is the story of eight-year-old Moon Shadow, who leaves his mother in China's Middle Kingdom to join his father in the bachelor society of turn-of-the-century San Francisco. Moon Shadow's father, Windrider, came to the United States not only to earn money for his family, but also to explore unknown frontiers. *Interracial Books for Children Bulletin* contributor Frank Chin observed that Windrider's "life here somehow brought the best out of him, and he had big ideas, daring plans and a Chinese American son to help him take to the air." Together the father and son fulfill Windrider's dream of flying his own plane.

"When I wrote of the aeroplane, called 'Dragonwings,'" Yep stated in the *Reading Teacher,* "I was actually dealing with the reach of our imagination.... Windrider and his son, Moon Shadow, are engaged not only in the process of discovering America and each other, but also in a pilgrimage, or even a quest for a special moment when they can reaffirm the power of the imagination; that power in each of us to grasp with the mind and heart what we cannot immediately grasp with the hand." Through their experiences and discoveries, Yep presents an encompassing view of Chinese-American history. "The story is narrated with humor and detail," Joe Stines summarized in *Dictionary of Literary Biography,* "blending Chinese folklore, myths, and legends with historical facts, such as the great San Francisco earthquake, the Chinese bachelor community of Chinatown, and the daring biplane flight of Fung Joe Guey." Critics applauded the complexity of Yep's characters and his sensitive portrayal of the prejudice they faced in the United States. Ruth H. Pelmas wrote in the *New York Times Book Review* that, "as an exquisitely written poem of praise to the courage and industry of the Chinese-American people, [*Dragonwings*] is a triumph."

Yep's 1977 young people's novel, *Child of the Owl,* is set in San Francisco's Chinatown of the 1960s. In this story Casey, a young girl brought up by a gambling father and then a suburban uncle, is confused by her dual American and Chinese heritage. Having been exposed only to American ways and therefore having no means by which to identify with her Chinese background, Casey finds new avenues opened to her when she is sent to live with her grandmother, Paw-Paw, in Chinatown. Paw-Paw tells Casey a long legend about an owl. To the grandmother the owl symbolizes family unity and tradition while to the granddaughter it provides a new, indirect way to speak of her feelings. A winner of the *Boston Globe-Horn Book* Award, *Child of the Owl* has been praised by critics for its vivid depiction of Chinatown as well as its skillful interweaving of myth with everyday reality.

Yep's 1979 semi-autobiographical novel, *Sea Glass,* is the story of Craig Chin, a boy whose feelings of rejection by both white and Chinese-American cultures pervade his search for identity. Uprooted from San Francisco's Chinatown to the small town of Concepcion, Craig is called names like "Buddha Man" by his schoolmates and yet told by a Chinese man that he is too much like "the white demons." Moreover, Craig's father, who had been a talented athlete, pushes him to be an "All-American" boy. His cousins ignore him. With the help of an eccentric uncle, Craig learns to accept himself as he is. Critics commended the fully developed characters in *Sea Glass,* as well as Yep's successful portrayal of the "outsider" position—a position shared by many characters in the novel. Yep, who believes that good writing is based on what an author knows, acknowledged that *Sea Glass* hit "close to home." Writing about himself and his Chinese heritage, he said in *Literature for Today's Young Adults,* "requires me to take a razor blade and cut through my defenses. I'm bleeding when I finish and I have to take time off by writing fantasy or something only marginally related to my Chinese heritage."

Yep has made significant contributions to several genres of children's fiction. During the 1980s he wrote three mysteries, two of which—*The Mark Twain Murders* and *The Tom Sawyer Fires*—feature as their main character nineteenth-century American writer Mark Twain as a young reporter in San Francisco. Yep also wrote two fantasy novels, *Dragon of the Lost Sea* and *Dragon Steel,* about Shimmer, a dragon princess who sets out with a young human boy to save her undersea world from the witch Civet. Reviewers applauded the characterizations, the high adventure, and the integration of Chinese myth into the structure of these fantasy novels. The early eighties also saw the publication of Yep's *Shadow Lord,* a "Star Trek" novel, and *Kind Hearts and Gentle Monsters,* a well-received psychological novel about a romance between a very logical teenage boy and a very emotional teenage girl.

Yep's 1984 book, *The Serpent's Children,* is a historical novel set in nineteenth-century China. Its main character is a young girl, Cassia, who, along with her family, becomes part of a revolutionary Brotherhood which seeks to rid China of corrupt influences and bring about an enlightened peace. Although Cassia's family suffers greatly from the widespread strife in the impoverished, drought-inflicted Kwangtung Province of China, she maintains the spirit to fight against the ruling clans of her village and to keep peace within her own family. In the book's sequel, *Mountain Light,* Cassia and her father return from a revolutionary quest in China's Middle Kingdom, meeting Squeaky Lau, the book's narrator, on their journey. On the eventful expedition, Squeaky—

Yep's fantasy novels, such as *Dragon of the Lost Sea,* often integrate Chinese myth into the high adventure of their plots. (Jacket illustration by David Weisner.)

who was considered a clown by the local villagers—finds his own inner strength by bringing out the good in others. Although he and Cassia fall in love, Squeaky sets off for America, "the land of the Golden Mountain," where he faces the violence and excess of the California gold rush. Although some reviewers held that Yep's narrative was not as strong in these two historical novels as in *Dragonwings* and *Child of the Owl,* many praised the insight into Chinese history and culture, the strong characterizations, and the debunking of stereotypes that these novels provide.

Yep, who also writes for adult readers, is an avid proponent of the power of children's literature. "To write for children, one must try to see things as they do; and trying to look at the world with the fresh, inexperienced eyes of a child enables the writer to approach the world with a sense of wonder," he wrote in *Reading Teacher.* Yep's empathetic understanding of young people has brought him acclaim from critics and readers alike. "There are scenes in *Child of the Owl,*" Maxine Hong Kingston wrote in *Washington Post Book World,* "that will make every Chinese-American child gasp with recognition. 'Hey! That happened to me. I did that. I saw that,' the young reader will say, and be glad that a

Yep's *The Star Fisher* reflects the struggles and triumphs of a family with a traditional Chinese heritage and a modern American identity.

writer set it down, and feel comforted, less eccentric, less alone."

WORKS CITED:

Chin, Frank, review of *Dragonwings, Interracial Books for Children Bulletin,* Vol. 7, numbers 2 & 3, 1976.

Kingston, Maxine Hong, "Middle Kingdom to Middle America," *Washington Post Book World,* May 1, 1977, pp. E1, E8.
Pelmas, Ruth H., review of *Dragonwings, New York Times Book Review,* November 16, 1975.
Something about the Author, Volume 7, Gale, 1975, pp. 206-07.
Stableford, Brian, review of *Sweetwater, Vector 78,* November/December, 1976.
Stines, Joe, *Dictionary of Literary Biography,* Volume 52, *American Writers for Children since 1960: Fiction,* Gale, 1986, pp. 392-98.
Yep, Laurence Michael, essay in *Literature for Today's Young Adults,* edited by Alleen Pace Nilsen and Kenneth L. Donelson, 2nd edition, Scott, Foresman, 1985, pp. 426-27.
Yep, Laurence Michael, "Writing *Dragonwings,*" *Reading Teacher,* January 1977, pp. 359-63.

FOR MORE INFORMATION SEE:

BOOKS

Children's Literature Review, Gale, Volume 3, 1978, Volume 17, 1989.
Huck, Charlotte S., *Children's Literature in the Elementary School,* 3rd edition, Holt, 1979.
Norton, Donna E., *Through the Eyes of a Child: An Introduction to Children's Literature,* 2nd edition, Merrill, 1987.
Twentieth-Century Children's Writers, 3rd edition, St. James Press, 1990.

PERIODICALS

Bulletin of the Center for Children's Books, March, 1984.
English Journal, Volume 71, Number 3, March, 1982.
Horn Book, April, 1978; November, 1979; July/August, 1985; May/June, 1989.
Lion and the Unicorn, Volume 5, 1981.
School Library Journal, January, 1986.*

—*Sketch by Sonia Benson*

*   *   *

YORK, Simon
See HEINLEIN, Robert A.

Cumulative Indexes

Illustrations Index

(In the following index, the number of the volume in which an illustrator's work appears is given *before* the colon, and the page number on which it appears is given *after* the colon. For example, a drawing by Adams, Adrienne appears in Volume 2 on page 6, another drawing by her appears in Volume 3 on page 80, another drawing in Volume 8 on page 1, and another drawing in Volume 15 on page 107.)

YABC

Index citations including this abbreviation refer to listings appearing in *Yesterday's Authors of Books for Children*, also published by Gale Research Inc., which covers authors who died prior to 1960.

Author Index

The following index gives the number of the volume in which an author's biographical sketch, Brief Entry, or Obituary appears.

This index includes references to all entries in the following series, which are also published by Gale Research Inc.

YABC—*Yesterday's Authors of Books for Children: Facts and Pictures about Authors and Illustrators of Books for Young People from Early Times to 1960*
CLR—*Children's Literature Review: Excerpts from Reviews, Criticism, and Commentary on Books for Children*
SAAS—*Something about the Author Autobiography Series*